Our Changing Journey to the End

Volume 1
New Paths of Engagement

Volume 2
New Venues in the Search for Dignity and Grace

Our Changing Journey to the End

Reshaping Death, Dying, and Grief in America

Volume 2

New Venues in the Search for Dignity and Grace

**Christina Staudt, PhD and
J. Harold Ellens, PhD, Editors**

 PRAEGER

AN IMPRINT OF ABC-CLIO, LLC
Santa Barbara, California • Denver, Colorado • Oxford, England

Library of Congress Cataloging-in-Publication Data

Our changing journey to the end : reshaping death, dying, and grief in America / Christina Staudt, PhD and J. Harold Ellens, PhD, editors.
   volumes cm
   Includes bibliographical references and index.
   ISBN 978-1-4408-2845-4 (hardcopy : alk. paper) — ISBN 978-1-4408-2846-1 (ebook)
1. Terminal care—United States.   2. Right to die—United States.   3. Death—Social aspects—United States.   4. Grief—Social aspects—United States.   I. Staudt, Christina, editor of compilation.   II. Ellens, J. Harold, 1932– editor of compilation.
   R726.8.O87   2014
   179.7—dc23   2013024633

ISBN: 978-1-4408-2845-4
EISBN: 978-1-4408-2846-1

18   17   16   15   14   1   2   3   4   5

This book is also available on the World Wide Web as an eBook.
Visit www.abc-clio.com for details.

Praeger
An Imprint of ABC-CLIO, LLC

ABC-CLIO, LLC
130 Cremona Drive, P.O. Box 1911
Santa Barbara, California 93116-1911

This book is printed on acid-free paper ∞

Manufactured in the United States of America

Contents

SECTION II: IMPROVING THE VEHICLES OF CARE

SECTION III: REDRAWING THE MAP

Our Changing Journey to the End

There Were Signs

Rose petals in the doorway
a penny turned up
tails on the street
the indoor plants
straining away from the light

even the famous oncologist
has a tin heart, they said,
a gift from Malta one night
his wife confirmed it
by cell phone

in the historic square
a grove of hanging trees
bear plums at Christmas

Catherine Rogers

Chapter 1

Introduction: The Need for Accommodation

Christina Staudt

*D*ying *with dignity and grace means different things to different people. It is a matter of cultural and religious traditions, ideology, and personal preference. It can mean dying on the battlefield for one's country—in the trenches of World War I, as a kamikaze pilot, or in the mountains of Afghanistan. Killing oneself may be perceived necessary to preserve one's honor within a particular cultural context such as a Japanese hara-kiri. It can mean committing suicide for a cause, as exemplified by Buddhist monks immolating themselves or suicide bombers killing others along with themselves for perceived rewards in the next life. Devout Catholics receive the sacrament of last rites, penance, anointing, and viaticum ("provisions for a journey") to lend grace to the spirit and meet suffering and death with dignity. To many Muslims who have the financial means, a dutiful life and an eventual good death calls for undertaking a Hajj, a pilgrimage to Mecca. Leopold Bloom, the partially Jewish protagonist of James Joyce's Ulysses, declared a good death to be unexpected and swift,[1] not an uncommon wish by many, regardless of religious background.*

The majority of people in the United States in the 21st century, surveys conclude, consider "dying well" to mean dying at home, surrounded by loved ones, at peace with themselves, and knowing that their families have not been unduly burdened by the process.[2] We need to strive to achieve this for those who desire it, while accommodating those who do not fit the norm. The chapters of this volume, briefly presented in this introduction, show that we are moving in the right direction toward such a goal and that, nevertheless, much still needs to be accomplished.

Our notion of how to "die well" is aligned with our personal attitude to death. Useful models for thinking about different approaches to death in Western culture include the traditional, the modern, and the neo-modern epistemes, outlined in Chapter 1 of Volume I, "A Bird's Eye View of the Territory." In the 21st century, the neo-modern model, embodied in the hospice and palliative care movements, increasingly dominates the picture. Adherents of this approach place a high value on the right to control the course and chart individual journeys. The dying person and his or her loved ones are the authority. The focus is on "living well until the end," rather than on the process of dying. Afthe the death personalized final rites and funeral services honor the deceased. The tendency is to promote caring relationships and personal expression in composing the last stage of life. The model allows for the election of a more traditional style of preparing for death, with authority given to medical staff and religious dogma, or dying in isolation and in silence, but only if that is the wish of the person who is at the end of life. The trajectory of the evolving neo-modern model in the United States points to an ideal that places individual choice at the center.

In tandem with choice emerges the notion that one has control over the situation. The number of new self-help handbooks on how to prepare for and cope with the end of life is undiminished since the early part of the decade and growing as we move further into this century. *Jane Brody's Guide to the Great Beyond—A Practical Primer to Help You and Your Loved Ones Prepare Medically, Legally, and Emotionally for the End of Life* (2009) is an example of an unsentimental approach that focuses on practical necessities for those who do not want to be caught unawares by what lies ahead.[3] Web-based tools to gain information and manage one's care have flourished in the decade since smartphones became popular and are the "go-to" resource for baby boomers as well as their children.

The idea that death is manageable appeals to baby boomers. They have been demanding control of their surroundings since their teenage years; and in their early old age they are determined to remain young. Barring the ability to hold death at bay, they intend to learn how to exit life as graciously and dignified as possible, first for the beenfit of their parents and then for themselves. The chapters in the first section of this volume, "Escaping the Quagmire," discuss some of the obstacles they have to overcome in order to achieve their objective.

In his chapter "The Future of Death and Two Challenges That Will Shape It," James W. Green focuses on the large number of baby boomers who are entering the Medicare system and demand control over their care and the need to accommodate those who will require that the system provide physician-assisted dying. In "Assisted Suicide in the Age of AIDS and Alzheimer's," Michael Teitelman discusses the complexities of maintaining control of one's medical care after being afflicted by late-stage Alzheimer's Disease (AD). Without approval of new legal provisions, the many AD patients who will enter the health-care system will not be able to take advantage of their right to end their lives by ceasing to eat or by receiving the aid of a physician to die—even if physician-assisted suicide were legalized in every state.

With between 2 and 3 million people dying every year in the United States, medical providers, the health-care system, and society as a whole cannot possibly accommodate every person's specialized wishes and needs at the end. Nevertheless, much can be done. We already see evidence that we are on a path to reframe end-of-life care to create a more family- and patient-friendly system that can better meet, at least, the needs of the many who have similar wishes, such as dying peacefully at home.

Joanne Lynn and Ira Byock, two palliative care physicians and long-term advocates for improved end-of-life care, have written treatises with similar proposals for how to improve care at the end of life: Lynn's *Sick to Death and Not Going to Take It Anymore—Reforming Health Care for the Last Years of Life* was published in 2004 and Byock's *The Best Care Possible: A Physician's Quest to Transform Care through the End of Life* in 2012. The similarities between their prescribed solutions suggest that progress has been slow in the intervening years. Both propose community-based comprehensive care solutions to make it possible for people with serious illness to remain at home instead of going into a nursing home. They both mention the Medicare- and Medicaid-funded Program of All-Inclusive Care for the Elderly (PACE) as a good model. A PACE site serves nursing-home eligible people in their own residences by providing a range of services: adult day care with nursing care and physical, occupational, and recreational therapies; meals and nutritional counseling; social work and personal care, as well as medical care by a PACE physician who is familiar with the history, needs, and preferences of each participant; home health care and personal care; all necessary prescription drugs; social services; medical specialists such as audiology, dentistry, optometry, podiatry, and speech therapy; and respite care and hospital and nursing home care when necessary. Lynn reports that in 2002, 28 PACE sites were serving more than 10,000 people and 10 were in development around the country.[4] In 2012, 88 PACE programs were operational in 29 states.

Private foundation grants have been infused to ascertain the expansion of PACE. Many other models of care are incorporated as not-for-profit organizations, notably "aging-in-place" initiatives and not-for-profit family services with a focus on the elderly. Individual states and counties have also invested in programs and services that support those with serious illness. The direction is clear even if the road to success and completion will be long and bumpy. Positive signs of the restructuring of end-of-life care include specialized training of medical staff in end-of-life care issues and increasingly incorporating new such programs into medical schools around the country. An innovative example of this at Columbia University is described in Chapter 6 of Volume I, "Stories of the End: A Narrative Medicine Curriculum to Reframe Death and Dying."

Wishing someone a good death sounds both reasonable and compassionate. However, more and more in the 21st century thoughtful practitioners are finding that the good death is not a meaningful concept without an understanding of the person's individual needs and wishes. Even when the goals are clear to one of the patient's primary physicians, diverging perspectives of other medical staff can confuse the patient and his or her family, ultimately marring the process. Unless changes are instituted so that all medical providers listen better to those who are dying, their families, and their loved ones, the notion of self-determination can be hollow. Such perplexities are the subject of Margaret Souza's chapter, "Dying Persons and Their Families."

Perhaps the most suprising development of the neo-modern model of death, since Tony Walter proposed it in a British contexr in 1993,[5] is that in 2013 in the United States it can mean seeking empowerment—and ease—by handing over major medical decisions to one's children and a trusted physician. The authority remains with the principal who can, given the law of self-determination, decide who should be involved in the decision-making process. We are seeing an intensified and increasingly nuanced discussion about decision making at the end of life. Unintended consequences of the self-determination acts that were passed in the late 20th century are becoming aparent. It is evident that the acts were drafted from a sociopolitical perspective that did not take into account the importance of the family in the decision-making process, nor the diversity of values that are a fact in the United States in the 21st century. The challenges this can present in appointing one single surrogate (i.e., an agent or proxy) to be the spokesperson, if the principal is not able to speak for himself or herself, are outlined by Lawrence A. Frolik in his chapter, "Decision Making at the End of Life: From Informed Consent to Family Consent."

The autonomous decision-making process that has as its purpose to prepare for a death commensurate with one's wishes is compromised in other ways. Long and debilitating illnesses frequently precede death. Advancing medical technology makes it possible to prolong the number of days, months, and even years that a person survives. The treatment, however, may reduce the quality of life to a point that the additional time does not seem warranted to the onlookers; and the onlookers—the patient's family and the health-care team—may not be in agreement about what they see. To help resolve such ethical dilemmas that first came about with the development of new, sophisticated life-sustaining machines, bioethics teams are set up in hospitals. Their work is complex and complicated. They are balancing the needs and rights of the dying person and those of his or her family, while also considering the resources and obligations of the medical team, the hospital, and the health-care system. Lingering taboos and a fear to face death are likely to be present among staff as well as families, adding to the quandary. Miraim Piven Cotler addresses this balancing act in her chapter "A Changing Landscape: Evolving Ethical Duties and Obligation of Patients, Families, and Providers."

Sara Waller radically questions medical ethical precepts that have been laid down for millennia and proposes a bold solution to care at the end of life in her chapter, "The Hippocratic and the Veterinary Oath: Medical Ethics at the End of Life." She suggests that the Hippocratic Oath can be an obstacle to good end-of-life care and argues that those who suffer would receive more humane treatment if physicians adopted the Veterinary Oath in place of the traditional Hippocratic Oath. (Daniel Callahan plays with the same idea in the conclusion of his chapter "Prognosis, Costs, and End-of-Life Care" in Volume I.)

Despite continuing unsolved problems and looming threats, crucial strides have been taken to improve the care we receive at the end, allowing many people to die in the manner and place of their choice. These ongoing developments are highlighted in the second section, "Improving the Vehicles of Care." Much, if not all, of the progress can, in one way or another, be attributed to the gains in palliative care. The last period of life for those who are frail or living with serious illness has been vastly improved by this growing medical specialty. Still in its adolescence, this holistic model of care is gaining acceptance and adherents among the medical profession, as well as awareness among the general public. The first chapter in this section, "Palliative Care and Hospice: Caring for Patients with Serious Illness" by Kerrianne P. Page and Maura L. Del Bene, reviews the history of palliative care and explains its place in the health-care system.

The following chapters discuss other measures and practices that are gaining strength and being redefined in the 21st century. They offer hope of a path to a dignified death for the majority of those at the end of their personal journey. Helping to overcome barriers to good end-of-life care, these strides are increasingly likely to change our journey to the end in a positive direction.

Linda Koebner presents the concept of health-care advocacy, a new and growing profession with specialists who help people navigate the complex health-care system. She explains how these guides serve patients and families after a diagnosis of serious illness in her chapter, "The Health Care Advocate in End-of-Life Care." Our kaleidoscopic society demands sensitivity to the multicultural dimensions of the care offered at the end of life, with attention paid to heritage and traditions, as well as current needs of each individual and family. In their chapter, "Culturally Competent Care in an Increasingly Diverse Society," Karen Bullock and Jasmin Vokel discuss how this is done appropriately and can be expanded to serve patients in different health-care settings.

With the humility of a long-time career as a nursing home physician, Anthony J. Lechich shows the contradictory forces at play in this setting in his chapter, "Attending to the Pain of the Dying: The Nursing Home Care

Paradox." He outlines the positive signs and potential future advances within this controversial and difficult model of care. The multidisciplinary team has become the norm for good end-of-life care. Developments toward a more patient- and family-centered care model have altered, to some extent, the contours and content of the work of all of the team members: doctors, nurses, other medical specialists and therapists, as well as nurses' assistants and aides, social workers, nutritionists, chaplains, and others.

Martha R. Jacobs and Linda S. Golding document a number of real-life cases in their chapter, "The Evolving Role of Hospital Chaplains at the End of Life." They demonstrate the growing need for spiritual care workers—chaplains—in the health-care system, despite, or perhaps because of, the decrease in the percentage of those who have a religious affiliation. The section concludes with Nathan Ionascu's chapter, "Before Their Time: The Need for Communication When They Die Young." A seasoned pediatrician with experience in multiple care settings, Ionascu presents the special case of children and adolescents with life-threatening conditions and discusses the movement toward better communication among medical staff and families as well as the need for drawing up clear medical plans that involve all stakeholders.

In addition to continuing to improve the services within health-care system, we need to broaden the engagement in the political and civic arenas, so that the avenues toward dignity and grace at the end of life can also widen and improve. The chapters in the third and final section of this volume, "Redrawing the Map" offer specific examples of steps that need to be taken—or avoided—to make room for those who are vulnerable and in need of care at the end of life. The chapter by Edward J. Lusk, Nellie Selander, and Michael Halperin, "Advance Directives and Hospice Care: Cost Savers at the End," analyzes and proposes savings that can be made in the health-care system that simultaneously improve the odds that people will die at peace and with dignity.

The inequalities on the road to the end have their roots in differences in education, group belonging, geographic location, social environment and personal relationships, and perhaps, most obviously, financial resources.[6] Kevin T. Keith's chapter "Conspicuous Metabolism: Life Support and Life Extension as Luxury Goods" focuses on the much-debated idea of life extensions, and points to the inherent inequities of this quest.

In his chapter, "Solidarity, Mortality: The Tolling Bell of Civic Palliative Care," Bruce Jennings urges us to see end-of-life care as a societal and civic problem—not just a medical and health-care issue. His chapter calls for active involvement by all segments of society. We need to do sensible planning for ourselves and our society so that everyone feels well accommodated at the end of life with, as David Kessler has expressed it, "a little psychology, a little medicine, and a little spirituality, mixed with a whole lot of love."[7] Or none of it, if that is the choice. This volume concludes with my comments to a personal letter from Richard Selzer, an octogenarian physician, reflecting on his career and current life.

NOTES

1. James Joyce, *Ulysses* (New York: Random House, 1990), 95.

2. Among others, see California Health Care Foundation, *S n a p s h o t: Final Chapter: Californians' Attitudes and Experiences with Death and Dying* (Oakland, CA, 2012), http://coalitionccc.org/documents/FinalChapterDeathDying.pdf

3. Jane Brody, *Jane Brody's Guide to the Great Beyond—A Practical Primer to Help You and Your Loved Ones Prepare Medically, Legally, and Emotionally for the End of Life* (New York: Random House, 2009).

4. Joanne Lynn, *Sick to Death and Not Going to Take It Anymore!* (Berkeley CA: University of California Press, 2004), 75.

5. Tony Walter, *The Revival of Death,* (London: Routledge, 1993).

6. See Christina Staudt and Marcelline Block, editors, *Unequal before Death* (Newcastle: Cambridge Scholars Press, 2012).

7. David Kessler, "Forward to the New Edition," *The Needs of the Dying: A Guide for Bringing Hope, Comfort, and Love to Life's Final Chapter* (New York: Harper Collins, 2000), xiv.

The Vet in the Coffee Shop

He is reading a book about God. It is sky blue, the book, like his sweater. And his wedding ring is nice and worn. He is not afraid of death and never has been, he says, probably because his sister died when she was six and he was three. And he is from a nice Jewish family of four kids: three of them, one who died, and then the sister who came later.

His wife is Catholic. When her father was dying they were all there: his wife, his wife's mother, his aunt. His wife's mother said, "Oh, thank God he's suffering so much now, so later he will be happier." His aunt said, "You're kidding, right?"

He has to put animals to sleep all the time, and he says that three things have to be ready: the animal, the animal's owner, and he himself, the vet. He says he can tell when the animal isn't ready. When all are ready, he does it. He says that he doesn't tell the owner, but he always says "I'm sorry" before putting the animal down. He also uses anesthetic first because it's a lot more controllable than the killing drug. Some animals go into shakes if they just get the killing drug. Others go right down. But with anesthetic, they are peaceful. He says he is always emotional when he puts them down, and if he ever loses that emotion he will stop the practice immediately.

He says when his mother died, at the moment she died, there was a whirlwind of energy. He said that he told his mother that each of her family members, and he named them all, released her. And that's when she died.

Catherine Rogers

Section I

Escaping the Quagmire

Chapter 2

The Future of Death and Two Challenges That Will Shape It

James W. Green

Changes in the medical management of death over the last half century combined with demographic shifts in the American population present two new challenges to how dying will be handled in the future. First, for aging baby boomers seeking increased medical control at the end of life, physician-aided dying will be more widely available. It is currently a choice in three states. An examination of the Oregon experience not only highlights some of its successes but also its weaknesses. The second challenge derives from the growing ethnic and religious diversity of the American population. Calls for cultural competence in patient care at the end of life are not new, but how it is practiced at the bedside is not always clear. Loosely conceived notions of a pan-human spirituality are often invoked although they may be culture-bound biases rather than anything useful as a guideline. Several ethnographic case studies suggest procedures for genuine cultural responsiveness in end-of-life care. Each of these two challenges demands new ways of thinking and acting in order to assure a dignified death for everyone, whatever their background or circumstance.

INTRODUCTION

In his magisterial history of death in the Western tradition, Philippe Ariès describes a style of dying he says was common to medieval Europe. He called it the "tame death" and it had two outstanding features that, he says, we have lost. One was "familiar simplicity": death was often prefigured and as it approached a ritual apparatus of confession, forgiveness took over to guide the dying into another world. Little instructional booklets of *ars moriendi,* the art of dying, contained everything the dying person and attending priest needed to know. The second element, says Ariès, "is its public aspect, which is to last until the 19th century. The dying person must be the center of a group of people"—family, friends, even a whole village.[1] An occasion of good dying, says a 15th-century English *ars moriendi,* should be so well planned and choreographed that "yf it were possyble all, an hole cyte oughte runne hastely to a persone that deyeth" both for moral edification and a good performance.[2]

Perhaps Ariès romanticizes but even as mythos his imagery of the tame death remains powerful. It suggests that perhaps in many places and times, dying was well understood because it occurred within a framework of etiquette and expectations familiar to all. Familiarity assured some degree of control, the commonly voiced concern of many who today request a physician's aid in dying. And it was a highly social event played out in an accustomed setting, with family and neighbors all gathered around. The 21st-century American setting is very different. The management of death—and "management" rather than "taming" seems the apt term—is divided among medical, commercial, and legal interests whose day-to-day functioning is perplexing if not invisible to outsiders. Nor is there an overriding *ars moriendi.* Instead, popular and varied notions of the good death, efficacious grief work, and speculation on where the dead are now compete for attention. In this cultural free market, which is not really so free, I want to look at two challenges that will be important to the future of all of us, as researchers, health-care providers, or anyone else who thinks they might die someday. They are both untamed in Ariès's sense, and that makes us all vulnerable when our time comes. Vulnerability is their common theme. I begin with physician-aided dying (PAD), the most political and controversial of the two.

PHYSICIAN-AIDED DYING

I do not use the phrase "physician-assisted suicide" since suicide in most jurisdictions is a legal term and a crime. Where aided dying with the help of a doctor is legal, assistance is not defined as criminal. I would add that while such dying is the public and hence more controversial issue, it is really part of a continuum of other life-ending practices that bring less public attention but have been discussed and debated in the bioethical literature. They include shutting down mechanical support, withholding supplemental oxygen or nutrition, and applying heavy doses of sedatives whose secondary effect is likely to be death.[3]

In early 2013, PAD is legal in three jurisdictions in the United States: the states of Oregon, Washington, and Montana. A ballot question that would have established an "Act Relative to Death with Dignity" that included the right to PAD was turned down by the electorate in Massachusetts in the November 2012 election. New Jersey, Vermont, and Connecticut are among the states where PAD is debated in the legislatures.

In Montana PAD was declared legal by the state Supreme Court; in Oregon and Washington it was approved by initiatives to the people. In *Baxter v. Montana* (2009), the state Supreme Court ruled in favor of Robert Baxter, a terminal patient suffering with lymphocytic leukemia. His request for a physician's aid with dying was denied so he sued in district court. His right to such aid was upheld and the court's order was issued; ironically, on the same day he died. The Montana Attorney General challenged that ruling in the Court but lost. In a narrowly phrased opinion, the majority justices argued they were not dealing with a constitutional right for aided dying but merely affirming an extension of public policy. An earlier state law on terminal dying already protected physicians who in withdrawing treatment from dying patients were not subject to a charge of homicide. Baxter's physician could have accommodated him without legal risk by offering medical aid that had the same effect. A commentator on that decision writes that "the statutory logic advanced by the Montana court, I assert, is boldly consequential. . . . For this reason, then, judges in Des Moines—or Sacramento, Juneau, or Cheyenne—could legalize PAID. . . ."[4]

In 1994, Oregon was the first state to approve PAD, when voters approved a Death with Dignity Act by a margin of 51 percent. Implementation was delayed until 1997 because a repeal initiative was immediately launched. It however lost 60 percent to 40 percent. In 2008, voters in Washington State approved an almost identical initiative by 58 percent, apparently reassured by the Oregon experience. Nationally, the public mood may be moving in that direction as well. In a 2010 Harris poll of 2,340 adults, 58 percent agreed with the statement: "the law should allow doctors to comply with the wishes of a dying patient in severe distress who asks to have his or her life ended."[5] Another 22 percent were not sure and only 20 percent disagreed. Given these trends, it seems likely that PAD will be legalized eventually in other states as well. It is worthwhile, then, looking at the Oregon experience to see if it works as well as the advocates promised in 1994.

Who uses the Death with Dignity law? According to the Oregon Health Authority, in 2010, a typical patient was a 72-year-old white married male (no minorities requested PAD), with baccalaureate degree or higher, who lived on the more urban west side of the state. His underlying illness was some form of cancer; he was enrolled in hospice and had discussed his choice for dying with his family. His prescribing physician, whom he knew for 18 weeks, issued an order for phenobarbital and he died within a half hour of ingesting a large dose.

The physician may or may not have been present. One other bit of data is noteworthy: in 2010, 96 fatal prescriptions were written statewide; 37 were not used.[6]

From the beginning, opponents of PAD raised a number of objections. Early and vague warnings of a "slippery slope" toward medicalized murder ("death panels" is the more recent characterization) were common. So too were fears that Oregon would become a magnet for elderly people traveling from all over the country to end their lives there. Neither of these things happened. Instead, what has evolved in law and in practice is an emphasis on protecting the vulnerable. For example, those who are clinically depressed, or might be, are much discussed in the medical literature on PAD. This is as it should be. Both Oregon and Washington laws specify that a fatal medication cannot be dispensed to a patient who is "suffering from a psychiatric or psychological disorder or depression causing impaired judgment."[7] But do errors happen? In a frequently cited 2008 study, individuals who contacted Oregon Compassion and Choices about information on aid in dying, and patients who made an explicit request of a physician, were evaluated by the study team to determine their competence for making a fatal choice.[8] Following a series of standardized tests, those diagnosed with major depressive disorder were so advised and counseling was recommended as an option to active dying. However, at the end of the study and after 18 participants received a lethal prescription, 3 among them met the study's criteria for depression. They slipped through the law's safety net. How did this happen?

One answer comes from a Dutch researcher whose country is familiar with aided dying.[9] Marije Van der Lee of the Helen Dowling Institute in Utrecht suggests that, firstly, a single mandatory consultation with a second physician for a second opinion is hardly adequate for diagnosing depression. Secondly, it is also possible that the attending physicians did not recognize the symptoms of depression as established in the *Diagnostic and Statistical Manual of Mental Disorder* (DSM4, 4th edition, published by the American Psychiatric Association). Van der Lee also suggests one difference from Dutch practice that, in her view, makes all the difference. To be eligible for aid in dying in Oregon, a patient must be judged to have six months or less to live. By contrast, the Dutch criterion for eligibility is "unbearable suffering," something that the patient, not the doctor, decides. There, the job of the physician is to determine that the complaint is voluntary and well considered, and that no relief of any kind is available. An informed decision is what counts; medicine's role in Holland is to protect patients against depression, not against assisted dying. For the unfortunate three in the Oregon study, that might have made the difference. Implementation of the Oregon model is not perfect but, as we will see, neither is the Dutch practice. The door is open for other states to develop their own PAD criteria for eligibility as the U.S. Supreme Court has not explicitly banned the matter. A 1997 Supreme Court ruling in *Washington v Glucksburg* referred to the "laboratory of the states" as the place to work these issues out.[10]

In those states where the families of the clinically depressed struggle with the implications of PAD as policy and practice, the medical community too has its sense of vulnerability. Many physicians in Oregon approved of PAD when it was an initiative to the voters but most do not welcome a PAD request from a patient. In a 2004 study, the most thorough on this to date, many said they felt anxiety when so approached, especially if working with the elderly was rare in their practice or if the patient was not well known to them. Many were surprised at the persistence and determination of some patients and felt their control and even competence was being questioned. Said one, "I see it as rejection of care . . . somehow the patient is saying, 'Whatever you are doing isn't good enough.' " Whether or not they accede to the request, some were profoundly uncomfortable discussing it with someone who seemed fully functional. One remarked, "I avoided it . . . I kind of dealt with the [patient's] medical issues and didn't square up with it."[11]

All agreed that following through with a PAD request was intense, time consuming, and emotionally draining. They were pulled by a sense of obligation and professional dedication and by the urgency of the patient's need. Over time, they said a momentum developed and they were drawn into it. Typical comments were "it was astonishingly intense. There wasn't much else I thought about for the last days of her life beside her." Said another, "And so I cried, and the nurses cried, and the son cried. It's wow! It's a big responsibility."[12] Some expressed relief if a patient died of the underlying illness first. Those who saw the process through, however, expressed satisfaction that things went well, that the death was peaceful and quick, and the patients had time with their family. Some doctors wanted to be present, feeling it was their responsibility. Others did not. One said he felt an outsider to the family and being there at the moment of death was not his place. Where there were regrets, they were for not communicating well or taking enough time with the patient. Yet even those who said they were satisfied with how they handled the experience did not welcome future requests. But they said they learned from it and were now better, more attentive physicians. Commented one: "There's something very serene and very magnificent in that. And it just gives you the power to go."[13]

A quietly powerful documentary film entitled "Death on Request," directed by Maarten Nederhorst (1994), is currently used with first year American medical students in bioethics courses. It tracks the experience of a Dutch physician, Wilfred Sidney van Oijen, whose patient Kees van Wendel de Joode is dying of ALS. Dr. van Oijen meets regularly with de Joode and his wife Antoinette in their home in Amsterdam and he is as sympathetic as he is unhurried. van Oijen keeps urging de Joode to put off dying until he reaches an upcoming birthday. At home with his own wife, in his car and on his bicycle, he ruminates constantly on what he is doing and why he went into medicine. It "leaves its mark on my whole body" he tells the camera, yet he handles up to four such cases a year. Killing, he insists, it is not. He wants only to relieve suffering despite the anguish it brings him.[14]

Another notable film, from a patient perspective, is *How to Die in Oregon.* Directed by Peter Richardson and released in 2011, it offers some remarkably candid vignettes and follows closely several patients and their families. Viewers are gently brought into each story. The story of a woman who dies in the final scene, tastefully shot from outside her house through a thinly veiled window, is especially moving. The film won the top documentary prize at the 2011 Sundance Film Festival.[15]

But beyond the bedside, there are other problems. Oregon physicians reported that collegial support was rare. In fact, they preferred not to talk about it at all with doctors they knew or worked with every day. Instead, like the Dutch physician, they discussed it with a spouse. Many felt poorly trained for handling the task (although that is changing) and those in rural areas and more conservative parts of the state, where the vote against PAD was substantial, often felt isolated and vulnerable. In small towns, doctors and health-care providers know each other, sometimes quite well. If a physician agrees to a request for PAD, he will have to order a prescription. Then the pharmacist knows, perhaps also the drugstore staff, and customers may learn of it. The word will get out that this doctor is the town's "death doctor," which is not good for business—nor for getting along at the weekly rotary club lunch.

Despite these difficulties, I predict the movement for legalized aid in dying will expand beyond its current Western states foothold. The aging of the baby boomers toward their final years will likely accelerate that. In addition, assisted dying was promoted, in part, to replace medical practices that are less visible, lack regulation, and hence accountability. Timothy Quill, a professor in the University of Rochester School of Medicine and active participant in this discussion, speaks of "the secret practice of physician-assisted death" in the rest of the country. There, he says, "to admit to participation, a physician has to admit to a crime and, along with any family present, run the risk of prosecution. On the other hand, there appears to be very little interest in prosecuting such cases provided they are not discovered or flaunted, leading to a 'don't ask, don't tell' policy. That is unpredictable and potentially dangerous."[16] He adds that about one to two percent of deaths nationally occur this way, although there is little data on it—understandably so.

The Dutch and Oregon practices, although different, both respond to Quill's concern. They bring conversations between patients and doctors out into the open and, for patients with unacceptable suffering, offer a "last resort option," as he calls it, rather than arbitrarily withholding it. Yet there remain problems with each approach, a point of murkiness and vulnerability. In Oregon and Washington, the issue is the space between regulatory language and the reality of doctor/patient encounters in the office or at the bedside. According to the law, only patients with six months or less to live are eligible. But how accurate can such a prognosis be? As it happens, not very. In one large study, Christakis and Lamont found that only 20 percent of medical practitioners got it right; 63 percent were overly optimistic and 17 percent were too pessimistic.[17] This has consequences for patients and offers challenges to physician credibility on a critical legal and medical question. So would the Dutch model be an improvement, by letting the patient decide instead? This too has its problems.

In a survey of over 1,000 Dutch physicians, fully a quarter said it was difficult to know if a patient's suffering was truly unbearable, as required by law. Those who had experience helping patients die had greater doubts about it than those who did not. To examine this more closely, a University of Nijmegen research group did a qualitative follow-up to their quantitative survey, hoping to find how the loss of meaningful activities hardened into suffering that became unbearable. The group determined at the end that assessing suffering cannot be done objectively and thus concluded, "it can be questioned whether placing emphasis on (purely) subjective aspects is an adequate fulfillment of the duties imposed on physicians, as laid down in the Dutch Euthanasia Act."[18]

Here we get to a researchable challenge: What is suffering at the end of life? Years ago, a wise physician wrote in the *New England Journal of Medicine* that "suffering is experienced by persons, not merely bodies, and has its source in challenges that threaten the intactness of the person as a complex social and psychological entity."[19] It is more than pain—the medical problem—or dread—the psychological problem. Suffering has a social dimension made evident in discourse, not any discourse but one embedded in a genre familiar to a patient and to a specific community and its traditions. Within this genre, the patient declares the meaning of his or her own dying experience. Two contrasting examples illustrate how that happens.

The first is reported in a long article by Atul Gawande, physician, author, and public intellectual on medical matters, appearing in a 2010 issue of *The New Yorker*. He writes of a dying cancer patient, aged 34 and pregnant with her first child. The storyline is of a family and doctor doing all they can to slow the inevitable, ceasing only on her dying day. As her condition became more desperate, Gawande says the family went into "battle mode," to which he offered this philosophical aside: "Death is the enemy. But the enemy has superior forces. Eventually it wins. And in a war you cannot win. . . . You don't want Custer. You want Robert E. Lee, someone who knew how to fight for territory when he could and how to surrender when he couldn't, someone who understood that the damage is greatest if all you do is fight to the bitter end." Gawande quotes approvingly from Stephen Jay Gould, who hedged a bit when considering his own incurable cancer. Noting Ecclesiastes's advice that there is a time for everything, Gould's view was that "when my skein runs out I hope to face the end calmly and in my own way. For most situations, however, I prefer the more martial view that death is the ultimate enemy—and I find nothing reproachable in those who rage mightily against the dying of the light."[20]

Gawande's genre here is that of military war stories, a discourse of great struggle, fighting on, calling up reserves, and always with hope that one will return home victorious from the chemo front. We commonly see this motif in obituaries in their references to bravery and heroism, and in the survivorship stories of those who live to run—sometimes literally—on another day. Such has been called "heroic dying," an expression typical of the individualism of our predominantly secular culture.[21]

Compare this to a very different kind of discourse. Ronald K. Barrett is a scholar of African American dying and funerals. Describing the importance of religion in his community, he says that suffering, while not glorified, is nevertheless ennobling. One replicates Christ's suffering on the cross and, he says, for many that is "somehow a better way to go than [that chosen by] people who have been medicated and thereby have chosen a 'softer' way . . . there are some people who really identify the dying process and the critical moment of transition as being times of *necessary* suffering."[22] Like Gawande's patient, many African American families want a full press at the end of life and there are good historical reasons for this. But for them, the governing imagery is less that of battle than the beginnings of transcendence toward another reality. This is a very different genre indeed.

The Dutch researchers acknowledged that subjectivity alone is not a reliable guide in thinking through requests for aided dying. Something more is needed. A discourse approach suggests that additional information, potentially useful, is available if one wants to move beyond the diagnostic categories of the DSM4. When someone says they are suffering, what is the larger context, the communal storyline of which their personal version is an exemplar? How can one elicit that information and use it in making wise decisions? No one expects physicians to do ethnography at the bedside. But the value of that information cannot be known until it is retrieved. How that is done leads me to death's second new challenge.

CULTURAL DIVERSITY AND DISCOURSES OF SUFFERING

As early as 2001, the U.S. Department of Health and Human Services issued a report with the lofty title of *National Standards for Culturally and Linguistically Appropriate Service in Health Care*. Known in the literature as the CLAS standards, it called for "cultural competence," meaning respect for the health beliefs and practices of diverse populations and training and staffing to make that respect evident. But just what is "cultural competence" at the bedside at the end of life? That unfortunate term has its origins in the social services literature of the 1980s. Unfortunate, I say, because most of the people who promoted it then thought of a culture—other than their own—as an assortment of unusual and distinctive customs and beliefs and, if they knew some of the really important ones, they could better persuade their minority clients and patients to do what was good for them. "Compliance" was the term for that. Thus, a small industry in "cultural competence" training arose, partly in response to the expectation in many "Request for Proposal" funding announcements that staff be trained for it. One of the best-known explorations of the difficulties of cultural competence in medical practice is Anne Fadiman's *The Spirit Catches You and You Fall Down* (New York: Farrar, Straus and Giroux, 1997). The story is of a Hmong child with severe epilepsy and the mighty contest between her tradition-minded parents and the medical professionals at a California hospital. The book is widely read in medical schools and has remained popular with the general public as well.

Fortunately, improvements are being made on how we think about cultural diversity and the delivery of health care. For most anthropologists, a "culture" is not a list of specific traits presumed to be typical of a given community; it is rather a set of "competing discourses and practices, within situations characterized by the unequal distribution of power." In other words, "'culture' is not a 'thing,' something 'out there,' that books are about. It is a process of making meanings, making social relations, and making the world that we inhabit, in which all of us are engaged—when we read and teach, and when we diagnose and treat."[23] In working with minority patients—and all patients really—meaning-making models are more powerful tools for understanding than trait lists presumed to be uniformly descriptive of *all* members of a given community.

Reflecting on the diversity of the Canadian medical scene, Lisa Chan and colleagues suggest something similar.[24] She begins by separating the idea of ethnicity from that of culture. We all have an ethnicity, but in the medical consultation our concern is the "culture of care." This, she says, is a dynamic and sometimes confrontational mix of three traditions: the practices of scientific medicine, the institutional culture of the hospital, and the range of preferences and expectations in the patient's family and home community. By culture, she means a context—the dialogue, gestures, assumptions, and appearances that shape the flow of a specific clinical event. It is flexible, negotiable, and contested, and the power of the players is decidedly unequal. Patients and families are visitors, outsiders in a territory that is unfamiliar; health professionals are insiders and have their own formal and informal agendas.

When ethnic distinctions are part of the mix, variations in understanding and disparities of power may be exaggerated. Although proponents of cultural competence tend to focus on patients as central to their inquiry, the social organization of hospitals and how that shapes dying is an old theme in medical anthropology.[25] In her work on dying in hospitals, Sharon Kaufman adds an important caution. Her view is that ethnic identity in the clinic is less important than the bureaucratic culture of the hospital: "it is the structure of the hospital system itself—along with the politics of hospital staff practice—that, more than anything else, affects how death is made."[26] What is critical in this setting is knowing what is at stake for the varying participants. How does one do that?

As natives on their own turf, care providers have the burden of knowing about how life's end is handled in the communities represented in their patient load. That should not be difficult since the medical literature is rich on this topic.[27] The search term "cultural diversity and end of life care" run through the PubMed database in early 2012 produced 410 hits and there are probably more now; Google Scholar is even more prolific. The problem is not a lack of information, but rather, narrowing it down to what one needs. That usually means focusing on a few critical areas: delivering bad news, decision making, life support, and advanced directives. These stand out because the default position of most whites, and therefore, health care generally, is informed consent, patient autonomy, and anticipatory decision making. But people in other communities may have different priorities.

Delivering bad news, for example, is problematic for many physicians, which is why there is a number of "how to" books and professional articles on the subject. While whites generally choose whether or not they want to hear the raw facts of their condition, in some communities that is not a choice. The rationales for that vary and are well documented. They include the idea that openly discussing death with a patient is disrespectful, or destroys hope, provokes anxiety, is unnecessarily cruel, or is "directly harmful to health" and that "a patient who is already in pain should not have to grapple with feelings of depression as well."[28]

How, then, does one learn what a patient or family prefers? Years ago, physician-anthropologist Arthur Kleinman suggested that like doctors, patients have in mind an explanatory model, in his terms, an "EM" of what is wrong with them, revealed in the plot lines and metaphors through which they give voice to their illness. Note the word "illness" here. Patients experience illness and their explanatory models are the stories they tell about it. Doctors' explanatory models are about disease, which is a scientific and medical construct. The task for the alert practitioner, then, is to elicit the patient's model with open-ended questions to determine precisely what is at stake in the illness as it is being experienced. Kleinman's short list (and others like it) provides a useful first step toward what some might call a more genuine sense of cultural competence. His questions are as follows:[29]

1. What do you call this problem?
2. What do you believe is the cause of this problem?
3. What course do you expect it to take? How serious is it?
4. What do you think this problem does inside your body?
5. How does it affect your body and your mind?

6. What do you most fear about this condition?

7. What do you most fear about the treatment?

Obviously, not all of these questions are part of an initial consultation, and they have to be adapted to one's personal style, but used over time they direct attention to what the patient knows, believes, and experiences—the localized meaning of suffering—and they alert others to what is more easily discussed and what is not.[30]

There is another way of honing clinical cross-cultural skills, one particularly apt when working with end-of-life patients and families. Every anthropological field-worker who enters an unfamiliar community knows to look for knowledgeable insiders. They are the real experts on the local scene. A recent study in Denver used a variant of that idea—focus groups with whites and with African Americans—to identify preferences in end-of-life communication.[31] There were some similarities across the groups. All agreed, it is better to have a familiar and sympathetic physician, or a social worker or nurse, present when critical family decisions are made. But there were differences of emphasis. African Americans were concerned that doctors be "respectful" and acknowledge all family members present. The attention of whites was more on the details of prognosis, therapeutic choices, the effects of medications, and the psychological and physical comfort of the patient. African Americans strongly favored aggressive care right through to the end of life and were more likely to insist on CPR, artificial ventilation, and tube feeding and were less willing to sign a DNR order or accept a referral to hospice. Nor were they as interested in advance directives. One study suggests that many African Americans are more attuned to God's timetable than human ones, timing and advance preparations for dying being a secondary concern. Latinos, by contrast, sometimes avoid planning as illness for them reflects unfavorably on the family.[32] Needless to say, for African Americans, who fit the dominant model for that race, PAD was *not* an option. They were looking for something else, made explicit in a snippet of conversation reported by a physician with the daughter of a 68-year-old woman dying from ovarian cancer:

Doctor: "We're not optimistic."
Daughter: "We understand that *you're* not optimistic, but *we* are."
Doctor: "We want to be realistic."
Daughter: "Well . . . *we're* looking for a miracle . . . "[33]

How might this physician have spoken in a way more attuned to the anxieties of the daughter and the expectations of her community? He says that his initial comment, "We are not optimistic," could have been rephrased as "We are not optimistic but we are always hopeful. . . . " This, he felt, could change the tone of the conversation, validating the daughter's commitment to faith and assuring her that the medical staff was not giving up. As rephrased, he says his comment "balances the prognostic realities with a measure of sensitivity to the patient's spiritual beliefs and needs."[34] The miracle in this case was not a metaphor but rather, a realistic expectation, a theme that recurs in the literature on end-of-life care in some minority communities.

So should this doctor or other health-care professionals with their scientifically grounded medical education seriously make hints about miracles? Apparently, in an interesting way, some do and they write about it. Search the phrase "spiritual or spirituality" in the PubMed data base—peer-reviewed, quantitative journal articles—and you will be inundated with over 10,000 hits, more than half of which were published in the last 10 years. The recent proliferation of articles on this topic is suggestive of something almost faddish. For the decade of the 1980s, there were 423 titles; in the 1990s 1,554 and since 2000 there have been 7,564.[35] Even *The Journal of the American Medical Association (JAMA)* has the occasional item. What is it about spirituality that interests health-care professionals and what does it have to do with diversity in clinical care? A literature review in the *Journal of Pain and Symptom Management* (February 2012) sought to identify significant "existential and spiritual concerns in relation to palliative and end-of-life care."[36] Not surprising, the authors' conclusion is that there is a significant lack of consistency in how these core concepts are defined. Many of the studies reviewed sought to measure an association between religious or spiritual coping and medical outcomes. Standard protocols such as RCOPE, the Brief Religious Coping Scale, are common. But are spiritual assessment tools like this, a methodology of choice in much of the literature, sufficient for health-care providers seeking to better know patients whose cultural background is unfamiliar? A meta-study of qualitative research on the topic concluded that they are not.[37]

The attractiveness of terms like "existential suffering" and "spirituality" when used generically is, as one critic has pointed out, in how they serve as "glow words"[38]: They suggest a profound and universal human activity, something we all desire. Those who use this language in their surveys, patient questionnaires, and workshops often have in mind a diffuse, individualized interior process of "meaning making" leading to reconciliation with fate and perhaps knowing a bit of triumph along the way. We can see here the ghost of Kübler-Ross's fascination with personal growth in dying.[39] But in that glow something important is omitted, the specific social and historical contexts we usually draw on to formulate these notions. Spirituality thus becomes an acultural and ahistorical phenomenon, something diffuse and universalized. But there is a flaw in that. Any such notion of spirituality is, in actuality, culture bound. Sociologist Tony Walter argues that it is a feature of "late-modern Anglophone societies," a "discourse that arises from the experience of a particular generation and a particular segment of the population, namely those moving beyond formal religion" and that includes many—but not all—highly educated individuals.[40]

More than that, however, I suggest that the focus on a generalized spirituality is for some professionals a shortcut, ultimately illusory, for the harder work of learning about specific sets of cultural and religious preferences and their importance to patients from distinctive communities. Yet these details are what care providers need to know to navigate the give-and-take of the intimate occasion Chan calls the "culture of care."[41] In practice, how might this look?

Fortunately, there is in the medical literature a suggestive case study, that of a young Spanish-speaking cancer patient, which is almost a syllabus of what a team of culturally alert professionals would want to know.[42] Even the format of this *JAMA* article is instructive. The authors, three physicians, begin with an overview of the patient's story. There follows a series of commentaries from the attending physician, a nurse, a social worker, the chaplain, and a medical student fluent in Spanish. Each is quoted at length about their understanding of some aspect of a difficult situation. The physician speaks of the husband, who has some English, and his insistence throughout that his wife will get better if they would just do more. He is certain a medical miracle is possible. The social worker learns of their fear of deportation: They are both undocumented, which helps explain the husband's evasiveness when questioned about family resources for social and emotional support. It also impedes acting on the wife's desire to contact her family in Central America one last time. The medical student appreciates the difficulty of translating English medical terms and concepts into everyday Spanish. He works to evaluate the family's "health literacy," their explanatory model in Kleinman's sense, what they understand about the prognosis, and what they misunderstand or ignore.

This mode of inquiry led the team into other challenging areas. Given the great value accorded family life, the woman wanted a final visit with parents and relatives in another country. She wanted to talk about her hopes for her surviving daughter. But these issues were pushed into the background by the husband who, given traditional gender roles, saw himself as her protector. When she spoke of what she wanted to do before dying, he redirected the conversation to treatment issues instead. Unfortunately, dissension between doctor and husband became a serious obstacle and so someone suggested bringing in a priest to mediate. Good suggestion until the chaplain discovered the notation "Catholic" on the hospital intake form was an incorrect assumption: rather, they were actually evangelical Protestants.

The patient, we presume, died in the hospital. But she inspired an unintended legacy, a story made known to the rest of us by a care team alert to genre, the context of her specific storyline. Their research choice was a qualitative methodology and a tight focus on a single, difficult case and their conclusions went well beyond the usual call for sensitive care. It led them to identify additional critical areas for inquiry—religion, family values, gender roles, fatalism, and the use of interpreters—for which they offer lists of opening questions clinicians can use for identifying patient expectations and preferences. That is the real strength of their approach. They build on and expand Kleinman's original suggestions. Some of what they propose are simple and immediately useful: during a consultation rather than asking if the patient has any questions, assume she does. Give her center stage with "What questions do you have for me?" and then wait. The husband's male protectiveness was more complicated; for him it was essential to his sense of familial responsibility. But it might have been redirected over time toward the unborn infant, his being asked to help the team assure its survival. And should cases like this come up with any regularity, ongoing reviews among staff of what worked and what did not could lead to protocols helpful to other care providers working with culturally similar patients.

In addition, this care team proposed an interesting and challenging metaphor to describe what they learned from working with this family. They came to see the woman who was dying as something of a navigator of the terrain at the end of her life, their role being map makers for what she described and why it was important to her. They began to see something of the larger cultural territory of her dying as she saw it, each team member filling in spaces on their expanding mental map as their clinical role and understanding of her and her husband directed. They called their method one of "teach-back." One "simply asks patients or family members to restate what was just discussed . . . placing the onus of achieving good patient understanding on the clinician."[43] Thus they were able to formulate new questions, specify in cultural terms the rationale for asking them, and suggest ways they might best be phrased. Knowing more of how patients construct meaning, invoke personal and communal resources, and identify issues that may not be obvious to outsiders is critical if one is to be culturally responsive in any sense at all.

Where does an ethnographic approach like this take us in rethinking "cultural competence" and its weak fellow traveler, "spirituality," in the culture of care at the end of life? It tells us that any alleged cross-cultural capability has a long learning curve and that Chan's model is a useful starting point. It directs us not to an ethnographic Other abstractly conceived but to the dynamics of a tri-part clinical event. Patients are one part; they represent not only particular communities but also particular slices within them. And they are worried strangers not wishing to be in this unfamiliar place. The professionals have their traditions and preferences too, developed over years of training, plus—invisible mostly—their relations with coworkers, medical hierarchies, and the politics of life on the ward. The hospital is a third presence. More than just a stage set, it has its own priorities and at the end of life matters of policy, staffing, scheduling, and finances (again, largely invisible) profoundly shape how dying happens. How hospital procedures shape dying has been well analyzed in Kaufman's book, referenced above, and among others, by Helen Stanton Chapple.[44] Kaufman's theme is the power of hospitals to move dying patients along a well-defined but not obvious institutional pathway, one she likens to the moving walkways of airports. Once on the track, it is difficult to get off of it and there are unexpected consequences right on through to the end. Gawande's case, described above, is a dramatic example. Chapple is a critical care nurse, a bioethicist, and an anthropologist. She examines what she calls a dominant rescue ideology that makes hospitals difficult places to die peacefully. She offers a useful and often-overlooked emphasis on institutional policies and hospital economics in two settings and how they shaped the care received by end-of-life patients. Both authors make extensive use of illustrative cases, befitting good ethnography.

This is complex territory. It makes us all vulnerable when our time comes, whether we choose to take command with a hefty dose of phenobarbital or attempt to delay the inevitable using all available technology. We bring to that decision a lifetime of learning, acting, and believing—and no two of us are the same. Perhaps the better starting point, then, is not "cultural competence" at all, but rather, a more modest "cultural humility" as some have suggested.[45] What works for understanding diversity in the clinic may be useful in responding to human suffering whatever its face. And from that starting point, something unexpected just might occur—the resurrection of Philippe Ariès's tame death.

* * * * *

My thanks to George E. Dickinson, Margaret F. Gaines, MD, and especially Susan Chapin, RN, for their critical reading of the manuscript and helpful suggestions. Also, thanks to the participants at the Columbia University 2012 Seminar on Death whose comments on the paper were useful. A special thanks goes to Margaret Souza who first suggested I participate and then offered generous hospitality while attending.

NOTES

1. Philippe Ariès, *The Hour of Our Death* (New York: Vintage Books, 1982), 18.

2. David William Atkinson, *The English Ars Moriendi* (New York: Peter Lang, 1992), 31.

3. My thanks to Susan Chapin for advice on this matter.

4. Arthur G. Svenson, "Montana's courting of physician aid in dying. Could Des Moines follow suit?" *Politics and the Life Science* 2 (2010): 3.

5. Available at www.harrisinteractive.com. (Search Harris poll assisted dying. Accessed February 28, 2013.)

6. This data is available at http://oregon.gov/DHS/ph/pas/index.shtml

7. The language of the Oregon Revised Statute is as follows: "127.825 s.3.03. Counseling referral. If in the opinion of the attending physician or the consulting physician a patient may be suffering from a psychiatric or psychological disorder or depression causing impaired judgment, either physician shall refer the patient for counseling. No medication to end a patient's life in a humane and dignified manner shall be prescribed until the person performing the counseling determines that the patient is not suffering from a psychiatric or psychological disorder or depression causing impaired judgment. 1995 c.3 s.3.03; 1999 c.423 s.4."

8. Linda Ganzini, Elizabeth R. Goy, Steven K. Dobscha, "Prevalence of Depression and Anxiety in Patients Requesting Physician's Aid in Dying: Cross Sectional Survey" *British Medical Journal* 337, 7676 (2008): 966–71.

9. Marije L. Van der Lee, "Depression and Physician Assisted Dying" *British Medical Journal* 337, 7676 (2008): 941–42.

10. The phrase is Justice O'Connor's.

11. Steven K. Dobsha, Ronald K. Heintz, Nancy Press, Linda Ganzini, "Oregon Physician's Responses to Requests for Assisted Suicide: a Qualitative Study," *Journal of Palliative Medicine* 7, 3 (2004): 455.

12. Ibid, 456.

13. Ibid, 458.

14. For a discussion of this film, see James W. Green, "Physician Assisted Suicide: Death on Request" in Henri Colt, Silvia Quadrelli, Lester Friedman eds., *The Picture of Health* (New York, Oxford University Press, 2011): 405–10.

15. Dir. and Prod. Peter Richardson, Supervising Prod. Jacqueline Glover/HBO, Assoc. Prod. Jordan Curnes, et al. Clear Cut Films is the producing company and the film is available from Amazon.com.

16. Timothy Quill, "Physician-Assisted Death in the United States: Are the Existing 'Last Resorts' Enough?" *Hastings Center Report* 38, 5 (2008): 17–22.

17. Nicolas A. Cristakis, Elizabeth E. Lamont, "Extent and Determinants of Error in Doctor's Prognoses in Terminally Ill Patients: Prospective Cohort Study," *British Medical Journal* 320, 7233 (2000): 469–73.

18. H. M. Buiting, J.K.M. Gevers, J.A.C. Rietjens, B.D. Onwuteaqka-Philipsen, P.J. van der Mass, A. van der Heide, J.J.M. van Delden, "Dutch Criteria for Due Care for Physician Assisted Dying in Medical Practice: a Physician Perspective," *Journal of Medical Ethics* 34, e12 (2008): 1.

19. E.J. Cassel, "The Nature of Suffering and the Goals of Medicine," *New England Journal of Medicine* 11, 6 (1982): 639–45.

20. Atul Gawande, "Letting Go," *The New Yorker* (August 2, 2010): 36–49.

21. This insight is elaborated by British sociologist Clive Seale in his article "Heroic Death," *Sociology* 29, 4 (1995): 597–613. A popular American critic of these practices, and a cancer survivor herself, is Barbara Ehrenreich. See her title, *Bright Sided, How Positive Thinking is Undermining America* (New York: Henry Holt and Company, 2009). Chapter 1 deals with cancer. The language of war, heroism and battle is widely used, in accounts of sports figures and celebrities who beat their disease and in the obituaries of ordinary people who did not.

22. Ronald K. Barrett, "Death and Dying in the Black Experience," *Journal of Palliative Medicine* 5, 5 (2002): 797.

23. Janelle S. Taylor, "The Story Catches You and You Fall Down: Tragedy, Ethnography, and 'Cultural Competence,'" *Medical Anthropology Quarterly* 17, 2, 556 (2003): 179.

24. Lisa S. Chan, Mary Ellen Macdonald, S. Robin Cohen, "Moving Culture Beyond Ethnicity: Examining Dying in Hospital Through a Cultural Lens" *Journal of Palliative Care* 25, 2 (2009): 117–24.

25. David Sudnow, *Passing On, the Social Organization of Dying* (Englewood Cliffs, Prentice-Hall, 1967).

26. Sharon R. Kaufman, *And a Time to Die, How American Hospitals Shape the End of Life* (New York: Scribner, 2005), 333.

27. One example among many is Roger Thomas, Donna M. Wilson, Christopher Justice, Stephen Birch, Sam Sheps, "A Literature Review of Preferences for End-of-Life Care in Developed Countries by Individuals with Different Cultural Affiliations and Ethnicity," *Journal of Hospice and Palliative Nursing* 10, 3 (2008): 142–61.

28. H. Russell Searight, Jennifer Gafford, "Cultural Diversity at the End of Life: Issues and Guidelines for Family Physicians," *American Family Physician* 71, 3 (2005): 515–22.

29. This list of questions appears in Arthur Kleinman, Peter Benson, "Anthropology in the Clinic: the Problem of Cultural Competency and How to Fix It," *PLoS Medicine* 3, 10 (2006): 1673–76. Its conceptual basis is described in Arthur Kleinman, *The Illness Narratives, Suffering, Healing and the Human Condition* (New York: Basic Books, 1988). See also Jacqueline Somerville, "The Paradox of Palliative Care Nursing Across Cultural Boundaries," *International Journal of Palliative Nursing* 13, 12 (2007): 580–87.

30. There are a number of examples. The following are useful as starting points. Stacy M. Fischer, Angela Sauaia, Jean Kutner, "Patient Navigation: a Culturally Competent Strategy to Address Disparities in Palliative Care," *Journal of Palliative Medicine* 10, 5 (2007): 1023–28. Joshua Hauser, "Navigation and Palliative Care," *Cancer* 117, S15 (2011): 3583–89. David A. Westbrook, *Navigators of the Contemporary, Why Ethnography Matters* (Chicago: University of Chicago Press, 2008). This is not dissimilar to what is now being called in some of the medical literature "patient navigation," a phrase that is catching on, and that seems apt since the biomedical disease model is not the only one at the bedside.

31. William H. Shrank, Jean S. Kutner, Terri Richardson, Richard A. Mularski, Stacy Fischer, Marjorie Kagawa-Singer, "Focus Groups Findings about the Influences of Culture on Communication Preferences in End-of-Life Care," *Journal of General Internal Medicine* 20, 8 (2005): 703–09.

32. Deborah Carr, "Racial Differences in End-of-Life Planning: Why Don't Blacks and Latinos Prepare for the Inevitable?" *Omega* 1 (2011): 1–20.

33. Brownsyne Tucker Edmonds, "Moving Beyond the Impasse: Discussing Death and Dying with African American Patients," *Obstetrics & Gynecology* 117, 2 (2011): 383–87.

34. Ibid, 385.

35. PubMed search February 9, 2012.

36. Patricia Boston, Anne Bruce, Rita Schreiber, "Existential Suffering in the Palliative Care Setting: an Integrated Literature Review," *Journal of Pain and Symptom Management* 41, 3 (2011): 385.

37. A. Edwards, N. Pang, V. Sjiu, C. Chan, "The Understanding of Spirituality and the Potential Role of Spiritual Care in End-of-Life and Palliative Care: a Meta-Study of Qualitative Research," *Palliative Medicine* 24, 8 (2010): 753–70.

38. Lucy Bregman, "Spirituality: a Glowing and Useful Term in Search of a Meaning," *Omega* 53, 1 (2006): 5–26.

39. Elizabeth Kübler-Ross, *On Death and Dying* (New York: Macmillan, 1969).

40. Tony Walter, "Spirituality in Palliative Care: Opportunity or Burden?" *Palliative Medicine* 16, 2 (2002): 133–39.

41. See note 24.

42. Alexander K. Smith, Rebecca L. Sudore, Eliseo J. Perez-Stable, "Palliative Care for Latino Patients and Their Families: Whenever We Prayed, She Wept," *Journal of the American Medical Association* 301, 10 (2009): 1047–57.

43. Ibid, 385.

44. *No Place for Dying, Hospitals and the Ideology of Rescue* (Walnut Creek, CA: Left Coast Press, 2010).

45. Melanie Tervalon, Jann Murray-Garcia, "Cultural Humility Versus Cultural Competence: a Critical Distinction in Defining Physician Training Outcomes in Multicultural Education," *Journal of Health care for the Poor and Underserved* 9, 2 (1998): 117–25.

Chapter 3

Assisted Suicide in the Age of AIDS and Alzheimer's

Michael Teitelman

*A*s the baby-boomer generation enters its senior years, the aging of U.S. society will accelerate. More people live longer and the prevalence of Alzheimer's disease will triple from 5 million to 15 million over the next three decades. This epidemiological change will be accompanied by a remarkable advance in the clinical diagnosis of Alzheimer's. The development of biomarkers of Alzheimer's will enable physicians to utilize noninvasive PET scan technology to diagnose the disease at its earliest stage while an individual's cognitive capacities are still intact. This diagnostic technology, which is already FDA approved and in clinical use, is indispensable for the development of new therapies. For the foreseeable future, aging boomers will face a mismatch between diagnosis and treatment. At the first sign of cognitive impairment, they will be able to know whether they are experiencing the expectable cognitive decline of aging or whether they are facing an inexorable journey into the profound dementia of end-stage Alzheimer's disease. The confluence of these changes in the epidemiology and science of Alzheimer's will reinvigorate debate regarding end-of-life ethical issues. Many boomers whose moral and social outlook has been grounded in an ethic of independence and individual autonomy will advocate for the morality of suicide. They will press for the legalization of euthanasia so that individuals who are cognitively competent can arrange for the future termination of their lives when they are no longer able to take action for themselves.

A teacher walks into the school office and stands in front of the secretary's desk. The teacher is at a loss as to why she is standing there. The secretary points to the pencil sharpener on the wall. The teacher is dumbfounded. "How did you know what I couldn't remember?" "Easy," says the secretary, "you are holding a bunch of pencils without points."

If this teacher were 25, you might think she forgot why she came into the office because she had too much on her mind. If she were 70, though, you might think there was not enough on her mind. You might wonder whether her momentary confusion was an early sign of Alzheimer's dementia, a disease whose hallmark manifestation is memory loss, and one in which age and memory are inextricably linked. Fifty percent of people over 85 are functionally impaired by their dementia.

Dementia is an observable clinical condition of the person. *Alzheimer's disease* (AD) is a pathophysiological process in the brain which results in clinical dementia. *Alzheimer's dementia* is the clinical condition that results from AD, which is the cause of most (more than 60%) clinical dementia. Other causes of dementia include vascular dementia, Lewy body dementia, Parkinson's disease, and Creutzfeldt-Jacob disease.

AD and other forms of dementia have become a part of daily life. Most of us know, by one or two degrees of separation, someone with dementia. As signs of the times, consider that the government of the City of New York transmits several text messages and e-mail alerts a day about missing elderly to subscribers to this service. Progress in AD research is front-page news worldwide.

This prominence of AD in social consciousness is recent. Back in the mid-1980s, there was an explosion of criticism and controversy about end-of-life medical issues such as physician paternalism and control, excessive utilization of medical technology, inadequate pain management, the neglect of palliative approaches to care, and the lack of hospice programs. AD was not part of that conversation.

Perhaps the most intensively debated issue was the legalization of physician-assisted suicide (PAS) for terminally ill individuals. PAS was catapulted into public awareness by the onset of the HIV epidemic. In the second half of the 1980s, rates of new AIDS cases and deaths were climbing steeply. Reports of markedly elevated suicide rates among AIDS patients sparked public discussion about the moral acceptability of suicide.[1] In 1988, a gynecology resident recounted how he ended the life of a young woman dying of leukemia. His anonymous article, provocatively entitled "It's Over, Debbie," contributed to a heated debate about the propriety of PAS.[2]

Cancer, amyotrophic lateral sclerosis (ALS), and HIV/AIDS were the biomedical backdrop of societal debate about PAS in the 1990s. They anchored the abstract legal, ethical, and professional arguments in the realities of disease, decline, and death. AD did not figure into the discussion.

When PAS was legalized in a 1997 electoral referendum in Oregon, it moved from the realm of theory to actual clinical practice. The vociferous debate over PAS simmered down. It continues to be studied and discussed in medical, legal, and intellectual venues, but it is no longer a "hot button" issue in the print and broadcast media.

I believe that this quiescence will not continue. The changing realities of AD will reanimate public discussion about assisted suicide. But it will be a radically different discussion because AD introduces morally vexing complications that are not raised by diseases like cancer or AIDS.

In the next section I will explain why I think we are going to have a second round of debate about assisted suicide. I then discuss how AD will reopen issues that were settled in the first round.

PART I. PHYSICIAN-ASSISTED SUICIDE: ROUND TWO

Over the next 25 years, renewed interest in assisted suicide will result from the confluence of epidemiological, scientific, and cultural factors.

1. Epidemiological. The prevalence of AD in the United States will more than triple in the next 40 years—5 million will increase to more than 15 million people living with AD.[3] This increasing prevalence is a consequence of longer life spans; the longer people live, the more likely they are to develop dementia. More importantly, the cohort born in the two decades after World War II, the baby-boomer generation numbering more than 70 million, is beginning to reach the 65-year mark. This will produce a "senior bulge" in the demographic profile. Currently, 13 percent of the population is over 65; in 2050, this will increase to 20 percent.[4]

As more Americans suffer from dementia, the psychological and financial burden will fall not only on patients, but also on families and society at large. More than 75 percent of affected individuals now finish their lives in nursing homes in which care is labor intensive and costly. With a tripling of the affected population, the strain on health-care institutions and health-care finances will be immense. The prevalence of AD will increase gradually. It won't arrive like the deluge of illness and death during the first decade of the HIV epidemic. But because so many people will be affected in so many ways, the issues raised by AD will fill the airwaves.

The epidemiological and social prominence of AD is new. Nobel laureate neuroscientist Eric Kandel and senior AD researchers recently concurred on a Charlie Rose program that four or five decades ago, AD received only passing notice in their medical school curriculum and that cases of AD in their clinical training were uncommon.[5] AD is a disease of postmodern times.

2. Scientific/Clinical. Like so much else in biomedical research, progress in understanding AD at molecular, cellular, and clinical levels in the last 30 years has been spectacular. The classic postmortem pathological triad that Alois Alzheimer delineated more than a century ago—amyloid plaques, neurofibrillary tangles, and cortical atrophy—has been yielding to the investigative tools of molecular biology. Over the last 30 years, the molecular structure of amyloid and the composition of neurofibrillary tangles have been analyzed in exquisite detail. Patterns of neuronal loss have been mapped out.[6]

One particularly impressive scientific achievement has been the development of a model of the pathogenesis of amyloid plaques. A key item in current etiological theory of AD is that the formation of beta-amyloid plaques creates a toxic environment for nerve cells. Understanding how neurons process amyloid is essential to understanding the diagnosis and treatment of the disease.[7]

We are on the verge of knowing how to diagnose AD with molecular and radiological tests whose validity will be comparable to routine diagnostic tests such as the measurement of cardiac enzymes to determine whether a person has suffered a heart attack. Validating levels of beta-amyloid and tau (a product of neuronal degeneration) as biomarkers for AD in the living brain and correlating their changing levels to the progression of clinical symptoms is a high-priority research objective.[8] Measurement of these molecules over time is yielding a picture of disease progression. Beta-amyloid concentration is elevated in the earliest stage of AD. As the disease progresses and neurons die off, amyloid concentration declines and tau increases.[9]

The introduction of biomarkers into clinical practice will fundamentally change the problem of diagnosis. At present, diagnosis in the presymptomatic phase is impossible: no symptoms, no diagnosis. With biomarkers, even before the first symptoms appear, it will be possible to detect the physiological process that will eventually progress to end-stage dementia.

Biomarker studies have already established that the physiological processes of AD are present 10 or 15 years *before* the onset of cognitive symptoms just as atherosclerosis of blood vessels precedes cardiac symptoms by many decades. Presymptomatic detection of AD physiology is essential to the development of medical interventions to prevent or retard disease progression. Serial measurement of biomarkers will be used to track the biological impact of new medications.[10]

The diagnosis of AD is not particularly problematic when symptoms are unmistakably present and are worsening. Diagnosis is based on patient and family reports, clinical observation, and neuropsychological testing.

The most vexing diagnostic problem resides in the earliest stage of the disease. At present, there is no reliable way to distinguish between the earliest manifestation of AD, which is designated "minimal cognitive impairment" (MCI), and the phenomenon of "age-associated memory impairment" (AAMI),[11] which was previously known as benign senescence.

Memory problems of aging (AAMI) are characterized by delayed information retrieval and the inability to remember familiar names and events. These disturbances can provoke considerable anxiety about whether they are manifestations of an incipient dementia. On a bad day, any aging person might experience several of these symptoms. But they do not portend a downhill course.

MCI is the first symptomatic step along the path toward dementia. Symptoms of MCI include forgetfulness, word finding difficulty, poor attention, difficulty with complex tasks, declining performance in work and social settings, difficulty retaining new information, and anxiety.

The problem is that there is no sure way for a clinician to distinguish between those who should be reassured that their memory problems are benign and those who will progress to dementia. At present, the diagnosis is made by serial observations of declining function. The diagnosis can be made with confidence only when a person is unmistakably symptomatic.

Biomarkers will have a transformative impact on diagnosis in this stage of AD. Measuring levels of beta-amyloid and tau protein in spinal fluid, quantifying radioisotope tagged amyloid plaques and neurofibrillary tangles in the living brain by PET scan, and integrating this data with MRI and CAT scan imaging will become routine and reliable ways to diagnose the disease.

Researchers are confident that clinically useful biomarkers will be available in the next few years. However, there is no comparable optimism about finding new treatments anytime soon. Basic research has opened up theoretically feasible paths to treatment but the problems of drug development are daunting. The science of AD has guided thinking about how to intervene in the disease process, but this has not yet led to effective treatments. Recent clinical trials have been disappointing.[12] Even when a potentially useful agent is identified, it can take a decade or more to move from insight to clinical research trials of a medication and even longer for its clinical use.

Thus, scientific progress is bringing us to the point of a mismatch between diagnostic and therapeutic capacities. Clinicians will be able to tell people with complaints of mild memory problems whether they are on the road to dementia and decline, but there will be no treatments to prevent or control the deterioration. This gap between diagnostic and therapeutic capacities is the second factor that I believe will revive discussion of assisted suicide.

3. Cultural. The value of individual autonomy has largely dominated the moral education of the boomer generation. The moral discourse of the culture, which is expressed in the vocabulary of rights and liberties, is grounded in the principle of autonomy, namely that people ought to be free to live according to their own desires and values. The desire to be in control of one's life is pervasive. In health care, the value of individual autonomy is the ethical foundation of the principle of informed consent. Respect for individual autonomy was at the heart of the debate over PAS in the 1990s.

In a 1995 study, just before legalization of assisted suicide in Oregon, patients in the late stages of ALS reported the desire to have control over when they would die. Most said they would choose PAS, were it legal, rather than endure total dependence in the final stage of their disease. They wanted control over when they would end their lives in order to prevent further deterioration of their independence.[13] In the 15 years since legalization of PAS in Oregon, most patients who opt for assisted suicide regarded the loss of independence in their final days as the principal reason for wanting to end their lives.[14]

So these are the three factors whose confluence I believe will stimulate discussion of assisted suicide: epidemiological, scientific, and cultural. Tens of millions of baby boomers will be at increasing risk for developing AD. Diagnostic tests will be available to determine whether they are in an early stage of Alzheimer's dementia or will be heading there. But there will be no meaningful therapeutic options anytime soon.

People diagnosed with early AD face a long, slow decline into dementia and death.[15] This progression has been well charted in the last three decades of clinical research. Eventually, and sadly, the afflicted person loses the ability to speak, to comprehend speech, and to recognize other people. Skills learned early in life wither away. There is a loss of the ability to dress and feed oneself and to control defecation and urination. Ultimately, the person is profoundly withdrawn and akinetic. End-stage dementia is grim.[16]

As the prevalence of AD increases, many more of us will have direct personal experience of this neurodegenerative process. Many in the boomer cohort have already lived through the dementia of parents, or grandparents, or other elderly people in their lives. People with advancing AD often remain at home until the burden of caring for them exceeds the psychological and financial resources of caregivers.

The decline into dementia is a gradual extinction of the self. Allowing for metaphysical brevity, the self is an aspect of mind that is produced by the brain: the cells of the brain that accomplish this are dying. In this condition, there is no living out one's days in a meaningful way. There is no finding meaning while enduring AD to the end of life. The biological machinery for finding meaning withers away. In a state of mindlessness, neither hope nor hopelessness is possible.

As the prevalence of AD accelerates and the new diagnostic technology comes into clinical use, I believe the generation of aging boomers will begin a conversation about the reasonableness of not going all the way down the neurodegenerative path. Discussion of assisted suicide will percolate beyond the precincts of universities and journals back into the public arena.

In the third part of this essay, I contend that the idea of assisted suicide for people with AD cannot be contained within the clinical-ethical paradigm of PAS that coalesced in the 1990s. However, before doing so, I explore what that paradigm is.

PART II. THE OREGON PROTOCOL: A TEMPLATE FOR ASSISTED SUICIDE

Oregon voters passed the Death with Dignity Act by a vote of 51 percent to 49 percent in 1994. The law allows a physician to provide a prescription for an oral medication, which a terminally ill person can use to end his or her life. After a few years of skirmishing in the courts, opponents of PAS, principally the Catholic Church, sponsored a 1997 initiative to repeal Death with Dignity. Voter support increased to 60 percent. From 1998 to 2010, 596 people ended their lives under provisions of the law. Popular support for the law has remained high.

The Oregon Health Authority promulgated a protocol for physician assistance:[17]

1. The patient requests assistance on two occasions at least 15 days apart. The patient also prepares a written request signed by two witnesses; one of them must be unrelated to the patient.

2. The physician and a medical consultant confirm the patient's diagnosis and that the patient's life expectancy is less than six months.

3. The physician and consultant ascertain that the patient is capable of deliberating about health-care decisions. If either believes that a mental condition, such as depression or delirium or psychosis, is compromising the patient's decision-making capacity, the patient is referred for psychiatric evaluation.

4. The physician ascertains that the patient is a resident of the state of Oregon. (This provision blocks the "suicide tourism" that occurs in Switzerland and the Netherlands.)

5. The physician counsels the patient that palliative care, hospice care, and pain control are available whether or not the requested medication is utilized.

6. The physician submits a report to the state health authority.

The Oregon protocol has recently been adopted in Montana and Washington. The protocol is likely to serve as a template for regulations in other states where PAS is under active consideration. In part, this is because the experience with PAS in Oregon has been unproblematic. It is also because the protocol expresses values and addresses criticisms that were central to the debate about PAS.

Opponents of legalization contended that assisted suicide would violate the ethics of the medical profession. Under the Oregon rules, physicians do not have an obligation to assist their patients' suicides. Because there is fundamental disagreement about what the profession's norms require or permit, no health-care provider is compelled to act against the values to which he or she is committed.

Respect for individual autonomy, which is the ethical foundation of the case for legalization, is embedded in the Oregon rules in several ways. Opponents of legalization contended that the mental and physical burdens of living with a terminal illness undermine a person's capacity for self-determination and sound decision making. Patients might request medication because they are in a depressed or delirious state and not because they have arrived at the decision through reflection and deliberation. The protocol addresses this by stipulating a 15-day waiting period to prevent impulsive suicide attempts and requires two physicians to make a clinical assessment of the patient's mental functioning. The rate of referral for psychiatric evaluation has been quite low: 6.7 percent.

Respect for individual autonomy is also reflected in the requirement of a six-month prognosis. People who are facing death are free to end their lives for reasons that make sense to them. Assistance is not limited to people who are actually experiencing pain. The protocol permits them to request medication before they experience significant pain. According to the Oregon Public Health Division, end-of-life concerns were loss of autonomy (91%), loss of ability to engage in enjoyable activity (88%), and loss of dignity (83%). Inadequate pain control, or fear of it, was near the bottom of the list (23%). Virtually no one (2%) cited financial considerations.[18]

The most serious criticism of PAS was that legalization would open the door to euthanasia or worse, to murder. Assisted suicide is voluntary. Patients decide whether ending life is the best course of action according to their circumstances, desires, and values. In contrast, euthanasia is a special form of paternalism. Someone else decides, without a person's knowledge or agreement, that death would be better than continued illness. The decision might be made by a family member who knows the person well or by others, such as hospital staff, who do not. One giant moral step beyond euthanasia is deciding to end a person's life to benefit other people, which is murder.

The Oregon protocol addresses this problem in several ways. First, from start to finish, the patient is in control. The patient decides to request the medication. The patient can choose to take it or not; 64 percent who received prescriptions in Oregon actually used the medication. The patient decides on the time and place; 94.8 percent ended their lives in their homes.[19]

Second, the method of administering a legal agent is ethically significant. Oral administration of numerous pills requires the active participation of the patient. Intravenous infusion and inhalation do not. The protocol blocks the slide from voluntary assisted suicide to euthanasia by not allowing either.

Third, in all other medical contexts, advanced directives are recognized as valid authorizations of medical care in circumstances delineated in the directive. In an advanced directive, a person speaks to future circumstances and decisions. Typically, a person addressing end-of-life issues indicates which technologies should be used or withheld. Substituted judgment is also recognized. A patient can designate a surrogate who is authorized to make decisions based on the treatment preferences previously expressed by the patient.

Advanced directives and proxy decisions are enormously useful in medical care. They are indispensable for squaring the moral principle of informed consent with the realities of disease and trauma in which the capacity for deliberation and decision unravels. They also have their limitations. Circumstances arise that have not been anticipated in advanced directives or in the conversations of patient and proxy. They are inescapably vague. Interpretation and extrapolation are unavoidable.

The Oregon protocol makes no provision for substituted judgment. Neither advanced directives nor proxy decisions have a place in the protocol. No document or person can substitute for the actual choice of the individual who requests suicide assistance. Their exclusion from the protocol is another safeguard against the slide into euthanasia.

PART III. ALZHEIMER'S DISEASE
AND THE OREGON PROTOCOL

Thus far, I have been exploring two propositions:

First, the sharp increase of an aging population coupled with the advent of new methods of diagnosing AD will lead to renewed interest in assisted suicide.

Second, the Oregon protocol, which is becoming a template for the legalization and regulation of assisted suicide, expresses the moral consensus that emerged from the debate about PAS.

This leads to the question whether the issues that will be raised in debate about assisted suicide for people with AD can be resolved without major departures from the Oregon protocol. I believe this is not possible because the protocol clashes with several features of the AD process.

Of the 596 Oregonians who received prescriptions, 80.9 percent were dying from cancer, 7.4 percent had ALS, and 4.2 percent had chronic obstructive pulmonary disease.[20] The requirements of the protocol mesh with the temporal contours of these diseases. Patients by and large retain the capacity to think and communicate. When they reach the point of having a life expectancy of six months, they are still able to make decisions for themselves. They can, if they choose to, request a prescription to end their lives. If they choose to use the prescription, they are alert and determined so that they are able to administer it to themselves.

In contrast, people with AD suffer significant deterioration in cognitive capacity long before they reach the six-month mark. By the time they cross that threshold, they are unable to deal with existential questions. So they do not qualify for assistance under the Oregon protocol: they are terminal but not competent. Somebody else would have to request medication for them, and somebody else would also have to administer a lethal agent by injection or inhalation. This is euthanasia. It is a significant departure from the moral consensus that underwrites the legalization of euthanasia.

If the requirement of a short life expectancy is set aside, a different problem emerges. A revised protocol could stipulate that patients with a well-established diagnosis of AD may request assistance if their minds are still functioning well even though they are not terminally ill. However, it isn't possible to make a definite clinical diagnosis while cognitive capacities are fully intact. The loss of the capacity to keep thinking on track and to deliberate about complicated problems on a sustained basis is itself a turning point at which the diagnosis can be made. So when people can be reliably diagnosed because of their cognitive deterioration, they may be too far along to request a prescription under the protocol.

Before a person reaches a level of cognitive impairment that compromises decision making, still another problem emerges. While cognitive capacity is still more or less intact, it may not be possible to distinguish between earliest stage of AD, MIC, and AAMI. A person with MIC might want to begin thinking about how he or she would like to plan for an inevitable decline even when it lies many years off. However, clinical differentiation of MIC from AAMI is uncertain and provisional. Sometimes the best the diagnostician can say in these circumstances is: "We can't be sure and time will tell."

This is where the new diagnostic technology will make a difference. The introduction of biomarkers into routine clinical practice will mean that people who are either asymptomatic or in the very earliest stage of AD will know, with a high degree of certainty, that they will ultimately face a decline into end-stage dementia. At this early stage, people still have the requisite capacity to live their lives and make their own medical decisions. But they will have no interest in ending their lives long before their brains begin to fail. They are still capable of meaningful activity and experiencing the satisfactions of life.

However, while they are still able to, they may want to prepare an advanced directive indicating the circumstances in which they would like to have a request for suicide assistance made on their behalf. Or, if they find it difficult to compose a clear, specific directive, they might want to formally designate a surrogate to act in their behalf. But this would require a serious emendation of the Oregon protocol, which does not recognize advanced directives or substituted judgment. Another person must mediate a patient's intentions in unpredictable future circumstances. If the AD patient is unable to ingest sufficient medication, someone may have to administer a lethal agent intravenously or by inhalation. This is euthanasia with the prior consent of the patient.

Thus, when the diagnosis of AD can be made with confidence through laboratory testing and when treatment alternatives do not exist, the idea of autonomous termination of life will begin to gain traction and the debate over assisted suicide will be renewed. In the first round of debate, autonomous suicide did not encompass euthanasia. In the second round, assessing the request for suicide assistance by a person with AD will not be possible just with clinical interviews and the writing of a prescription. It will require the participation of a second person to effectuate the intentions of the person whose cognitive competence has failed.

A more morally complex and legally more complicated arrangement will be required to help people to make the kind of graceful exit they previously decided upon for themselves before their brains began to fail. The intricacies of this problem will be the core of the next round of debate about assisted suicide.

PART IV. AIDS AND ALZHEIMER'S DISEASE: THE DYNAMIC OF DESPAIR AND HOPE

In the 1980s, the idea of PAS was propelled into public awareness in the deluge of the AIDS epidemic. Autonomous suicide began to be seen as a morally acceptable option for people with a terrible disease that would cut them down in short order. Their despair was understandable. The horror of the epidemic and the plight of AIDS patients swayed sympathies and convictions

Observers note that assisted suicides are a minuscule percentage of deaths in Oregon. People did not rush for the exit when it became available. Those who did choose to end their lives have been younger, more educated, and economically better off than patients with comparable illnesses who did not seek suicide assistance. They are, in a sense, early boomers. So the frequency of assisted death may increase in the coming decades.

Interestingly, very few individuals with HIV/AIDS sought suicide assistance after it was legalized in 1997. This might seem surprising in view of how the epidemic and PAS were so entangled, but something happened along the way. Treatment took a dramatic turn. A multidrug regimen that reduced the viral load and rescued the immune system was brought into clinical practice. Death rates and hospitalizations started to fall. Despair gave way to hope. Autonomous suicide became irrelevant.

Probably, in coming years, as the prevalence of AD triples and the new diagnostic technology brings bad news to many, there will be quiet despair. The fact that it is quiet does not mean it should be ignored. In time, new treatments will shift the balance from despair to hope. But before then, respect should be paid to the quiet despair of the aging and their families.

* * *

I would like to thank Emma Teitelman for her editorial assistance.

NOTES

1. Peter Marzuk et al., "Increased Risk of Suicide in Persons with AIDS," *Journal of the American Medical Association* 259 (1988): 1333–37.

2. Anonymous. "A Piece of My Mind. It's over, Debbie," *Journal of the American Medical Association* 259, 2 (January 8,1988): 272.

3. Alzheimer's Association, "2011 Alzheimer's disease facts and figures," *Alzheimer's & Dementia* 7 (2011): 208–44.

4. Laura Shrestha et al., *The Changing Demographic Profile of the United States,* Congressional Research Service, March 31, 2011.

5. Charlie Rose, "Alzheimer's Disease," *Brain Series* 2, February 23, 2012.

6. George M. Savva et al., "Age, Neuropathology and Dementia," *New England Journal of Medicine* 360 (2009): 2302–9.

7. Henry Querfurth and Frank LaFerla, "Alzheimer's Disease," *New England Journal of Medicine* 362 (2010): 329–44.

8. Mary Naylor et al., "Advancing Alzheimer's disease diagnosis, treatment and care: Recommendations from the Ware Invitational Summit," *Alzheimer's & Dementia* 8 (2012): 445–52. Lucie Yang et al. "Brain Amyloid Imaging—FDA Approval of Florbetapir F18 Injection," *New England Journal of Medicine* 367 (2012): 885–87.

9. Rebecca Craig-Shapiro et al., "Biomarkers of Alzheimer's disease," *Neurobiology of Disease* 35 (2009): 128–40. Harald Hampel et al., "Biomarkers for Alzheimer's disease: academic, industry, and regulatory perspectives," Nature *Reviews Drug Discovery* 9 (2010): 560–74.

10. Jack Clifford, Jr et al., "Hypothetical model of dynamic biomarkers of the Alzheimer's pathological cascade," Lancet *Neurology* 9 (2010): 119–28.

11. Marilyn Albert et al., "The diagnosis of mild cognitive impairment due to Alzheimer's disease: Recommendations from National Institute from Aging and Alzheimer's Association work group," *Alzheimer's & Dementia* 7 (2011): 1–10. Richard Mayeux, "Early Alzheimer's Disease," *New England Journal of Medicine* 362 (2010): 2194–201.

12. Katie Thomas, "Trials for Alzheimer's Drug Halted after Poor Result," *New York Times,* August 6, 2012. Gina Kolata, "Doubt on Tactic in Alzheimer's Battle," *New York Times,* August, 18, 2010.

13. Linda Ganzini et al., "Attitudes of Patients with Amyotrophic Lateral Sclerosis and Their Caregivers toward Assisted Suicide," *New England Journal of Medicine* 339 (1998): 967–73.

14. Oregon Public Health Division, "Characteristics and end-of-life care of 596 DWDA patients who have died from ingesting a lethal dose of medication as of February 29, 2012, by year, Oregon 1998–2011," http://public.health.oregon.gov/ProviderPartnerResources/EvaluationResearch/DeathwithDignityAct/Documents/year14-tbl-1.pdf

15. Susan Mitchell et al., "The Clinical Course of Advanced Dementia," *New England Journal of Medicine* 361 (2009): 1529–38.

16. Greg Sachs, "Dying from Dementia," *New England Journal of Medicine* 361 (2009): 1595–96.

17. Oregon Public Health Division. "Death with Dignity Act Requirements," http://public.health.oregon.gov/ProviderPartnerResources/EvaluationResearch/DeathwithDignityAct/Documents/requirements.pdf

18. Oregon Public Health Division. "Oregon's Death with Dignity Act—2011" http://public.health.oregon.gov/ProviderPartnerResources/EvaluationResearch/ DeathwithDignityAct/Documents/year14

19. Ibid.

20. Oregon Public Health Division. "Characteristics and end-of-life care of 596 DWDA patiens who have died from ingesting a lethal dose of medication as of February 29, 2012, by year, Oregon 1998–2011," http://public.health.oregon.gov/Provider PartnerResources/EvaluationResearch/DeathwithDignityAct/Documents/year14-tbl-1.pdf

Chapter 4

Dying Persons and Their Families

Margaret Souza

*T*his chapter provides a window into the way that dying occurs from the various perspectives of family members, dying persons, and the medical profession. It underscores the complexity that exists in the process of dying in the 21st century. In particular it focuses on the difficulties involved in decision making. Diverse perspectives from medical professionals provide contradictory messages for family members who are called upon to make such decisions. The differing ways in which family members and the health-care team approach the dying process is made visible. The chapter then goes on to discuss the ways in which care is rendered based on the location of the dying person in a facility and those who are administering the care highlighting the need for a personal advocate.

Although some would suggest that dying in previous times was easier because it was more visible, happened earlier in the life cycle, and occurred in previous cultures that were more religious,[1] there are scholars who question that assumption. Archeological evidence as well as art and poetry provide a different perspective.[2] They suggest and I would agree that dying has always been a troubling occurrence.

Since I assert that dying presents a problem to the human community and ruptures our social fabric,[3] it is important to understand what the experience of dying is, particularly in the 21st century and what it means for the individuals who are dying and their kin. This information provides a window into the U.S. culture. Because of the change of the demographics of dying, only 20 percent of all deaths occur suddenly with 80 percent being the result of long-term and terminal illness. Thus, the problem of dying has taken on new dimensions becoming a longer-term process and in most situations a medical event.

The medical/nursing response to the dying process has been hospice and the newer medical specialty developed in the later part of the 20th century, palliative care. The proponents of these two approaches, which vary, suggest that they are able to provide a "good death," that is pain free and peaceful.[4] In this sense, they seek to eliminate the sting of death. In this they underscore a Western cultural value of life without pain and suffering. In my research,* in general, I found that many individuals involved in these approaches to dying often were reacting to the difficult situations that they had experienced in the intensive care units as medical residents where dying persons were treated long after any hope of stability or improvement seemed possible to them. They described to me how they saw the patient treatment that was being administered as torturous.

In this chapter I provide a close examination of the dying process and develop two themes surrounding it. First, although the moment of death can be peaceful and simple, the process to that moment can be most difficult for individuals who are dying and for their kin. The focus in this chapter is mainly about the experiences of kin. The ideology of a good death is an ideal, but something that is an oxymoron. Death is a difficult process particularly for those who are personally involved in it. It entails loss. Presently in the U.S. context, dying persons or their family members usually have to make decisions about withholding or ending treatment, which adds to the burden of dying. I am not suggesting that dying persons or their family members should not be involved in this process, but simply underscoring the difficulties involved in this process. Second, even though there are many dedicated persons delivering care to the dying the quality of care that anyone receives in a hospice or palliative care program is only equal to the individuals who are providing it. I will describe some of the ways in which the responses by individuals who work in these programs also add to the burden of those personally involved.

First, I address dying and its difficulties. Most individuals when they are healthy speak of how they would not want any unnecessary interventions, - even interventions that potentially could sustain their life. The complexity comes into the picture when someone has a serious diagnosis, particularly one that is considered terminal. Cancer is probably the most common dreaded and feared disease. As a person's condition deteriorates and then plateaus, individuals often agree to continued intervention to sustain their life

---

* I was the principal investigator in a Fan and Samuel Fox research grant focused on end-of-life care in nursing homes. The research included various methodologies; this data is from the participant observation I completed in five nursing homes in New York City, which included one in each borough.

and gradually accept the limitations that occur as their deterioration ensues. Since the decline often occurs incrementally, individuals adjust and compensate for losses they have experienced that come to be viewed as normal, albeit a new normal. These limitations are experienced as better than no life, namely death.

At some point the person or family member needs to decide when to stop these interventions or a person dies as interventions that can often be invasive and painful are continued. The problem is when is it time to stop. The need to make such a decision may come from a recommendation or direction for care from one of the medical professionals, a physician who objects to continuing treatment or a member of the health-care team. It also could come from the individual who is receiving such treatment and finds it too burdensome. Another source for recognizing the need for decision making could come from a friend or family member who has had previous experiences with the difficulties of continued treatment in relation to the end of life.

Another type of scenario is that in which someone has an acute episode of a disease or a catastrophic accident. The initial response is to seek interventions to restore the individual's health. As interventions get under way the outcome is uncertain. If the individual's condition remains in an extremely deteriorated state decisions can be made to stop the interventions and allow death to occur. The alternative is to continue interventions until the individual has reached a stable plateau in a physical condition that may be severely compromised or the individual may die despise the interventions.

The difficulty in situations in which interventions have begun is discerning when you decide to stop and if so when you stop. Although most individuals wish that the person be restored to his or her prior physical condition, often continued life in whatever condition is more acceptable than death. Family members or the person often do not know the outcome of these interventions. Medical professionals also may not be able to predict the result of interventions. What is also unknown and remains invisible is how multiple interventions might impact the process of dying.

Decision making to stop medical interventions is difficult. Since death occurs as the result of terminating or refusing interventions, many of those involved experience it as the cause of death instead of death being the result of the individual's health status. Medical personnel indicate the difficulty in terminating treatment.[5] Terminating treatment that results in the death of a person often is experienced by all involved as causing the person to die or in its most exaggerated form the feeling that you were involved in killing someone. Considering the difficulty that professionals experience, it should not be surprising that in the research I have done when a health-care proxy is asked to sign a form in order either to forego interventions or to discontinue them, they experience the feeling of choosing to end the life of their loved one. The advances in medical technology that provide increased assistance and ongoing life for many also cause difficulty when they do not produce the desired outcome. Then a consideration to terminate treatment can become visible. If more can be done and life can be sustained, should the treatments be stopped and if so when?

Within the biomedical system when someone is seriously ill major interventions usually are painful and traumatic. However, for the individual persons and their loved ones life is precious and it is difficult to finally say it is not worth undergoing these difficulties. The hardship is endured hoping the outcome will be positive. When it is not, decisions can be made. Decision making to forego or terminate treatment is a process and one that is not usually arrived at easily. From the research I have done it is usually kin who have to make the decision, otherwise intervention that not only is invasive but also traumatic continues until the person's body finally gives out.

For those kin who do decide to terminate or not begin some interventions, their time frame and that of the medical professionals do not always coincide. So we find at times that some medical professionals want to continue interventions while families and individuals do not. It also is important to note that different medical professionals do not always agree on issues of continuing or terminating treatment.[6] With this uncertainty as to the timing of stopping interventions or discontinuing them even among medical professionals it is understandable that those unfamiliar with the health-care system as well as those who are dying or have someone in their family dying have a difficult time in determining when is the appropriate time to make such decisions.

A feature of the good death ideology is that dying can occur in a peaceful context once decisions to forego interventions have been made. Within this hospice ideology each dying person can live life to the fullest each day until death occurs. There are accounts in books that deal with end-of-life care that describe these types of deaths.[7] Certainly in these stories we always hear of those situations that seem to indicate that death can be "good," but these books are written from the perspective of the providers of care. A reasonable expectation would be that the "best" accounts are the ones that get published. It is uncertain what the individuals and families think of these deaths because we do not hear their voices. Also even if these dying experiences are as good as portrayed, are these deaths representative of most deaths or are they exceptions?

I cite the ethnography by Lawton[8] who writes that when bodies become unbound hospice staff tell the families that they no longer need to visit. These individuals whose bodies are oozing are placed in back rooms so they become invisible to the larger hospice social environment. Chapple in her ethnography writes that in acute care hospitals when decisions are finally reached that the individual will be placed on the hospice unit death is hastened.[9] It seems doubtful that hastening death would be the choice that was made either by the individual or the family. The general feeling that hospice programs hasten death may be part of the reason that these programs are rejected by many.

During my research in five nursing homes in New York City, I discovered a vast difference between the notion that the institution had about ongoing intervention and those that families held. As opposed to the time in which I was employed in these institutions as a professional, I had the opportunity during my participant observation to sit with residents and/or their families. During this time I realized that family members often acquiesced to the ways in which the professionals describe the situation. However, they had their covert means to protect their loved ones. In nursing homes it is noteworthy how many family members are present at meal times to assist their loved one. Families know if the patients' appetites decrease and they stop eating, death is imminent and so they insure as best they can, that the person they have had to place in the nursing home receives as much nutrition as he or she can to prolong life. They are aware of the limited time staff may have to provide assistance with this task for their relative so they provide it themselves.

How do family members comply with nursing home personnel, but yet maintain their differing views? Here are two such examples. Coleen had her mother placed on a palliative care program after discussing with me what it meant. However, when her mother was in a critical condition the doctor on the unit called her suggesting her mother be admitted to the hospital. She immediately complied. This was done in a nursing home that had a palliative care program developed and fostered by the medical director who strongly disagreed with any individual going to the hospital if they were on the program. In this situation two medical doctors were providing two different messages to the family member. Coleen's mother went to hospital and died there.

When I asked Colleen the reason for the hospitalization after placing her mother on the palliative care program that rejected such a move she indicated that she had admitted her mother to the program not because she thought she was dying. Rather her mother was on the program because all persons on the program received a weekly visit from the nurse practitioner who would evaluate their condition and make recommendations regarding their ongoing care. It was not because she was prepared for her mother to die that she had her placed on the program but for the extra care she would receive. However, her mother's dying in the hospital provided peace to Colleen because she had provided her mother with whatever kinds of interventions might sustain her ongoing life, even though she indicated she would reject intubation for her mother.

At the same nursing home, Rubin had rejected surgery for his wife when she fractured her hip after a fall in their home. He had admitted her to the nursing home after the fall and her subsequent hospitalization. The hospital would not discharge his wife unless he agreed to a nursing home placement for her. Once in the nursing home Rubin rejected the idea that his wife be readmitted to a hospital for any further intervention. Yet if there was any episode that indicated a change in her physical stability he insisted that it be attended to by the nursing/medical staff. He was able to monitor her condition closely because of his daily visits, but also because he developed relationships with the nonprofessional staff, the private duty aides of other residents, and residents who were alert and oriented. These relationships insured his 24-hour monitoring of her condition. They all had his cell phone number.

However, all would have denied being in contact with him if his wife's condition changed and he called the facility for some intervention. He monitored her care extremely closely although she was unable to respond to him even nonverbally. She could not even tolerate being in a room with many other persons. He daily sat with her outside of the dining/recreation area in a quiet corner. For her birthday, he brought her into the dining room with the other residents and staff on the unit. However, he only wheeled her into the room for the singing of happy birthday and blowing out of the candles on the cake. Then he had to immediately take her out because of her inability to tolerate such a gathering. Yet for him it was his wife that he loved. He had a difficult time thinking about how he could possibly have any life for himself after her death. When she died he told me he had had five years with her at home, five years in the nursing home and he wanted five more and when that was done he would want another five and then another.

Neither Colleen nor Rubin would directly confront the perceptions of the staff yet each had alternate ways in which to insure that the care they wanted for their family member was given. In both of these situations, Colleen and Rubin responded to the medical professionals' wishes ostensibly. Each one had a limit as to the type of intervention they would accept, but also those upon which they would insist. They did not simply let the institutional perspective or response limit their choices or involvement.

This leads into the second point in my chapter. The way in which care is rendered is based on the institution, the unit in which the person is receiving care, the doctor who has the authority to authorize the direct care because several doctors may be involved, the nurse on duty, and the direct care providers. At each of these levels, care can be rendered or withheld overtly or covertly depending on the perspective of the provider who is on duty at a particular time.

Although the ideology of hospice and palliative care is for persons to live their lives to the fullest, it is often the case that because of the multiple interventions that person has had, the dying process can be painful and difficult as well as long term. Hospice care also promotes the ideology of a peaceful, pain-free death. Hospice juxtaposes this concept to a high-tech death in medical institutions, which palliative care providers say is medically engineered, painful, and only prolongs the dying process. However, palliative and hospice providers do not recognize the medical engineering of their interventions.

They remain invisible as interventions since their focus is comfort and they do not include high technology. Also what remains invisible to the consumers of care are multiple interventions that may not be high-tech or invasive, but could sustain life in an acceptable condition from the family's and person's perspective.

The notion driving the promotion of palliative and hospice care is that it provides for a "natural" death. Since many interventions which impact the dying process occur prior to dying, it is impossible to think of any death as "natural." Even in hospice and palliative care as indicated above, death is medicalized through interventions provided by staff in their effort to alleviate pain and suffering and provide comfort.

Although doctors rarely indicate the relationship between a long and difficult dying process and the interventions that have been undertaken, one physician did admit to me the relationship. A 24-year-old Pakistani man was dying. His pain was palpable as he responded to it incessantly. I was perplexed at his continued life and said to his oncologist: "I cannot understand why he doesn't die." His response was "the chemo is working." I was surprised to hear that he had been treated with chemo when his diagnosis was terminal and that it was the treatment that was causing him to be in excruciating pain and from this doctor's perspective prolonging his death.

This incident occurred when I was doing research, training, and education for a palliative care grant in a community hospital.[†] However, it was not the first or only time in which I witnessed oncologists continuing to provide chemotherapy to patients who had been referred by utilization review nurses to the palliative program because of their admission diagnosis.

Another incident occurred when I had been asked by the radiation oncologist to speak to a patient who had a young daughter. The oncologist also had a daughter who was a friend of this patient's daughter. The patient was a neighbor of his and he recognized that her condition was terminal. He wanted his neighbor to be aware of her diagnosis so she and her husband could help their child through this process and all prepare for the impending death. When the medical oncologist realized that I was seeing her patient she insisted I was to have no further contact with the patient. She also demanded that I not be allowed to see any of her patients until she authorized approval of my working with them.

The specification for the hospital protocol was that I would see all patients referred by the utilization nurses depending on the admitting diagnosis, which the grant had designated as possible candidates for admission to the palliative care service. Doctors would have to sign for a patient to be exempted from

[†] This research was supported by United Hospital Fund grant and conducted in a local community hospital in the borough of Brooklyn. Grants were given to five New York City hospitals to enable them to implement palliative care programs in their facilities.

this protocol. However, she demanded a change for her patients despite the protocol and I was not allowed to see any patient on her service unless she gave me permission. She never did. In this situation there were two medical doctors, one a radiation oncologist, the other a medical oncologist having very different responses to a patient in relation to her condition and prognosis. The situation also highlights how patients in the same hospital and presumably on the same unit in the hospital can receive different care based on the decisions and directions of the medical personnel involved.

Prior to this incident I had met with one of the medical oncologist's patients who was having a terrible reaction to her chemotherapy treatment. This patient also had been referred to me. The patient said that she had already accepted that her condition was terminal. She was distressed knowing that she was going to die. However, this oncologist had insisted that she receive more chemotherapy. The patient told me at the interview that it was not worth it, but she complied with what her oncologist wanted.

In these situations, we see the complexity of the dying process because of the insistence that treatment be sustained. The result is a mixed message for the patient whose body is deteriorating and the idea that there is still an available treatment that seems to indicate cure or at least stabilization for a period of time, the idea that more life may be possible. Knowing that oncologists' income from chemotherapy is considerable, it makes the reality of a health-care system for profit—an issue that usually remains invisible to the general public who seek life from their doctors and want to believe that doctors can provide it. Medical residents told me "oncologists' children eat chemotherapy." Their recognition of the continuation of chemotherapy for profit after its usefulness for palliation or cure underscored the issue for me.

Turning to the discourse in hospice about dying, the focus is on helping families and the person through the dying process.[‡] In this endeavor, however, there are ways in which the direction hospice provides is not always assisting the people involved. Some of the ways in which they approach families will illustrate this point. One line familiar in this context is that in order to die well the person has to "get their ducks in order." If the person involved is not dying within an appropriate time frame, staff may question what needs to occur in order for death to be reached in a time that they believe to be reasonable. This type of comment can cause the dying person and/or family members to feel as if they are doing something wrong.

[‡] Some of the data for this chapter are based on the numerous conversations I have had with individuals who have experienced the death of a family member that occurred in a medical facility. Because of my research individuals often wish to share their experiences in an effort to make others aware of the difficulties involved. Data also is based on my personal experience of being a health-care agent for a friend who was dying.

Another example, in an effort to assist the individual who is dying, staff might suggest that family members tell the dying person "it is okay to die." The staff suggests this particularly when death does not seem to be happening quickly enough. The words are often difficult for family members to utter. I often wonder how the dying person responds to such a statement.

Informants also report that the staff has described deteriorating conditions through which the dying person will suffer if they do not follow the directive of the physician in refusing or eliminating certain interventions. This discussion of impending discomfort and doom for the dying person usually occurs when family members are making a request for some type of intervention. The intervention may not be for curative purposes, but for what they perceive as comfort or perhaps as providing more time for and with their loved one and one that does not cause pain or discomfort. In an effort to limit the duration of the dying process, well-intentioned hospice staff unintentionally exacerbate the problems that can happen by describing graphic details of conditions that might occur. Then family members face added worries and fears in regard to what is happening to someone they love. Often the individual dies without the dire events occurring.

During my research it was obvious that most staff that provided hospice and palliative care services wanted to be helpful. However, the research also revealed that many of the ways in which they tried to assist, with their focus on the notion of creating a "good" death, unknowingly created problems for dying persons and their families. Often the notion was that death should occur quickly in order for comfort to occur. It does seem in these situations that it is not clear whose comfort is the focus of attention.

The last issue I will mention is the use of pain medication. Certainly for years individuals have died in pain because of a reluctance of providers to prescribe adequate pain medicine. Within the present context pain appears to be paramount in the minds of practitioners in both hospice and palliative care. At every meeting or talk at a conference about palliative care and/or hospice, there is at least one session on pain control. The talk illustrates the various ways in which physical pain can be alleviated. In this present environment, individuals should not have to deal with physical pain or should have the right to have their pain relieved if they wish.

During my research providers and staff at all levels often saw physical pain even if there were no obvious signs that it was present. In focus groups respondents indicated that death must be painful. It is a common belief held by most. The difficulty may involve the discomfort that death causes to the medical staff or at times family members. The focus on physical pain also obfuscates the different types of pain that can exist when death is imminent. Emotional pain, fear, anxiety can exacerbate and be inherent in physical pain. I am not suggesting that these types of pain are not experienced physically nor am I suggesting they are not real pain. Rather, I am arguing that the mind/body dichotomy with which we think may limit our ability to recognize the intersection of the experience of pain. Only treating or addressing it as a physical component may make it difficult if not impossible to alleviate.

One informant explained how she enrolled her husband in an in-patient hospice program because of his physical needs. When they arrived the nurse brought in the pole on which hung the pain medication, which was standard procedure at the facility. Her husband had not experienced any pain. When she saw the pole she took her husband home. This informant worked as a certified nurse's aide in a long-term care facility and was aware of the difficulties of providing pain medication when it was not needed. She also was concerned that the facility in their use of pain medication would hasten her husband's death.

Although palliative care is supposed to be a holistic response to the dying individual and his or her family, controlling physical pain often has been the priority. However, the other types of pain, emotional, existential, spiritual, psychic, which I believe, as indicated above, have an impact on the physical, is much less prominent often receiving nothing more than lip service.

Chapple cites in her ethnography that during her research once the patient was moved from a hospital bed to the hospice unit death was hastened. This reality is the fear that many families have. Facing death is difficult enough, but dealing with the notion that the health-care system hastens death is unacceptable for many. One nurse during my research was discussing with the director of social work withholding all of the regular medication for a patient. The social work director asked if that would hasten death. The nurse's response was "isn't that what this is about?" This nurse was the regular day nurse on the hospice unit with little understanding of the hospice concept for caring for dying persons and responding to their families. Another nurse who worked in this facility, but not on the hospice unit, told me she refused to give her patients medicine from the brown bottle (morphine) because she believed it hastened their death.

These realities underscore that when a dying person interfaces with the health-care system regardless of how benign that system is or how it purports to provide comfort, families must be involved and advocate for the person they have entrusted to the medical professionals' care. Hopefully this chapter has presented ways in which the perspective of families of dying persons can differ from that of the providers even those who are supposed to be insuring the "good" death. Hopefully it has validated those perspectives and made them visible.

NOTES

1. Philippe Aries, *At the Hour of Our Death* (Oxford: Oxford University Press, 1991).

2. Lynn Akesson, "The Message of Dead Bodies," in *Bodytime: On the Interaction of Body, Identity and Society*, ed. Susanne Lund and Lynn Akesson (Lund, Sweden: Lund University Press, 1996), 157–82.

3. Emile Durkheim, *The Elementary Forms of Religious Life* (New York: Free Press, 1965).

4. Ira Byock, *Dying Well: Peace and Possibilities at the End of Life* (New York: Riverhead Books, 1987).

5. Daniel Chambliss, *Beyond Caring: Hospitals, Nurses, and the Social Organization of Ethics* (Chicago: University of Chicago Press, 1996).

6. Joan Cassell, *Life and Death in Intensive Care* (Philadelphia: Temple University Press, 2005).

7. Maggie Callanan and Patricia Kelly, *Final Gifts: Understanding the Special Awareness, Needs, and Communications of the Dying* (New York: Bantam Books, 1993).

8. Julia Lawton, *The Dying Process: Patients' Experiences of Palliative Care* (London: Routledge, 1997).

9. Helen Stanton Chapple, *No Place for Dying: Hospitals and the Ideology of Rescue* (Walnut Creek, CA: Left Coast Press, 2010).

Chapter 5

Decision Making at the End of Life: From Informed Consent to Family Consent

Lawrence A. Frolik

*U*nder the doctrine of informed consent, individuals have the right to control their medical care, including the right to refuse medical care even if the proposed treatment is necessary to sustain the patient's life. If the patient loses the mental capacity to consent to medical care, the right is not lost because the patient can sign a living will that directs his or her medical care at the end of life. The patient also has the right to name a surrogate health-care decision maker to make health-care decisions, including end-of-life care, on behalf of the patient. By law, the surrogate is supposed to apply substituted judgment and make the same treatment decisions that the patient would have. In reality, it is difficult for a surrogate to apply substituted judgment because the surrogate is often uncertain as to patient's end-of-life treatment preferences. However, even when the patient's preferences are clear, the surrogate may be reluctant to end treatment, particularly if the patient's family prefers that treatment continue. As a result, at the end of life, the doctrine of informed consent often gives way to family consent.

INTRODUCTION

In the United States, by virtue of the legal doctrine of informed consent, patients control their medical care.[1] Although medical providers can propose a procedure or course of treatment, the patient must consent to any medical treatment, except in the case of an emergency. The patient's right to control his or her medical care arises from the federal and state constitutional rights of personal autonomy, self-determination, and the right of an individual to control his or her body. As stated by the U.S. Supreme Court in *Cruzan v. Director, Missouri Department of Health,* "a competent individual has a constitutionally protected liberty interest in refusing unwanted medical treatment."[2]

Some dying patients, however, cannot exercise the right to control their medical care because they have lost the capacity to make critical end-of-life treatment decisions. Some have lost mental clarity because of their illness. Others have lost the capacity to understand or reason about their medical condition because of medical treatments and therapies. Still others have lost mental capacity because of dementia or other related illness. Yet the need for their consent continues; the doctor cannot make the decision because the right of an individual to control his or her care does not end even if the patient has lost capacity.[3]

WHOSE BODY IS IT ANYWAY?

The legal rule, that a patient has an absolute right to control his or her medical care, is of relatively recent origin. In the past, many physicians believed, because of their professional training and understanding of medicine, that they should be the ultimate decision maker. Whatever the merits of that position, in 1914, the highest state court in New York, when faced with whether a physician could provide medical treatment without the permission of the patient, held that "every human being of adult years and sound mind has the right to determine what should be done with his own body."[4]

Over time, this right became known as the doctrine of informed consent, which requires patients to be informed about the benefits, burdens, and risks of the proposed treatment as well as possible alternative treatments, so that they can give informed and knowledgeable consent to their medical care.

THE RIGHTS OF AN INCAPACITATED PATIENT

In 1976, a New Jersey court was asked to decide who has the right to make medical decisions for a patient who lacked the capacity to give informed consent. Karen Quinlan, at age 21, was in an auto accident and for a few minutes stopped breathing. Thanks to emergency medical care, she survived, but she remained in a coma with no hope of recovery and was kept alive on a respirator and a feeding tube. Her father sought to be appointed Karen's legal guardian for the express purpose of discontinuing the respirator, thereby allowing his daughter to die. His request worked its way through the court system and was finally decided by the New Jersey Supreme Court, which held that a competent patient had a constitutional right to refuse treatment, and that right was not lost even if the patient lost capacity.[5] Therefore, Karen's father could be appointed her guardian with the authority to demand the removal of the respirator even if that resulted in Karen's death.

By 1990, a number of courts had considered similar cases that raised the issue of the right of a patient, or someone acting on behalf of the patient, to refuse life-sustaining treatment.[6] Almost without exception, the courts held that a competent person has the right to refuse life-sustaining treatment and that right was not lost even if the person became incapacitated.

In response to the need for incapacitated, terminally ill patients to control their health care, beginning with California in 1976, every state eventually enacted a living will statute, which permits individuals to create a written set of instructions about the kind of end-of-life medical care that the individual would find acceptable. Living wills are usually written to limit care by giving instructions as to when to withhold or withdraw treatment, but they can also be used to demand treatment.[7] Although a living will can be custom-drafted, most are versions of some standard form, and many states' living will statutes contain a non-mandatory form.

Individuals sign living wills for a variety of reasons. Some fear futile medical treatment that may prolong their pain or suffering. Others want to avoid the indignity of being kept alive by machines and so want to "pull the plug." A few believe it is wrong to waste costly medical care on hopeless treatments when death is near. Yet despite the attractions of a living will, public use is modest. One study found that fewer than 25 percent of Americans have executed a living will or any other form that would govern their care in the event of their incapacity.[8]

THE COURTS SPEAK: BUT DOES THE PUBLIC LISTEN?

In 1990, the U.S. Supreme Court took its first case that dealt with the issue of end-of-life care—*Cruzan v. Director, Missouri Department of Health*.[9] In 1993, Nancy Cruzan suffered severe injuries in an automobile accident that left her comatose and hospitalized. She was kept alive by the use of a feeding tube. Her father, who had been appointed her guardian, asked the hospital to remove the feeding tube. The hospital refused to do so without a court order. The father sued to have the tube removed, and, over the objections of the State of Missouri, won in the trial court. The Missouri Supreme Court reversed the decision on the basis that the state's interest in the preservation of life outweighed the burden of continuing the treatment for Nancy. The father appealed to the

U.S. Supreme Court, which upheld the State of Missouri's objection to the removal of the feeding tube on the basis that the state could demand clear and convincing evidence that Nancy would have wanted the tube removed. In a subsequent court proceeding in Missouri, the father was able to provide sufficient evidence of Nancy's wishes to convince a judge to approve the removal of her feeding tube.

The Supreme Court's decision in *Cruzan* affirmed the right of incapacitated patients to control their medical care by providing advance instructions, and the right of the surrogate decision maker, relying on the wishes of the patient, to order the termination of life-sustaining treatment. Although the Court upheld the right of a state to demand clear and convincing evidence of the patient's wishes, only a handful of states have adopted that standard of proof, which is higher than the "more likely than not" standard that is used in most states.

In another 1990 court case, the Florida Supreme Court was asked to determine the fate of Estelle Browning, age 90, who had suffered a stroke, was bedridden and kept alive on a feeding tube.[10] Her nephew, who had been appointed by the court as Estelle's legal guardian, asked for the authority to remove the feeding tube, the use of which is considered by the American Medical Association to be a medical procedure.

Estelle had signed a living will that stated if she was terminally ill she did not want to be kept alive by artificial nutrition and hydration. The Florida Court held that a patient has a constitutional right to refuse life-sustaining treatment and that right can be effectuated by a guardian or other surrogate. The Court emphasized that an individual can designate a surrogate to make health-care decisions, including the right to terminate life-sustaining care. Because Estelle had expressed her wishes in her living will, the guardian, without the need to ask for court permission, had the authority to remove the feeding tube.

LIVING WILLS—LESS THAN MEETS THE EYE?

Although the *Cruzan* and *Browning* decisions increased the public awareness of living wills, unfortunately this document has significant limitations. Under state law, a living will typically only takes effect if the patient is both incapacitated and is either terminally ill or permanently unconscious, also known as being in a permanent vegetative state. It does not apply if the patient is very ill but not terminally ill. As a result, a living will frequently does not apply to the prevailing medical circumstances. For example, in most states, if an incapacitated patient is in great pain, but not terminally ill, a living will has no legal effect on the patient's medical treatment.

Sometimes living wills are difficult to enforce because they contain ambiguous language. For example, would language in a living will, which called for the termination of care to avoid an unnecessarily drawn-out death, apply if death were very likely but not certain?

Some people object to living wills on the grounds that an end-of-life medical decision should be made only after a full discussion about the alternatives and consequences of the possible choices. The need for consent, after all, is referred to as "informed consent" and a patient cannot make an informed decision about end-of-life care without knowing all the benefits and burdens of the proposed course of action.

At times, a direction in a living will to terminate treatment runs up against deeply held beliefs of the patient's family that it is not right to terminate medical care so long as there is any hope for recovery. One study found that 44 percent of adult African Americans and Latinos believe that "everything possible should be done in all circumstances to save a life."[11] Faced with determined family opposition to termination of care, the treating physician may hesitate to follow the dictates of a living will.[12]

Even if the patient has signed a living will, it may not be available when needed. Although hospitals are required to ask patients when they are admitted if they have executed a living will,[13] the request will be futile if the patient has lost capacity prior to being admitted. A spouse is likely to know if the patient signed a living will, but other family members may not. Even if they believe that the patient signed a living will, family members may not be able to locate it because individuals are notorious for failing to save important documents where they can be located when needed.

Even if the living will is available, if it is more than a few years old, the "staleness" of the document, while usually not affecting its legal validity, may give pause to others as to whether to follow its directives. A living will that was signed 15 years ago, for example, may not represent the patient's current views[14] or it may have been created for a world of far different kinds of medical treatments.

As a result of these problems, in 2004 the Hastings Center Report declared that living wills were a failure and that they did not and cannot achieve the goal of preserving patient autonomy. According to the Report, it is impossible for individuals to predict their "preferences for an unspecifiable future confronted with unidentifiable maladies with unpredictable treatments."[15]

THE SURROGATE DECISION MAKER: DON'T CHECK IN TO THE HOSPITAL WITHOUT ONE

In response to the shortcomings of living wills, today every state permits an individual to sign a document, variously referred to as an advance directive, a surrogate health-care power of attorney or a health-care proxy, by which the individual appoints someone as his or her surrogate health-care decision maker if the individual loses capacity. The surrogate, who in some states is referred to as a proxy or an agent, is expected to consider the possible treatment decisions, weigh the benefits and burdens of the choices presented, and make a decision on behalf of the incapacitated patient. Unless the document provides otherwise, the surrogate has full authority to make all health-care decisions for the incapacitated person, including the right to refuse or terminate life-sustaining treatment.

In some states, an advance directive can contain instructions to the surrogate as to how the incapacitated person wants to be treated. The instructions can be mandatory such as "no tube feeding;" advisory, such as "I prefer not be tube fed;" or merely express the incapacitated person's values or beliefs, such as "I believe that tube feeding is usually not a good idea." Other states permit the patient to combine the living will with the appointment of a surrogate, with the understanding that the surrogate will enforce the treatment dictates that the patient included in the living will.

The use of advance health-care directives and the naming of a surrogate were encouraged by the 1990 passage of the federal Patient Self-Determination Act,[16] which requires that health-care facilities, upon the admitting patients, give them written notice of their right to make their health-care decisions and inform them of their state law regarding advance health-care directives.

Although medical professionals and lawyers urge individuals to sign an advance health-care directive and appoint a surrogate, and there is even a National Health care Decisions Day (April 16) designed to increase public awareness of the need to sign a directive, it is unlikely that most patients will do so.

Many patients never sign an advance health-care directive because they never thought to do so, or, if they did thought about it, they decided not to. The low numbers of individuals who have signed an advance directive may be partly a result of their unwillingness to think about the possibility of dying.

Some patients may not choose to appoint a surrogate because they expect their spouse or family to make decisions for them without the need for a formal appointment. They are often right, for in reality many health-care decisions for incapacitated patients are not made by a formal surrogate. Instead, the spouse or family works informally with the physician to make treatment decisions. As long as no one objects, and if the family agrees to the course of treatment, it is highly unlikely that anyone will institute legal action to block the proposed course of treatment.

When family members cannot agree about the proper medical treatment, however, things can get nasty. In 1990, a 27-year-old Florida resident, Terri Schiavo, suffered cardiac arrest. She survived, but never regained consciousness and was eventually diagnosed as being in a permanent vegetative state. Ten years later, her husband, who was her legal guardian, requested court approval for the removal of her feeding tube. He testified that Terri, who had not signed an advance health-care directive, had indicated in discussions with him that she would not want to be kept alive in her condition. After the Florida

Supreme Court upheld a lower court's approval of the removal of the feeding tube, Terri's parents sued to have the feeding tube kept in place, insisting that she was not in a permanent vegetative state, and that she deserved additional medical treatment that might improve her condition. They also claimed that Terri had never said that she did not want to be kept alive if she were in a permanent vegetative state or terminally ill.

The case soon became a national storm of conflicting arguments as to whether Terri was in a persistent vegetative state and whether her feeding tube should be removed. In an attempt to override the court decisions that permitted the removal of the feeding tube, the Florida legislature and Congress passed laws that applied specifically to Terri. In the end, however, the courts determined that she was in a persistent vegetative state, and, if she had the capacity to do so, would have chosen to remove her feeding tube. Fifteen years after her heart attack, her feeding tube was removed, and Terri died.[17]

The *Schiavo* case raised public awareness about the need to appoint a surrogate to make life-sustaining treatment decisions. The case also showed how important it is for the surrogate to know how the patient would like to be treated if terminally ill, permanently unconscious, or very ill and not expected to recover or regain capacity.

STATUTORY SURROGATES—IF YOU WON'T APPOINT A SURROGATE, THE STATE WILL

If an individual, who has lost capacity, did not appoint a surrogate health-care decision maker, the state can appoint one for that individual in one of two ways. The traditional method is to appoint a guardian, which requires someone to petition the appropriate court and ask for the appointment of a guardian with the authority to make health-care decisions for the incapacitated person.[18] After a hearing on the petition, if the court determines that the individual lacks sufficient mental capacity to make health-care decisions, and if the court finds that a guardian would be in the individual's best interest, the court can appoint a guardian with the authority to make health-care decisions.

Because guardianships are costly and time-consuming, in many states the appointment of a guardian for health-care decision making has been replaced by laws that automatically appoint a surrogate health-care decision maker for incapacitated individuals who have failed to do so. Sometimes referred to as "default" surrogate decision maker statutes, the laws provide that if a patient's physician declares the patient is unable to provide consent for medical care, a surrogate is automatically named without any need to go to a court. The statutes have a list of who has priority to be the surrogate, beginning with the spouse, but if there is none, then the adult children, siblings, and continuing on through a statutory list.[19] The statutes also grant the surrogate the right to terminate life-sustaining treatment under appropriate conditions.

SURROGATE DECISION-MAKING STANDARDS—BE AS ME OR DO WHAT IS BEST FOR ME

Regardless of how a surrogate is named, whether by an advance directive, statute, or a court, a surrogate decision maker is an agent—a fiduciary—who has a duty of loyalty to do what is best for the patient.[20]

Substituted Judgment

Under state statutes and case law, a surrogate, when faced with an end-of-life decision, is expected to apply the doctrine of substituted judgment when possible; if not, do what is in the best interest of the patient. The substituted judgment standard directs the guardian to do what the incapacitated person would have chosen to do if still able to make decisions. The best interest standard directs the surrogate to do whatever produces the greatest good or most benefit for the incapacitated person.[21]

The law's preference for substituted judgment reflects the concept that a surrogate is the incapacitated person's alter-ego, who has been empowered with the right to make decisions as a way of preserving the autonomy and self-determination of the incapacitated person. Therefore, the surrogate should do what the incapacitated person would have done.[22]

Of course, to apply substituted judgment requires the surrogate to know what the incapacitated person would have wanted. Ideally, the patient will have written down or discussed his or her attitudes about end-of-life treatment with the surrogate, so that the surrogate will understand the patient's values, desires and concerns. Sometimes, in the document appointing the surrogate, the patient will include a description of his or her attitude about life-sustaining treatment or may have specifically rejected or accepted certain procedures, such as a feeding tube.

If the patient never put his or her views in writing, the patient may have talked to the surrogate about what he or she considers appropriate end-of-life care. Unfortunately, that conversation often never takes place, or if it does, it may be perfunctory or not noteworthy enough for the surrogate to recall the details. Moreover, memories of conversations rarely are accurate because the listener may have misheard, only partially heard, or misremembered what was said.[23] And memories of a critical subject, such as end-of-life care, are susceptible to the surrogate recalling what is most comforting or what comports with his or her own values and desires.[24]

When the patient does not discuss end-of-life care or provide written instructions, the surrogate may be able to rely on more general discussions with the patient about health care and try to translate the general values of the patient into specific treatment decisions. In short, surrogates are supposed to do the best that they can to make decisions that the patient would have approved.

Often, however, the surrogate will not be sure what the patient would want despite prior statements by the patient. Studies show that often a patient's prior request to terminate treatment does not represent what the same patient wants when actually faced with the decision to terminate life-sustaining treatment. Many dying, mentally competent patients want very aggressive treatment even if it has little probability of success.[25] Apparently the old Mexican saying, "The appearance of the bull changes once you enter the ring," applies to end-of-life medical decisions.

Best Interest

In some, but not all, states, a surrogate, who has no knowledge as to what the incapacitated person would want, may make treatment decisions that are in the incapacitated person's best interest.[26] A few state courts have ruled that under some circumstances the termination of life-sustaining treatment by the surrogate can be in the best interest of the incapacitated person.[27] Possibly the clearest example is when it is necessary to increase the incapacitated person's pain relief medicine, such as a morphine drip, to such a high level that death is the likely result. Known as the double effect, such treatment is considered appropriate if it is necessary to relieve the patient's suffering.[28]

Reliance by the surrogate on the best interest test usually is only necessary when the incapacitated person and the surrogate are strangers or such distant relatives that the surrogate has no knowledge of what the incapacitated person would want. A surrogate, who is a spouse, adult child or other relative of the patient, will almost always be able to apply substituted judgment because the surrogate will usually have some idea as to the patient's attitude about life-sustaining treatment and so will not have to resort to the best interest test.

The Reality of Substituted Judgment: The Law Orders but Surrogates Decide

Although the application of substituted judgment may appear to dictate what the surrogate must do, in reality it does not. Ideally, a surrogate applies substituted judgment based upon a statement by the patient about end-of-life treatment preferences. However, even an apparently clear directive by the patient may prove difficult to apply. For example, suppose a patient, who has left explicit instructions to never be kept alive by artificial hydration or nutrition, becomes mentally incapacitated. Imagine that the physician asks the surrogate to approve a feeding tube. The surrogate applies substituted judgment and so denies the request. Or so it would seem. Certainly if the patient was suffering from the later stages of Alzheimer's dementia and was semi-comatose, the surrogate's refusal of a feeding tube would be consistent with the wishes of the patient.

However, suppose that the patient was not demented, but merely in a coma from which he or she was expected to recover. Without the feeding tube the patient might die before awaking from the coma. Under these facts, despite the explicit instructions by the patient, the surrogate should reject substituted judgment, rely on what would be in the patient's best interest, and approve the feeding tube. In the alternative, the surrogate could contend that substituted judgment requires approval of the feeding tube, because the patient's directive, to not use artificial hydration or nutrition, was intended to apply only if the patient were severely demented or near death; not when the use of a feeding tube might result in her recovery to health and full mental capacity.

This example illustrates that substituted judgment rests upon the surrogate believing that the patient intended the instructions to apply to the facts at hand. As one court put it, substituted judgment requires the surrogate to do what the surrogate believes the patient would want done if the patient were to suddenly regain capacity for a moment and was perceptive of his or her condition.[29]

And for some surrogates, substituted judgment may offer emotional relief because, according to that doctrine, it is the patient, not the surrogate, who has made the decision. The surrogate can take comfort in not having to make the decision—"I am only carrying out the patient's wishes."

The Surrogate as a Mind Reader

Substituted judgment cannot be mechanically applied because the doctrine of substituted judgment requires several decisions by the surrogate. First, what are the apparent instructions or desires of the incapacitated person, and second, is that instruction or desire applicable to the decision faced by the surrogate? If not, then the surrogate must answer a third question: what treatment decision will serve the best interest of the incapacitated person. Because each of these questions is subject to the judgment of the surrogate, it is apparent that the values of the surrogate are likely to influence the surrogate's decisions.[30]

Even a conscientious surrogate, who thinks that he or she is doing what the patient would want, may be doing what the surrogate subconsciously wants. Alternatively, the surrogate may recognize the difficulty of being sure about what the patient would want, and so resorts to doing what he or she believes is in the patient's best interest.

Whose Best Interest—the Patient's or the Surrogate's?

Determining what is in the patient's best interest is also difficult when making end-of-life health-care decisions. At some point, perhaps because of pain or the hopelessness of the patient's condition, terminating treatment may be what is best for the patient. However, expecting a surrogate to permit the patient to die, is asking a lot. If the patient is suffering pain that cannot be relieved short of measures that lead to the patient's death, a surrogate may believe that the patient's death is the best choice. But, without the need to end pain it is hard to imagine a situation in which a surrogate, who is likely to be the spouse, relative or close friend of the patient, would not be terribly conflicted and distraught when trying to decide whether death is the best option for the patient.

Unless surrogates have almost robotic control of their emotions, it is likely that under these circumstances surrogates may conflate what is best for the patient with what is most acceptable to the surrogate; that is, to agree to continue life-sustaining treatment. Even if the surrogate decides that death is the patient's best option, there is nothing to force the surrogate to act on that decision. Without the need to relieve the patient of pain, the surrogate might correctly conclude that the person who has the greatest stake in the decision is the surrogate. The incapacitated patient will not know nor be frustrated if the surrogate fails to terminate life-support treatment. In contrast, the surrogate will likely experience emotional pain and guilt by terminating treatment and letting the patient die.

The Surrogate—Neither a Robot nor the Alter-Ego of the Patient

A surrogate's decisions are not simple, mechanical executions of the patient's prior decisions. The indeterminacy of diagnostic predictions and the uncertainty among health-care providers as to what is the appropriate course of treatment often defeat patients' attempts to dictate their end-of-life care. The best the patient can do is to provide the surrogate with general guidance about how he or she would prefer to be treated. In the end, however, it is the surrogate who must make the final, critical decisions.

Talking to the Physician—But Not Hearing Answers

Surrogates do not make decisions in a vacuum; they make decisions in consultation with physicians and other health-care providers. In stark terms, a surrogate often must choose whether to terminate treatment and allow the patient to die. Naturally, when faced with such a choice, the surrogate is likely to ask the physician for advice.

Suppose the patient told her surrogate to terminate treatment if she ever becomes "very sick and demented." Later she becomes severely demented and develops pneumonia, which can be treated with antibiotics. If not treated, however, it is highly likely that she will die. The treating physician strongly recommends the use of antibiotics because the likelihood of success is great and there are no downsides to doing so. The surrogate is likely to consent to treatment of the pneumonia despite the prior statement by the patient.

Even if the surrogate is determined to apply substituted judgment, in many instances it will not be possible to do so. If the physician offers several care options, the patient's statements about how he or she wants to be treated may not help the surrogate chose among those options.

When a physician presents the treatment options but does not offer a recommendation, the surrogate must look to some value to choose among those options and may make a decision that reflects the values of the surrogate rather than the values of the patient. For example, without clear direction from prior statements by the patient, if the surrogate believes that preservation of life is paramount, the surrogate may insist on continued medical treatment. Even if the patient had left instructions that the surrogate should terminate treatment under appropriate circumstances, the surrogate might decide that the circumstances are not "appropriate" and so do not justify the termination of treatment.

Talking to the Family—and Listening Carefully

Surrogates not only consult with the physician, they also discuss difficult end-of-life decisions with the patient's spouse, adult children, siblings, life partners, and friends, and sometimes religious advisers or counselors. Not in all cases, to be sure. Some surrogates make decisions on their own. But many find themselves being the recipient of advice, instructions, pleas, complaints, and criticism from family members who are not easily ignored.

A surrogate, who is the patient's child, is likely to be heavily influenced by the advice given by other members of the family, including various in-laws. For example, a spouse, when faced with a physician's advice to terminate treatment, may turn to her adult children for support for this painful decision. An adult daughter, who was named as the surrogate for her dying father, will discuss with her brother and sister what should be done. Sometimes the advice is not sought. A son, the surrogate for his mother, is accosted by his brother, who objects to the surrogate's decision to terminate treatment. A daughter's insistence upon further chemotherapy for her father is berated by her physician brother-in-law, who claims that additional treatment is pointless.

Conversations with other family members may interfere with the surrogate's application of substituted judgment or best interest, but it is also possible that the patient would have preferred that end-of-life treatment decisions be made by the surrogate in consultation with the family. The patient may have wanted the surrogate to be the ultimate decision maker, but the patient nevertheless hoped that the surrogate would consider the views of other family members. In some cases, involving the family may improve the decision making, as all the options and consequences are fully explored. Even if the other family members add little, the patient may have preferred that the surrogate listen respectfully to the views and emotional needs of other family members.[31] For the patient, the delay in reaching family harmony may be more valuable than a swift decision to terminate life-sustaining treatment.

All in the Family?

The extent of disagreement among family members about a patient's end-of-life care is unknown. What is apparent is that the doctrine of informed consent can lead to the surrogate essentially forgoing making the decision and letting the family make it. Such family decision making surely means disagreements that at times may become very emotional and lead to hostility among family members. In time those disagreements can usually be resolved, and the family will finally agree to terminate life-sustaining treatment.

Of course, agreement does not mean that "all is forgiven." Some members of the family may believe that others were too quick to terminate treatment because of their lack of love and concern for the patient. The pro-treatment family members may also be angry because they may think that those who wanted to end treatment do not appreciate the sanctity of life or are blind to the dictates of their religion. Some may even believe that those who were willing to let the patient die wanted to accelerate an inheritance or avoid additional medical expenses.

The surrogate may not wish to terminate treatment in the face of opposition from the family because the surrogate will have to live with the family and face their criticism of the decision to terminate treatment. In contrast, continuing treatment until most, if not all, family members finally agree with the decision to end life-sustaining treatment may seem like a small price to pay for future family harmony.

The Role of the Physician—More Than Meets the Eye?

Sometime surrogates must overcome the reluctance of the treating physician to terminate care in the face of family opposition. While physicians certainly understand the right of the surrogate to make the decision, some prefer to delay termination of treatment until they are able to convince the family of the futility of further medical care.[32]

Physician preference for family unanimity arises from a variety of motives. At the most fundamental level, physicians take no pleasure in the death of a patient, and so agreeing to the request of family members that treatment be continued may be acceptable to the physician. Physicians may also want to avoid emotional outbursts or recriminations by family members. Better to wait a few days, than to have a child berate the physician for "killing my father!" Some physicians may fear being sued for malpractice by a family member who believes that the physician unnecessarily hastened the patient's death. From a physician's perspective, even if a malpractice suit or the threat of a suit is unfounded, and the physician eventually prevails, the physician still "loses" because of the loss of reputation and the emotional cost of being accused of failing his or her professional duty.

When end-of-life decisions must be made, family conferences, which include the physician, are frequently held.[33] The medical community supports family conferences and has issued guidelines as to how they should proceed. Not surprisingly, the guidelines suggest that family conferences be organized and led by physicians and attended by other treating personnel, including nurses, hospital social workers, and spiritual advisers. Research shows that interdisciplinary communication leads to quicker family agreement to emphasis palliative care rather than life-sustaining treatment.[34] This likely reflects the need of family members for professional advice and guidance before they agree to terminate life-sustaining treatment.

One study found that family satisfaction about their decisions involving a patient in an Intensive Care Institution increased in proportion to the amount of time that the family members talked about what should be done, as opposed to the medical professionals telling them what is best.[35] This is understandable because family members are trying to work through their emotion and confusion as to what is the right thing to do. While they want professional advice, in the end, they must come to grips with the decision to terminate care. Professionals need to lay out the facts and the options, and then let the family come to a decision. A little professional empathy for the difficulties faced by families who are making end-of-life decisions can go a long way to move the decision forward.

One response to the family's need to come to terms with the imminent death of the patient is the "stuttering withdrawal" in which some procedures and treatments are removed while others continue. This measured withdrawal delays death and may convince families that they are not abandoning the patient, but are only taking sensible steps in light of the diminishing possibilities of survival. They are not giving in to death. Rather than letting the patient die they are engaged in a measured retreat in the face of medical reality.

POLST AND HOSPICE CARE: ADVANCE DIRECTIVE ALLIES OR OPPONENTS?

Although the medical profession has accepted the concept that patients should control their care, it has never been entirely comfortable with advance directives. A sizeable body of research has found that advance directives are often ignored in the clinical setting.[36] Medical personnel complain that the documents are often ambiguous, too general or too detailed, not applicable to the patient's condition, not responsive to changes in medical care, and they are not satisfied that a patient's care should be dictated by a document written years ago. Physicians also claim that they don't have the time to read through a many paged advance health-care decision in an attempt to learn what the patient wants done.

In an attempt to reassert the physician's role, as well as to ensure that patients' treatment decisions are respected, many hospitals and physicians recommend the adoption of the Physician Orders for Life-Sustaining Treatment or POLST, in some states known as MOLST (Medical Orders for Life-Sustaining Treatment) or POST (Physicians Orders for Scope of Treatment).

First adopted in Oregon in the early 1990s, POLST focuses on the importance of physicians' orders and clinical procedures in the delivery of end-of-life health care. POSLT is designed for patients with advanced progressive chronic conditions who are expected to die within a year. The creation of a POLST begins with a conversation between the attending physician and the patient, or surrogate, if the patient lacks capacity. The conversation lays the groundwork for a set of physician's orders that will govern the patient's care in light of the patient's treatment goals. To ensure that the orders on the form are followed, the POLST is printed on brightly colored paper—pink in Oregon and green in West Virginia. It is the cover sheet for the patient's medical record and follows the patient wherever the patient may be transferred—a nursing home, a hospital, or a hospice. The POLST is supposed to be periodically reviewed and updated in light of the patient's condition and treatment desires.

The POLST is not an advance directive; rather it is a set of medical orders that attempt to carry out a patient's current treatment goals. If the patient has an advance directive, the POLST can translate that directive into meaningful medical care instructions. POLST forms appear to accurately convey patient treatment wishes, and POLST directives are apparently effective. One study found 90 percent of patients had their treatment wishes followed when they had a POLST.[37]

Other approaches to end-of-life care are an increasing focus on palliative care and the use of hospice. Many believe that many patients and their families often demand treatment because they fear that if treatment is removed, the patient will experience increased pain. The fear of dying a painful death is not unfounded. While improvements in pain management have occurred in recent years, only a decade ago indications were that up to 50 percent of those who die are in pain.[38] That need not be the case. Palliative care can almost always control a patient's pain at the end of life. Unfortunately, too often patients and their families focus on a cure, which may be impossible, rather than on mitigating pain.

One response to the desire to encourage the use of palliative care was the 2011 enactment of the New York Palliative Care Information Act, which requires physicians and nurse practitioners to offer terminally ill patients information and counseling concerning palliative care and end-of-life options. Patients are considered terminally ill if they have an illness or condition that is reasonably expected to cause death within six months. Palliative care, as defined by the law, is "health care treatment, including interdisciplinary end-of-life care, and consultation with patients and family members, to prevent or relieve pain and suffering and to enhance the patient's quality of life, including hospice care." Presumably, if patients, surrogates and families better understand palliative care, they will be more open to a physician's suggestion that the time has come to terminate life-sustaining treatment.

Increased use of hospice is another way for patients to control their end-of-life care. Hospice tries to implement a patient's end-of-life goals and make him or her as comfortable and free of suffering as possible, rather than pursue futile attempts to extend life. Hospice is the provision of medical care to terminal patients with the goal of improving the patient's last days by offering comfort, dignity, and aggressive control of pain. Originally conceived and developed in Great Britain in the 1960s, hospice is designed to provide comfort and support to terminally ill patients and their families. Hospice does not hasten death, but it also does not attempt to prolong the patient's life. By agreeing to hospice, a terminally ill patient has consented to care that focuses on palliation and given a clear signal to the surrogate that the patient wants to forego extreme life-sustaining treatment, such as feeding tubes and ventilators.

NOW AND IN THE FUTURE

Although POLST, palliative care, and hospice can assist terminally ill patients to control their end-of-life medical care, advance health-care directives and the appointment of health-care surrogates are not going to disappear. Patients will continue to sign advance health-care directives. Lawyers will continue to urge their clients to use them and, because of the Patient Self-Determination Act, hospitals will continue to inform their patients of their right to sign an advance directive. If the patient does not appoint a surrogate, state default statutes will appoint one for the patient.

However, the right of an incapacitated patient to control medical decisions by a surrogate who makes decisions according to the substitute judgment standard is not what many patients want. Patients often prefer that the surrogate consider what the patient's family thinks would be best.[39] Small wonder that surrogates often seem reluctant to act without the support of the family, who in turn may be reluctant to agree to the termination of life-sustaining treatment without the support and approval of the treating physician and other medical personnel.

None of this should be surprising. The reluctance of a surrogate to terminate life-sustaining care by applying substituted judgment, the desire for family harmony, and the dependence of the family on professional advice and approval is all predictable.[40] Surrogates and families are often faced with a stark choice: continue care and try to keep the patient alive or discontinue care and let the patient die. It is not surprising that families often prevaricate and delay the decision. They need time to accept that the patient's death is inevitable.

The doctrine of informed consent and its application through substituted judgment were the law's attempt to preserve and promote autonomy of the patient. State advance directive statutes and judicial pronouncements, however, did not incorporate the desire of many patients, that if they are incapacitated their families should have a say in the patient's medical decisions. As a result, for many incapacitated patients, informed consent has been replaced by family consent, which has no foundation in law, but has deep roots in the emotional need of the family to not allow a loved one to die. Requiring a surrogate to make a decision that will result in the death of a patient is asking a great deal. It should be no surprise that the sterile logic of the law is often tempered by the emotional needs of the surrogate and the patient's family. That is what many patients want—they are willing to forego some of their autonomy and control over their health care for the sake of serving the emotional needs of their family.

NOTES

1. Alan Meisel and Kathy L. Cerminara, *The Right to Die, The Law of End-of-Life Decisionmaking,* 3rd ed. (New York: Wolters Kluwer, 2004), 1–17.

2. 497 U.S. 261, 279 (1986).

3. Meisel and Cerminara, *The Right to Die,* 2–17.

4. Schoendorff v. Society of New York Hosptial, 105, NE. 92, 93 (N.Y. 1914).

5. In re Quinlan, 355 A.2d 647 (N.N. 1976).

6. Meisel and Cerminara, *The Right to Die,* §1.04. (3rd ed. 2004).

7. Ibid. at 7.01[B][3].

8. Dorothy D. Nachman, "Living Wills: Is It Time to Pull the Plug?" *The Elder Law Journal* 18, 2 (2011): 289, 299.

9. 497 U.S. 261 (1990).

10. In re Guardianship of Browning, 568 So. 2d 4 (Fla. 1990).

11. California Health Care Foundation, "Attitudes towards end-of-life care in California," http://www.chcf.org/publications/2006/11/attitudes-toward-endoflife-care-in-california

12. Erin Webley, "Law, Insouciance, and Death in the Emergency Room," *The Elder Law Journal* 19, 1 (2011): 256–87.

13. Patient Self-Determination Act of 1990, Pub. L. No. 101–508.

14. T. R. Fried, J. O'Leary, P. Van Ness, and L. Fraenkel, "Inconsistency Over Time in the Preferences of Older Persons with Advanced Illness for Life-Sustaining Treatment," *Journal of the American Geriatrics Society* 55 (2007): 1007.

15. Angela Fagerlin and Carl E. Schneider, "Enough: The Failure of the Living Will," *The Hastings Center Report* 34 (March–April 2004): 30, 33.

16. 42 U.S.C. 1395 cc (a).

17. Kant Patel and Mark Rushefsky, *Health Law Politics and Policy in the United States,* 3d ed. (Armonk, NY: M.E. Sharpe, 2006), 354.

18. Vaughn E. James, "No Help for the Helpless: How the Law Has Failed to Serve and Protect Persons Suffering from Alzheimer's Disease," *Journal of Health & Biomedical Law* 7 (2012): 407.

19. Charles P. Sabatino, "The Evolution of Health Care Advance Planning Law and Policy," *The Milbank Quarterly* 88, 2 (2010): 211, 216.

20. Jeffrey A. Marshall, "Power of Attorney—Key Issues for Elder Care Planning," *Pennsylvania Bar Association Quarterly* 74 (2003): 160.

21. Lawrence A. Frolik and Linda S. Whitton, "The UPC Substituted Judgment/Best Interest Standard for Guardian Decisions—A Proposal for Reform," *University of Michigan Journal of Law Reform* 45 (2012): 739.

22. Lawrence A. Frolik, "Is a Guardian the Alter Ego of the Ward?" *Stetson Law Review* 37 (2007): 53.

23. Robert Trivers, *The Folly of Fools: The Logic of Deceit and Self-Deception in Human Life* (New York: Basic Books, 2011), 143–45.

24. Ibid.

25. Thomas E. Finucane, "Care of Patients Nearing Death: Another View," *Journal of American Geriatrics Society* 50 (2002): 551.

26. Frolik and Whitton, "The UPC Substituted Judgment/Best Interest Standard," 6–8.

27. For example, In re Grant, 747 P.2d 445 (Wash. 1987), *modified,* 757 P.2d 534 (Wash. 1988).

28. Compassion in Dying v. Washington, 79 F.3d 790, 823 (9th Cir. 1996).

29. In re Quinlan, 355 A.2d 647, 663 (N.J. 1976).

30. P. M. Abadir, T. E. Finucane, and M. K. McNabney, "When Doctors and Daughters Disagree: Twenty-Two Days and Two Blinks of an Eye," *Journal of the American Geriatrics Society* 59 (2011): 2337.

31. M. T. Nolan, D. P. Narendra, J. R. Sood, P. B. Terry, A.B. Astrow, J. Kub, R. E. Thompson, and D. P. Sulmasy., "When Patients Lack Capacity: The Roles that Patients with Terminal Diagnoses Would Choose for Their Physician and Love Ones in Medical Decisions," *Journal of Pain and Symptom Management* 30 (2005): 342.

32. S. B. Hardin and Y. A. Yusufaly, "Difficult End-of-Life Treatment Decisions: Do Other Factors Trump Advance Directives?" *Archives of Internal Medicine* 164 (2004): 1531.

33. John M. Luce, "End-of-Life Decision Making in the Intensive Care Unit," *American Journal of Respiratory Critical Care Medicine* 182 (2010): 6.

34. Ibid.

35. Ibid., 9.

36. Fagerlin and Schneider, *The Hastings Center Report,* 30–42.

37. Patricia Bomba and Charles P. Sabitino, "POLST: An Emerging Model for End-of-Life Care Planning," *The Elderlaw Report* XX, 7 (February 2009): 1–5.

38. Terrie Lewis, "Pain Management for the Elderly," *William Mitchell Law Review* 29 (2002): 223.

39. Daniel P. Sulmasy, M. T. Hughes, R. E. Thompson, A. B. Astrow, P. B. Terry, J. Kub, and M. T. Nolan, "How Would Terminally Ill Patients Have Others Make Decisions for Them in the Event of Decisional Incapacity?" *Journal of the American Geriatric Society* 55 (2007): 1981.

40. Karen B. Hirschman, Jennifer M. Kapo, and Jason H. T. Karlawish, "Why Doesn't a Family Member of a Person with Advanced Dementia Use Substituted Judgment When Making a Decision for That Person?" *American Journal of Geriatric Psychiatry* 14 (2006): 659.

Chapter 6

A Changing Landscape: Evolving Ethical Duties and Obligation of Patients, Families, and Providers

Miriam Piven Cotler

*T**he health-care landscape has changed considerably. Advances in technology have brought higher costs and altered where and how health care is delivered as well as caused changes in payment mechanisms and the organization of care. Innovation has fundamentally changed the delivery system at the macro level and at the bedside. However, relationships have often suffered and communication has been lost. New challenges face professionals and patients as they share common goals to maintain health, cure ailments, and provide a good death when that becomes imminent. Focusing on dying persons, this chapter explores the evolved ethical rights and obligation of dying patients as well as their families and providers. The chapter looks at the principles supporting patient and professional rights and obligations, as well as organizational and professional efforts to clarify the decision-making process to patients who are actively dying. The new structures compress time, discourage and impede traditional patient/physician relationships, and provide unrealistic, false expectations. While the hope to keep living is ultimately in vain, the hope for a good death that treats pain, minimizes suffering, and respects the dignity and values of the person are all obtainable. The process requires clarity, communication, and time. It is a central tenet of this chapter that we owe the time. It is respectful, effective, and ultimately efficient.*

INTRODUCTION

Since the middle of the 20th century, the U.S. health-care delivery system and the dying process have changed considerably. Technological advances effected a transformation from a cottage industry with close health-care professional–patient relationships often maintained in a home or office into a complex, turbulent, expensive, and resource intensive environment. People now die most often in a hospital, surrounded by strangers. These changes in the health-care system fundamentally altered the challenges facing both professionals and patients as they share common goals to maintain health and provide a good death when that becomes inevitable. Technology created choices; arriving at the best decision for the patient consistent with the medical facts requires a relationship and it requires time. The new time pressures have become a serious obstacle to optimal end-of-life decision making. Furthermore, given that the decisions are unprecedented, and that we have had no consistent ethical, religious, or legal code, the dilemmas facing the dying and their families have been exacerbated by much confusion and variability. With the invention of mechanical ventilators, dialysis machines, and other technologies intended to support life in the decades following World War II, it became gradually and increasingly clear that, in addition to purely physiological choices, patients' values were at stake and the physicians' traditional decision-making role and authority was challenged. Physicians had typically told patients what was right for them, and the good patient accepted his judgment (indeed, it was a male profession). The new paradigm of patient self-determination was initially legally mandated. Since 1976, the courts have consistently found in favor of persons' clear authority to accept or reject recommended treatments. At first physicians were reluctant to accept patients' decisions to forgo recommended therapies, since such refusals seemed to violate physicians' obligation to do no harm, to cure if possible.

This principle of patient self-determination, known as autonomy, has been grossly misapplied and misunderstood. After half a century, the health-care professionals and the administrators who run our hospitals encounter increasing numbers of families who demand aggressive technology for relatives who are dying, cannot speak for themselves, have no advance directive, and for whom aggressive technology provides no benefit. Other patients have a directive that the family challenges. For these and a variety of systemic reasons, there is a growing effort to develop policies and procedures in response to care which the professional team deems inappropriate or nonbeneficial.

This chapter discusses the evolved ethical duties and obligation of dying patients as well as their families and providers, given changes in the delivery system. Case review of typical scenarios is presented along with arguments for and against limiting families' authority, and suggestions to improve decisions for the dying patient.

Waiting for Miracles

What does it mean to accept that death is imminent?
That technology is useless to obtain benefit, to reverse the dying?

I am waiting for a miracle, but in the meanwhile,
I insist that you employ every means of technology, every resource
available.

As if the machines will do the trick.

Tricks—
As if we are not each going to die
'And each is entitled to a peaceful death.

"It is useless"
"I give up hope"
"I still hope"
Hope for what?

And each is entitled to a peaceful death.

Miriam Piven Cotler (2012)

This chapter is about persons for whom death is imminent. It explores the decision-making process, false hope, and the time necessary to arrive at an authentic treatment decision consistent with the patient's preferences, best interests, and medical facts. While rational people intellectually acknowledge the inevitability of death, fear and denial are significant and common. Furthermore, expectations and dreams facilitated by modern medical advances have allowed some of us to behave as if death might be avoided—or certainly, forestalled indefinitely. Health professionals, patients, and families ask for time. Time for what? To wake up? To leave the hospital? To recover? To see if he or she doesn't die? Our very questions reflect the denial and confusion. Treatment decisions, and the processes by which they are made, have evolved as innovations have changed the options and as the courts have weighed in on landmark cases. Ethical duties, rights, and responsibilities sometimes become power struggles, and the trusting relationships necessary for good outcomes have been lost. While most deaths have not become ethical dilemmas, some decisions surrounding the dying do become sites of conflict when the principles are confused and authority is unclear. The problems are compounded by the machines that are breathing, feeding, and urinating for our loved ones. Patients do not look as if they are dying, and families see what looks like life (movement of the chest and the dials). Where there is life, there is hope. Hope for what?

Our attitudes and very language surrounding the machines do not help. We talk about life supports as if removing them is what causes an otherwise avoidable death. Although the law does not distinguish between withdrawing and withholding treatment, health professionals and the public frequently see a significant difference, for example between never beginning and stopping ventilator support, dialysis, or artificial feeding. Some religious groups permit withholding treatment under particular circumstances, but their doctrine forbids withdrawing it.

We pray for miracles while demanding aggressive treatments and we cast blame when patients do not improve. In extreme cases, families' demands for continued aggressive technology contradict prudent management, may increase the patient's pain and suffering, and challenge professional responsibility of stewardship. These situations have been labeled "futility cases" and have been the subject of legal and ethical debate. To some degree, they reflect a backlash from the patients' rights movements of the last 50 years. The evolving landscape includes efforts to establish a coherent, broadly acceptable ethic for end-of-life care: to find a common ground from which to manage a successful dialogue that respects the medical facts along with personal and professional values.

This chapter briefly reviews events that have led to these dilemmas; the principles underlying models of patient self-determination and professional rights and obligations; expectations of family and patients; and major current organizational and professional efforts to clarify obligations to patients who are actively dying. Most of the persons who are the subjects of these concerns are not awake or alert and they are unable to make informed choices. Indeed, most terminally ill patients in this condition will never regain the ability to communicate with us. The dilemmas are somewhat modified if the person had completed an advance directive, but there is often ethical confusion even under those circumstances.

BACKGROUND

The Hippocratic code, written around the 5th century BCE, was not modified until 1847, and it remains the hallmark. However, it addresses the physician's duties rather than physician's rights and patient's rights and responsibilities. Patients were the passive recipients; physicians were the providers and their tools were primarily compassion and caring. The history of modern medicine is not long; simple technology such as anesthesia and microscopes has been available for less than 150 years, and antibiotics were not available until the mid-20th century. The physician/patient relationship was the center of healing, and "father knows best" was an accepted maxim. In the period around and shortly after World War II, trust in the family doctor was the norm, and people in the United States tended to remain with their same physician. The technological explosion in the mid-20th century required capital-intensive facilities and equipment, the transfer of patients to these facilities, and a new third party mechanism to pay the charges. It soon became impossible for one physician to be an expert in all aspects of practice, and specialization further advances health care delivered by strangers in an unfamiliar place. Thus, these advances now force us to deal with the clinical, financial, and personal costs.

The public was faced with complex care, expensive financing, and new psychosocial adjustments along with the physical illness. These are often emotion-laden and confusing. Patients' abilities to sift through those decisions are further complicated by the illness itself—pain, exhaustion, and fear. Health-care decisions include a choice between accepting and rejecting recommended therapy, and between continuing and stopping treatments already begun. Self-determination is implemented through the informed consent process, and conversation between a competent patient and the physician is critical to the process. When patients have capacity to make choices, they listen and possibly read the information, process it, ask the questions that they believe are relevant, and then decide. Sometimes, they get another opinion or wait a while.

Until there were meaningful options, patients had generally been passive recipients of physicians' treatments. As medicine became more effective and options increased, decisions carried significant weight. Patients' values increasingly drove their decisions. At first, physicians resisted choices they felt were not in the patient's best interests. Their ethics demanded "doing good" which usually meant aggressive therapies, and when patients opted for palliation or other nontraditional treatments, physicians objected. The new model is very different from the old paternalism that assumed adequate justification for overriding the patient's wishes. It acknowledges that there are more than facts at stake, there are values as well. It may be more important to a patient to avoid limb amputation than it is to have a few more years of life; or to give children some inheritance, rather than hang on as long as there is brain function.

These conversations take time. Managed care, pressures on organizations about "the bottom line," discharging patients earlier, and production pressures on physicians are often the limiting factors. Furthermore, the absence of a long-term physician/patient relationship increases the time necessary to know each other.

We have gone from an empty toolbox, reportedly with an ample supply of tenderness and caring, to significant technological competence demanding specialization in an unsystematic arrangement. While modern medicine has been quite effective in preventing or treating acute and infectious diseases, trauma and chronic illness increasingly burden the population and the system. They challenge justice and beneficence, as well as good management. These claims are true not only with reference to trauma services or intensive care; all medical care is subject to these challenges. The old community hospital seems obsolete, along with the old family physician. Modern technology is conducted in a turbulent environment. It is capital intensive and it requires complex institutions and centralization. In the United States, the only industrialized nation without a national system of universal health-care coverage, most hospitals have entered into for-profit, religious, or not-for-profit corporate arrangements; public and private third parties reimburse for selected services; physicians have become so subspecialized that the primary care practitioner often does not see hospitalized patients; and administrators have achieved ever-increasing power and control. It is truly health care from strangers.[1] Patient satisfaction has declined along with the familiar and kindly comforting that substituted for effectiveness. Furthermore, if patients are among the approximately 16 percent of Americans without insurance, their care has been sporadic, late, and carried out in expensive settings such as an Emergency Department. It is not clear how effective or efficient the Patient Protection and Affordable Care Act (PPACA or ACA) enacted in 2010 will be when it is implemented, but it does not appear to require structural changes in current practices.

When does a person with a terminal illness begin to die? That acknowledgement and its implications may be challenged or ignored by families resisting the loss of a loved one. The glib response that we begin to die when we are born may be sincere, but it is fatuous. Of course we will die, but we are not dying in the sense that our bodies are shutting down, that healing or cure will not occur, and that life itself will shortly be extinguished. The inefficiencies and confusion are exacerbated when patients are dying, and the very language we use in calling the technology "life supports" adds to the problem. Loving families do not want to choose death. Of course dying is not a choice, but we do not make that clear in our verbal language or in our attitudes. Asking a grieving loved one if they would like to continue a treatment, without sufficient context, is a cop-out. Of course it is difficult to tell a family member their loved one is going to die soon no matter what treatments are imposed, but it is necessary to reframe the question so that the conversation acknowledges the imminence of death so that options and recommendations reflect reality. We are often not clear whether we are supporting life or prolonging the dying. This assumes the conversation occurs at all. While we have an ethical obligation to discuss these critical issues, families and physicians may avoid them and the current system does not provide adequate time for them.

The process of dying has been explored by Robert J. Kastenbaum. He suggests that dying begins when the medical facts are recognized by a physician, when those facts are communicated, and when the patient realizes or accepts the facts.[2] Since death will occur whether or not we acknowledge dying, and, since the process is independent of the label, I am suggesting that we have a very large stake in providing the best dying situation possible. Kastenbaum's model assumes a rational patient, and we know that patients are often far more accepting of their condition and clear about their choices than their families. However, as reported by the American College of Physicians' End of Life Treatment Panel, 60–70 percent of seriously ill patients in an Intensive Care Unit (ICU) are unable to speak for themselves when decisions to limit treatment are considered.[3] Most dying patients are not awake or alert. Physicians may also be in denial. "She's dead when I say she is!" exclaimed a physician to the ICU nurse. Our denial of dying disrespects and disadvantages the patient, their loved ones, and those who care for them.

Slowly over the past 40 years in the United States, several changes have occurred:

1. Most physicians have become educated or resigned to patients' alternate choices or refusals of recommended treatments.

2. Patients' expectations of medical technology to cure and at least sustain life have expanded and are often unrealistic.

3. Given insurance and other reimbursement changes along with specialization, the long-term patient/physician relationship is rarer than it used to be. Trust is more difficult to establish in the frequently short relationships between patient and physician.

4. Given public and professional confusion along with specialization and the decline of the long-term physician–patient relationship, end-of-life decisions have become increasingly problematic. Indeed, family dissatisfaction and perception of poor quality of life and care for the dying patient translate to perception of poor hospital and physician quality.

Autonomy remains a misunderstood and misinterpreted principle at both ends of the curve. Some physicians cede too much, the "I'll do whatever you want" model versus others who offer little or no decision-making authority, that is, "If you turn off the machines, it is homicide."

Although alert patients are often likely to acknowledge and accept their condition, professionals and family members may resist the fact of impending death and the change of course from aggressive technology to comfort measures may be impeded. According to Herman Feifel, dying persons want very much to talk about their feelings and thoughts concerning death, but feel that we, the living, close off the avenues for accomplishing this.[4] Discomfort and false hope are often accompanied by failure to place relief of pain and suffering above other medical needs. Failure to acknowledge imminent death is also associated with physicians' difficulty in acknowledging their own needs and making the transition in a system geared to intensity of machines rather than care. Consider the following scenarios.

A family is resisting a diagnosis of death by neurological criteria. Their confusion is increased by the fact that the patient remains on machines and drugs that make him look alive are still being administered. The family asks the physician to continue terminal care. He replies, "He is dead when I say he is dead," and he walks away.

A patient suffering end-stage cancer is experiencing multisystem failure. This is a common and peaceful way for the body to shut down. As part of this process, the patient stops eating or "fails a swallow test." The physician offers a surgical feeding tube insertion. This offer does not acknowledge that the procedure may not improve the patient's condition.

The first example is extreme. Was the physician trying to cope with his own needs while dealing with an angry, unaccepting family? It is not uncommon for families and professionals alike to be confused about death by neurological criteria; it is often difficult to establish and communicate that a patient is "brain" dead. The second story exemplifies cases in which there is no effective treatment or cure, but in which physicians feel internal or external pressure to act; such situations occur regularly, probably in every hospital, and despite guidelines indicating significant risks with little benefit. These cases may be associated with physician discomfort or fear of liability; both require conversation, empathy, and time.

PRINCIPLES SUPPORTING PATIENT AND PROFESSIONAL RIGHTS, OBLIGATIONS, AND EXPECTATIONS

The availability of new treatments allows patients choices, and their values influence their decisions. Since the United States is religiously pluralistic, ethnically diverse, and lacks a uniform ethos, conflicts occasionally arise among the parties involved and necessitate a court settlement. Some of these court battles have become landmark cases.[5] Health policy and practices have responded to judicial decisions, and over time patients' rights have largely become accepted. The principles serve as a guide to right actions. However, ethical dilemmas often involve conflicts over principles, which have no clear ranking. So, for example, if a patient with metastatic cancer chooses to forego chemotherapy a physician may be morally distressed. This becomes a conflict between the patient's self-determination and the physician's mandate to do good while avoiding harm. Disagreements also occur between patients or their surrogates and physicians, and within families. How should controversy be resolved when patients and physicians disagree on best practices?

The primary principle underlying patients' decisions is autonomy and self-determination. In the courts, it has trumped beneficence (doing good), but in practice, in the clinical setting, the two have continually conflicted. Historically, less attention has been paid in the clinical setting to other factors or legal principles, such as distributive justice and organizational ethics. Autonomy is based on liberty, respect, privacy, and the recognition that once we have choices, there are more than facts at issue. The individual's values, goals, and expectations may drive the decision. Autonomy provides the rationale for informed consent and the basis for a legal charge of battery or abuse. The principle acknowledges that we own our bodies, and it forbids touching without permission. The maxim according to H. Tristram Engelhardt states: "Do not do unto others that which they would not have done unto them and do for them that which one has contracted to do."[6] It is grounded in mutual respect.

While autonomy has provided the framework for ethical behavior in clinical settings, it has also been gravely misunderstood. The very notion of self-determination sounds like the right to demand. However, it is a negative right, the right to be left alone, and does not give one a claim on another. Thus, Engelhardt has renamed it the principle of permission.[7] This principle has been so widely misinterpreted that one may hear practitioners tell patients they will do whatever the patient wants. That is disingenuous and may be cowardly. It is also impossible. The following examples are from my experience as a clinical bioethicist.

> A physician asks for an ethics consultation with the family of a critically ill elderly man. His stated goals are assisting the devoted son and daughter-in-law to understand the futility of surgery despite their father's heavy internal bleeding. Almost all the organs are shutting down. His first words to the family are: "Your father's heart is doing better today." He does not, or cannot, admit that the kidneys and lungs are failing, and that the patient would not survive surgery. Naturally, the family hears the first words of encouragement and they want to schedule a surgery.

Professionals' discomfort or disinclination to be clear ignores responsibility. It has been fostered by loss of relationship with patients and by time pressures, and fueled by fear of litigation. We unnecessarily set up an adversarial relationship that does not account properly for duty, respect, and the importance of peaceable negotiation.

The principle of beneficence, which has been the underpinning of medical practice since Hippocrates, often comes into conflict with autonomy. Particularly from around 1965 through 1990, at the beginning of modern bioethics, health professionals had great difficulty with patients' decisions that seemed unwise and perhaps life threatening. That still occurs. For example, a surgeon recently told a family that it would be homicide to withdraw life supports from their old and failing mother who had expressed concerns about quality of life and who feared potential dependence. While honest exploration and discussion of these controversies is excellent practice, the word "homicide" obviously implies a coercive and inaccurate polemic. In present times, neither nurses nor social workers nor families accept coercion quietly.

Where are the patients in all of this? Patients who are deemed to have "capacity" know what they feel and what they want in the way of care and comfort.[8] However, what a patient needs—as contrasted with what the patient wants—is a physician-determined professional construct. Physicians have legal responsibility for determining appropriateness of treatments, and they order approximately 85 percent of health-care services. Patients entering the system often, understandably, have unrealistic expectations. Their lack of objectivity is understandable given successes in public health and in preventing and treating infectious and acute diseases. Their belief in the system has also been fostered by exaggerated claims and heavy reliance on the beneficent professional into whose hands they have entrusted themselves. Is that bad or good? If we accept the view that end-of-life care should respect the person's treatment preferences and address the various needs, we must also acknowledge that we are failing to provide valuable support and we may be failing to honor prior directives. This is particularly problematic when patients cannot speak for themselves.

Several important factors are associated with medically inappropriate family demands when patients are dying. One factor is iatrogenic complications, that is, complications caused by medical treatment, caused sometimes by hubris and at other times by physicians disagreeing among themselves—perhaps from fear of litigation. Barriers also arise from resistance and discomfort among the professionals who are responsible for communicating with the family. This may be seen in physicians' attitudes about code status, referral to hospice, and other end-of-life care supports intended to respect patients and their families physically and emotionally. Although palliation and hospice are now part of mainstream medical care, we still talk about referring to hospice as "doing nothing more" and "giving up," rather than as turning from futile attempts to cure, to caring for the whole patient's needs: psychological, physical, spiritual, and social.

Physicians have a well-codified ethos acknowledging fiduciary obligations to the patient, collegial duties as part of a medical staff, and stewardship of professional resources. Despite the ability of patients to consult internet sources, physicians, on the whole, have more knowledge and better control of how to use medical information. They make the diagnoses, recommend treatments, and sanctify need. The profession remains highly respected. However, as Jerome Groopman has pointed out:

> The effects of a doctor's inner feelings on his thinking get short shrift in medical training and in research on decision-making. "Most people assume that medical decision-making is an objective and rational process, free from the intrusion of emotion. . . ." Yet the opposite is true. The physician's internal state, his state of tension, enters into and strongly influences his clinical judgments and actions. . . . Cognition and emotion are inseparable. The two mix in every encounter with every patient.[9]

Physicians' personal values also play a role in how they treat patients. In a large community hospital we can expect to find physicians who are opposed in principle to acknowledging the need for palliation and pursue aggressive, futile attempts to treat. Their motives cover the gamut from personal denial, to ego, to reimbursement and may make the family's decision-making role overwhelming. How much status should we give the physician's personal values? The ethical model says a physician should transfer a case when there is a conscientious objection to the patient's or agent's decisions. In practice, that choice may be difficult or it may not be offered.

While appropriateness is a medical determination, the attribution of inappropriateness may be disputed by other practitioners. When physicians disagree or do not communicate, thus giving patients conflicting and confusing information, the appropriateness of requests are themselves arguable. For example, different oncologists may have very different levels of optimism and aggressiveness, as well as treatment recommendations. Sometimes, these physicians are associates in one practice. Or, several physicians recommend against amputation of a limb for a dying patient, yet a vascular surgeon can be found who will perform the surgery. Another example is recommendations against dialysis in the final weeks of life for a patient dying of other causes. Patients in multisystem failure may experience loss of kidney function. Indeed, that is reportedly a pain free and, to the observer, apparently pleasant way to die. Yet, families may find a nephrologist willing to begin dialysis. Are they treating a person or an organ? We treat systems and when the whole person begins to die, we may be so busy with the part that we do not recognize the whole.

The following case illustrates some of the difficulties in trying to adhere to the different and contradictory principles that support patient rights and honors professional obligations.

Mrs. M., a 70-year-old woman, had survived nine years with ovarian cancer. She had received several procedures and bouts of medical therapy, but she remained functional and in good spirits. She was married to her second husband who was her designated health agent, and she had three children from her first marriage. She was admitted to the hospital for another, supposedly routine, debulking of the tumor. However, Mrs. M. suffered an internal bleed that required another surgery and then a stroke during the second procedure. After more than 60 days on a ventilator, receiving dialysis and other aggressive treatments in the ICU, her nurses and social worker felt they were violating her advance directive. The patient had stated she did not want to be maintained on life supports if her condition was terminal. An ethics consultation disclosed several medical and family problems. The primary block was disagreement about the patient's status among the six physicians present in person or on speaker phone. The oncologic/gynecologic surgeon and the general surgeon both felt that Mrs. M. was not necessarily dying, and that she could recover from the complications. The primary care physician and the nephrologist both believed they were violating the directive of a dying woman. The infectious disease specialist and pulmonologist were not sure if her lungs could recover or her infection would be controlled. How was her husband to know what to do? He was not concerned about violating the directive, but he cared very deeply that he not violate Mrs. M's children who maintained an optimistic vigil. They wanted all aggressive treatments continued. Several members of the nursing staff were refusing to continue to care for Mrs. M. They looked to the directive, to her quality of life, and to their sense of despair. The surgeon had no patience with their conscience.

ORGANIZATIONAL AND PROFESSIONAL EFFORTS TO CLARIFY OBLIGATIONS TO PATIENTS WHO ARE ACTIVELY DYING

Professional and organizational views partly reflect their institutional culture and the personal values of the members of those professions or organizations. Physicians' practice patterns often continue to follow outmoded reimbursement systems, which once both appeared generous and protected consumers from the costs of treatment. These mechanisms now pressure patients and organizations to control costs. Thus, while physicians are reimbursed for services, hospitals are usually paid by diagnostic groups. The former maximizes revenue with a longer length of stay and greater use of resources; the latter pressures in the opposite direction. This may lead to misaligned incentives among organizations, physicians, and patients.

It takes time and patience to explain the uncertainty surrounding many therapies, and those conversations are difficult for some physicians. Patients and families are also frequently confused about physicians' obligations to not offer inappropriate treatment or those they deem nonbeneficial. This disconnect between families' demands and providers' perceptions of appropriateness is further exacerbated by the changing health-care delivery system. The family physician has been largely replaced in the hospital setting. Indeed, many office-based generalists do not see their hospitalized patients. New specialties have arisen to meet the needs of technology and in response to managed care structures. Hospitalists will take care of patients in the hospital and intensivists increasingly cover the ICU. Indeed, widespread reorganizations are under review from the standpoint of cost effectiveness and professional relationships. The organizational environment is less caring despite efforts to promote patient satisfaction.

Hospitals are under severe cost constraints from Medicare, Medicaid, and private insurers as well as health-care corporations who demand increasing percentages of revenue. Nurses may be unionized and they may be temporary staff from an agency. The impact of these variables may be unclear. The hospital physicians are often strangers to their patients.[10] The dying patient is usually not able to express or assure compliance with his or her values. On its own merits, the effort on the part of hospitals and physicians to limit care that they judge inappropriate or ineffective also represents an ongoing struggle for control over the decision-making process. The fact that it is pursued in an extreme cost-controlling context intensifies the dilemmas. Some see families' demands for inappropriate or nonbeneficial care for the dying patient as unreasonable, others as too costly, and still others as patients' rights issues.

CONCLUSIONS

Dying persons who are awake, alert, and have capacity to make their own decisions are usually more accepting of death, and there is little or no question of the validity of their choices. However, all too often we encounter situations in which dying patients do not have that capacity and are hospitalized in an ICU. Their end-of-life care is being decided by family members, whether loving or not and functional or not, often without advance directives from the patient, while being given advice from physicians they do not know. Ideally, the health-care team itself is unified and in agreement with the family regarding appropriate and effective treatment.

Families may need time to process the situation. They are usually able to accept the imminence of death and the importance of a good dying, including adequate pain management and the limitations of technology. However, as U.S. health care has evolved, expectations, technology, strangers, the reimbursement system, as well as misaligned provider and family incentives sometimes conspire to estrange the relationships between patient/family and health professionals, thus making it impossible to establish trust. Those problematic situations may trigger an ethics consultation, but by that time, positions may be intractable. Given priority of the best interests and dignity of the dying, these dilemmas must be addressed. Therefore, some communities and institutions have established policies and procedures to address demands for inappropriate or nonbeneficial care at the end of life. While ethicists disagree about whether these are efforts to regain control and subvert patient autonomy, there is agreement about the importance of addressing the problem. Emphasis should be on shared decision making, meeting early and often with families in conversation rather than the monologue historically provided by physicians in a hurry. This time spent in conversation may be difficult for professional and patient/family alike, but it is morally obligatory, it is efficient in the present, and effective in the longer run.

We do not have a model to assess or identify "adequate" time. The imposition of time constraints and the lack of time allotted for individual patient visits is a common complaint about present reimbursement arrangements. Yet, the ACA deliberations shut down compensation for these conversations, calling them "death panels." How much time does it take the doctor or patient to learn to trust, to ask the right questions, to understand the underlying problem? Patients and families require time to internalize bad news, and often there is a significant learning curve for the physician to become familiar with the case—and the person. There may be a start-up time between visits for the patient or family member. Will she see the same doctor next time or is there a rotation among providers? What is all this talk about communication and comprehensiveness?

What do families mean by "do everything"? The goals of care must be articulated and reevaluated as necessary. It is important to acknowledge uncertainty. Asking families their understanding of the patient's condition usually reveals significant knowledge that can facilitate goal setting. It is also important to glean the patient's preferences if possible and the family's as well. We need to hear the story, and we all need to be clear about preferences. Are they authentic and stable? A chance of what? The end of what? Spiritual care from chaplains or the patient's pastor may also be helpful—indeed, crucial.

Most cases will be peaceably and respectfully resolved. In rare cases, the physician may have a conscientious objection to patient or family demands or refusals. Those should be discussed, and the physician may have to transfer care. The rules of the game are changing, and we are not clear what reciprocal time is owed to professionals and patients.

Specific cases require different responses and approaches. They all demand respect and clear communication among the major players: the dying patient whose son insists on surgery to correct the bleed despite widespread system failure; the grieving family from an ethnic minority with no money or insurance and sincere generic distrust of the system; the wife who insists the lawyer did not explain the meaning of the advance directives she and her husband signed. We must hear the story and try to understand the history. We must keep talking, without violating mutual respect, good judgment, our morals, or our ethics, and we must have the requisite time to have the conversations.

Rules and policies, based on principles, do matter. Not because of power. Power is not inherently bad; it is insufficient. We have been so concerned with violations of the patients' right to be left alone, with ignoring treatment refusals based on personal values, belief, and rational choice, that we run the risk of abandoning the critical distinction between unreasonable refusals and unreasonable demands. Personal, professional, and systemic factors all contribute to poor outcomes when physicians don't talk with each other and are unclear with families; when hospitals are where people die and they seem forbidding;

when families expect miracles right here and now. While most cases do not carry the drama that is referred for ethics consultation, the less dramatic infractions are real and they are significant. Yes, dying is inevitable. Good deaths take courage from the bystanders: the family, the professionals, the organization, and the system. Few of us want to die surrounded by tubes, machines, and strangers.

Finally, we have bastardized and falsified hope. The hope to keep living is ultimately in vain; the hope for a good death that treats pain, minimizes suffering, as well as respects the dignity and values of the person are all obtainable. They require clarity and communication. They may also require time. It is a central tenet of this chapter that we owe the time. It is respectful, effective, and ultimately efficient.

Does it matter if he dies on his own?

He was still intubated.

Why not?
The family was spared telling us to extubate,
and it was only a few more days,
or a week,
or somewhat longer.

What were the costs?
ICU resources;
did someone else need the bed?

Did the patient feel anything?
or did we prolong pain and suffering?

Does it matter that the nurses practice futile care?
That's their dilemma

Were we honest with the family?
With each other?

What was with the physician?
so lacking in courage?
Was he dis-honorable?

Does it matter?
This patient is dead.
Until the next one.

Miriam Piven Cotler (2012)

NOTES

1. Charles E. Rosenberg, *The Care of Strangers; the Rise of the American Hospital System* (New York: Basic Books, 1987).

2. Robert J. Kastenbaum, *Death, Society, and Human Experience* (Boston: Allyn and Bacon, 2001).

3. Kathy Faber-Langendoen and Paul Lanken, "Dying Patients in the Intensive Care Unit: Forgoing Treatment, Maintaining Care," *Annals of Internal Medicine* 133 (December 2000): 11.

4. H. Feifel, ed., *The Meaning of Death* (New York: McGraw-Hill, 1959), xi.

5. See Lawrence Frolik's chapter in this volume.

6. Tristram H. Engelhardt, *The Foundations of Bioethics,* 2nd ed. (New York: Oxford University Press, 1996), 123.

7. Ibid., 103.

8. "Adult patients are presumed to have capacity unless otherwise determined by the physician or the court. Capacity assumes ability to make decisions and to be responsible for those decisions, including ability to understand nature and consequences of proposed health care treatment and procedures, including significant risks, benefits and alternatives" (California Probate Code 4609).

9. Jerome Groopman, *How Doctors Think* (Boston: Houghton Mifflin, 2007), 36, 39.

10. Rosenberg, *The Care of Strangers.*

Chapter 7

The Hippocratic and the Veterinary Oaths: Medical Ethics at the End of Life

Sara Waller

*I*n this chapter I will present an interpretation of important differences between *the Hippocratic and Veterinary oaths by examining how each might relate to the human fascination with and fear of death. It is often considered a kindness to kill an animal that suffers, but controversial at best to kill a suffering human. I suggest that this commonly manifested notion that it is frequently right to kill animals but seldom right to kill humans can be explained through the psychology of death-terror.*

INTRODUCTION

A commonly used and very representative version of the current Hippocratic Oath states:

> I do solemnly swear by that which I hold most sacred: That I will be loyal to the profession of medicine and just and generous to its members; that I will lead my life and practice my art in uprightness and honor; that into whatsoever house I shall enter, it shall be for the good of the sick to the utmost of my power, holding myself aloof from wrong, from corruption, from the tempting of others to vice; that I will exercise my art solely for the care of my patients, and will give no drug, perform

no operation for a criminal purpose, even if solicited, far less suggest it; that whatsoever I shall see or hear of the lives of people which is not fitting to be spoken, I will keep inviolably secret. These things I do promise and in proportion as I am faithful to this my oath may happiness and good repute be ever mine—the opposite if I shall be forsworn.[1]

The American Medical Association formally approved this very similar version of the Hippocratic Oath in 2000:

You do solemnly swear, each by whatever he or she holds most sacred, that you will be loyal to the Profession of Medicine and just and generous to its members; that you will lead your lives and practice your art in uprightness and honor. That into whatsoever house you shall enter, it shall be for the good of the sick to the utmost of your power, your holding yourselves far aloof from wrong, from corruption, from the tempting of others to vice. That you will exercise your art solely for the cure of your patients, and will give no drug, perform no operation, for a criminal purpose, even if solicited, far less suggest it. That whatsoever you shall see or hear of the lives of men or women, which is not fitting to be spoken, you will keep inviolably secret. These things do you swear. Let each bow the head in sign of acquiescence. And now, if you will be true to this, your oath, may prosperity and good repute be ever yours; the opposite, if you shall prove yourselves forsworn.[2]

In contrast, the current (2010) Veterinary Oath as approved by the executive board of the American Veterinary Medical Association states:

Being admitted to the profession of veterinary medicine, I solemnly swear to use my scientific knowledge and skills for the benefit of society through the protection of animal health and welfare, the prevention and relief of animal suffering, the conservation of animal resources, the promotion of public health, and the advancement of medical knowledge. I will practice my profession conscientiously, with dignity, and in keeping with the principles of veterinary medical ethics. I accept as a lifelong obligation the continual improvement of my professional knowledge and competence.[3]

THE OATHS, THEIR DIFFERENCES, AND THE CONNECTION TO EUTHANASIA

The contemporary Hippocratic Oath commonly in use today asks new Medical Doctors (MDs) to promise to "benefit the sick" and to take seriously their powers of healing, and thus their powers of potentially harming, a patient. The Oath urges us away from euthanasia, stating that doctors "will give no drug, perform no operation, for a criminal purpose, even if solicited" and so shall refuse to kill or violate any legally stated rights and responsibilities even if asked to do so by the patient or the patient's family. In short, doctors who care for humans are to preserve human life in the face of human suffering. In contrast, the Veterinary Oath asks new veterinarians to use their knowledge and skill to "benefit society through the protection of animal health and welfare" and toward "the prevention and relief of animal suffering." Nowhere in the Hippocratic Oath is there explicit mention of maintaining or improving the quality of the lives of humans being treated, although there is mention in most versions of the Oath about treating patients with concern for justice and protecting patients from injustice. Nowhere in the Veterinary Oath is there a clause asking animal caretakers to avoid the death of the animal in the name of the law or moral compunction. Indeed, prevention of suffering is a cornerstone of the Veterinary Oath, even at the expense of life, while prevention of death is a cornerstone of the Hippocratic Oath, even if it means the propagation of suffering. Why?

Goldenberg et al. report that humans eagerly separate themselves from animals in an effort to avoid thoughts of their own mortality.[4] Cox et al. have argued that when people are reminded of their similarity to animals, thoughts of death and mortality become more easily accessed and more prominent.[5] To be able to claim moral justification to euthanize an animal is to claim a certain amount of control over life and death as well as suffering; and it is to place humans in a position of power above animals as separate from them. Animals do not euthanize each other. This is a job for humans with rational decision-making processes, with good judgment, and with kindness and ethical concern. However, to make a similar claim regarding ending the life of a human is to once again lose that control by allowing an equal, namely another human, to have judgment regarding, and power over, life and death. To offer such power to an equal, to someone like in kind, is to erode the boundary between ourselves and death. If we control the mortality of others, implicitly that control sets us apart from others. If we control the mortality of ourselves, we are forced to confront the fact that we will die, because we see creatures like us dying. We cannot easily say to ourselves "this happens to you and creatures like you, but not to me." Further, we may well harbor immense fear, envy, and resentment toward those who have the temerity to wield power over life and death.

Using this background as a foundation for my interpretation, I argue two points in this chapter. First, I suggest that the contemporary Hippocratic Oath and the policies and politics that stem from it should be changed to be more in line with the Veterinary Oath, because quality of life, in light of our death terror, is potentially more beneficial to society than quantity of life. Such a change will not be easy because it demands that we confront the terror of death when we lack the cultural and psychological resources to do so. Nevertheless, it is my belief that we would have a higher quality of human life if we changed the Hippocratic Oath, and a better understanding of ourselves if we practice confrontation of our own finitude. Second, I argue that the two oaths evolved differently because humans have a fascination with death that allows us to take animal lives "morally," for example, in the name of avoiding their suffering, or for food for ourselves, but not human lives. This chapter offers the interpretation that, in our fear of death, we more comfortably inflict death upon others who are unlike humans in an effort to separate ourselves from death. We mask this willingness to kill under many veils, including one of "kindness" as reified in the Veterinary Oath. This in no way suggests that euthanasia is not in fact kind, but rather that we are motivated to believe that euthanasia for nonhuman animals is kind because it allows us to avoid our own fear of ego-dissolution at the point of death; and that we are not so motivated regarding human euthanasia because it confronts us with that inherent fear.

EUTHANASIA

The moral concerns surrounding euthanasia, as well as our human fears about death, are well played out in the differences between the two oaths. I will quickly survey common arguments against human euthanasia to demonstrate that, at least in the United States, the deliberate use of medical skill to bring about human death is highly controversial and usually condemned; and that this view has persistent philosophical history.

Two well-used arguments against euthanasia for humans include the argument of "Playing God" and the argument of "Nature." Arguments that assert that we should not *play God* or violate *nature* tell us that only a being with superior wisdom or knowledge of the consequences of our actions should have power over life and death. Humans simply do not have the knowledge or intellectual capacity to make decisions about such matters for beings that are equal or similar to ourselves. But it is not just the physicians who must introject humility into their non-divine judgments. Patients who wish to be euthanized today may be thought to have wrongly sacrificed themselves should a cure become available tomorrow. Ultimately, the "playing God" argument states that the beginning and ending of the life of the patient is not a matter to be decided by any human but only by a divine force.

A related argument is the "cure" argument, which states that a patient should not be euthanized because the disease may fail to progress as expected. We, as doctors, patients, or loved ones, never know fully when a cure might suddenly become available, or how a disease will progress, therefore, we should not euthanize human beings. Some take the progression of the disease to be something only known or controlled by—or rightly controlled by—a divine or supernatural power. Others interpret this argument about the potential for a cure to appear to be fully natural, that is, science may progress in such a way as to reveal a cure for a terminal disease independent of the existence or action of divine will.

Similarly, the argument based on nature suggests that euthanasia is "unnatural" because it interferes with the "natural course" or the expected prognosis that the disease would take without a drastic, life-ending intervention. Since we do not and cannot, without being omniscient, know with certainty what the natural course of any individual's disease is, the nature-based argument suggests that we should never prematurely end a life. After all, the natural course of the disease may lead to spontaneous healing, an expansion of human knowledge of the disease, or some deep lesson of the nature of human existence that may occur if the suffering victim is allowed to progress through the disease in its entirety, until death. Some might take the "nature" argument to be the "playing God" argument used by those who want to avoid appeals to divinity or the supernatural.

Our current Hippocratic Oath in the United States demands that we do not even suggest euthanasia, nor treat our patients in any way that is criminal or in violation of the law. This conservative command asks that we think only within social boundaries already delineated by attorneys, lawmakers, and existing policy; in other words, it asks us to stay within the bounds of human works and human knowledge, and thus avoid "playing God." Likewise, a medical provider who does not violate legal parameters is likely to refrain from "unnatural" acts such as hastening death. Why, then, does the Veterinary Oath allow euthanasia? Aren't we "playing God" and radically altering the "natural" course of the disease in the case of animals in our care?

The Veterinary Oath also circumscribes and limits treatments provided by, and actions of, the health professional, and while some principles of circumscription are similar, that is, we are to use our knowledge in responsible and beneficial ways, we are also to use our powers to further needs of society as plausibly indicated by law and policy. We should attempt to advance medical knowledge; a phrase that, taken by itself, might lead us to H.G. Wells' *Island of Dr. Moreau* (1896), in which disturbing animal–human hybrids were created using surgical means, all in the name of scientific exploration. Happily, the Oath provides principles such as the relief of animal suffering, conservation of animals as resources, and promotion of public health. Interestingly, in contrast to those in the Hippocratic Oath, these ideals take precedence over matters of life and death. In the Veterinary Oath, knowledge is cast as knowledge possessed by a human community with needs and goals of human and animal health and quality of life. While the original Hippocratic Oath is sworn to the Greek gods, and contemporary versions ask medical doctors to swear on whatever they hold sacred, no divine knowledge is mentioned in the Veterinary Oath and what is natural seems to be encompassed in, or overshadowed by human needs and social welfare. "Playing God" does not enter into consideration here, perhaps because humans see themselves as godlike in respect to animals, with more knowledge and power. We take ourselves to have better judgment over their lives and welfare than they do. We somehow feel that we cannot answer moral questions about the value of a human life and the importance of the quality of that life, but we can answer questions about the usefulness of animals to us, and the conservation of animal resources relative to us. Thus, if we play God to nonhuman animals, we do so in the belief that we know more than they do: our knowledge is godlike in comparison to theirs. The philosopher Rudolf Carnap tells us "all deliberate action presupposes knowledge of the world,"[6] and so we take comfort in making decisions when we convince ourselves that we do have knowledge, and we take equal comfort in refraining from decisions when the world outstrips our knowledge of it. We include ourselves and our own deaths in the category of what we cannot know so well.

SEPARATING OURSELVES FROM ANIMALS, AND DEATH

Cox et al. suggest that humans are eager to separate themselves from any aspect of their animality. We deny, ignore, and hide many bodily functions, for example, we are disgusted by excrement, sweat, mucous, and so on, because they remind us of the ultimate limit of the body: death. The Cox study revealed that people who are presented with disgusting stimuli more readily have death-related thoughts. Culturally, we often take animals to be less than human, and Wise notes that we have a preoccupation with "drawing the line" between animals and humans that runs back 2,400 years to Aristotle's *De Anima* in which animals are given only vegetative and sensitive souls, allowing them to have bodily functions and sensations; of course, humans are given these souls plus rational souls that increases our knowledge, judgment, and wisdom beyond the animals' capacity.[7] Descartes is famous for maintaining that animals are only mechanistic, because they are less flexible in their response to stimuli and do not exhibit language that suggests an understanding of abstract concepts in any clearly discernible way.[8] Since crows have been found to make tools,[9] and dolphins, according to Lou Herman and his research team, use syntax-based language when trained,[10] the line between humans and animals has shifted. Merlin Donald suggests that the distinction between animals and humans is that humans possess forethought, music, humor, and laughter while animals lack them.[11] Philosophers and psychologists alike have spent much time and energy on attempting to draw the line between humans and animals. Cox and others give us hints as to why it is so important to us to make clear the line of human–animal demarcation.

Like Kierkegaard, Ernest Becker suggests that the human struggle is one of reconciling the idea of being abstract and infinite with the noisome reality of being housed in a physical, limited, and finite body that dies.[12] Psychopathology emerges from ineffective cognitive modes of death transcendence. A growing body of evidence likewise supports the notion that we struggle to defend ourselves against myriad sources of death anxiety, and we languish when we are unable to deny and distance ourselves from the dread of vulnerability, bodily decay, and actual or symbolic annihilation. Becker also calls death a complex symbol. When one fears death, one may actually fear the loss of life due to aging, injury, or disease. One can fear death symbolically when one feels (even unconsciously) the loss of identity or loved ones; is overwhelmed by one's own needs, desires, and anger; or when separation from community, ideology, or God threatens to annihilate the self. One can fear destruction of the ego just as intensely as one can fear the death of the body.[13]

While Becker separates humans from animals, claiming that this existential tension is human and not experienced by animals, he also notes that disowning our animal nature and physical finitude is one of our urges because such a separation quells the fear of death. This urge may explain the difference between the two oaths taken by medical professionals dedicated to healing and treating physical bodies. Physicians and veterinarians have much in common: They undergo very similar training and screening. Both treat the body. Both must take the well-being of the living system being treated into account. Both must stand at some point defeated in the face of death. Both have the power to palliate and to kill. But two oaths emerged, arguably because it is important to us to see ourselves as different from animals, and each oath is governed by a different set of principles. We like the fact that Aristotle described us as rational as well as sensitive, but deemed the animals as only sensitive. This principle of separation makes us different. In order to preserve ourselves, psychologically, from death, we cling to Leibniz' notion that "[I]t is the knowledge of necessary and eternal truths that distinguishes us from the mere animals."[14]

TERROR MANAGEMENT THEORY EXPLAINS THE OATHS[15]

Terror management theory (TMT) is the exciting new discipline focusing on human psychological responses and reactions that emerge when we recognize death and contemplate our finitude. TMT takes as its foundation the conflict between our comprehension of death and our deep instinctive urge to continue to live. That conflict creates terror within us that is often eagerly pushed away from ordinary daily consciousness. Mundane tasks such as doing dishes and obeying traffic laws may well be overwhelming if one is possessed of full knowledge about how short and precious life is, and how final death will be for each of us. TMT, as explained by Greenberg et al. is based on two vital notions: the "anxiety buffer" hypothesis and the "mortality salience" hypothesis. The anxiety buffer consists of self-esteem, and soothing cultural worldviews that mitigate death-anxiety. The mortality salience conjecture suggests that people will forcefully defend irrational cultural worldviews when reminded of death.[16] Such worldviews mitigate anxiety by "imbuing the universe with order and meaning, by providing standards of value, and by promising protection and death transcendence to those who meet those standards of value."[17] In cultural worldviews, Greenberg et al. include nationalistic beliefs, moral codes, and religious values as well as in-group codes of conduct and social mores. As such, oaths for both physicians and veterinarians present to medical professionals a shared code of conduct unifying their communities and highlighting individual membership in an in-group.

A shared value for many in the United States is *kindness,* whether based on a religion such as Christianity or simple community values. This shared value, I suggest, functions as a buffer against death-based terror when we are reminded of our own finite existence. Euthanizing animals when they are suffering is considered to be an act of kindness; thus the word's meaning "the good death." When one is kind, one increases one's self-esteem, and death-based anxiety is reduced. TMT suggests that challenging deeply held cultural worldviews increases death anxiety. Of course, the contradictory notion that human beings cannot be euthanized, that such action is criminal, or against God or nature, is also a deeply held cultural belief. To subscribe to and uphold these beliefs affords opportunities to reinforce our feelings of in-group belonging and concurrently, according to TMT, reduce our anxiety about death. I conclude that our current policy and practice of upholding two rather contradictory sets of principles for the treatment of humans and animals can be well explained by TMT.

WHY THE HIPPOCRATIC OATH SHOULD BE CHANGED

I argue that we will have a higher quality of human life if we change the Hippocratic Oath, as well as a better understanding of ourselves if we practice confrontation of our own finitude. Thus, the "should" here is not strictly a moral "should" but one of the pragmatics of better living and a healthier psychological approach to death. I suggest that the erosion of the anxiety buffer, and the confrontation of our own fear of ego-annihilation, will help us recognize the difference between kindness held up as a moral façade against the eventuality of death, and real kindness that removes suffering and affords a stance that is in fact more "godlike" in its objectivity and less motivated by fear. While some policies rightly take our fears into account, for example, policies ensuring equal rights and treatment, the difference between the oaths is likely motivated by the factors suggested by TMT. While some might argue that keeping the anxiety buffer intact will preserve much that is good in the human psyche and society, I suggest that artificial distinctions such as the one found here, false moralizing based on fear, and egocentrically motivated "kindness" is not the path to an authentic existence. To embrace death as an event that is shared by all, albeit experienced alone, and one that is an inevitable part of life, is to own one's existence authentically.

We do not in most other cases base policy or law simply on the fear of inevitable eventualities, such as the aging process in general. For example, a law based on the fear of being over 30 would not serve personal or social interests, though it may be great fuel for fiction such as *Logan's Run,* a film in which people are executed on their 30th birthday based simply on a fear of aging shared by the younger members of that society. There is ample evidence that at least some people over 30 both enjoy life and contribute a great deal of quality to the lives of others, even if it does seem scary to be 30 when one is 25. Likewise, our practices and laws are not, for the most part, based only on positive-but-irrational emotions. While we celebrate aging with parties, congratulate the 16-year-old on being eligible to get a driver's license, and extol the 35-year-old's eligibility to run for President, we make laws about driving and presidency based on expected rationality, competency, and life experience, not merely on *joie de vivre.* Other practices and laws that rule us are also not based entirely on irrational motives such as fear, celebration, or outrage. We make an exception when we base social practices such as those that govern medical and veterinary societies on the avoidance of something unavoidable, and we make such policy and law both irrationally and in false conscience.

I suggest, finally, that if we accept death as part of life, we will opt for quality of life rather than quantity, and so choose the Veterinary Oath for humans and replace the Hippocratic Oath as it is currently written. A life lived with low quality and with high pain and suffering is not one that most of us would choose, barring a self-punishing allegiance to arguments against "playing God" or interfering with the "natural order" of things. As we see in current law in Montana, Oregon, and Washington, the majority of voters want the option to control their dying when faced with prolonged, severe ill health, although some do choose to live with such suffering.

The policy that might emerge would allow us to have *autonomy* over our lives, a common moral principle used in policy creation, to such a degree that we are able to request assisted suicide or euthanasia if we are suffering with a course of terminal illness that predictably leads to more suffering. That is, we could replace concerns about "playing God" with policies that allow us to be our own masters. My conclusion can be summarized: while our human knowledge will never be the perfect knowledge imagined by those who discuss divine omniscience, we do have a profound acquaintance with our own subjective experiences, and that, combined with our best sciences, is an excellent data set on which to ground decisions, and practices of life and death.

Humans and human skills—technological, medical, legal, and social—can both be understood as part of the natural order and capable of changing the "natural" progression of disease. We can use these same skills to contribute to policy and practice in a way that gives more profound respect to human autonomy and human quality of life. That is, as humans we have great power to shape our reality. Whether we are using biological technology, such as stem cells or antibiotics, or working with the social skill of understanding human interaction, behavior, and flourishing, we can, and very often do, change the way our lives are lived and ended. Indeed, the Hippocratic Oath as it stands now virtually commands medical professionals to interfere with the natural course of injury and disease toward the prolongation of human life. If we are to choose to be authentic, we will finally reject our anxiety buffers and embrace death as something that can also be changed in terms of its "natural" course: both by its being avoided for the present through competent and careful treatments based on medical advances, and by its being welcomed through the natural progression of medicine, ethical reflection, and our willingness to face and incorporate a deeper understanding of ourselves and our authentic existential realities.

NOTES

1. George Washington University School of Medicine and Health Sciences, Graduate Medical Education Resident Manual (2004).

2. "Hippocratic Oath," Microsoft® Encarta® Online Encyclopedia 2000.

3. https://www.avma.org/KB/Policies/Pages/veterinarians-oath.aspx.

4. Jamie L. Goldenberg, Tom Pyszczynski, Jeff Greenberg, Sheldon Solomon, Benjamin Kluck, and Robin Cornwell, "I Am Not an Animal: Mortality Salience, Disgust, and the Denial of Human Creatureliness," *Journal of Experimental Psychology* 130, 3 (2001): 427–35.

5. Cathy R. Cox, Jamie L. Goldenberg, Tom Pyszczynski, and David Weise, "Disgust, Creatureliness and the Accessibility of Death-Related Thoughts," *European Journal of Social Psychology* 37 (2007): 494–507.

6. A. W. Cairnes, *Carnap and 20th Century Thought: Explication and Enlightenment* (Cambridge: Cambridge University Press, 2007), 123.

7. Stephen M. Wise, *Drawing the Line: Science and the Case for Animal Rights* (New York: Basic Books, 2003).

8. Daisie Radner and Michael Radner, *Animal Consciousness* (New York: Prometheus Books, 1996).

9. Nathan J. Emery and Nicola S. Clayton, "The Mentality of Crows: Convergent Evolution of Intelligence in Corvids and Apes," *Science: New Series* 306 (5703) (December 2007): 1903–7.

10. Louis M. Herman, "Cognition and Language Competencies of Bottlenosed Dolphins," in *Dolphin Cognition and Behavior: A Comparative Approach*, ed. R. J. Schusterman, J. Thomas, and F. G. Woods (Hilldale, NJ: Laurence Erlbaum Associates, 1986), 221–51.

11. Merlin Donald, *A Mind So Rare* (New York: Norton & Norton & Co., 2002).

12. Ernest Becker, *The Denial of Death* (New York: Free Press, 1973).

13. For evidence on the complex dimensions of death anxiety and their impact on psychopathology, see for example, Robert Firestone and Joyce Catlett, *Beyond Death Anxiety* (New York: Springer, 2009); Robert J. Lifton, *The Broken Connection* (Washington, DC: American Psychiatric Press, 1979); J. S. Piven, *Death and Delusion* (Westport, CT: Information Age Publishing, 2004); and Irvin Yalom, *Existential Psychotherapy* (New York: Basic Books, 1980).

14. Gottfried Leibniz, *Monadology* http://www.rbjones.com/rbjpub/philos/classics/leibniz/monad.htm, 1714: Paragraph 29.

15. Special thanks to Omar Shehryar, PhD and Jerry Piven, PhD for their assistance with this section.

16. Jeff Greenberg, Tom Pyszczynski, and Sheldon Solomon, "The Causes and Consequences of a Need for Self-Esteem: A Terror Management Theory," in *Public Self and Private Self*, ed. R. F. Baumeister (New York, NY: Springer-Verlag, 1986), 189–212.

17. Jeff Greenberg, Sheldon Solomon, and Tom Pyszczynski, "Terror Management Theory of Self-Esteem and Cultural Worldviews," *Advances in Experimental Social Psychology* 29, 61 (1997): 65.

When it was all over, when the last call finally came, Jack took Phoebe by the elbow through the long corridors, the hermetic metal doors and clicking floors. The nurses met them, the doctor, all wearing white.

The boy came out of the iron lung with legs like a bird. He flapped his arm and wiggled his fingers. With legs like a bird, Phoebe said. She hovered over the hospital crib, loosened her scarf. Only they're not moving. She took off her sunglasses and put them back on. You hold him, Jack, she said. You pick him up. You hold him. I don't want to hurt him.

From "Flight," by Catherine Rogers

Section II

Improving the Vehicles of Care

Chapter 8

Palliative Care and Hospice: Caring for Patients with Serious Illness

Kerrianne P. Page and Maura L. Del Bene

*A*pproximately 90 million Americans are currently living with serious and
*life-threatening illness, a number that is expected to more than double in the next
25 years. How will we care for them? Are we prepared? Can we afford it? Hospice
and palliative medicine is a new medical subspecialty and paradigm of care that
allows the health-care system to respond to the needs of seriously ill patients and
their families, through expert, interdisciplinary care that provides for comprehensive, compassionate treatment from the diagnosis of a serious illness through
death and bereavement. This chapter explores the current state of serious illness
in the United States, the emergence and growth of palliative care and hospice in
the health-care system, the scope of palliative care and hospice services today,
and the barriers and opportunities for growth of this promising new medical
subspecialty.*

INTRODUCTION

Any examination of the current status of death and dying in America requires
an understanding of the prevalent causes of death and how the American
health-care system has responded to the needs of people with serious and life-
limiting illnesses. In the last century, there has been a profound shift in both
the causes of death and the health-care system's management of patients who

are nearing the end of life. Prior to the 1940s, most deaths in the United States were due to acute illness (such as infections) and accidents, typically resulting in a short course of illness and disability, often followed by death at home. Advances in medical technology and treatments, which have resulted in marked improvements in life expectancy and effective treatment for what were once fatal illnesses, shifted the major causes of death to chronic illnesses, often with a prolonged phase of disability and functional decline. Approximately 90 million Americans are living with serious and life-threatening illness, a number that is expected to more than double over the next 25 years.[1] In 2011, the most common causes of death in United States were heart disease, cancers, chronic lower respiratory diseases, and cerebrovascular diseases (stroke). Alzheimer's disease and diabetes mellitus were the sixth and seventh leading causes of death, respectively.[2] A result of gains in life expectancy is that the U.S. population is growing substantially older; by 2030, 20 percent of the U.S. population will be more than 65 years old.[3] With these changes, the locus of care and dying shift away from the home toward the hospital and nursing home setting. As a result, many Americans have never experienced the death of a loved one in the home setting, despite the fact that home is strongly preferred as the site of death by American adults.

The growing burden of chronic illness and its management has led to substantial increases in U.S. health-care spending, which has now become a focal point of social, political, and economic policy. Data indicate that individuals with five or more chronic illnesses are responsible for two-thirds of Medicare spending, but only represent 20 percent of all Medicare beneficiaries.[4] Additionally, 5 percent of the most seriously ill Americans account for more than 50 percent of health-care spending, with most costs incurred in the last year of life as a result of hospital-based treatment.[5] Despite these large expenditures on this subpopulation, numerous studies have detailed unmet needs, including persistent pain and other physical symptoms, significant emotional and psychological distress, poor communication with health-care providers, lack of caregiving resources, and personal financial indebtedness. The SUPPORT study, published in 1995, crystallized these problems: it revealed a picture of seriously ill hospitalized adults with unmet physical, psychosocial, and communication needs that were not impacted by attempts to improve communication between patients and physicians within the standard medical framework.[6] This growing gap between increasing resource utilization and persistent, suboptimal quality of care set the stage for the growth of hospice and palliative medicine as a new medical subspecialty and as a paradigm of care.

HISTORY OF HOSPICE AND PALLIATIVE CARE

The discipline of hospice and palliative medicine traces its roots to medieval times, when hospices were places of rest established along pilgrimage routes for sick and weary travelers. The term "hospice" derives from the Latin *hospitium,* implying care and refreshment. Throughout the 18th, 19th, and 20th centuries, religious organizations founded institutions called hospices—physical places that provided care for dying and indigent people. In 1967, Dr. Cicely Saunders, founder of the modern hospice movement, opened St. Christopher's Hospice in South London. Through her work, Dr. Saunders, herself a nurse, social worker, and physician, established the core principles of hospice care as a system of care rather than a location: the management of pain and physical symptoms, psychosocial support for the patient and family, education of health-care providers in the management of dying patients, and research into treatments to alleviate suffering.

Dr. Saunders' collaborative work with Florence Wald, Dean of the Yale University School of Nursing, led to the opening of Connecticut Hospice in 1974, the first hospice in United States. At that time, hospice was viewed as an alternative approach to standard medical care in the face of terminal illness. Hospice organizations were developed across the United States by volunteers and through grant-funded programs, utilizing a model that focused on care delivered in the patient's home in partnership with the patient's family as caregivers. By 1982, the success of this model led to the creation of the Medicare Hospice Benefit as part of the Tax Equity of Fiscal Responsibility Act (TEFRA). The Medicare Hospice Benefit defined a comprehensive array of services that address the needs of patients and families related to the terminal illness. Importantly, the Hospice Benefit defined terminal illness as "a life expectancy of 6 months or less should the disease run its usual course" and stipulated that the patient forgo curative treatments.[7] While an important step forward, the design of the Hospice Benefit limited the scope of services and eligibility of patients living with serious illness, such that only a subset of this population qualify for these needed services.

Around the same time hospice services were being developed in the United States, Dr. Balfour Mount at the Royal Victoria Hospital in Montréal, Canada coined the term "palliative care" to address symptom management and quality of life in hospitalized patients with serious illness. The term arises from the Latin *palliare,* "to cloak," referring to the treatment of symptoms apart from the underlying disease. The concept of specialized, interdisciplinary services for patients dying from serious illness was broadened to include a larger population of patients suffering from the effects of serious illness but who were not yet at the end of life. Through the financial support of philanthropic organizations such as the Robert Wood Johnson Foundation and Open Society Institute, palliative care services were formed in academic hospitals in United States and Canada to promote symptom directed care focusing on quality of life and goals of care. Additional forces spurred the growth of the field, including the Institute of Medicine's 1997 report *Approaching Death: Improving Care at the End of Life,* the formation of the National Consensus

Project for Palliative Care, the development of the Center to Advance Palliative Care (CAPC), and the recognition of hospice and palliative medicine as a medical subspecialty by the American Board of Medical Specialties in 2007. As of 2010, nearly 66 percent of American hospitals had palliative care services.[8] Current expansion of palliative care services includes outpatient palliative care services as well as services in hospital emergency departments and intensive care units.

PALLIATIVE CARE AND HOSPICE—WHAT'S IN A NAME?

The terms "palliative care" and "hospice" have been variably used, confused, and poorly understood by both health-care professionals and the public. Due to long and cumbersome definitions, such as that of the World Health Organization,[9] health-care providers have struggled to describe the concept of palliative care to patients, the services it provides, and its relevance to their medical situation. In 2011, the CAPC commissioned public opinion research on palliative care to assess the knowledge and attitudes of the American public toward palliative care in a sample of 800 adults. That research demonstrated that 70 percent of the sample described themselves as "not at all knowledgeable" about palliative care. When informed about the meaning of palliative care, respondents overwhelmingly agreed about the importance of education about palliative care and the availability of palliative care for patients with serious illness and their families.[10] Qualitative research within the poll identified a description of palliative care that resonates with the public and has been adopted by CAPC as a new definition of the discipline:

> *Palliative care is specialized medical care for people with serious illnesses. This type of care is focused on providing patients with relief from the symptoms, pain, and stress of a serious illness—whatever the diagnosis.*
>
> *The goal is to improve quality of life for both the patient and the family. Palliative care is provided by a team of doctors, nurses, and other specialists who work with a patient's other doctors to provide an extra layer of support. Palliative care is appropriate at any age and at any stage in a serious illness, and can be provided together with curative treatment.*[11]

Key elements in this definition include the concept of "extra layer of support" as an addition to standard medical care; appropriateness at any stage of illness, not just at the end of life; and the simultaneous delivery of services together with curative treatment. These latter two elements differentiate the broader scope of palliative care services when contrasted with hospice.

Hospice is a specialized form of palliative care, directed at patients at the end of life. The definition of "end of life" varies amongst experts and organizations, but is widely considered to encompass the last 6–12 months of life in the setting of an incurable illness. The National Hospice and Palliative Care Organization provides the following definition of hospice:

> *Considered the model for quality compassionate care for people facing a life-limiting illness, hospice provides expert medical care, pain management, and emotional and spiritual support expressly tailored to the patient's needs and wishes. Support is provided to the patient's loved ones as well.*
>
> *Hospice focuses on caring, not curing. In most cases, care is provided in the patient's home but may also be provided in freestanding hospice centers, hospitals, nursing homes, and other long-term care facilities. Hospice services are available to patients with any terminal illness or of any age, religion, or race.*[12]

Hospice services seek to improve the quality of life when time is limited, and when treatments that are directed at the underlying disease may no longer be effective or desired. It shifts the focus of care to symptom control and quality of life as the main priorities of treatment. The origin of the term "hospice" sometimes lends to the misperception of hospice as a "place" or location of care, rather than a system or "philosophy" of care. Likewise, the term is often used to describe the financial and regulatory provisions of the Medicare Hospice Benefit, which has largely defined the scope of hospice services in the current U.S. health-care system.

Additional terms, such as "comfort care" and "supportive care," have also been used to describe care that is focused on symptoms and quality of life. These terms do not have standard definitions or specific elements of care, and are often used to describe the avoidance of components of disease-directed care—for example, forgoing transfusions, chemotherapy, operative procedures, and so on. They are often used by non-hospice and palliative medicine professionals, especially when the terms "hospice" or "palliative care" are assumed to have negative connotations. The public opinion research described above suggests this is an unfounded fear, and that the public responds to language that describes palliative care as specific, action-oriented elements of medical care.

HOW DOES PALLIATIVE CARE IMPROVE THE CARE OF SERIOUSLY ILL PATIENTS?

At the heart of hospice and palliative care is a "whole person" approach to the patient. Beyond understanding the specific illness, great importance is paid to understanding the person who suffers from illness, the impact of the illness on that individual's life, and the impact on his or her family and loved ones. Interdisciplinary care from a variety of professionals is critical to achieving this goal: palliative care teams are comprised of a combination of physicians, advanced practice nurses, nurses, social workers, chaplains, nursing aides, and others, such as physical therapists, nutritionists, and pharmacists. Each discipline brings its unique perspective and expertise to the assessment of the patient and family and participates in developing a plan of care to meet their needs.

Palliative care teams enhance care through expert management in several areas:

Symptom control: This includes the management of distress and physical symptoms that are common in serious illness including pain, depression/anxiety, fatigue, weakness, nausea/vomiting, respiratory distress, and delirium. In some situations, this may include managing difficult medical interventions including the withdrawal of life-sustaining treatments such as mechanical ventilation or hemodialysis, palliative sedation for intractable suffering that is unresponsive to other treatments, and addressing the discontinuation of futile care. Palliative medicine physicians and nurses have specialized knowledge and training to provide management of these often complex problems.

Prognostication, goals of care, and help with decision making: Through honest and sensitive discussion, palliative care providers help patients and their families understand the nature of their illness, its response to treatment, and the trajectory of the illness over time. Many illnesses, especially noncancer diagnoses, may have an inherent variable or uncertain prognosis; this is compounded by an optimistic bias of physicians in judging prognosis, and patients' and caregivers' tendencies to minimize information about poor prognoses. Palliative care providers help patients and families understand and process this information by attending to both the factual and emotional components of these discussions. They help patients and families identify their goals of care—for example, cure, life prolongation, and comfort—in the context of the specific illness and its available treatments, as well as the things they value—for example, being at home, spending time with family, achieving professional milestones, and so on. Through this process, palliative care teams help align treatments with patients' preferences and priorities, helping patients to avoid unnecessary or unwanted treatments, or to pursue treatments that may be beneficial in meeting their goals.

Communication and conflict management: Palliative care teams facilitate communication between physicians and patients as well as between patients and families. They evaluate patient and family health literacy, that is, their familiarity with health-care terminology and practices, to help present information in a format that patients and caregivers will understand. They address both the cognitive and emotional components of medical information, responding to the need for support and empathic presence. Palliative care professionals help other health-care providers present information to patients and families in an accurate, sensitive, and digestible way that promotes understanding, allows for questions, and minimizes misunderstandings or misconceptions. They also help facilitate communication within families, by addressing "the elephant in the room" of fears and expectations related to serious illness. When conflict occurs, either between health-care providers and the patient/family, or between family members, palliative care teams can negotiate consensus and provide conflict resolution by clarifying factual information about the situation, each parties' goals and intentions, and the benefits and burdens of treatments to arrive at an acceptable plan of care.

Psychosocial and spiritual concerns: The interdisciplinary expertise of the palliative care team incorporates the skills of social workers and chaplains to help manage the stress, anxiety, and spiritual pain that commonly occur in serious illness. These elements are key factors in determining patients' perception of quality of life as well as their ability to adhere to medical treatment regimens for the underlying illness. The support and counseling of the palliative care team helps patients normalize their emotional response to illness, decrease a sense of isolation, and reframe hopefulness. The team also plays a critical role in providing support to family and caregivers, who often minimize their own stress and emotional response to the patient's illness. Additionally, palliative care teams may provide bereavement support to caregivers after the death of the patient to facilitate appropriate grieving. This feature is a standard component of hospice programs, and may be offered by some, but not all, palliative care programs.

Practical caregiving and financial concerns: Many patients and families are overwhelmed by the tasks of providing hands-on care or arranging for the appropriate care for the patient. Additionally, the financial burdens associated with serious illness can be staggering, causing many families to spend their life-savings to provide care. Palliative care teams can help patients and families with these concerns by providing education in direct caregiving skills; identifying services available through the patient's insurance benefits, such as home care or hospice services; identifying community resources that may be able to assist with care; advising patients and families about the benefits of financial planning to maximize existing resources; and assessing potential eligibility for support through programs such as Medicaid, Social Security Disability, or Veteran's benefits.

Coordination of care and ensuring continuity across settings: Palliative care providers help to ensure that the patient's goals and preferences for care are consistent in all settings where care is provided, whether in the hospital, at home, or in a nursing facility. This is often accomplished through communication among providers to transition care between different settings, as individual palliative care teams are often limited to providing care in a single setting. Hospice services are unique in this regard, as they retain professional management of the patient's care across all venues as the patient's care needs change and can provide care in all of these settings.

Clinical research has borne out the effectiveness of the comprehensive approach of palliative care and hospice to serious illness. Studies in both palliative care and hospice populations have demonstrated improvements in symptom control, survival compared with usual care, patient and family satisfaction, outcomes for caregivers, as well as cost savings and decreases in the use of inappropriate health system resources. A notable study in 2010 demonstrated the impact of palliative care services when utilized early in the course of serious illness: patients with newly diagnosed metastatic non–small cell lung cancer who received palliative care from the time of diagnosis reported better quality-of-life scores and fewer depressive symptoms while receiving the same rates of chemotherapy as the population not receiving palliative care services. The palliative care group utilized less aggressive end-of-life care (defined by less hospitalization and ICU utilization and increased hospice utilization) but still demonstrated a median survival improvement of three months compared to the non-palliative care population; this gain in life expectancy is equivalent to that conferred by chemotherapy treatment in this disease.[13] Recent research comparing Medicare decedents who received hospice services with those who did not demonstrated reduced hospital and ICU admissions, shorter overall hospital stays, and fewer in-hospital deaths over a range of hospice lengths of stay, while at the same time reducing Medicare expenditures.[14]

PRACTICAL DIFFERENCES BETWEEN PALLIATIVE CARE AND HOSPICE SERVICES

Both palliative care and hospice services improve care for seriously ill individuals and their families through the elements described above. By its nature of providing an extra layer of support throughout the course of illness, most palliative care services are structured to provide assistance with symptom management, psychosocial support, and coordination of care while the provision of services such as specific medical treatments for the illness, home care, medications, and other services are accomplished through separate providers and paid for through standard insurance benefits. There are no specific payment mechanisms for palliative care services outside of the typical reimbursement mechanisms for the professional services of physicians and advanced practice nurses. As such, many of the services provided by the palliative care team do not generate revenue, and thus must be supported by the hospital or health system in which the palliative care team practices. A model of "cost avoidance," which describes how the work of palliative care services curtail unnecessary and unwanted expenditures, along with improved quality outcomes, such as improved pain scores and higher patient and family satisfaction rates, support the business case for palliative care services as an essential component of quality health care.

In contrast, hospice is a unique care service designed specifically to meet the needs of patients near the end of life. In the United States, the scope of hospice services is largely defined by the Medicare Hospice Benefit, which is the major payor for hospice services. Patients qualify for hospice services if they are certified by their attending physician and the hospice medical director to have a terminal illness with a life expectancy of six months or less based on the natural course of the disease, and they agree to forego curative treatments for that illness. The hospice is responsible for providing and paying for all care related to the terminal illness based on its plan of care for the patient, including nursing services, social work, pastoral care, volunteer services, medications and treatments, durable medical equipment, home health aide services to supplement family or private caregivers, and access to emergency nursing services around the clock to manage acute problems. Hospice provides respite care to relieve family caregivers for short periods, continuous care in the home to manage acute symptom crises if needed, and short-term inpatient care for the management of complex medical problems that cannot be adequately managed in the home setting. The patient's attending physician works with the hospice interdisciplinary team to provide the patient's medical care, and a hospice medical director, a physician with expertise in hospice and palliative medicine, ensures the care provided to the patient appropriately manages the patient's symptoms and underlying illness. Bereavement services are also provided to the patient's caregivers for 13 months after the death of the patient.

Hospice services are available to appropriate patients wherever they live, whether in a private home or nursing home. Hospice services may also be appropriate in the hospital setting, based on the complexity of the patient's symptom management. As described above, hospice services move with the patient should he or she require transfer from one setting to another, for example, from a private home to a nursing home setting. Hospice services are reimbursed on a per diem basis, with higher rates paid for the more intense continuous care and general inpatient services.

CURRENT SCOPE OF PALLIATIVE CARE AND HOSPICE SERVICES

In the first decade of the 21st century, palliative care and hospice services have grown substantially, serving an increasing number of patients with serious illness. Data demonstrate that palliative care has been one of the fastest growing trends in health care, with the number of hospital-based palliative care teams increasing approximately 148 percent between 2000 and 2010.[15] As of 2010, 66 percent of U.S. hospitals with more than 50 beds have a palliative care team. However, it is important to note that access to palliative care varies significantly by hospital size, with 88 percent of large hospitals (more than 300 beds) having services, compared with 23 percent of small hospitals (less than 50 beds). Additionally, geography matters—approximately 53 percent of hospitals in the southern region of the United States have palliative care programs, compared with rates exceeding 70 percent in other areas of the country. Other hospital characteristics also influence access: public hospitals, for-profit hospitals, and sole community provider hospitals are less likely to report palliative care services. The lower rates of services in public hospitals and sole community provider hospitals suggest that underserved populations may have limited access to palliative care.[16] Currently, there are no available data about the prevalence of outpatient palliative care programs, although reports within the hospice and palliative medicine professional community indicate they are growing. Varying models of outpatient palliative care practices are employed in different settings, making aggregation of data and comparisons more difficult.

Data about the scope of hospice services are published annually by the National Hospice and Palliative Care Organization in *NHPCO Facts and Figures: Hospice Care in America.*[17] As of 2011, 1.65 million Americans were cared for by more than 5,300 hospice programs; this represents 45 percent of all deaths in the United States. Medicare beneficiaries comprised 84 percent of all hospice patients, 39 percent of whom were 85 years or older. There was a slight predominance of females (56%), but a marked predominance of the white/Caucasian population (83%). The median (50th percentile) length of hospice service was 19 days, with a mean (average) length of service of 69 days. Nearly 36 percent of patients died or were discharged from hospice with the length of service less than seven days. Eleven percent of patients received hospice services for more than 180 days (six months). Cancer diagnoses represented 38 percent of admissions to hospice, while the remainder comprised diagnoses such as heart disease (11%), lung disease (9%), dementia (13%), and debility (14%). Nearly two-thirds of deaths (66%) occurred in the home or nursing home setting, while 26 percent occurred in a hospice inpatient facility, and 7 percent occurred in an acute care hospital. It is important to note that while the number of patients served by hospice continues to increase, the length of time enrolled in hospice has declined in the past several years. Although the Medicare Hospice Benefit was designed to provide services for patients in the last six months of life, 50 percent of patients received hospice services for less than three weeks.

LIMITATIONS, CHALLENGES, AND OPPORTUNITIES IN THE GROWTH OF PALLIATIVE CARE AND HOSPICE SERVICES

Workforce

Perhaps the most significant limitation to the growth of hospice and palliative care services is the manpower supply of qualified professionals in this small but rapidly growing field, especially among physicians. Subspecialty board certification in hospice and palliative medicine is the principal route for physicians to obtain expertise and credentialing in this discipline. The initial phase of board certification allowed for experiential training in the practice setting as a foundation for board certification eligibility; this pathway to certification ended in 2012 for allopathic physicians (those with a Medical Doctor, or MD, degree) and will end in 2013 for osteopathic physicians (those with a Doctor of Osteopathy, or DO, degree). Subsequently, board certification will only be available to those physicians who have completed a fellowship training program in palliative care. The growth and development of hospice and palliative medicine fellowship training programs is limited by a cap on Medicare-funded Graduate Medical Education (GME) positions imposed by the 1997 Balanced Budget Act.[18] As of May 2012, there are 85 active programs offering more than 234 fellowship positions.[19] Most of these positions are funded by philanthropic grants rather than by the Medicare-funded mechanisms that support position training and education in other medical specialties.

Although it represents an important element in insuring quality and expertise in hospice and palliative medicine physicians, the board certification process falls woefully short in meeting the discipline's workforce needs. A 2010 analysis indicated that there were approximately 4,400 current hospice and palliative medicine physicians, most of whom practice the specialty part time, providing a current manpower pool of 1,700–3,300 full-time equivalents (FTE). The analysis estimated that in order to fully staff existing hospice and hospital-based palliative care programs at that time, a workforce between 4,487 and 10,810 FTE would be required.[20] A report from the CAPC and the National Palliative Care Research Center emphasizes the physician workforce shortage in a different way: it highlights that while there is one cardiologist for every 71 patients who suffer a heart attack and one oncologist for every 141 patients newly diagnosed with cancer, there is only one palliative medicine physician for every 1,200 patients living with serious or life-threatening illness.[21]

Several strategies are currently in development to close the gap between the workforce need and manpower supply. The model of *primary palliative care,* skills that all clinicians should have, supported by the availability of *specialty palliative care,* delivered by experts with advanced training in managing complex and difficult problems, has been proposed as a means to meet demand for palliative care services.[22] The success of this model relies on adequate education and training of all clinicians in the core principles and skills of palliative care (discussed below). Alternate training pathways to board certification for mid-career physicians are also being considered. A credential for Hospice Medical Director certification, which will focus on the specific competencies for physicians practicing in hospice organizations, is expected to be initiated in the Spring of 2014.[23]

Education and Training

The key to providing a sizable and competent workforce in palliative care is broad availability of education and training for all disciplines in the health-care system, at every level of experience. Currently most training in hospice and palliative care is provided through the efforts of professional societies supported by educational funding grants. Programs such as the End-of-Life Physician Education Consortium (EPEC) and the End-of-Life Nursing Education Consortium (ELNEC) are examples of training for practicing clinicians. Similar training programs are in development and implementation for practicing social workers and chaplains. At the medical school and nursing school level, however, educational exposure and requirements are not standardized, leading to significant variations in instruction in the core elements of palliative care. A report from the American Association of American Medical Colleges acknowledges this, noting that while basic teaching about these principles occurs in the nonclinical years in medical school, there is not enough exposure to clinical palliative care as most rotations are elective, models vary, and funding for this type of education is limited.[24] At the postgraduate residency training level, similar variations in exposure and standardized curriculum exist. Fellowship programs designed to provide advanced training in subspecialty palliative care are relatively few in number and inadequately funded, as previously discussed. Additionally, limited availability of qualified clinician educators exists in all these settings.

Attempts to expand educational initiatives in palliative care are underway at both the legislative and professional society level. The Palliative Care and Hospice Education and Training Act (PCHETA) was introduced into Congress in July 2012. This legislation would authorize the development of Palliative Care Academic Career Awards to develop career paths for clinician educators in palliative care and the development of interdisciplinary Palliative Care Training Centers funded with federal support.[25] An array of palliative care organizations continue to advocate for mandatory palliative care curricula both at the medical school and residency training level, and a repeal of the cap on Medicare-funded GME fellowship positions to allow for growth in specialty palliative care training.

Research

Academic and clinical research in palliative care continues to grow as the field develops but remains a small component of the nation's research health-care agenda. In 2009, there were only 114 active awarded National Institutes of Health (NIH) grants supporting palliative care research,[26] compared with 21,704 NIH grants funded through the American Recovery and Reinvestment Act in that year.[27] It is important to recognize that the activities of philanthropic organizations such as the Kellogg Institute, The Robert Wood Johnson Foundation, The Hartford Foundation, The Open Society Institute, and others have been crucial to the support of research in this field.

Organizations such as the National Palliative Care Research Center have called for the NIH and Agency for Health care Research and Quality (AHRQ) to allocate 2 percent of their current budgets to focus on palliative care research, and for the development of an Office of Palliative Care Research within the NIH to oversee and coordinate research efforts in palliative care. The ongoing funding of research through private foundation grants will remain a key element in this arena.

Access and Quality

The success of palliative care and hospice as a model of care requires widespread access to services that consistently demonstrate quality and consistency, regardless of location. As discussed earlier, access to hospital-based palliative care services is growing, but remains variable based on hospital size, classification, and geographic locale. As of 2013, the availability of palliative care services is not a required element in the accreditation standards for hospitals and nursing homes. Furthermore, the composition of palliative care services in terms of multidiscipline involvement and the model of practice, for example, consultation only versus direct clinical management, varies from location to location based on available resources. Resources for longitudinal care after hospital discharge are limited, as most hospital-based programs have limited or no outpatient services, although this is an area of active expansion. Finally, the lower rates of available palliative care services in public and sole community provider hospitals as well as hospice enrollment statistics demonstrating low rates of utilization by minority groups indicate the need for improved outreach and services for underserved and minority populations.

Efforts to improve access to palliative care services have taken multiple forms. The CAPC provides training, mentorship, and expertise to hospitals in developing and implementing quality palliative care services through its Palliative Care Leadership CentersTM program.[28] Several organizations have called for the inclusion of palliative care services in the accreditation standards for hospitals and nursing homes as a means of enhancing access to services. Additional efforts through legislative advocacy are beginning to bear fruit: in 2011, New York enacted the Palliative Care Access Act, a groundbreaking initiative requiring health-care entities to "facilitate access to appropriate palliative care consultation and services."[29] Quality improvement efforts are also ongoing. The National Consensus Project for Quality Palliative Care, a collaboration between multiple hospice and palliative care professional organizations, has published and revised *Clinical Practice Guidelines for Quality Palliative Care*[30] to promote standardized, quality palliative care services across all settings.

This group issued its most recent guidelines in 2013. In 2011, The Joint Commission, a national organization that provides Medicare accreditation for hospitals, developed a voluntary *Advanced Certification Program in Palliative Care*[31] that recognizes hospital-based palliative care programs for their quality services and expertise. To support these efforts, The LIVE**STRONG**™ Foundation, in collaboration with CAPC, has provided grant funding to programs to assist in preparing for and obtaining certification.[32]

Hospices providing services to Medicare beneficiaries are subject to Medicare's *Hospice Conditions of Participation,*[33] which identifies required elements and core services in the provision of hospice care. Programs are subject to federal and state surveys for compliance with these conditions as a measure of quality care. In addition, beginning in 2013, Medicare will require the public reporting of certain hospice quality measures. In addition to governmental oversight of the quality of hospice care, the National Hospice and Palliative Care Organization has developed the *NHPCO Standards for Hospice Care*[34] and sponsors a Quality Partners Program to assist hospice organizations in developing quality measures and improving performance.

The development of outpatient palliative care services is a growing aspect of the discipline utilizing different models including clinic-based and home-based services. The scope and sustainability of some of these models are unclear in this early phase of development. Some experts have called for the development of a new model of care, community-based palliative care, which transcends the silos of the current U.S. health-care structure to deliver care based on patient and family needs, regardless of location.[35] This model is promising, but requires further exploration of how to operationalize these services on a widespread basis.

Reimbursement Models

In any service delivery system, the opportunity for growth and expansion is dependent upon financial sustainability. This is particularly true for palliative care and hospice services, which have unique reimbursement structures within the current health-care system. As discussed earlier, palliative care services are not compensated as a single entity; while the professional services of physicians and the advanced practice nurse team members are reimbursable, the important contributions of other interdisciplinary team members, such as social work and chaplains, are uncompensated. Typically, revenue generated from professional billing will cover only 20–30 percent of the cost of an average palliative care program; the remainder of the expense is supported by the health-care institution. The business case for hospital palliative care is predicated upon a cost avoidance model, which accounts for savings achieved through the elimination of unnecessary or unwanted treatments and decreased utilization of expensive resources when they are likely to be ineffective. These models are difficult to integrate into hospital's current operating metrics[36] and have limited relevance in financing outpatient palliative care services.

Hospice services are currently reimbursed through a fixed dollar per diem methodology, which is designed to provide all care related to the hospice diagnosis. The per diem payment in 2013 for Medicare home hospice services is $153 per day, prior to wage adjustment.[37] This payment methodology is not well matched with the intensity of care throughout a hospice stay, where service intensity is greater—and hence, more costly—at the beginning and end of the stay, thus making short hospice stays particularly costly to a hospice provider. Overall Medicare spending for hospice in 2011 was $13.8 billion, up from $2.9 billion in 2000. This rapid growth is attributable not only to an increasing number of Medicare beneficiaries utilizing hospice services, but also a growth in the duration of long hospice stays (which account for approximately 11% of all hospice stays), particularly among for-profit hospice providers. This rapid increase in spending has increased the scrutiny of hospice providers by the federal government, resulting in audits and fraud and abuse investigations over improper enrollment of Medicare beneficiaries in hospice services. The Medicare Payment Advisory Commission (MedPAC) has recognized the mismatch between service intensity and the current payment structure, and has proposed payment system reform to better match service intensity.[38] Such models remain under consideration but are not yet implemented.

Health-care reform involving new models of care delivery and reimbursement offer opportunities for palliative care and hospice to secure financial sustainability. Both palliative care services and hospice services have demonstrated value—defined as the ratio of quality and cost—across a number of care settings. As health-care services become more integrated through initiatives such as bundled payments and accountable care organizations, the value of palliative care and hospice services becomes more evident and essential to the success of health-care systems in these new payment methodologies. Palliative care experts advocate that this must lead to improved resource allocation for the growth and expansion of palliative care and hospice services for seriously ill populations.

Cultural Acceptance

Ultimately, the ability of palliative care and hospice to meet needs of patients living with serious illness depends on how American society and its health-care system accept and support the principles of this discipline, not only from a financial and programmatic standpoint, but most importantly, through the society's cultural attitudes toward serious illness and death. The United States has long been described as a "death denying" culture, and a recent public opinion poll suggests these attitudes remain well entrenched. In addition, these attitudes differ significantly from opinions of American health-care providers.

In a poll entitled "Living Well at the End of Life: A National Conversation"[39],[40] by *National Journal* and The Regence Foundation in 2011, 71 percent of public respondents believed that enhancing quality of life for seriously ill patients is more important than extending life as long as possible, compared with 96 percent of the 500 board certified physicians who were surveyed. Only 37 percent of Americans agreed that the health-care system spends too much trying to extend the lives of seriously ill patients, and 55 percent of respondents said the health-care system has the responsibility to spend "whatever it takes." This contrasts starkly with the physicians in the poll, 79 percent of whom said the system spends too much on life prolongation in this population. Despite physicians' beliefs in the importance of palliative care, they report substantial concerns about the role of palliative care services and identify barriers to referring patients for palliative care. A large percentage of the physicians surveyed (42%) felt that emphasizing palliative care could interfere with doing whatever it takes to help patients extend their lives as long as possible, and 24 percent of physicians were reluctant to recommend palliative care out of the concern that patients may conclude that they were not doing everything possible to extend the patient's life. Additionally, 25 percent reported they were not prepared to counsel patients about the options for end-of-life care. These opinion surveys coincide with the CAPC public opinion research findings that most Americans are not knowledgeable about the basic tenets of palliative care.[41] Consistent with these recent data about attitudes toward serious illness, actual patterns of health-care utilization suggest continued growth in the provision of intensive, life–prolonging, and often ineffective medical care near the end of life. A recent study of Medicare beneficiaries demonstrates that while the site of death has shifted away from the hospital toward the home setting in the last decade (2000–2009), the rate of ICU use in the last month of life has increased, as has repeated hospitalizations—three or more—in the last 90 days of life. Additionally, transitions in the site of care (home to hospital, hospital to nursing home, hospital to hospice, and so on) at the end of life have increased— in 2009, 43 percent of decedents had a health-care transition in the last two weeks of life. During this time hospice utilization increased, but length of stay dropped, with 28 percent of beneficiaries receiving hospice services for less than three days. Approximately one-third of the short hospice stays were preceded by an ICU stay in the last month of life.[42] One commentator aptly points out "the study paints a picture of increasing commotion in the final weeks of patients' lives."[43] It also underscores the late utilization of palliative care and hospice services, curtailing the benefits that these models of care offer to patients and families.

The provision of some palliative care services in legislative health-care reform has proven to be a focal point for political debate and exploitation. In 2009, a provision in the proposed Affordable Care Act that would require Medicare to pay for physician communication and counseling sessions about patient preferences, advance directives, and end-of-life care options was famously labeled a "death panel," asserting that this was "a government run plan to decide when to pull the plug on grandma."[44] A political firestorm ensued, and the provision was dropped from the legislation.

As a society, we are yet to form a cogent philosophy about our approach to health care: we decry the expense and lack of quality in our current health-care structure, yet we assail initiatives to curb ineffective or unnecessary treatments as rationing or impingement on individuals' rights. Palliative care and hospice are not immune to these tensions, and are especially vulnerable to being misconstrued as "second rate care" in a society that views highly technological interventions as the vanguard of progress and a marker of excellence. This has led some in the field to propose a name change for hospice and palliative medicine as a discipline, citing that a change in "branding" would help expand access to the population of seriously ill patients who are never referred for palliative care or hospice services or who decline these services because of assumptions and unfavorable stereotypes.[45] In 2012, the American Academy of Hospice and Palliative Medicine surveyed its membership about this topic; results indicated that a majority of practitioners wished to keep the current name intact. These issues magnify the need for continuous education of both the American public and health-care providers about the principles, practices, and benefits of palliative care and hospice in providing care for people with serious illness that meets their needs and aligns with their goals and values.

CONCLUSION

Palliative care services possess all the attributes to provide optimal care to patients living with serious illness: expert symptom management, focus on quality of life, and goals of care aligned with curative treatments that allow patients to live each day in the best way possible. Hospice, as a specialized form of palliative care, provides essential services to patients and families at the end of life to allow for death in a way that reflects individual's values and meaning.

In an introductory paper to the *Perspectives at the Close of Life* series published in the *Journal of the American Medical Association* in 2000, the editors summarized the importance of palliative care to both patients and medical professionals:

Death is inevitable, and while there is no way out, there is a way through. Caring for patients at the close of life is one of the greatest challenges most clinicians ever face yet it can be one of the most appreciated and personally rewarding experiences. . . . At the close of life clinicians can learn to attend to patients' hopes to have their symptoms controlled, their emotions understood, their relationships supported, and their spiritual concerns addressed. One of the greatest gifts in confronting death is the perspective it offers about living life. Perhaps we too can achieve some perspective and under-standing of how to share fully in the lives of those we love, all of whom will inevitably die, and how to live our own lives well in the time we have.[46]

In the words of Hubert Humphrey, "it was once said that the moral test of government is how that government treats those who are in the dawn of life, the children; those who are in the twilight of life, the elderly; those who are in the shadows of life, the sick, the needy, and the handicapped."[47] It is also a test of our health-care system and our society to provide care that alleviates suffering and enhances the quality of life for the millions of Americans living with serious illness and their families—high quality, accessible palliative care services.

NOTES

1. The Dartmouth Institute for Health Care Policy and Clinical Practice, *The Dartmouth Atlas of Health Care.* www.dartmouthatlas.org/keyissues/issue.aspx?con=2944. Accessed March 24, 2013.

2. Centers for Disease Control, "Deaths: Preliminary Data for 2011," *National Vital Statistics Reports* 61, 6 (October 10): 2012. www.cdc.gov/nchs/data/nvsr/nvsr61/ nvsr61_06.pdf. Accessed March 17, 2013.

3. The Administration on Aging, "Aging Statistics," *The Administration on Aging (AoA) Website.* www.aoa.gov/AoARoot/Aging_Statistics/index.aspx. Accessed March 18, 2013.

4. The Commonwealth Fund, "Two Thirds of Medicare Spending is for People with Five or More Chronic Illnesses." www.commonwealthfund.org/Charts/Testimony/Car ing-for-an-Aging-America/T/Two-thirds-of-Medicare-Spending-is-for-People-with-Five-or-More-Chronic-Conditions.aspx. Accessed March 25, 2013.

5. National Institute for Health Care Management Foundation, "The Concentration of Health Care Spending," *NIHCM Foundation Data Brief,* July 2012. www.nihcm .org/images/stories/DataBrief3_Final.pdf. Accessed March 18, 2013.

6. The SUPPORT Principal Investigators, "A Controlled Trial to improve CARE for Seriously Ill Hospitalized Patients: The Study to Understand Prognoses and Preferences for Outcomes and Risks of Treatments (SUPPORT)," *Journal of American Medical Association* 274, 20 (1995): 1591–8.

7. Medicare Benefit Policy Manual, "Chapter 9—Coverage of Hospice Services Under Hospital Insurance." www.cms.gov/Regulations-and-Guidance/Guidance/ Manuals/Downloads/bp102c09.pdf. Accessed March 25, 2013.

8. Center to Advance Palliative Care, "2012 Snapshot," *A State by State Report Card on Access to Palliative Care in Our Nation's Hospitals.* www.reportcard-live.capc .stackop.com/pdf/capc-growth-analysis-snapshot-2011.pdf. Accessed March 18, 2013.

9. World Health Organization, *WHO Definition of Palliative Care.* www.who.int/ cancer/palliative/definition/en/. Accessed March 18, 2013.

10. Center to Advance Palliative Care, *2011 Public Opinion Research on Palliative Care.* www.capc.org/tools-for-palliative-care-programs/marketing/public-opinion-re search/2011-public-opinion-research-on-palliative-care.pdf. Accessed March 19, 2013.

11. Ibid.

12. National Hospice and Palliative Care Organization, *2012 Edition NHPCO Facts and Figures: Hospice Care in America.* www.nhpco.org/sites/default/files/public/Statistics_Research/2012_Facts_Figures.pdf. Accessed March 1, 2013.

13. Jennifer S. Temel, Joseph A. Greer, Alona Muzikansky, Emily R. Gallagher, Sonal Admane, Vicki A. Jackson, Constance M. Dahlin, Craig D. Blinderman, Juliet Jacobsen, William F. Pirl, J. Andrew Billings, and Thomas J. Lynch, "Early Palliative Care for Patients with Metastatic Non-Small-Cell Lung Cancer," *New England Journal of Medicine*363 (2010): 733–42.

14. Amy S. Kelley et al., "Hospice Enrollment Saves Money for Medicare and Improves Care Quality Across a Number of Different Lengths-of-Stay," *Health Affairs* 32, 3 (2013): 552–61.

15. Center to Advance Palliative Care, "2012 Snapshot."

16. Center to Advance Palliative Care, "Key Findings," *A State by State Report Card on Access to Palliative Care in Our Nation's Hospitals.* www.capc.org/reportcard/findings. Accessed March 18, 2013.

17. National Hospice and Palliative Care Organization, *2012 Edition NHPCO Facts and Figures: Hospice Care in America.*

18. Center to Advance Palliative Care, "Recommendations for Action," *A State by State Report Card on Access to Palliative Care in Our Nation's Hospitals.* www.capc.org/reportcard/recommendations. Accessed March 18, 2013.

19. American Academy of Hospice and Palliative Medicine, *Fellowship Directory.* www.aahpm.org/fellowship/default/fellowshipdirectory.html. Accessed March 22, 2013.

20. Dale Lupu, "Estimate of Current Hospice and Palliative Medicine Physician Workforce Shortage," *Journal of Pain Symptom Management* 40, 6 (December 2010): 899–911.

21. Center to Advance Palliative Care, "Recommendations for Action."

22. Timothy E. Quill and Amy P. Abernethy, "Generalist plus Specialist Palliative Care—Creating a More Sustainable Model," *New England Journal of Medicine* (March 6, 2013) (Epub at NEJM.org). Accessed March 17, 2013.

23. American Academy of Hospice and Palliative Medicine, *Hospice Medical Director Certification.* www.aahpm.org/certification/default/hmdcert.html. Accessed March 23, 2013.

24. Gina Shaw, "New Opportunities for Palliative Care in Medical Education," *AAMC Reporter,* July 2012. www.aamc.org/newsroom/reporter/july2012/297224/palliative-care.html. Accessed March 22, 2013.

25. American Academy of Hospice and Palliative Medicine, *Palliative Care & Hospice Education and Training Act.* www.aahpm.org/uploads/pcheta_summary2012.pdf. Accessed March 22, 2013.

26. Center to Advance Palliative Care, "Recommendations for Action."

27. National Institutes of Health Report, *NIH Grants Funded by the American Recovery and Reinvestment Act of 2009.* www.report.nih.gov/recovery/arragrants.cfm. Accessed March 22, 2013.

28. Center to Advance Palliative Care, *Palliative Care Leadership CentersTM.* www.capc.org/palliative-care-leadership-initiative/overview. Accessed March 24, 2013.

29. New York State Department of Health, *Palliative Care Access Act (PHL Section 2997-d): Palliative Care Requirements for Hospitals, Nursing Homes, Home Care and Assisted Living Residences (Enhanced and Special Needs).* www.health.ny.gov/professionals/patients/patient_rights/palliative_care/phl_2997_d_memo.htm. Accessed March 24, 2013.

30. National Consensus Project for Quality Palliative Care, *Clinical Practice Guidelines for Quality Palliative Care*, 3rd edition, 2013. www.nationalconsensusproject.org/ Guidelines_Download2.aspx. Accessed March 24, 2013.

31. The Joint Commission, *Advanced Certification for Palliative Care Programs.* www.jointcommission.org/certification/palliative_care.aspx. Accessed March 22, 2013.

32. **LIVESTRONG**™, "Advancing Joint Commission Palliative Care Certification in Cancer Centers." www.livestrong.org/What-We-Do/Our-Actions/Programs-Partnerships/Community-Engagement/Programs/Advancing-Palliative-Care. Accessed March 24, 2013.

33. U.S. Government Printing Office, "Part 418-Hospice Care." *Electronic Code of Federal Regulations.* www.ecfr.gov/cgi-bin/text-idx?c=ecfr&sid=818258235647b14d 2961ad30fa3e68e6&rgn=div5&view=text&node=42:3.0.1.1.5&idno=42. Accessed March 25, 2013.

34. National Hospice and Palliative Care Organization, *NHPCO Standards of Care for Hospice Programs.* www.nhpco.org/standards. Accessed March 24, 2013.

35. Arif H. Kamal et al., "Community-Based Palliative Care: The Natural Evolution for Palliative Care Delivery in the U.S," *Journal of Pain and Symptom Management* (November 15, 2012) (Epub ahead of print).

36. Center to Advance Palliative Care, "Recommendations for Action."

37. Center for Medicare & Medicaid Services, *MLN MattersR,* Number MM7857. July 20, 2012. www.cms.gov/Outreach-and-Education/Medicare-Learning-Network-MLN/MLNMattersArticles/Downloads/MM7857.pdf. Accessed March 24, 2013.

38. Medicare Payment Advisory Commission, "Chapter 12: Hospice Services," *Report to the Congress: Medicare Payment Policy* (March 2013): 265–7. www.medpac.gov/ chapters/Mar13_Ch12.pdf. Accessed March 25, 2013.

39. *National Journal* and The Regence Foundation, *Living Well at the End of Life: A National Conversation* (Public Data). http://syndication.nationaljournal.com/ communications/NationalJournalRegenceToplines.pdf. Accessed July 31, 2013.

40. *National Journal* and The Regence Foundation, *Living Well at the End of Life: A National Conversation* (Physicians' Data). ttp://www.cambiahealthfoundation.org/ media/release/11152011njeol.html. Accessed July 31, 2013.

41. Center to Advance Palliative Care, *2011 Public Opinion Research on Palliative Care.*

42. Joan M. Teno et al., "Change in End-of-Life Care for Medicare Beneficiaries," *Journal of the American Medical Association* 309, 5 (2013): 470–7.

43. Melissa Healy, "Quiet Deaths Don't Come Easy," *Los Angeles Times,* February 05, 2013.

44. Justin Bank, "Palin vs. Obama: Death Panels," *The Factcheck Wire.* August 14, 2009. www.factcheck.org/2009/08/palin-vs-obama-death-panels/. Accessed March 22, 2013.

45. Timothy E. Quill, "Personal Reflections n the Meaning of Our Brand," *AAHPM Quarterly* 13, 2 (Summer 2012): 4–5.

46. McPhee, S. J. et al., "Finding Our Way-Perspectives on the Close of life," *Journal of the American Medical Association* 284, 19 (2000): 2512–13.

47. Hubert H. Humphrey, Remarks at the dedication of the Hubert H. Humphrey Building, November 1, 1977, Congressional Record, November 4, 1977, vol. 123, p. 37287.

Chapter 9

The Health Advocate in End-of-Life Care

Linda Koebner

When a person faces a life-threatening illness there is no standard of care. Each individual must choose from a variety of medical and personal options to determine how he or she wishes to spend the last part of life. In today's health-care system the range of therapeutic treatments is vast and the path to the best choices is often burdensome, especially at a time of confusion and fear.

Health advocates are a growing part of the medical team and are also referred to by titles such as patient advocate, patient representative, or patient naviga-tor, usually dependent on their place of employment. Health advocates serve cli-ents in hospitals and corporations, and sometimes maintain their own private practices. Their expertise guides policy, legislation, and grassroots strategies to develop safer medical models and affect the quality of health care in their com-munity and globally. A recently recognized and growing field, health advocacy is playing a significant role in ensuring access to palliative care and hospice, thereby broadening the conversation about end-of-life care in the United States.

No matter how they are labeled or what population they serve, the health ad-vocates' primary mission is to secure patient-centered care: assisting patients in defining and preserving their wishes as they steer through the complexities of the health-care system. Perhaps at no time is this more important than when a per-son progresses to the end of life. This chapter explores the growing field of health advocacy and the work of professional health advocates, especially the role they play in assuring that every individual may die with dignity and grace.

INTRODUCTION

As a person nears the end of life, through illness or the frailty of old age, there are many decisions to be made and resources to gather. To help the patient facilitate the kind of care he or she wishes to receive, by whom and where, the addition of a health advocate to the medical team provides important expertise. End-of-life care may include aggressive medical treatment, palliative care, or the support of hospice, all of which can be very confusing and upsetting. The encouragement and guidance a health advocate provides is always beneficial to a patient but especially critical when confronting life-limiting or life-threatening illness. It is a time when critical decisions about treatment and support services must be made for the patient and family, often in haste at a very stressful time. The health advocate serves many important functions, primarily supporting the patient's voice so it is heard in an often confusing labyrinth of medical care.

There are many different labels and roles given to professionals who advocate for patients as they do their work in a variety of settings. Ultimately, their primary responsibility is to support the patient and assure he or she receives the best possible care, in line with his or her wishes. They educate and open the lines of communication between providers, and between providers and clients. Health advocates are mediators in the complex American health-care system.

In addition to direct patient service, a health advocate may pursue policy work in a nonprofit organization, corporation, or government entity. There is a role for the health advocate in the local community as well as nationally and globally doing policy work on health-related issues. This chapter focuses on the direct service role of health advocates, specifically in end-of-life care.

The benefit of having a health advocate as part of the health-care team is increasingly recognized and has given rise to an expanding number of educational programs around the country—from weekend certificates to Master's level programs. Although steps are taken to develop national standards, as of 2013 there are no professional requirements for health advocates. However, it is clear that the well-trained health advocate will acquire increasing responsibility in an evolving health-care system, and most importantly, play a pivotal role in support of the person navigating the final journey toward death.

BACKGROUND

An 86-year-old man loved his life. He was active, felt blessed to have a sharp mind, caring family, and to sleep in his home of 50 years. The wrenching diagnosis of pancreatic cancer, with metastasis in bone and brain, left him—and his loved ones—whirling. What to do, what doctor to listen to, even what to have for lunch became impossible. One omission in his treatment plan sent him from the comfort of palliative care during his remaining days to a painful, restless death—one that was also considerably more stressful for his family.

His oncologist was the best, the medical facility one of the world's finest, and his family was available but overworked and overcome with grief. The inclusion of a health advocate at the time of diagnosis might have provided the focus, knowledge, and know-how to advise the patient and family about other options for his care and further support for medical, spiritual, and psychosocial care for him and his family—easing him gracefully to the end of his rich life.[1]

Not so many decades ago, death came swiftly or the extended family was available to care for the chronically ill or aging loved one. Advances in medical technology and a weakened family structure have changed how we die. As baby-boomers age and medical choices are more complicated, there will be an ever-increasing role for professionals trained to support the needs of patients at the end of life. The academically and practically trained professional health advocate is both a resource and a support to the dying. Increasingly, as we move further into the 21st century, health advocates will be called on to take on a number of roles within America's complex health-care system to improve patient-centered care and access to care choices at the end of life. The Institute of Medicine defines patient-centered care as "Health care that establishes a partnership among practitioners, patients, and their families to ensure that decisions respect patients' wants, needs, and preferences and that patients have the education and support they need to make decision and participate in their own care."[2]

HISTORY

Professional health advocates were not necessary in America's early history. The family cared for the ill at home and buried the dead. With the industrial revolution, the urban population turned increasingly to hospitals for its medical care. For several decades in the late 19th and early 20th century, hospitals were more noteworthy as places to die than to be cured—the wealthy stayed at home or, to prevent contagion, left congested cities.[3] By the 1950s, medical advances were burgeoning and the hospital, with patients under the care of all-knowing, even deified, physicians, was the place for the ill. People were living longer and their hospital stays lengthening. The patient could be lost in the increasingly depersonalized, institutional care setting and often became a "subject" rather than an individual. In the 1970s, the patient rights movement grew out of this impersonal situation and many patient's rights documents were formed in hospitals and state governments. A Patient's Bill of Rights accompanies the Affordable Care Act of 2010, outlining what entitlements an individual has when passing into the world of the ill.[4] Assuring the patient is knowledgeable about those rights and receives them is a primary function of the health advocate.

The high cost of medical care, the complexities of treatments, and a confusing health-care system has focused the need for a professional who can synthesize and interpret for the patient. Health advocates have emerged as professional members of the medical community. Their vocation and training direct them to become a growing force in efforts to enhance communication in the medical setting as well as lead efforts to advocate for systems and policies to secure good health in communities.

THE WORK OF HEALTH ADVOCATES

Health advocates support patients as they find their way in today's complex medical system; both within and outside the walls of the hospital. Within a hospital or other kind of medical institution, the health advocates represent the patient and facilitate the communication process in an often complex and confusing conversation with providers. Outside of a medical facility, they work as independent practitioners alone or in groups. At the same time, national and community organizations employ health advocates to advance research on a particular disease or medical condition such as muscular dystrophy, breast cancer, or autism. Such organizations are usually nonprofit and may offer individualized advocacy services gratis or on a sliding fee scale.

Health advocates are also employed in the corporate sector, including pharmaceutical and insurance companies. Health advocates who are employed by these for-profit entities often walk a fine line and may encounter conflicts between the patient's and the company's interests. On a smaller scale, an example of a for-profit business model is a so-called concierge service. Employees of these companies help patients, who can pay premium prices, obtain very personalized service. These for-profit companies may arrange appointments with top specialists and lead clients to the head of the appointment line, remind them of the appointment, and even sit with them during the doctor's appointment to take notes and ask salient questions. Concierge health advocates may also assure the client's medications are ordered, delivered, and taken on schedule.

The health advocate offers a holistic and multifaceted approach toward serious illness and end-of-life care across many levels. On a case level the advocate not only helps the patient and family coordinate care across various settings but also connects them with resources from multiple agencies, institutions, and other care providers. On an institutional level, advocates serve not only as fierce defenders of patient autonomy and self-determination but also represent the voice of the patient to the institution. By speaking up, they demand better care for their patient and raise the standard of care not only for their charges but for all patients in the institution.

On a community level, advocates guide people to appropriate end-of-life care through their work in education and social change. Julie Buyon, MA, a health advocate specializing in end-of-life care states that "Advocates are effective change agents at the system level, using legislation and grassroots strategies to ensure access to palliative care and hospice. Across all levels advocates are altering the landscape of end of life in America, reclaiming the dying process from an often impersonal medical establishment, and restoring agency to those at the end of life so they may die with dignity."[5]

In an increasingly complex medical system health advocates ease the way and help make sense of what often appears as a "senseless" system—one that is going through many complex changes as the Affordable Care Act is implemented. As American hospitals come to depend increasingly on patient satisfaction in order to receive reimbursement for services, it is key to have happy customers who are comfortable with the care and treatment they receive. Hospitals in the United States have a lot at stake. Almost $1 billion of the federal money allotted to hospitals will be based, in large part, on surveys measuring how pleased patients are with the outcome of their stay, part of the pay-for-performance mandate of the Affordable Care Act.

High patient satisfaction will lead to bonuses; poor performance will lead to reduced payments to the institution. It is in the hospital's best interest to put in place systems to reduce infection rates and readmissions as well as health advocates to make sure the patient and family feel well cared for on all levels. To be well cared for in an overtaxed medical system is far easier with a health advocate at one's side. In a situation with a very ill patient or distraught family, a health advocate is able to speak on behalf of a patient to the medical staff and administration, often assuring the patient receives the necessary attention. By hearing and understanding what the patient wants and assuring needs are met, the health advocate offers support that translates into greater satisfaction ratings from patients.[6] Being well cared for, from the patient's perspective, may mean not only receiving excellent medical service but also the comfort of compassionate care from the nursing staff, good food, and being in a clean environment.

"Aren't social workers meant to help patients navigate medical care?" one might ask. "Why do we need health advocates?" Increasingly, social workers in institutions are overwhelmed with paperwork and discharge plans and must often battle with insurance companies. It has become increasingly difficult for professional social workers to provide the psychosocial support for which they are well trained. Time is limited to sit with a patient, or family, and listen to concerns or help with the difficulties of managing an illness. Sporadic family meetings with hospital personnel may be the only time this is possible. Generally, social workers are employed by an institution or agency and have many patients and demands, and therefore they are not able to fully focus on wishes and needs of the one patient. On the other hand, the sole function of health advocates is to assist and support patients.

And, what about the nurse? Chaplain? Physician? Aren't they the ones to help tackle complex issues for the patient? Yes, they are there for the patient yet their responsibilities are not focused solely on one patient; they all have many other responsibilities in the treatment plan. Few of them can center their attention on the complex needs of one patient. The health advocate can.

And, how about the ethicists? Their role is generally to help sort out issues and conflicts in medical care. Most hospitals are now required to have an ethics committee, and some states require other institutions such as nursing homes and hospices, to retain one as well. Ethics committees involve groups of individuals from diverse backgrounds (physicians, chaplains, social workers, and community representatives) who assist patients in the promotion of their rights within the institution and assist them or their surrogates in making difficult and often complex medical decisions about end of life within an ethical and legal framework. A health advocate can be an important addition to this complex effort, especially at the end of life.[7]

WHAT IS IN A NAME?

In the emerging profession of health advocacy, practitioners vary considerably in their experience, knowledge, training, and credentials. The terms health advocate, patient advocate, patient representative, and patient navigator are often used interchangeably. All of these terms define the work of a professional advocating for the patient or patient group. Yet, to the consumer, and even the medical profession, the terms are often confusing and unclear. No matter what the name, their roles are similar, and shaped primarily by their place of employment. Here I will describe the most commonly used titles—health advocate, patient representative, and patient navigator—and explain the duties and tasks most commonly associated with each, and how they are usually differentiated.

The health advocate may be employed by an institution or, as mentioned earlier, may choose to work as an independent contractor. The health advocate may work one on one with a patient or represent a patient group. Most commonly, he or she works directly with individual patients and families, assisting in the exploration of resources across the many systems and institutions that meet the patient's unique and individualized needs, helping the patient gain access to appropriate resources.

Most importantly, health advocates are the communicators and mediators between all the branches of the health-care industry and other stakeholders to assure patient-centered care. Marsha Hurst, PhD, former director of the Health Advocacy Master's Program at Sarah Lawrence College, explains, "The advocacy model puts the patient/client in the pilot's seat and uses the advocate as an educator, a resource, a voice of the patient when the patient cannot give voice herself."[8] The patient is often in a weak state, in a frightening and alien environment. The role of the health advocate is crucial for the patient to feel heard and respected, especially if there is no family or friend at the bedside to advocate for him or her. The advocate's job is to formulate the best treatment plan for the patient and make certain the patient's wishes are clearly heard by the medical team and family. Sometimes, at the end of life, it is to hold a hand, quietly.

The health advocate is the person who will be there when there is no family or friend. She may also be there for the patient's support system. The advocate serves as an interpreter for the language of medicine and provides a voice of comfort and calm for the patient. The role of the advocate in a medical setting can be essential when a family is trying to determine the pros and cons of surgery or a particular course of treatment.

While health advocates are most commonly found working with patients directly, they may also support or represent a patient group, thereby serving a broader landscape of policy and education. They may, for example, advocate for populations with certain medical conditions through organizations such as the Alzheimer's Association, The American Cancer Society, or work for not-for-profit organizations that support the advancement of hospice or palliative care. The health advocate may also design medical research protocols, assure patient rights are upheld in clinical trials, struggle with ethical decisions in medicine in a think tank, implement medical narrative programs in educational institutions, or advise on the construction of websites and other tools that can facilitate patients' access to medical and nonmedical resources.

The patient representative—the common term in hospitals—serves much the same function as a health advocate who has direct patient contact. In nursing homes the preferred term for the person in this role is sometimes customer service representative or client representative. These titles also reference a patient advocate who is based in, and paid by, an institution to increase the patients' access to specific resources within the parameters of the institution's mandate. The agenda of the institution is not necessarily in conflict with that of the individual patient, but it is not always aligned either. The responsibilities of a patient representative are variable and dependent on the culture of the organization where they are employed. The hospital patient representative is often—but not exclusively—requested to carry out singular tasks that help the patient in specific ways. She may take a report about a patient's missing cell phone, accept a complaint about the pancakes that came cold to the bedside, or help a family understand the medical jargon coming from

10 different health professionals trying to save their dying child—not trivial issues for a sick person or parent who is overwhelmed. A professional health advocate can help the patient in the same way but additionally provide an ongoing personalized holistic support system.

The concept of a patient navigator was first introduced by oncologist Harold Freeman to help remove obstacles his low-income patients might encounter, preventing them from receiving treatment for breast cancer.[9] Women from the community were trained to help newly diagnosed women "navigate" the path a physician had laid out for their care and assist with nonmedical issues that might interfere with their care, such as lack of transportation, child care, or the means to make and follow up on appointments. There is a reference to the role of patient navigator in the Affordable Care Act but as yet it has not been fully defined or made operational.

With all these nuances on a common theme, one can understand why the terms "patient advocate" and "health advocate," "patient representative," "patient navigator," and "customer service representative" are often confused and not necessarily informative. In the public's mind, and even within the professions, the distinctions are often as unclear as the credentials they can be expected to possess.

PROFESSIONAL TRAINING

The name may not be so important. Of greater concern is that health-care consumers have limited reliable means to find a health advocate with appropriate professional training. As of 2013, there is no standardized curriculum, no outline of what must be taught, what experience in the medical field an advocate must have to be credentialed, and, perhaps most importantly, how to gauge how much supervised experience they have caring for patients.

We can expect in the near future that the training, credentials, and experience of health advocates will become consistent and well understood by the public. Health advocates will gain recognition for their professional expertise and will be considered essential to any medical team or organization. Health advocate will most likely be the prevailing title of these highly trained, experienced, and compassionate individuals. However, just as the roles and titles of people working to assist patients navigate the health-care field varies in the second decade of the 21st century, so too do their training and education.

As of this writing, there are several professional organizations for patient advocates: The Alliance of Professional Health Advocates (APHA), National Association of Health Advocacy Consultants (NAHAC), and Professional Patient Advocate Institute (PPAI). NAHAC has developed ethical standards for the profession. Yet, to date none of the organizations have created a national professional credentialing system or association for health advocates.

Health advocacy may be a new field, yet there is an exploding need for its services as patients flounder in the complexities of care. The demand has given birth to a deluge of programs and certificates touted as comprehensive training for health advocates or patient advocates. Without standards of training, a comprehensive curriculum, or even a consistent definition of what a health advocate is, health-care consumers are vulnerable to inadequate and potentially incompetent guidance.

The current educational landscape for training health advocates range from short-term certificate programs to concentrations within undergraduate departments and full-fledged graduate programs. Unfortunately, many of the certificate programs do not even require applicants to hold a bachelor or nursing degree, so the advocacy education may be built upon a shaky scaffold with little substance or practical application. Some programs cloak themselves in the language of advocacy, yet in reality are little more than training programs for medical billing or patient admissions.

There are programs sponsored by accredited institutions, but the curriculum and practicums are not consistent across the field. Buyon makes note of the following four programs:[10]

- The Health Advocacy Program at Sarah Lawrence College offers the only Master's degree in health advocacy.
- The Center for Patient Partnerships of the University of Wisconsin offers a graduate level education model targeted to professionals, graduate, and returning adult students, and draws upon interdisciplinary faculty from the University's graduate schools.
- Stanford School of Medicine has a patient advocacy program for undergraduate students focusing on community health for underserved populations.
- The University of North Carolina at Chapel Hill School of Public Health offers an advocacy course.

Linda Adler of Pathfinders Medical Advocacy points out:

An advocate may have received a certificate, but this is not a substitute for training and experience. A certificate means that they took a course, not that they have any supervised training or passed a professional exam from a professional organization that requires certain standards to be met. Currently, there is no national organization that either licenses or credentials health care advocates. Certificates are great additions to existing healt hcare knowledge and experience, but are not a substitute for them. . . . A qualified advocate will not only hold a degree, but will typically have spent several years working within the medical community and will have a solid understanding of how it works, including the resources that are available, the personnel involved, and the challenges that may be encountered.[11]

The Master of Arts in Health Advocacy founded in 1980 at Sarah Lawrence College is the only full graduate—Master's level—program in the discipline. The program was the first of its kind when it was established and it remains, in 2013, the only comprehensive, professional two-year program in the country. The Health Advocacy Program prepares graduates for leadership roles in shaping the future of this field. By integrating analytical discussions of issues that face the nation's health-care systems with hands-on experiential fieldwork assignments, students are prepared to influence health policy at the systems level as well as to serve individuals with health-care advising and advocacy. Director of the Sarah Lawrence College Health Advocacy Master's Program, Vicki Breitbart, MSW, Ed D., feels that the program's strong curriculum covering social, political, intellectual, legal, and medical care issues, and underscored by over 600 hours of practical experience launch model health advocates into the community, and have done so for decades. "The breadth and opportunities in a multidisciplinary approach prepares students to advocate for change within a complex and evolving health care system."[12]

HEALTH ADVOCATES IN END-OF-LIFE CARE

The diagnosis was grim. Ray had fourth stage lung cancer. The cough he had tried to ignore for so long had taken on a life of its own and the malignant cells had quietly planted themselves throughout his body. After learning the news from his primary care physician, he had been sent to an oncologist. He didn't like this doctor, but what could he do? It had already taken weeks and the pulling of strings to see this man with the impeccable credentials.

With the help of a health advocate, he went to a consultation with a different oncologist in the same institution—one he felt much more comfortable with and who would work with the first physician to develop a plan of action. During the coming two years, he and his health advocate were in constant communication. She remained a constant presence in his life, someone who came to know him, not just his disease. She helped find a nutritionist when he needed one. When he had little strength to argue with insurance companies, she was his voice. When he did not like his care provider, but his family insisted she stay, mostly because they could not go through the effort to find another, the health advocate made new arrangements.

When he had to weigh the advantages versus the pain of more treatment, she listened. She arranged for him to receive hospice care. He spent his final months at home with his wife, his dog, and the music he loved. He had no pain or anxiety. He knew he had an ally by his side; someone who had understood his wishes and would stay connected with his family after he was gone. He was able to die on his terms, in peace, comfort, and with dignity.[13]

The health advocate is playing an ever-increasing role in end-of-life care. Progressively, the country is allowing the reality of death to enter the conversation, in part because the aging baby-boom generation is coming face to face with the inevitable, and in part because of soaring health-care costs. Breitbart, says, both from her professional point of reference and personal experience, "Patient advocates can play an important role with individuals and with changing a system that will give choices back to the elderly individuals in need of care."[14] These choices are life and death decisions and must be made with knowledge, care, and coordination. The health advocate is in the perfect place to facilitate conversation about end-of-life care, coordinate various care options, and support a person's wishes.

Since discussion in the United States about the end of life has been limited or nonexistent in recent decades, most people are unaware or uncomfortable talking about options when they themselves are dying or they are in the presence of a loved one near death. The general population is unfamiliar with the meaning of palliative and has misinformation about hospice.[15] Uninformed at the time of a life-limiting diagnosis, patients often have little choice but to go headlong into death with aggressive treatment, no matter how costly or painful for the patients and their families. This is where the health advocate can be especially helpful.

There is a growing need for advocates in all areas of health care, but there may be no greater role than standing with an individual who is approaching death and must make treatment choices or choose to forgo further intervention and allow death to come. Even when comfort care is chosen, there may be much to consider and many services to find and coordinate. The patient may have wishes that are not in line with his family's—wishes he is unable or unwilling to express; or he may have needs or desires that require more attention than he is able to give for any number of reasons. Almost always the road to the end of life is complicated to navigate.

For the person facing life-limiting or life-threatening illness, having an advocate to help understand the barrage of modern medical intervention and choices of care can be indispensable. Sorting out the patient's wishes, discerning the family's needs, knowing what the options are, and assuring the patient he is not alone during this challenge is what the professional health advocate is trained to do. More importantly, it often takes an advocate to educate all stakeholders—patient, family, and health-care personnel—on the availability and appropriateness of certain models of care, including palliative, complementary, and hospice, all or none of which are not consistently offered to the seriously ill.

The health advocate is available to research appropriate medical services and help explain the medical options to the dying person. Connecting services and professionals, the health advocate is prepared to work with physicians as well as the patient to determine what treatment choices are best. As a trained listener, communicator, and facilitator, the health advocate has a critical role in this arena of health care.

When a newly diagnosed patient has a health advocate by the bedside, it is possible to explore more options when locating the right physician for aggressive treatment, finding a clinical trial, or choosing comfort care. Training and experience allow the health advocate, right from the time of diagnosis, to make sure the patient has the best services available and that the family does, too. Loved ones also suffer through the serious illness of a patient and require support. The medical provider is the first person to discuss options with the patient, but the health advocate is an excellent surrogate for ongoing discussion and support when the medical team has limited time.

If a palliative care team is not available or in place for the patient, the health advocate can take on that role, replicating many of the roles in a palliative care team, for example, arranging family meetings, setting goals of care, coordinating with the medical team, and finding complementary services for the patient.

If a palliative care team is in place through the hospital, it usually consists of experts in many fields, including palliative care doctors, nurses and social workers, chaplains, massage therapists, pharmacists, nutritionists, and other complementary care providers, whose sole role is to work with the patient and family to improve the quality of life as they manage the illness through curative treatment or comfort care. The health advocate is also an important part of the palliative care team in a hospital and plays an immensely important role if the institution has no formal palliative care program inside its walls. Then the health advocate is an excellent person to help locate the best complementary care for the patient and family, and to facilitate the monumental transition back to health or on to death. Additionally, the advocate may help guide the patient by addressing any legal or ethical concerns around the illness, recovery, or death, including offering information about advance care planning and long-term care planning.[16]

The health advocate is a well-trained, compassionate supporter. Nothing can replace a caring family at the bedside of a critically ill person. Yet, dying sometimes also "takes a village." Since the American Board of Medical Specialties approved Hospice and Palliative Care as a subspecialty in 2006, palliative care has found a place alongside other specialties and pharmaceutical care in the treatment of serious illness. This newly recognized specialty provides complementary therapies to address the psychological, social, and spiritual distress of the patient and family, supporting them through the course of their treatment, whether the outcome is a cure or death and bereavement. Health advocates may be part of those complementary therapies and are well placed to support caregivers, the bereaved, and friends as they make the journey with the patient.

> The child lay swaddled in a crib which was far too big for the tiny body. Machines and lights surrounded the crib. They were too harsh for anyone, let alone a six-week-old recovering from surgery to correct an imperfect heart. Nurses, pediatricians, surgeons, intensivists, respiratory therapists, chaplains, interns, and cleaning staff moved in and out of the intensive care room all day and night. To be sure who this little body was and what ailed her, they often had to check her chart. Shifts changed, residents passed through, weekends came and went.
>
> Every day the mother came to stand by her child's bed and take the tiny hand in hers. Every day the health advocate came to see the mother to stand with her to listen or to be with her in the silence. With the mother, too exhausted and distraught to do more than be with her baby, the health advocate acted for her to get answers from doctors and arrange for a child life specialist to be with the siblings when they came to visit their baby sister. She organized paperwork, arranged for a parking pass when the father could visit. She was a constant in the short life of the baby and her family, and when the end came, the health advocate and the chaplain helped make final arrangements.[17]

When we think of death, it is generally with the old in mind but children die too. Palliative care and the support of health advocates are important resources for the life-limited or life-threatened child. Today, it is possible to live with excruciating physical or emotional suffering in order to extend life. Respirators and feeding tubes are part of the tool kit to prolong life. The decision to allow nature to take its course, even while assuring a pain free, comfortable death through other medical means can be difficult enough when someone is at the end of a long life. For a young person to struggle with this choice is heart wrenching and impossibly hard. Imagine just turning 18 and in a position perhaps to go against parental wishes. For the parents of a beloved child, teen or infant, it is almost too much to ask. But it is often and repeatedly asked. When the family hopes for a miracle, religious convictions impact decisions, or the impossible choice to surrender to death must be accepted, it is especially important to have someone with an impartial, educated ear to listen.

Once it was expected that the doctor knew best, and the decision was his, or nature took its course. Today, with advanced technology, the doctor has access to many treatments to prolong life, sometimes even for decades, making it even harder for parents and sometimes a young adult to make life and death decisions.

The guidance of the health advocate in these situations can be of enormous value, as has been demonstrated in the growing number of palliative care programs in children's hospitals. Outside of these hospitals, there is minimal information about the services they are able to provide. Existing programs have many components and providers available for the patients, parents, and siblings. This is a positive development from the days less than 50 years ago when parents were not allowed to visit their sick children in the hospital.[18]

Health advocates maintain focus on the autonomy and the rights of patients, a service that encourages the medical team to concentrate on aligning the direct services of the hospital with the goals of patient. Although the doctors and other institutional staff are dedicated to the mission of healing the patient, demands on their time, as well as hospital-related imperatives, may divert them from focusing entirely on the goals and rights of their patients. A health advocate will broaden the patient's horizon by adding a nonmedical and noninstitutional perspective to the decision-making process. Through their reach into the community and contact with other advocates, they can find additional services and options, provided in or outside of the hospital.

Many hospitals offer formal ethics consultation services, which not only provide legal and ethical guidance but also assist in mediating conflicts between stakeholders—within the family unit, between members of the care team, and between the care team and the patient or the surrogate decision maker when the patient cannot speak for himself or herself. Such mediation is similar to what many palliative care teams and patient advocates do: facilitate communication among a fragmented care team, provide a framework for understanding and evaluating a complex diagnosis, overcome inhibitions and disinclination to talk about death, and align hopes with medical reality.[19] Ideally, the health advocate, with the patient's perspective in mind, is part of the hospital's ethics committee.

Even when palliative care is available in a hospital, physicians do not always make referrals to the palliative care team. The doctors may not really understand what the team does, they may not wish other care providers involved in their patient's care, reimbursements may not be supportive in the hospital, or they may confuse palliative care with hospice care.

THE HEALTH ADVOCATE AS EDUCATOR
AND POLICYMAKER ON END-OF-LIFE CARE

Physicians state that poor communication is the primary reason more patients are not referred to palliative care.[20] If doctors and physician assistants do not have the time to become knowledgeable about palliative care options in their community and/or do not communicate the option to their patients, the health advocate is in a good position to facilitate the conversation alongside the medical practitioner. When the patient has questions after the initial conversation with his physician, the health advocate is available for subsequent discussion and to provide follow-up and ongoing information.

To supplement or even to replace conversations, information can be transmitted through printed materials, video, websites, and seminars, but such resources are sparse. Health advocates are in an excellent position to develop these tools to support physician's conversations with patients and to educate the public in an ongoing fashion.

Numerous coalitions and organizations provide resources and education about end of life, a service they provide because these matters continue to be so inadequately addressed in the health-care setting until death is imminent. They often rely on health advocates to formulate the material they disseminate. In policy work, the health advocate can assist in making it the "norm" for medical providers to easily and routinely provide their critically ill patients with information about all available treatment options, including comfort care, which may potentially create a huge savings for the country in health-care costs, and the toll of human suffering. It is in this context, the Palliative Care Information Act was passed in New York State (2011).[21] It followed a similar 2008 ruling in California. The effort to draft and pass the law was led primarily by health advocates affiliated with Compassion & Choices and other organizations advocating for better discussion of end-of-life issues at a national, state, and local level. Working through the courts such laws are expanding the individual's choice at the end of life and opening a better dialogue between care providers and patients as well as fostering a more open discourse in the larger community. This law mandates that health-care providers inform their gravely ill patients about all their end-of-life options, including palliative care. These laws encourage conversation and the health advocate will likely have a growing role as supporter and educator; providing information, follow-up, and guidance to implement a plan with the patient, if the patient desires.

THE FUTURE OF HEALTH ADVOCACY

The training and experience of professional health advocates position them to expand their role as leaders, communicators, and gentle listeners in the quest to make end-of-life care something our society can address openly and truthfully, and dying something we can accept with grace and dignity.

In the coming decades we foresee professionally trained health advocates as standard bearers for a paradigm shift toward patient-centered, holistic care at the end of life. Knowledgeable both in the technology and methodology of medicine, as well as the humanistic needs of the dying, the health advocate is positioned to be a guide and support.

The profession will provide space for an open discussion about all care alternatives when death approaches—from highly mechanized interventions in institutionalized environments to palliative and hospice care in viable and safe home, or homelike, settings. The health advocate is a partner for the entire voyage. Through her work she will help each person clarify his or her goals while assisting medical care providers endorse a humane and dignified passage to the end of life for their patient—a death that respects each individual's wish for a unique journey.

* * *

Special thanks to Julie Buyon, MA, for her guidance and generosity and Vicki Breitbart, MSW, EdD, for her leadership and encouragement.

NOTES

1. Julie Buyon, Fictionalized account of an actual case, communicated in personal communication, September 15, 2012.

2. Institute of Medicine of the National Academies. www.iom.edu. Accessed January 18, 2012.

3. Paul Starr,*The Social Transformation of American Medicine* (New York: Basic Books, 1982), 75.

4. Department of Health and Human Services, Health Care.Gov. http://www .healthcare.gov/law/features/rights/bill-of-rights/index.html. Accessed November 10, 2012.

5. Julie Buyon, Personal communication, January 6, 2013.

6. Janet Adamy, "US Ties Hospital Payments to Making Patients Happy," *The Wall Street Journal,* October 14, 2012. http://online.wsj.com/article/SB10000872396390443 8903045780102641560731 32.html.

7. Robert A. Perlman, "Ethics in Medicine," Department of Bioethics and Medicine, Seattle, University of Washington, Medical School, 2010. http://depts.washington .edu/bioethx/topics/ethics.html.

8. Marsha Hurst, Jo Anne L. Earp, Elizabeth A. French, and Melissa B. Gilkey, "Patient Advocacy for Health Care Quality," in *Strategies for Achieving Patient-Centered Care,*ed. Jo Anne L. Earp, Elizabeth A. French, and Melissa B. Gilkey(Sudbury, MA: Jones and Bartlett Publishers, 2008), 484.

9. Marsha Hurst, Personal communication, October 29, 2012.

10. Buyon, Marsha, Personal communication, October 29, 2012.

11. Linda Adler, http://www.pathfindersmedical.com. Accessed October 27, 2012.

12. Vicki Breitbart, Personal communication, January 5, 2013.

13. Linda Koebner, Fictionalized account of an actual case, August 2012.

14. Vicki Breitbart, "My Mother Was Not Alone," *Health Advocacy Bulletin: The Journal of the Health Advocacy Program at Sarah Lawrence College* 19, 2. (Fall 2012): 1.

15. James Fausto, Palliative Care PowerPoint Presentation to St. Barnabas Hospital and Montefiore Medical Center, December 8, 2011.

16. Julie Buyon, Personal communication, October 22, 2012.

17. Linda Koebner, Fictionalized Account from the Pediatric Intensive Care Unit, The Children's Hospital of Montefiore Medical Center, May 2012.

18. Howard Markel, "When Hospitals Kept Children from Parents," *The New York Times,* Health Section, January 1, 2008. http://www.nytimes.com/2008/01/01/health/01visi.html

19. Nancy N. Dubler and Carol B. Liebman,*Bioethics Mediation: A Guide to Shaping Shared Solutions* (New York: United Hospital Fund, 2004), 5.

20. Ibid.

21. New York State Department of Health, *Information for a Healthy New York.* http://www.health.ny.gov/professionals/patients/patient_rights/palliative_care/information_act.htm

Chapter 10

Culturally Competent Care in an Increasingly Diverse Society

Karen Bullock and Jasmin Volkel

Culture influences patients' reactions to serious and life-threatening illnesses, decisions about treatment and who to involve in their care at end of life. In the United States, end-of-life care providers emphasize patients' autonomy, advance care planning, palliation versus life prolongation, and nuclear family involvement versus extended social support systems. In a diverse society, perspectives on palliation and advance care planning may be predisposed by a history of disparities and discrimination in health-care systems. Other factors may include the lack of acceptance, understanding, and attention that is afforded; individuals and families that do not represent the mainstream ideal; and Western-based medicine philosophy. Because generalizations about particular cultures are not always applicable to specific patients, understanding when and how to engage a culturally competent care plan and pattern can be challenging for practitioners. To identify areas of cultural diversity in care, offer guidelines for cultural competence and ways to apply these guidelines to a diverse patient population. This assists providers in achieving cultural competence and increasing the likelihood that all patients and families experience optimal care at end of life.

INTRODUCTION

As the population in the United States is becoming more culturally diverse, so too is the patient population for whom we care. Culture represents race, class, ethnicity, and a whole host of other factors that can facilitate or impede end-of-life care. If we are to provide optimal care for all patients, cultural factors that influence end-of-life care must be better understood.

Historically, one racial group has dominated mainstream culture in the United States and is considered to be the majority. This racial/ethnic group identifies as "white/non-Hispanic" or "Caucasian/non-Hispanic." All other race/ethnic groups tend to be grouped together as "minorities" in the academic research as well as public speech. However, in the past two centuries the people represented in these racial/ethnic minorities in the United States have increased in numbers across the country. In 2000, ethnic minorities comprised almost 25 percent of the population, whereas in 2010, ethnic minorities comprised almost 28 percent of the total population.[1] Federal projections predict that current identified minority groups will become the new majority by the year 2050.[2] The federal government expects African Americans, Asians, Alaskan Natives, Pacific Islanders, Native Americans, and the elderly to increase in population.[3] The largest increase will occur with the Latino population who will outnumber all other minority groups by 2050 with approximately, one-third of the population identifying as Latino.

The challenge for practitioners in an increasingly diverse society is to ensure that all patients and families receive optimal care. It behooves us as end-of-life care providers to consider factors that influence our ability to provide culturally competent care in an increasingly diverse society because lived experiences, customs, traditions, and values affect how individuals and families make decisions about care. Furthermore, attention must be given to under-represented and disenfranchised populations.

Minority and elderly persons report lower rates of excellent or good health and higher rates of fair or poor health than their white, non-Hispanic counterparts.[4] Research suggests that these health disparities carry over into end-of-life care treatments. Mistrust of the health-care systems, opposing cultural beliefs, strength of religiosity, and lack of understanding of health-care options account for most barriers to adequate treatment.[5] Therefore, it is important to understand the role of culture in caring relationships between patients and their medical providers.

The range of diversity within specific racial/ethnic groups as well as family structures and types pose tremendous challenges for providers who lack cultural competence. Particularly, compared to whites of European descent, racial/ethnic minorities exhibit greater variability in their preferences for and against end-of-life treatments.[6] Also, as U.S. families increasingly consist of unmarried couples, single parents, blended (previously divorced) households, extended social systems of family—in which none of the members are related by marriage or biological heritage—and same sex couples, it is imperative that we as care providers make a shift in our definition of family and what it means to be family-focused in our approaches to caring for patients. Self-determination is a key component of culturally competent care and thus, patients should be able to decide who is, and who is not, involved in their care.

The extent to which specific attitudes, including preferences for end-of-life care, beliefs about dying, spiritual practices, and mistrust of the health-care system, individually or collectively explain racial differences in the completion of advance directives and beliefs about hospice needs to be considered through a culturally competent lens.[7],[8] Research results have shown that minorities have greater preferences for life-sustaining therapies, less comfort discussing death, greater distrust of the health-care system, and spiritual beliefs that may conflict with the goals of hospice care.[9]

The surmounting diversity that is confronting our U.S. health-care systems gives rise to the need for greater attention on how best to care for patient in this society. Given that minority groups are predicted to double within some populations and triple in others, it is essential that providers recognize the impact that culture has on patients' behavior and decision-making patterns associated with care at end of life so that they can adjust their practices accordingly.[10] They must learn how to discuss cultural issues that affect end-of-life care, such as truth-telling, hope-preserving, autonomous decision-making, and collective decision-making. Most specially because people who make up the largest U.S. minority groups—Latinos, Asians, and African Americans—tend to have different beliefs systems, values, and preferences for engaging in these health-care system behaviors than people of the Caucasian American majority. Furthermore, minorities often rely on their nontangible resources such as spirituality, cultural beliefs, and intuition for guidance in decision making.[11] In the health-care system these practices can be viewed as barriers to care.

CULTURAL COMPETENCE

Cultural competence is necessary to break down barriers and ensure each patient receives optimal care while coping with the dying and loss process. It is impossible to know everything about every cultural group, but we can be culturally competent in recognizing factors that influence differences in preference for and decisions about end-of-life care. According to the National Association of Social Workers, cultural competence means understanding culture and its function in human behavior and society and recognizing the strengths that exist in distinct cultures.[12] A practitioner who delivers hospice and/or palliative care has an obligation to treat individuals and families according to their preferences, when possible. The problem for some patients is that they do not feel that enough is done on the part of the practitioner to identify and incorporate the value and norms of the patient's culture.[13]

Establishing standards of care that are derived from culture-based assessments and community involvement is a recommended evidence-based practice approach.[14] Assumptions about race, structural racism, power, and privilege differentials should be considered in the search for cultural competency strategies and care models. Using an assessment technique and/or tool that incorporates collective decision making and exploration of care options in the context of cultural norms, values, and beliefs will enable practitioners to:

1) gain knowledge about the family structure and function that can influence health behaviors as well as practices, values, and attitudes toward the health-care system;

2) assess communication style in the decision-making processes, acculturation, and degree of integration into the larger community; and

3) evaluate the capacity of the patient and members of the informal support network to navigate the health-care system and cope with the disease or illness in a culturally acceptable manner.

It is important for practitioners to learn what patients and families, whom they care for, prefer. Often times, people of minority groups do not prefer the treatment philosophies, approaches, and even care settings that are consistent with Western-based medicine's recommendations. This is evidenced by longitudinal data, which shows that consistently over the past decade, white/non-Hispanics are overrepresented among hospice and palliative care recipients, while black and Hispanic individuals are underrepresented as care recipients.[15] It is important to understand that these differences exist in our diverse society.

The American Academy of Family Physicians (AAFP) has developed a set of guiding principles and position statements about diversity.[16] In the framework of ethical principles they make clear that "Care at end of life should recognize, assess and address the psychological, social, spiritual/religious issues, and cultural taboos realizing that different cultures may require significantly different approaches." The, biomedical ethicist Matthew Crawley argues that to effectively understand and address the needs of underrepresented populations require the application of a framework that considers the context of equity and strategies for eliminating disparities. To do so, one must identify sources of bias and discrimination in the provision of care and increase the representation of a range of diverse populations groups in care systems.[17]

USE OF HOSPICE AND PALLIATIVE CARE

Hospice and palliative care are broad terms that describe the type and philosophy of care that is offered to people with life-threatening and terminal illnesses. The work of hospice professionals is critical in the care of the dying and typically includes palliative care, pain management, attention to psycho-social needs and techniques delivered in-home or in a home-like setting by doctors, nurses, social workers, and other trained professionals.[18] The com-plex, multidimensional nature of the care highlights the importance of cultural understanding and acceptance between the medical community and ethnic minorities.

Hospice and palliative care provides individuals and families with the best possible quality of life by promoting dignity, comfort, and freedom from pain in a multidisciplinary, team-based approach. It also offers emotional and spiri-tual support, while respecting cultures and traditions. Of particular concern is the fact that ethnic minorities and nontraditional family types, that is, those not connected by marriage or blood lineage, are underrepresented in these care settings when they are dying.[19]

Research that explores ethnic and racial differences in end-of-life care deci-sion making and treatment preferences document the need for further atten-tion to advance care planning and greater understanding of health behavior change.[20] Although racial and ethnic minority groups tend to have higher morbidity and mortality rates, they tend not to complete advance directives and often refuse hospice and palliative care.[21]

The benefits of advance directives as reported in the interdisciplinary health-care literature include autonomy in decision making regarding wishes and preferences for care, congruence between personal values and end-of-life choices increased likelihood that patient's wishes will be honored, less burden on family and health-care providers as wishes are known, and potential to pro-mote death with dignity.[22] Considering these potential benefits and the likeli-hood that they can assist a patient with having a good death, another challenge for end-of-life care providers is to figure out why racial/ethnic minorities tend not to take advantage of these benefits.

The recent data show that the overwhelming majority of hospice-care recip-ients are white (83%). Black (8%) and Latino (3%) Americans are less likely to utilize hospice and black Americans are least likely to want to die in the home due to fear of overburdening their families.[23] However, when exploring other types of diversity and cultural challenges, we find that there is less systematic review of factors that influence end-of-life care among Asian-Pacific Islanders and American-Indians/Alaskans, as well as a dearth of information on how nontraditional family systems such as those headed by cohabitating or same-sex partnerships experience death, dying, and end-of-life care.

WHAT IS CULTURE?

Patients' values may not always be consistent with those of traditional Western-based medicine, and culture can have significant impact on decision making at the end of life. An individual's beliefs, value systems, interpretations of care-giver discussions, and the expectations about what care may entail may vary greatly. Ruhnke et al. define culture as a "set of learned values, beliefs, customs, and behaviors that is shared by a group of interacting individuals".[24] Every cultural group defines concept and constructs of health for its members, and prescribes methods for maintaining health, dealing with illness and death.[25] If conflicts arise between the norms, beliefs, and value systems of the health-care provider and the patient, failure to deal with them properly may result in improper care or no care. In some cultures, family is the prevailing determinant in patient outcomes and not the individual or doctor as is common in Western medical practice.[26]

DIVERSITY

Diversity has been defined as physical or social attributes that are not easily subsumed in the larger culture.[27] These attributes may differ by socioeconomic status, gender, sexual orientation, age, and differential ability. Awareness of diversity and its role in influencing end-of-life practices among different ethnic minorities should be a priority for end-of-life care providers.

Increasingly, those of us who provide care in regions where there are people represented from countries around the globe, different family types and structures, understand that we must not make assumptions about the degree to which any of these attributes predict the patterns of decision making at end of life. It is imperative that we examine the role of diversity within groups and the relationship to good patient outcomes. Not all people of any group will always adhere to the preference of the dominant group.

RACE

Race is a difficult concept to pinpoint due to disagreements about its exact meaning among different populations and cultures. The definition is also dependent on the era. In 1997, the U.S. Census Bureau only accepted five categories of race: white, black or African American, American Indian or Alaskan Native, Asian, and Native Hawaiian or Other Pacific Islander.[28] In 2000, the bureau expanded upon the race concept by including a "some other race" category for those who did not identify with the five accepted designations. Although meaning of the word "race" differs by group, there is a general consensus that it has no biological significance, although it has tremendous significance in social and political arenas. In other words, race can be defined as a social construct in which individuals are grouped together based on physical attributes, but not based on biology, anthropology, or genetics. Race is often used interchangeably with ethnicity, both of which are variables for identifying culture.[29]

ETHNICITY

Race and ethnicity are used interchangeably, but they differ.[30] A person can identify his or her race as "black," but their ethnicity may be African American, Caribbean, Haitian, African, or even Latino depending on their geographical location and cultural identification. This concept of race/ethnicity is probably understood by most through the reference to people in the Anglo "white" race who are of Italian, Polish, Irish, German, or other European ancestry. The important point here is that there is shared culture that develops within racial groups, but may be distinctly different across ethnic groups. Johnson, Kuchibhatla, and Tulsky consider race to be a social classification in which each member is bound together by a shared set of beliefs, values, and cultural behaviors.[31]

FACTORS THAT INFLUENCE CULTURE

Many factors routinely influence a person's culture and guide their belief system. Race, ethnicity, gender, age, sexual orientation, religiosity and spirituality, socioeconomic status, indigenous heritage, and years of citizenship all interconnect to formulate culture. Lived experiences also influence culture. Therefore Italian, Irish, English, and other Anglo white persons may be extremely well-acculturated into the white/race culture and their distinct ethnic culture may be secondary or completely whitewashed to nonexistence. Furthermore, people who have historically experienced discrimination and oppression, for example, people of color, tend to develop coping strategies and mechanisms for survival that cultivate norms, behaviors, values, and preferences. Understanding why and how cultural differences emerge is helpful in working toward achieving cultural competence. The AAFP's cultural proficiency guidelines points practitioners to health diversity as an entry into achieving the goals of ethical care.

HEALTH DISPARITIES

One could argue that minorities in the United States have a legacy of discrimination that plagues them from birth to death. Research suggests that people of color, that is, black, Latino, Native Americans, and other ethnic minorities disproportionately report poor health outcomes.[32] Minorities tend to die younger than their Anglo white counterparts, tend to live in poverty longer, and are least likely to use hospice care.[33,34] Reports show that minorities, specifically African Americans, are least likely to utilize hospice and advance directives, but are more likely to request aggressive care at end of life than Anglo whites.[35,36]

LATINOS

Latinos, categorized as people of Cuban, Mexican, Puerto Rican, South or Central American, or other Spanish culture or origin regardless of race, generally prefer collective decision making and to have relatives receive information about the patient's diagnosis and prognosis.[37,38] However, it has been documented that Mexican-Americans who are acculturated are more likely to agree that patients should be directly informed of their medical conditions than those who lack acculturation.[39] Furthermore, research shows that, in general, Latinos prefer to seek hospitalization for end-of-life care instead of remaining at home or in nursing home.[40,41] Those who identify as highly religious prefer life-sustaining measures and are more likely to not have advanced directives than non-Hispanic white persons. Latina women are more likely to want life-sustaining procedures such as breathing machines, dialysis, and feeding tubes than Latino men.[42] Although there is diversity within Latino culture, a common language, attitudes, beliefs, and practices make up an identifiable Latino culture that influences end-of-life care.[43]

ASIAN AMERICANS

Studies of Asians and Asian Americans, which included Japanese, Korean, and Chinese American patients, have examined their perspectives on death, dying, and the grieving process. In general, most of the self-identified Asians in both the United States and parts of Asia disprove of life-sustaining measures, telling patient of terminal diagnosis, and advanced directives.[44] Among many Asian cultural groups, illness is considered a family affair and not an individual experience.[45] Therefore extended family members are likely to be involved in the care. However, the ultimate decision about end-of-life care is deferred to the physician because of the high regard, authority, and respect accorded to physicians in these cultural groups. The doctor has the final say and the authority to go against the patient's wishes. Patients look to the doctor for the answers about medical decisions as opposed to preferring autonomous decision making.[46]

AFRICAN AMERICANS

African American patients are less likely than other race/ethnic groups to use advanced directives, especially those individuals who identify themselves as being religious and believe that God has final say in life or death.[47] There is culture incongruence for African Americans to interfere with what they view to be the "will of God." Furthermore, the legacy of discrimination and oppression contribute to African Americans' perceptions of bias in, and mistrust of, the current U.S. systems of care.[48] Negative past experiences have shaped cultural norms, values, and beliefs about end-of-life care. So much so that their preference for more aggressive, life-prolonging intervention may well be the result of black/African Americans experiences of having been denied access to care historically.[49] In contemporary times, there is evidence that African

Americans tend to avoid the use of advance directives and other mechanisms that they believe may hasten death, which is a likely explanation for why they are less likely than other racial groups to utilize hospice and palliative care at end of life.[50]

LESBIAN, GAY, BISEXUAL, AND TRANSGENDERED

Persons who are lesbian, gay, bisexual, or transgendered often experience discrimination and lack of equal access and treatment when faced with end-of-life care issues. Almack, Seymour, and Bellamy report that as gays, lesbians, bisexuals, and transgender individuals age there will become more of a need to incorporate their partner's wishes in their caregiving and/or family support even if their family structure is not that of the typical family in the care system.[51] To document attitudes on end-of-life care in a gay and lesbian community, 575 respondents were surveyed.[52] The majority supported legalization of physician-assisted suicide and preferred a palliative approach to end-of-life care. There was stronger support for these approaches among men than women. Noteworthy is the finding that male respondents completed advance directives at a higher rate than women generally, which points to the importance of understanding diversity among and across diverse groups.

GUIDELINES FOR CULTURAL COMPETENCE

A basic set of guiding principles of care include respecting the goals, wishes, and choices of our patients. It is expected that we will attend to the medical, emotional, social, and spiritual needs of the patient and when possible, the family. We should be committed to assisting our patients with identifying and accessing appropriate care, so that optimal, holistic care is available to all patients.

Many of the challenges that end-of-life care providers face stem from that lack of understanding about how to apply cultural competence guidelines. Care providers must address their capacity to work effectively across cultural differences by examining their own behaviors and attitudes toward their patients' differences. This requires that providers be aware of cultural norms and values that they bring into the care relationship. Some specific areas of cultural diversity to pay attention to are values, acceptance, and understanding. These areas are further explained as follows.

1. Values for and against individualism versus collectivism; independence versus interdependence; self-reliance versus interconnectedness; and future-oriented versus present-oriented
2. Acceptance of nontraditional family types and structures; nontraditional gender roles and boundaries; and direct disclosure versus nondirect disclosure

3. Understanding of views on suffering, divine intervention, afterlife, the supernatural, as well as culturally variant communication patterns, for example, direct versus indirect, verbal versus nonverbal[53]

On a larger scale, institutions and organizations have their own cultural biases as individual practice skills, attitudes, policies, and structures influence the systems or group of professionals who provide the care. The stakeholders in these systems have to undergo ongoing, continuous learning in order to value and integrate diversity into their infrastructures.

RECOMMENDATIONS

The United States will be an increasingly diverse society as we move further into the 21st century. Documented differences in end-of-life care needs across diverse groups require that health-care providers adjust their practices to ensure that all patients, regardless of race, ethnicity, sexual self-identification or other markers of identity, receive optimal care, according to their wishes. This includes communicating with patients in ways that invite and welcome preferences and opinions with consideration for the literacy level of the person. Strategies include offering translations by culturally attuned translators, when needed, and to avoid conveying attitudes of disregard and disrespect. While certain styles of communication and decision making may be more common in some cultures than others, stereotypes should be avoided.

Generalizations about specific cultures are not always applicable to specific patients. As individuals more and more self-identify as belonging to more than one culture, it will be even more important to rely on appropriate assessment tools to determine the degree to which patients and family are acculturated to the standard practices of the setting where they are treated. We need to create environments that are inviting and welcoming to all individuals, including significant others; we need to broaden definitions of family to include unmarried and same-sex family members. A set of questions that ask about family type, structure, and functioning as well as values, beliefs, and attitude toward health-care systems will be helpful in developing a culturally competent care plan. Appropriate treatment will consider the culturally specific social, emotional, and spiritual needs of the patient and family.

Ko, Cho, and Bonilla studied life-sustaining measures among Korean-American and Mexican-American patients.[54] They found that when health-care providers adhered to comprehensive written directives such as the Medical Orders for Life-Sustaining Treatment (MOLST) or the Physician Order for Life-Sustaining Treatment (POLST), patients and their caregivers reported better interactions with the provider. To bridge the gap in the development and delivery of culturally competent care, it is important to identify tools that help to facilitate patient-centered care. Rather than conclude that underrepresented populations will not be willing to take advantage of hospice and palliative care, which has been deemed the gold standard of care with its attention to psychosocial, emotional, spiritual, and comfort needs, the final recommendation for providers is to commit to achieving cultural competence through continuing education and training that is evidence-based and multidisciplinary.

NOTES

1. U.S. Census Bureau, "Overview of Race and Hispanic Origin: 2010," last modified 2011, http://www.census.gov/prod/cen2010/briefs/c2010br-02.pdf

2. U.S. Census Bureau, "An Older and More Diverse Nation by Midcentury," last modified 2008, http://www.census.gov/newsroom/releases/archives/population/cb08-123.html

3. Ibid.

4. U.S. Census Bureau, 2011.

5. Iraida Carrión, "When do Latinos Use Hospice Services? Studying the Utilization of Hospice Services by Hispanic/Latinos," *Social Work in Health Care* 49, 3 (2010): 197–210. Karen Bullock, "The Influence of Culture on End-of-Life Decision Making," *Journal of Social Work in End-of-Life & Palliative Care* 7, 1 (2011): 83–98, 10.1080/15524256.2011.548048 (accessed January 21, 2013). Kimberly Johnson, Maragatha Kuchibhatla, and James Tulsky, "What Explains Racial Differences in the Use of Advance Directives and Attitudes Toward Hospice Care?" *Journal of the American Geriatrics Society* 56, 10 (2008): 1953–58.

6. Gala True, Etienne Phipps, Leonard Braitman, Tina Harralson, Diana Harris, and William Tester, "Treatment Preferences and Advance Care Planning at End of Life: The Role of Ethnicity and Spiritual Coping in Cancer Patients," *Annals of Behavioral Medicine* 30, 2 (2005): 174–79.

7. Iraida Carriòn and Karen Bullock, "A Case of Hispanics and Hospice Care," *International Journal of Humanities and Social Sciences* 2, 4 (2012): 9–16.

8. Johnson, Kuchibhatla, and Tulsky, "What Explains Racial Differences in the Use of Advance Directives and Attitudes Toward Hospice Care?"

9. Lilian Cohen, "Racial/Ethnic Disparities in Hospice Care: A Systematic Review," *Journal of Palliative Medicine* 11, 5 (2008): 763–68.

10. U.S. Census Bureau, 2008.

11. Bullock, "The Influence of Culture on End-of-Life Decision Making." Lavera Crawley, "Racial, Cultural, and Ethnic Factors Influencing End-of-Life Care," *Journal of Palliative Medicine* 8, Supplement 1 (2005): S-58–69. K. Allen Grenier, Subashan Perera, and Jasjit Ahluwalia, "Hospice Usage by Minorities in the Last Year of Life: Results from the National Mortality Followback Survey," *Journal of American Geriatric Society* 51, 7 (2003): 970–78. Marjorie Kagawa-Singer and Leslie Blackhall, "Negotiating Cross-Cultural Issues at the End of Life: 'You Got to Go Where He Lives,'" *Journal of the American Medical Association* 286, 6 (2001): 2993–3001.

12. National Association of Social Workers, "Code of Ethics," last modified 2008, http://www.socialworkers.org/pubs/code/code.asp?print=1

13. Carrión and Bullock, "A Case of Hispanics and Hospice Care."

14. Gary Stein, Patricia Sherman, and Karen Bullock, "Educating Gerontologists for Cultural Proficiency in End-of-Life Care Practice," *Journal of Educational Gerontology* 35, 11 (2009): 1008–25.

15. National Hospice and Palliative Care Organization, "Hospice and Palliative Care," last modified 2012, http://www.nhpco.org/i4a/pages/index.cfm?pageid= 4648&openpage=4648

16. American Academy of Family Physicians, "Positions and Policies: Cultural Proficiency Guidelines," last modified 2011. Accessed December 10, 2012, www.aafp.org/ x6711.xml

17. Crawley, "Racial, Cultural, and Ethnic Factors Influencing End-of-Life Care."

18. National Hospice and Palliative Care Organization, 2012.

19. Ibid.

20. Bullock, "The Influence of Culture on End-of-Life Decision Making." Sonia Duffy, Frances Jackson, Stephanie Schim, David Ronis, and Karen Fowler, "Racial/Ethnic Preferences, Sex Preferences, and Perceived Discrimination Related to End-of-Life Care," *Journal of American Geriatric Society* 51, 7 (2006): 150–57.

21. Bullock, "The Influence of Culture on End-of-Life Decision Making." Alexander Smith, Revecca Sudore, and Eliseo Pérez-Stable, "Palliative Care for Latino Patients and their Families: Whenever We Prayed, She Wept," *Journal of the American Medical Association* 301, 10 (2009): 1047–57.

22. Ellen Csikai and Elizabeth Chaitin, *Ethics in End-of-Life Decisions of Social Work Practice* (Chicago: Lyceum Books Inc, 2006). Margaret Reith and Malcolm Payne, *Social Work in End-of-Life and Palliative Care* (Chicago: Lyceum Books Inc, 2009).

23. Duffy et al., "Racial/Ethnic Preferences, Sex Preferences, and Perceived Discrimination Related to End-of-Life Care."

24. Gregory Ruhnke, Sandra Wilson, Takashi Akamatsu, Takaaki Kinoue, Yutaka Takashima, Mary Goldstein, Barbara Koenig, John Hornberger, and Thomas Raffin, "Ethical Decision Making and Patient Autonomy: A Comparison of Physicians and Patients in Japan and the United States," *CHEST* 118, 4 (2000): 1173.

25. Bullock, "The Influence of Culture on End-of-Life Decision Making."

26. Karen Bullock, Sarah McGraw, Karen Blank, and Elizabeth Bradley, "What Matters to Older African Americans Facing End-of-Life Decisions? A Focus Group Study," *Journal of Social Work in End-of-Life & Palliative Care* 1, 3 (2005): 3–19.

27. Jose Sisneros, Catherine Stakeman, Mildred Joyner, and Catheryne Schmitz, *Critical Multicultural Social Work* (Chicago: Lyceum Books Inc, 2008).

28. U.S. Census Bureau, 2011.

29. Bullock, "The Influence of Culture on End-of-Life Decision Making."

30. Ibid.

31. Johnson, Kuchibhatla, and Tulsky, "What Explains Racial Differences in the Use of Advance Directives and Attitudes Toward Hospice Care?"

32. Todd Jenkins, Kathryn Chapman, Christine Ritchie, Donna Arnett, Gerald McGwin, Stacey Cofield, and H. Michael Maetz, "Hospice Use in Alabama, 2002–2005," *Journal of Pain and Symptom Management* 41, 2 (2011): 374–82.

33. Ibid

34. Johnson, Kuchibhatla, and Tulsky, "What Explains Racial Differences in the Use of Advance Directives and Attitudes Toward Hospice Care?"

35. Polly Mazanec, Barbara Daly, and Aloen Townsend, "Hospice Utilization and End-of-Life Care Decision Making of African Americans," *American Journal of Hospice & Palliative Medicine* 27, 8 (2010): 560–66.

36. Kagawa-Singer and Blackhall, "Negotiating Cross-Cultural Issues at the End of Life: 'You Got to Go Where He Lives.' "

37. U.S. Census Bureau, 2011.

38. Smith, Sudore, and Pérez-Stable, "Palliative Care for Latino Patients and their Families: Whenever We Prayed, She Wept."

39. Kagawa-Singer and Blackhall, "Negotiating Cross-Cultural Issues at the End of Life: 'You Got to Go Where He Lives.' "

40. Amber Barnato, Denise Anthony, Jonathan Skinner, Patricia Gallagher, and Elliott Fisher, "Racial and Ethnic Differences in Preferences for End-of-Life Treatment," *Journal of General Internal Medicine* 24, 6 (2009): 695–701.

41. Duffy et al., "Racial/Ethnic Preferences, Sex Preferences, and Perceived Discrimination Related to End-of-Life Care," 150–57.

42. Barnato et al., "Racial and Ethnic Differences in Preferences for End-of-Life Treatment."

43. Smith, Sudore, and Pérez-Stable, "Palliative Care for Latino Patients and their Families: Whenever We Prayed, She Wept."

44. Eunjeong Ko, Sunhee Cho, and Monica Bonilla, "Attitudes Toward Life-Sustaining Treatment: The Role of Race/Ethnicity," *Geriatric Nursing* 33, 5 (2012): 341–49. Ruhnke et al., "Ethical Decision Making and Patient Autonomy: A Comparison of Physicians and Patients in Japan and the United States."

45. Gwen Yeo and Nancy Hikuyeda, "Cultural Issues in End-of-Life Decision Making Among Asians and Pacific Islanders in the United States," in *Cultural Issues in End-of-Life Decision Making*, ed. K. Braun, J. H. Pietsch, and P. L. Blanchette (Thousand Oaks, CA: Sage, 2000), 101–25.

46. Ibid.

47. Johnson, Kuchibhatla, and Tulsky, "What Explains Racial Differences in the Use of Advance Directives and Attitudes Toward Hospice Care?"

48. Bullock et al., "What Matters to Older African Americans Facing End-of-Life Decisions? A Focus Group Study."

49. Elizabeth McKinley, Joanne Garrett, Arthur Evans, and Marion Danis, "Differences in End-of-Life Decision Making Among Black and White Ambulatory Cancer Patients," *Journal of General Internal Medicine* 11 (1996): 651–56. Johnson, Kuchibhatla, and Tulsky, "What Explains Racial Differences in the Use of Advance Directives and Attitudes Toward Hospice Care?"

50. Johnson, Kuchibhatla, and Tulsky, "What Explains Racial Differences in the Use of Advance Directives and Attitudes Toward Hospice Care?"

51. Katheryn Almack, Jane Seymour, and Gary Bellamy, "Exploring the Impact of Sexual Orientation on Experiences and Concerns about End of Life Care and on Bereavement for Lesbian, Gay, and Bisexual Older People," *British Sociological Association* 44, 5 (2010): 908–24.

52. Gary Stein, and Karen Bonuk, "Physician–Patient Relationships Among the Lesbian and Gay Community," *Journal of the Gay and Lesbian Medical Association* 5, 3 (2001): 87–93.

53. Bullock, "The Influence of Culture on End-of-Life Decision Making."

54. Ko, Cho, and Bonilla, "Attitudes Toward Life-Sustaining Treatment: The Role of Race/Ethnicity."

Chapter 11

Attending to the Pain of the Dying: The Nursing Home Care Paradox

Anthony J. Lechich

*H*ere *I will explore an aspect of our changing journey to the end by focusing on the increasing probability that our death will occur in an institutional setting. I examine the care environment and how the standard nursing home setting presents many obstacles to a dignified death. A review of the evolution of the formidable regulatory apparatus of the nursing home industry will explain how some of these obstacles arise. Other barriers will be shown to relate to the essential communication elements that are often not present in contemporary medical encounters. In examining the regulations and the pervading care environment in the average long-term care setting, it will become clearer why the fate of the many who come to spend their last days in an institution is to be deprived of a dignified, peaceful death. In conclusion I offer a number of ways that the nursing home experience can be improved for the staff as well as, and more importantly, for its residents who live out their lives there.*

BACKGROUND

A brief sketch of my background and how I developed an interest in this subject illustrates how I—and similarly others in the helping professions—come to serve those who are dying. I am a physician licensed in the state of New

York, trained in the United States, and currently serve as the Chief Medical Of-ficer of the 729-bed Terence Cardinal Cooke Health Care Center in Manhattan (TCC). From the early days of medical school I have always favored special-izing in the care of the elderly, gravitating to situations where they would most likely be found: a private internal medical practice, hospital clinics, programs for the homebound elderly, nursing homes, and during hospital stays. In my case all of these facilities were located in and around Manhattan: The Chelsea-Village Homebound Elderly program at St. Vincent's Hospital in Greenwich Village, St, Clare's hospital in Hell's Kitchen, the Village Nursing Home, Kateri Residence, and now, in 2013, for the last 19 years, Terence Cardinal Cooke Health Care Center in upper Manhattan (TCC).

My family, of Croatian extraction—all of my four grandparents hailed from a small village on the island of Losinj on the Adriatic coast—always venerated the elderly. Maybe their esteem derived from having survived the spectacular challenges of the 20th century. The villagers, in essence, owed their survival to the ingenuity and strength of those who raised them. It was while living with my mother's parents that I first encountered mortal illness in an adult, and soon after, death. First, at age 8, it was my grandfather, who at age 79, devel-oped chest pain one evening at home, promptly went into cardiogenic shock, and in the upstairs bedroom, died quickly, surrounded by his sons and daugh-ters. The grandchildren including me were relegated to the kitchen, stunned by the somber voices, sobs, and the collective fathoming of his passing. Thirteen years later it was grandmother's time: at 84 she suffered a small stroke and was attended to by our iconic family physician. He made a house call and exam-ined her in that same bedroom. Just before he arrived she had experienced an episode of incontinence and promptly proclaimed in Croatian, "That's it." She was not about to accept the indignity of incontinence and dependency. It might be said that her quality of life vanished in that moment. The physician, aware and highly encouraging of my medical studies, invited me outside the house in the Bronx and on the sidewalk, by his Cadillac, quietly spoke to me for the first time as a colleague. He said, "She's having small cerebral bleeds and it will be best if we just keep her comfortable right here. I don't believe the trip to the hospital will do her any good." I took his words and the manner in which they were delivered as a right of passage into the realm of the physician. It was a deeply affecting gesture. As he drove off it fell to me to go back to the bedside and this time not to cower in the kitchen but rather to relate the doctor's words and offer myself up as a source of information and strength. Embracing her rosaries in a room lit by candles, she died peacefully in her bed, two days later, surrounded by her sons, daughters, grandchildren, and the novice physician, me. That tableau of grieving family, assault on dignity, terminal breathing, and the sacred duty that I was called upon to accept has remained with me ever since. Many deaths that followed in my career tapped into the same mosaic of understanding, duty, perseverance, and humility. When applied successfully, these sacred moments of care become a deeply gratifying affirmation of the physician's highest purpose: to allay suffering and to honor the dignity of the person in his or her time of great need. The essential elements of successful interventions at the time of dying could be applied to all caregivers, but these situations are uniquely served by the physician's clinical judgment, nimble communication skills, authority, and the station that is essential to gain trust of those left behind. Once this trust is earned, those in attendance become more attuned to the inevitability of the passing and will have a much less painful time in the aftermath than if doubts remain. Their decisions need to be secure for this process to proceed smoothly.

As my career in the study of geriatrics evolved I learned and continue to learn how to savor the company of the elderly in the face of mental and physical decline. I joined many others in the emerging field of geriatrics, as in it I found many kindred spirits with similar devotion to the elderly. In geriatrics we thrive on keeping the individual functioning at the highest possible level, preventing avoidable decline, treating chronic illnesses effectively, and constantly reminding ourselves that the treatment of one ailment may produce another, even worse. It is the duty of the physician to recognize this truth and apply the principles necessary to prepare for this possibility.

WHAT IS "QUALITY OF LIFE"?

In any nursing home it is the medical director's responsibility to oversee the performance of subordinate caregivers.[1] The strict responsibilities are now memorialized in federal regulation. They include the supervision of medical practitioner, of treatment orders, drug prescribing, the provision of a safe, clean, and dignified environment, and more. The position demands knowledge of the latest medical advances, federal and state regulations, financial economies, and constant attention to details that, when unattended, cause suffering, poor outcomes, and litigation.

As I began to see individuals in these nursing homes reach their time of dying it became clear to me that the process of end-of-life care was not really embraced as a fundamental duty of the physician and other caregivers. I saw it as a paradox that all the emphasis is on quality of care as it relates to those who are relatively stable and not on the quality of care relevant to death and dying. Paradox is defined as "A statement, proposition, or situation that seems to be absurd or contradictory, but in fact is or may be true: conflicting with expectation."[2] The paradox that I envisioned is that we are constantly attuned to regulatory prohibitions that presume to be indicators of poor care such as: loss of function, weight loss, lack of skin integrity, falling, hospitalization, and death. Yet, those residing in skilled nursing homes, currently estimated at approximately 1.5 million in the United States excluding the expanding population of subacute, short-term stays, will almost certainly die in that residence or in a related hospitalization. Simply stated, we speak constantly of quality of life but far less of quality of death.

There is a vast literature on quality of life with many scales, indices, and questionnaires that purport to measure the quality of life among the frail elderly, including that of patients with Alzheimer's Disease and Huntington's Disease (HD).[3] Such measures are not as suitable for examining the "quality of life" for someone who has begun the process of dying. Although some attempts at measures are now available to measure the quality of life of those who are dying.[4] Here, I believe that narrative literature provides us with the best examples of retained quality of life in the face of dying: Mitch Alborn's autobiographical *Tuesdays with Morrie* (1997), and Aldous Huxley's utopian vision *Island* (1962), to name two.[5]

How do we describe quality of life as it pertains to those homebound or residing in nursing homes? We all have our ideas about the quality of our lives. They can vary with our mood, impactful events, our health, and many yet unexplored influences. It would be safe to say that for all of us there is a distribution of such assessments; some people are naturally joyous, others negatively inclined, still others vacillate between the two poles in their assessment of their lives. Most important is that we define it for ourselves as an individualized self-reflection.

Even more of a challenge is how we define quality of life in the context of severe dependency, as it is experienced in the nursing home. Even among the scholars who study measures of quality of life there is much discord. For example, one definition in psychiatry states: "The degree to which a person is able to function at a usual level of activity without, or with minimal compromise of routine activities: QOL reflects overall enjoyment of life, sense of well-being, freedom from disease symptoms, comfort, and ability to pursue daily activities."[6] This one does not seem to be applicable to the nursing home population. An alternative definition is offered by Anita Stewart in the *Journal of Pain and Symptom Management*:

> The quality of a person's life is determined both by the nature of his or her experiences, and by the values and meaning that the person attaches to those experiences. People adapt to adverse circumstances and may continuously reevaluate the meaning inherent in those circumstances. Thus, it is essential to define quality of life in terms of subjective evaluation by individual, rather than in terms of the meaning others attribute to the experiences of the individual.[7]

This definition serves the discussion best as it pertains to the nursing home setting.

An example that might help to illustrate this is the image of the loving nurse who comes up to the old man in the bed immobilized with contractures, distressed with bedsores, in pain, and says, with a kiss on the cheek, "I love you even more today," and causing him to beam. To me, in that moment, his joy and the lingering thought of it counts high on that day's or moment's quality-of-life scale. When I saw this, I rejected all prior judgments about his quality of life. People adapt to adverse circumstances and they may continuously reevaluate the feelings inherent in those circumstances. It is essential to define quality of life as it relates to that individual in that circumstance, at that moment, rather than in terms of the meaning others may judge as the quality of life of that individual. I really believe this to be a notion to hold close when dealing with the decline of those in our care.

Many are appalled at what they see in the average nursing home. They often cannot see this setting as allowing for an acceptable quality of life and for some it may not be. After spending almost 40 years among nursing home patients I have come to understand that although drastically altered, life does go on and the value and quality that we can assign to it still defies any measure external to the patient's own experience.

Perhaps a description of a few of my memorable patients will help. In the early days as an attending physician in the Village Nursing Home in Greenwich Village I recall admitting a new patient, a 95-year-old Italian gentleman and noticed that in addition to some meager belongings he had brought boxes and boxes of Di Napoli Cigars, affectionately known as "stinkers." I asked him what was up with the boxes of cigars to which he replied "I donna wanna runna out!" For years I watched him chain smoke those things down to the nub. About three years after I had left the Village Nursing Home, I substituted for a colleague in the hospital and found the same man dying of pneumonia after a total of seven years of smoking enjoyment in the nursing home!

Another great lady whom I attended was none other than Marion T. She was the original aunt of Patrick Dennis and was later famously known as "Auntie Mame." In the four years that I took care of her in the Village Nursing Home she was in the depths of dementia and would not remember who was in her room minutes before. Yet, she was capable of great repartee and even of great advice instantly forgotten. One day, then First Lady Rosalyn Carter came to the Village Nursing Home for a memorable luncheon at which Mame and I were present. Afterward, a reporter from WOR television in New York City interviewed Ms. T. and asked her how she felt in the presence of the First Lady of the United States, to which she memorably replied: "My dear man, she is not the first First Lady in whose presence I have been . . . after all I was jumping rope on Bank Street with my neighbor Eleanor Roosevelt when I was a child!" She was always upbeat, altered, but not reduced by dementia, ever optimistic, humorous, and Mame to her last breath. If pressed, I would say she had a high quality of life to the end.

COMMENTS ON THE ETHICAL CONTEXT OF END-OF-LIFE CARE

The quality of death, or death with dignity, is defined from a religious perspective by Daniel Sulmasy, MD, PhD, as follows:

- "For Catholics, each individual, by virtue of being human, has an intrinsic value Catholics call dignity. This is the fundamental principle of all interpersonal morality.
- There is a duty to preserve life.
- There is a fact of finitude. Medicine is a finite craft; all patients ultimately die. Individual and collective resources are also finite.
- Diversity of the human: decisions must take into account the uniqueness of each case.[8]

Similarly, the former Cardinal Archbishop of New York, Terence Cardinal Cooke, wrote: "Life is no less beautiful when accompanied by illness or weakness, hunger or poverty, mental or physical handicaps, loneliness or old age."

These statements bear on the discussion of death in the nursing home. The notions of the finitude of life can advance a discussion with a family facing the death of a loved one. It is important to consider that health-care resources for all of us, such as time, material, emotional investment, and stamina, are also finite. It is becoming increasingly important to recognize that the expenditure of public and private health-care funds must now be better accounted for. The United States compares unfavorably against many countries in cost of health care and outcomes. While rationing has negative connotations, there needs to be an acknowledgement that resources deployed for one purpose are not available for another perhaps more worthy There needs to be an ethical context in which health-care decisions are made so that resources can be deployed for the greater good.

Every day in the nursing home we deal with individuals who are kept alive through what some may consider extraordinary means. "Extraordinary" must be defined in relation to each case individually. For example, in our pediatric unit for severely disabled children, it is not extraordinary to feed patients through a gastrostomy tube or ventilate them mechanically—measures essential to preserve their lives. These considerations introduce the weighty ethical dilemmas that commonly arise as folks in nursing homes turn toward death. No intervention can be judged ordinary or extraordinary apart from the clinical context.

Almost any intervention may be deemed extraordinary if it is futile. There-fore, in the context of end-of-life care, futility is another very important con-sideration that has received a great deal of attention in medical and legal circles in the past decades.[9] I believe that futility may be fairly narrowly defined as "the intervention strategy is not going to work, not going to add anything posi-tive to the person's end of life." The debate about futile strategies can also be framed as a matter of circumstances and as a matter of how tangential words, such as "cure," "hope," and "care" are used. End-of-life discussions may raise the question of what is meant by cure. A definition of cure might be: to reverse the condition or appreciably forestall imminent death or relieve a physical or psychological burden. We begin to see some limitations of these hard-to-pin-down artful terms as we embrace responsibility to address death and dying in the nursing home. For example, the word 'hope' is laden with meaning and must be carefully applied in conversations with the families and patients as they face the dying process, that is, "hope for what?"[10] It is our responsibility to carefully and lovingly explain the burdens of certain interventions in this context. There always needs to be a willingness to consider a shifting of the goals of care. One of the fundamental tenets of palliative care is to balance life prolongation efforts with life comfort efforts. When the comfort side of the equation takes precedence, there would be a noninitiation of burdensome measures and emphasis on comfort rather than cure. The following story from my experience is a case in point:

An 87-year-old Dominican woman with a large family and diagnoses of end-stage renal disease, congestive heart failure, insulin-dependent diabetes, previous cerebrovascular accidents, and dementia fell and broke her hip. She survived the surgery and came to our nursing home needing total care. Bed-ridden, communicating only through eye contact, she was fed via gastrostomy tube. The family insisted that all resuscitative measures be used should her heart or lungs stop. Her course was stable although all she could manage was some meaningful eye contact with family. Although she was basically stable it was clear that at her age, level of disability, and other diagnoses she would not likely be alive beyond six months. This six-month limit is an important mile-stone as it opens doors in Medicare for hospice election and other benefits. The notion, however, of predicting death from "this distance" is speculative at best and, I might add, often wrong in the nursing home setting.

One day I was called to see her for labored breathing and wheezing. She seemed to be entering respiratory failure and would soon be in need of venti-lator support. The family accepted this information from me and I convinced them that once intubated she might linger on a ventilator with burdensome or unwanted consequences. They agreed to keep her in the nursing home that night. The "goals of care" shifted from curing her respiratory condition by transferring her to the hospital for full workup and potentially ventila-tor support, to keeping her comfortable. Given her moribund appearance

I predicted, incorrectly, that she would soon die. I did this so that the family could be better prepared for the looming onslaught of grief. I administered morphine for the terminal relief of her respiratory distress and not only did it relieve the respiratory distress but probably reversed her pulmonary edema (a reversible filling of the lungs with fluid), a well-known property of morphine. She returned to baseline! I needed to regain some of the trust that I might have lost by turning her revival into a positive sign and attributed her rally to her great strength. The family accepted the support from me but from that day on camped out at the bedside every day, around the clock, until she died three months later.

That case demonstrated the many ways that such scenarios need to be navigated with the caregivers. For example, I knew at the outset, by the fact that she was on dialysis in the condition she had declined to, that her family was not going to quietly accept passivity as the theme of care. In fact, each time I passed by to check in on them I always felt that they relished every hint of eye contact that she could muster; they would argue and their mother seemed to respond to the eye contact. This case exemplified the delicate titration of the many elements that prevail during such times: family (including members with different opinions and sensibilities), clinical decision making by physicians, nurses and pastoral care staff, and others. Most importantly, we try to maintain their trust, and prevent that they opt for hospitalization. When the family insists on hospitalization, the unfortunate death in the hospital becomes a *fait accompli*. We were careful to keep the patient comfortable, clean, the room tidy, quiet, and to connect positively and supportively with whoever happened to be "on watch" for the family. Physical, psychological, and spiritual comfort has to be preeminent to minimize unnecessary suffering for the patient, family, and staff. Ideally, care in nursing home is a family and team endeavor. It is up to the person orchestrating the care—be it a physician, nurse, or priest—to imbue in the tag team of shift changes the essentials of this dynamic. Sadly, often no one is there to "orchestrate." Shift changes become a barrier in nursing home staffing as detailed sign-out on all 50 patients on a unit does not admit for much opportunity of nuanced exchanges of information.

Another instructive case involved an 86-year-old female (E.F), who was admitted following multiple falls at home, a hip fracture, and rapid mental decline from dementia. E.F. was ostensibly admitted for "rehabilitation" but soon it became obvious that she was unfit to return home to her apartment and two beloved cats. Devastated, she declined further, weeping openly each day for weeks. She appeared in constant pain despite heavy narcotics, pain consultations, and a doting staff. Not even occasional visits from her neighbors and cats helped. We all agreed that she was simply beyond consolation and left her with volunteers at the bedside and continuous playing of her favorite diversion, opera. After Ethics Committee guidance, it was decided that her death was not to be prolonged by tube feeding, although she was hydrated intravenously for a while in the expectation that it would offer palliative relief. When pneumonia finally came it was not treated and she succumbed. All involved caregivers felt a collective sense of defeat in this case as it appeared to all of us that she had endured unmitigated suffering all waking hours. In that sense her death was the exception from the norm at the nursing home, where for the most part we feel that we manage suffering well. We all felt diminished by not being able to console her or connect with her. Her loneliness during those days has stuck with all of us. The case was instructive by what we were unable to do.

In the nursing home or other advanced care venue, the challenge, then, is to identify the point at which the person begins to accelerate in his or her decline. It is incumbent on the staff to detect the signs that the sustaining measures of control for the ailments and inexorable aging of their bodies and mind are beginning to lose effectiveness. It is at that point that we begin to shift the goals of care from cure or even stabilization to palliation. In summation, we must

- Keep the patient as a person with individual wishes and goals. Monitor for physical comfort: minimize avoidable suffering on behalf of patients, family, and staff and control symptoms
- Monitor emotional well-being: anxiety, depression, sadness, loneliness, fear, and joy
- Social functioning and well-being: communication of important thoughts and feelings; verbalizing closure; and keeping (summoning) loved ones to be present
- Be mindful of the spiritual well-being and meaningfulness of life: consistent with the culture of the individual
- Honor advance directives
- Allow for the settlement of affairs.[11]

THE NURSING HOME PARADOX

Let us now set the stage for the paradox: the shift in the nature of nursing homes. The nursing home population in the second decade of the 21st century is characterized by higher degrees of frailty and higher percentages of dementia than in past decades. The residents have increased prevalence of chronic diseases, risk for weight loss, functional decline, hospital transfers, falls, and skin breakdown. Nursing homes are increasingly places where people arrive nearer to their death. Nursing home residents of today have shorter average lengths of stay and consequently nursing homes have higher annual mortality rates per bed. Nursing home administrations also have to contend with a punitive regulatory environment and unrealistic pay-for-performance–based clinical criteria.

In 2009 a relatively small number—1.5 million or 4.1 percent—of the 65+ population in the United States lived in institutional settings, with nursing homes accounting for 1.3 million. However, the percentage increases dramatically with age, ranging from 1.1 percent for persons 65–74 years and 3.5 percent for persons 75–84 years to 13.2 percent for persons over 85 years. In addition, approximately 2.4 percent of the elderly lived in senior housing with at least one supportive service available to their residents.[12]

That's a different picture from years past. In 2013, as nursing home revenue increasingly depends upon Medicare and managed care clients to offset low reimbursement Medicaid-only long-term care residents; we see subacute patients coming and going in much larger numbers than they used to. This subacute group also includes patients who are in their final decline. A lot of these patients are bouncing around from hospital to nursing home, making this discussion more compelling. Approximately one-fifth of all deaths in the United States were in nursing homes. One study has attempted to derive a personal severity index showing patients stratified by degree of disability.[13] In this study, 12 percent of all people studied were dead in six months. Those who were up and walking had 2.9 percent mortality with up to 70 percent mortality in six months for the most frail. Clients we deal with every day would be considered in the "more frail" category. We have primitive criteria by which to prognosticate in this group, but have found that prognostication is a dangerous game in the nursing home, and that is a fact that must be recognized. In this discussion, when we have patients who require maximum assistance, who have advanced major disease states, unrelenting decubitus ulcers (often hospital acquired), their prognosis could easily be set at less than six months. The point here, and the crux of the paradox, is if we have a better than one-in-five chance of dying in a nursing home shouldn't we devote more time and study on how this can be better addressed?

A provocative study recently showed that those who receive palliative care versus aggressive chemo actually live longer.[14] It was also shown in this study that the survivors are more likely to suffer depression in the late-term chemo group than in the palliative care group. The palliative care group seemed better prepared for death and therefore had less sense of defeat than the aggressive chemo group. The physician-author covers this well and challenges us to think about what's better for the individual and the family.

We don't seem to meet the responsibility for end-of-life care in nursing homes across the country. In its current state in hospitals and home care, palliative care services often stand too far apart from the primary care environment of the patient. Such services need to be much more integrated into the care teams than they are now. The palliative care consultation can sometimes cause the primary caregivers to withdraw in "defeat." I feel that it should be more adjunctive than preemptive. The following observations of mine and by others have been confirmed by audience interviews in various end-of-life nursing home presentations to medical director groups, to be discussed later in the chapter:

- The average nursing home does not meet the responsibility inherent in the reality that so many will die while in residence there
- Symptom management is notoriously poor
- Hospice referrals remain low
- Hospitalizations near the end of life are too high
- Inadequate use of advance care planning
- Family dissatisfaction is common
- Staff acknowledgment of impending death is variable

For the past 10 years I have presented a summary of the palliative care program experience at the Terence Cardinal Cooke Health Care Center at the American Medical Directors Association meetings. I present our experience with setting up the program, the outcome measures, the barriers, and shortcomings. The audiences are usually about 80–100 medical directors each representing facilities with 200–300 beds. Up to now, there has been unanimous agreement among medical directors present at these classes that end-of-life care is lacking when it comes to the anticipation and preparing for the death of nursing home residents.

EVOLUTION OF QUALITY IMPROVEMENT INITIATIVES IN THE NURSING HOME

A review of how quality of nursing home care has evolved helps illustrate how this evolution impedes end-of-life care in the nursing home. In the 1970s the epicenters of scandalous nursing home care were Texas and New York. In New York, two of the nursing homes operated by the discredited Bernard Bergman, the Village Nursing Home and the Park Crescent Nursing Home, were targeted. One night, in 1970, as an intern at the neighboring St. Vincent's hospital I was called from emergency room duty to pronounce a patient dead in the Village Nursing Home, then still under Rabbi Bergman. I recall the senior medical house officer at St. Vincent's warning me: "Oh man, I don't envy you." Off I went on in the middle of the night into the Village Nursing Home. Later, when I worked there in 1980, there were 200 residents. When I made that house call the facility held an astounding 360 residents. At 200 it was tight, and at 360 it was overrun.

Upon arrival I was greeted by a nurse with a flashlight who led me into a room where cots were lined up, four in a row. Her grim duty was to put the light on the deceased. Trying not to disturb those sleeping only inches away from the dead man, I quietly verified his death and completed the death certificate. That was the Village Nursing Home in the 1970s. It literally was, as President Nixon famously said, "a warehouse for the elderly." To my eyes, it was a junkyard for the dying. At the same time in Texas it was widely reported that the majority of the people in nursing homes there were overmedicated with tranquilizers and living in squalor.

Deplorable conditions such as these in New York and Texas, and other similar events, sparked the whole 1970s movement of nursing home reform led by David Pryor, Senator for Arkansas, with the creation of the Office of Nursing Home Affairs, Social Security Reforms, Standards, and Ombudsman programs. The next major milestone was in 1987, when the Omnibus Reconciliation Act (OBRA) of 1987 emerged from an Institute of Medicine report.[15]

OBRA '87

- Established nationwide standards for quality of care in nursing homes

- Designed a program to monitor and assure resident rights

- Established consistent procedures for the certification process that determined if nursing homes are meeting the quality goals

- Established training of nurse aides and use of the Resident Assessment Instrument of which the Minimum Data Set (MDS, described below) is a major descendant.

The MDS contains the core items necessary for a comprehensive assessment of nursing facility residents. It also provides triggers, that is, individual items or combinations of MDS elements, to identify residents for whom specific Resident Assessment Protocols (RAPs) are appropriate. RAPs are specific regulated approaches that should be undertaken to address the issues that the MDS questionnaire identifies.[16] In my experience, speaking with professionals in the nursing home field, consensus comments on the MDS include some positive factors, but also criticism of a reporting system that may not serve the nursing home residents well.

While MDS offers a powerful database for future demographic analysis, it may lead to premature conclusions about the quality of care in a given nursing home. To make the assessment accurate, it is necessary to add to the MDS reports risk-adjustment modifiers to allow for the presence of greater numbers of patients in decline. Let me explain: Nursing homes are monitored by state authorities that base their conclusions on the quality of care to a large extent on the MDS reports. Among the measurements is the progress of residents as compared with their "disability score" at the time of admission. Since the truth is that most residents are admitted with their or their families' expectation that the nursing home placement will be their final home, their physical decline is, if not "obligatory," at least the norm. For example: their decubitus ulcers get worse, their ability to perform activities of daily living diminishes, and they experience weight loss. MDS reports on the residents' changes in condition must be submitted to the authorities regularly. This means that a nursing home that offers its residents at the end of life palliative care in its own facility will report more incidents of decline and death—which gives them a negative score by the authority—than those nursing homes that send residents to a hospital to die or receive treatment.

In addition, the concerns are that MDS reports are grist for the litigation mill and that they cannot be effectively used for the correlation of staffing resources. A revised MDS—MDS 3.0—attempts to address some of the shortcomings. The applicability of this version to the nursing home environment in 2012 can be summarized as follows:[17]

- It remains a powerful tool for implementing standardized assessment and for facilitating care management in nursing homes and noncritical access hospital swing beds.
- Its content has implication for residents, families, providers, researchers, and policymakers.
- It has been designed to improve the reliability, accuracy, and usefulness of the MDS, to include the resident in the assessment process, and to use standard protocols used in other settings.
- Enhanced accuracy supports the primary legislative intent that MDS be a tool to improve clinical assessment and supports the credibility of programs that rely on MDS.

Importantly, a section of MDS 3.0 addresses Special Treatments, Procedures, and Programs relating to hospice care. The reporting for code residents identified as being in a hospice program for terminally ill will not be part of the same reporting as the general hospice population. This will help prevent some of the above referenced issues relating to the inevitable decline of residents but does not fully solve the problem, since it requires that the patient and family agree to hospice acceptance. Many will not and these residents will still be considered "care deficiencies" in the MDS database. The fundamental issue gets back to the conversations with the families and residents and whether the staff can successfully convey the information that a conservative end-of-life plan, or hospice election, is appropriate for their loved one.

THE PROS AND CONS OF THE REGULATIONS

A prominent piece of nursing home reform legislation is a mandatory annual survey. "The National Nursing Home Survey (NNHS) is a continuing series of national sample surveys of nursing homes, their residents, and their staff. Although each of these surveys emphasized different topics, they all provided some common basic information about nursing homes, their residents, and their staff."[18] Each state is responsible to administer the survey and the Federal Government is also empowered to conduct random unannounced surveys as well as a means to oversee state's performance of this obligation. Surveys can also be triggered in response to allegations of neglect or incidents that rise to a certain level of potential danger or evidence of poor care. As such, the survey process is another very powerful enforcement arm.

A negative survey can have ruinous consequences for a nursing home operator and, therefore, is generally a stressful exercise for provider staff, who, among other things, are asked to show chart compliance. In the case of our facility, TCC, the survey team will come in for an entire week at all hours and comb through the entire facility. Surveys have evolved into sophisticated screenings that direct the inspectors to the most vulnerable patients who require voluminous documentation. While generally objective and fairly effective in weeding out substandard performance the survey process still cannot really capture what goes on at the bedside.

To help consumers evaluate nursing homes, the official website for Medicare—www.medicare.gov—gives an up to five-star quality rating to every Medicare-and Medicaid-certified nursing home in the United States. These ratings derive from assessments in three areas: health inspections, staffing, and quality measures. The ratings are important tools for consumers who want to compare nursing homes. They are also of great importance to the nursing homes. A bad survey can reduce the nursing home's star rating for three years. The ratings are available on the "Nursing Home Compare" website.[19]

My personal assessment of the current status of nursing home reform is as follows: 25 years after OBRA '87 it remains difficult to comment on the overall quality of nursing home care in the second decade of the 21st century, an opinion shared by others.[20] The focus of survey assessments now is—rightly—on function, staff interaction, and the environment of care. There is a renewed interest in patient-centered care. There is greater interdisciplinary involvement in patient care and there is greater accountability for good care. The deck, however, remains stacked against palliation and demise on the premises of the nursing home as dying patients frequently have weight loss and decline in activities of daily living, as well as pain, emotional turmoil, family dissatisfaction and demands, and heavy personal care needs.

LESSONS FROM A SUCCESSFUL END-OF-LIFE CARE PROGRAM

Taking Stock and Educating Staff

As the medical director of two large nursing homes for over 25 years I estimate that I have been on watch for over 5,000 deaths. Early on, I observed too often that the deaths were inadequately anticipated, often unaccompanied, involved unnecessary hospitalization or emergency room visits, and were needlessly accompanied by controllable symptoms. To examine this I created a questionnaire that consisted of five incisive questions, relating to what I determined to be core responsibilities for each key discipline: social work, medicine, nursing, pastoral care, and administration. For example, the physician was asked, "Was the patient's death unexpected? Were you aware the patient was approaching death? Were symptoms managed adequately? Was family summoned? Were hospitalizations avoided, as appropriate?" Other disciplines were given similar questions based on their core duties.

The survey was done for 50 consecutive patients and the survey was also given to the next of kin of the same patients. The results showed that the professional staff rated themselves higher than the families rated them in turn, and that the professionals acknowledged that their accountability to this aspect of care was lacking.

At TCC the diversity of programs—AIDS medicine, Huntington's disease special unit, end-stage renal disease (ESRD) unit, pulmonary unit, and so on—intensified our interest in addressing palliative care needs. In 2000, we received a grant from the United Hospital Fund and Greater New York Hospital Association that was titled Palliative Care Quality Improvement Collaborative. The grant allowed us to receive training for our staff by expert teachers in palliative care. It was a valuable experience for our staff to receive extensive information on the subject and to utilize the teachings of Education in Palliative and End-of-life Care (EPEC), a program with the "mission to educate all health care professionals in the essential clinical competencies of palliative care."[21]

SETTING GOALS AND CRITICAL FACTORS IN IMPLEMENTATION

The targets for improvement developed then remain relevant: improve advanced care planning; improve communications with the patient and family; improve symptom control; improve pain control; provide pastoral care to patient and families; reduce unnecessary hospitalizations at end of life; and strive for a peaceful, dignified death in-house. To achieve these targets, we started by developing philosophy, goals, policy, and procedures. One of our goals was a reduction of pain at the end of life, and we were successfully able to demonstrate that. At the end of one year we had reduced pain scores by 80 percent. We looked at staff responsibilities and assigned marching orders for each level of staff and created a screening tool for palliative care upon admission. Early identification of patients in need of palliative care services remains an unmet obligation in many nursing homes. It is imperative that we be prepared for cases, in which a patient is in the hospital for a short admission and has a terminal diagnosis, and the hospital physicians and care teams have not even broached the subject of prognosis. Such cases are sent to the nursing home for "rehab," although the patients are in fact beginning the process of dying.

Clearly, the nursing home staff needs to better ally with the hospital teams so that such cases may benefit from the palliative care teams in the hospital or at least to establish reasonable advance directives discussions. The hospital teams should also convey better information about the patient's family and how its members are coping with the situation.

At TCC, the key to our early success was to buy-in to the idea of better palliative care by all involved, from the bedside staff all the way up to the Board of Directors. We created a steering committee that set program objectives, timelines, and deliverables. We also established a collaborative consultation team that could come together quickly around a new client. We dubbed one of the physicians "project champion;" his job was to keep track of active end-of-life patients, collect data, educate ever-changing staff, and performing check lists surveys after the death of the patient.

BARRIERS TO GOOD NURSING HOME CARE

We encountered many barriers, some of which still stand today and many which are likely to be present in other nursing homes, as well. These obstacles prevented us from achieving our goals of successful anticipation, assessment, management, and the attainment of the peaceful, dignified death of our clients. To this day, they still require constant effort to overcome. Here are some to consider:

1. *Cold environment:* The average nursing home remains an inhospitable place. It takes a great deal of training to change the culture and design prevalent in most homes.

2. *Regulatory restrictions:* Nursing homes are regulation-driven, as mentioned above, and many of the regulations don't favor the best care for those at the end of life.

3. *Staff turnover:* The need to constantly retrain, remind, and supervise staff, especially "floater staff," is time-consuming and reduces the amount of attention to the residents.

4. *Staff stress:* Staff members' encounters with doubting, untrusting, and conflicted families are stressful. Staff can balk at the added attention that actively dying patients require, and giving that time may not always be possible

5. *Cultural differences about death among families and staff:* Some serious cultural dictums can preclude direct care of people when they are

dying. Some cultures do not share the conservative ideology that we at TCC embrace.

6. *Lack of physician availability:* For the nursing home to function optimally the physician must be available, possess a measure of charisma, communication skill, and patience. The best palliative care training is through role modeling at the bedside. It is important that the staff physician takes the time to speak with the nurses and aides, and other care staff, to answer their questions—including questions about why a patient may not benefit from going to the hospital—and to understand their limitations and stress factors. If the attending physician fails to communicate clearly with the staff, the family may get a different message from the staff than the physician intended.

7. *Inadequately trained physicians:* Many physicians are poorly prepared and downright clumsy when it comes to the nuanced discussions around death; they absolutely need to be scripted and trained, and watched and mentored. An article by Atul Gawande in the *New Yorker,* "Letting Go," beautifully describes Dr. Susan Block broaching the subject of end-of-life care with a family, describing it almost as an operation, a procedure that has to be nuanced, carefully orchestrated, or else will "lose the trust and the opportunity."[22] Ironically, she goes on to report how she admitted being speechless when discussing the issues of advance directives with her own father.

8. *Hostile financial environment:* The majority of nursing home care is Medicaid funded, meaning limited money for bedside care. It is expensive at times to take care of patients at the end of life; it may require additional staff, medication, and treatments.

9. *Negatively perceived language:* The semantic weight given to certain words has become a significant barrier to good care. For example, "palliative care" is a concept that is poorly understood by the general public and unless good explanations are given to patients and families when it is offered, they may refuse this form of care which can be very beneficial in chronic serious illness as well as at the end of life. Other words are equally fraught.

THE COMPLICATED IDEAS OF "TERMINAL" AND "BURDEN"

The word "terminal" is not a precise diagnosis. In the context of nursing home medical care, its usage has become extremely complicated. If the current length of stay for the majority of nursing home patients is dropping down into months rather than years then it may soon be fair to say that the majority of the entrants to nursing homes could be deemed "terminal" on admission.

That would make it even more difficult to square the current regulatory focus on not declining with the actual fate of the clientele in question. There are many confounders in our quest to detect when the "tipping point" occurs in the nursing home resident, the point at which he or she actually begins the decline toward death. I trust in Joanne Lynn's findings that those in nursing homes with standard chronic illnesses are a select group for whom the usual prognosticative guidelines for such diseases under-estimate survival.[23] The disease trajectories so important for family discussion are largely speculative. In the end, it's always the *individual* with chronic obstructive pulmonary disease (COPD or ESRD whose course we are trying to predict.

Standard and average measures do not seem very useful in individual cases. The variations are too broad. I have had in my care for over two years patients with COPD, on oxygen, who have been on and off hospice three times, meaning that two physicians each time predicted that their life expectancy was less than six months—a requirement for hospice eligibility. Predicting life expectancy for someone with dementia or Alzheimer's, both "terminal" conditions, is even more difficult. Likewise, on our HD unit when we studied death and dying of our HD residents, we found the closest answer to the question of how HD patients die to be: very slowly. Patients with HD somehow survive through emaciation, repeated infections, trauma, and hospitalizations. There have even been examples on the HD unit of patients who were tube fed for years and became "do not replace tube if it comes out" candidates only to survive with resumed, laborious—for the staff and the patient—oral feeding for another year. We have similar experience with ESRD patients. We tried to apply the information in *The New England Journal of Medicine* (2009, October 15) on ESRD prognosis that tied negative survival to patients with poor abilities in toileting, transferring, and feeding. We found that our patients who met the criteria for probable death in under six months remain alive long after that.[24]

The operative lesson in managing these open-ended "terminal" cases is to involve the patient and the family in the discussion about the burdens of care and the eventual diminishing returns on going to the hospital or continuing with burdensome treatments. With ESRD it is often the comorbidity that overtakes the patient. Examples are: congestive heart failure, recurrent septicemia, or bleeding that set the patient up for earlier demise. The significance of such complications need to be explained to the patient and families and they need to be assisted in factoring them into the burden of treatments and changing goals of care from curing and containing to comforting and accepting decline and death. The discussion always seems to come back to the issue of burden, a key tenet of palliative care dogma. We really must present the burdens of treatment versus comfort in the most tactful way, respecting that the patient and family are struggling to assess just what that means for their loved one. However, a burden to one person is not so to another. Two cases in point:

J.B. is a 57-year-old Hispanic man with a long history of intravenous drug abuse (IVDA), diabetes, Hepatitis C with cirrhosis, ESRD on dialysis for 24 years, peripheral arterial disease, and previous below-the-knee amputation. He has been somber and depressed unrelieved by antidepressants or psychological sessions. He is estranged from his family and has only one regular visitor. He announced suddenly one night that "I had enough of this shit. I want to stop it and will not go back to dialysis. Quality of life? I have NO quality of life!"

There is a rigidly fixed protocol for the termination of dialysis. The patient has to have mental capacity when he decides to discontinue treatment, as it is uniformly fatal. This man had a percutaneous catheter for dialysis via his subclavian vein (in the upper chest). One psychiatrist said that J.B. did not have capacity. I felt that he in fact did have capacity to understand what he wanted to do. I asked another more senior psychiatrist to see him and his comment was "he really doesn't have capacity. He gets it, yes, but he doesn't understand to a great enough degree what he wants to decide." So, at the 11th hour, after that consult, when he was sitting alone with a plate of food in front of him, dejected, I said, "I think you need to go to the hospital," and he said, "I don't want to go to the hospital." I said, "You are really not in the right mind about all of this, and our experts say that this decision is not really something you can live with right now." In the end, he went to the hospital, after a call to 911. He was resistant to the ambulance force at first, and then said, "No, I'll walk out."

The psychiatrist's point was that the perception of his quality of life at that exact moment was terrible, and he (the psychiatrist) was unwilling to allow him to commit passive suicide. J.B. was brought to the hospital on medicine, and liaison psychiatry followed him to try to reverse the depression in time for him to again accept dialysis. The rub here is that if you don't cooperate with the dialysis procedure you will die in a matter of days. So if he continued to refuse or if he reached for the dialysis tubes during dialysis and exsanguinated on the spot, he would accomplish his wish. If the patient will not allow the machine to be attached, the patient, even without capacity, is then allowed to succumb to renal failure. The end-of-life discussion takes a different but no less complex turn. Many cases we have seen have dealt with waffling back and forth about stopping treatment. Again, with ESRD there is an avowed willingness to accept a burdensome intervention: dialysis. These individuals usually need a second "burden" to push them to stop dialysis.

Mr. B has long-standing oxygen-dependent COPD, is frequently near respiratory failure, and then he recovers. His disease course looks like a sawtooth. In fact, when we look at the end-of-life trajectory of COPD we often see such a pattern of decline, measured either in oxygen saturation decline or hospitalizations prior to death. This pattern may assist us in conversations with the patient and family. When the hospitalizations come more and more frequently we can predict that the patient may be nearing an admission when he or she will require ventilatory support, and thereafter possibly unable to be weaned. The patient will best be served to know that, and what life will be like on the ventilator, most likely permanently.

LOOKING AHEAD

For successful palliative care we need role models in all disciplines. We need to train them; we need to have them train more trainers. We need to turn the culture around and encourage communication between all team members. The lesson that we learned at TCC is that a champion is not enough. The unit teams must accept the responsibility to perform the day-to-day tasks on patients known to be at the end of life, as well as be vigilant to identify those who are beginning to approach the end of life right before their eyes.

There is evidence that the political climate is opening up to more acceptance and encouragement of the professional's responsibility to provide good palliative care. New York State passed the Family Health Care Decisions Act (FHCDA) in June, 2010, which is a huge advance that enables family members who are not health-care proxies to come in and rule on the future care of their demented mother or father or loved one.[25] Prior to the passage of the FHCDA we had not been able to do that unless there was written evidence of what the patient wanted. Now, the family can base the end-of-life decision on all accumulated evidence of preferences of a beloved father with dementia in the nursing home; with their knowledge of him, his family members can assess, to the best of their ability, how he might have considered potential burdens such as, tube feeding, ventilatory support, and resuscitation. That is a major advancement.

A significant potential improvement in end-of-life care is derived from the push to reduce rehospitalizations, a focus of the Affordable Care Act (H.R. 3590). It stipulates, among other rules, that rehospitalizations for certain conditions such as pneumonia, after a myocardial infarction (MI), will incur financial penalties. This establishes a significant change in that there is now an incentive to reduce the futile hospital admissions so frequently seen, for example, in the last three months of dementia care.[26] Another initiative is called INTERACT 2.0 (Interventions to Reduce Acute Care Transfers).[27] It is an ingenious program of communication enhancement that was developed to help keep rehospitalizations down. It utilizes early recognition of acute changes in clinical condition and the early treatment that follows. It demands greater clinical detail from the nurse when calling the outside physician so a better, more informed, decision to hospitalize or not hospitalize can be made. It also provides scripting for the conversations on advance directives by the doctor. Through our own experience with this program and our dramatic decrease in hospitalizations from TCC, I have come to believe its effectiveness in reducing rehospitalizations.

Another useful vehicle that has advanced the cause of better end-of-life care is the, POLST (Physician's Order for Life-Sustaining Treatment), or MOLST (Medical Orders for Life-Sustaining Treatment) as it is known in New York and a few other states, or—in yet other states—MOST (Medical Orders for Scope of Treatment) or POST (Physician's Orders for Scope of Treatment). Regardless of the name, the document has essentially the same purpose and use in all states that promote them.[28] These medical forms—variations on the same theme—outline the patient's wishes in regard to life-sustaining treatments and interventions, and are appropriately filled out when a physician estimates that the frailty of the person suggests that his or her remaining life is relatively short—maybe around a year or less. One copy of the form is kept with the patient regardless of his or her place of residence or treatment; another copy stays with the medical professional who has filled out the form according to the patient' values and wishes; the patient's health-care agent (surrogate) should also have a copy and be informed of its content.

Our experience with the MOLST form in our nursing home in New York has been successful in that the clinicians have been better equipped to have the conversations needed for them to accurately enter the desired advance directive for the client. At a minimum it is an excellent tool to help those with serious illness talk about their wishes regarding potential future care options and interventions; at its best it becomes a seamless and reliable way for the patient to transfer that information from one care setting to the next.

These programs have succeeded in getting more acceptance of the utilization of hospice, and improving our application of palliative care principles. The proof of our success in these programs comes from the increase in the percentage of deaths in the nursing home—now around 80 percent. We have conducted satisfaction surveys after death and demonstrated greater staff and family appreciation of the burdens of ineffective interventions.

A brief mention of student contributions to this effort is in order. I have been graced with one or two students each summer and some throughout the school year from Columbia University's Center for the Study of Science and Religion.[29] They have been extremely important in keeping our efforts fresh, informed, and chronicled. For example, one student developed a scale to measure spiritual pain. He learned that how, and in what setting, the questions were asked could swing the results dramatically. Another project took an inventory of the documentation and steps expected to be applied to those identified as being at the end of life. He found slippage. Many of the students sat with and got to know the dying patients and their loved ones taking from those experiences impressions that will accompany and guide them in their medical careers. All of the students became familiar with the many challenges that detract from the avowed mission of death with dignity. I am especially grateful to Ashley Shaw of Columbia University for her invaluable insights and assistance in organizing this work.

In closing, I must emphasize how important it is for those of us leading the way to improved end-of-life nursing home care, to exemplify and to learn from the humanity of the endeavor. We need to embrace the responsibility to effectively lead staff by example and to continue to learn how to measure our successes and shortcomings. The quality markers that emanated from early Nursing Home Reform legislation have gotten us far from the warehouses that I once visited. While I acknowledge that the survey process is being refined and improved upon, I maintain that it still does not effectively address the quality of the care surrounding a client's death. I see good death as a responsibility absolutely fundamental to our care mission. Until we succeed much more often to effectively accompany our clients and their families through their final journey in the best way possible our work will not be done.

NOTES

1. American Medical Directors Association, "The Nursing Home Medical Director: Leader and Manager," http://www.amda.com/governance/whitepapers/A11.cfm. Accessed October 1, 2012.

2. *Oxford English Dictionary,* 3rd edition, s.v. "paradox."

3. "Construction of the SF-36," http://www.sf-36.org/tools/sf36.shtml#CONSTRUCT. Accessed September 29, 2012. S. M. Albert, "Quality of Life in Patients with Alzheimer's Disease as Reported by Patient Proxies," *Journal of the American Geriatrics Society* no. 44 (1996): 1342–47.

4. Anita L. Stewart, "The Concept of Quality of Life of Dying Persons in the Context of Health Care," *Journal of Pain and Symptom Management* 2 (February 1999): 93–108.

5. Mitch Alborn, *Tuesdays with Morrie* (Read How You Want, 2010). Aldous Huxley, *Island* (Harper Perennial Modern Classics, October 2009).

6. *McGraw-Hill Concise Dictionary of Modern Medicine,* s.v. "quality of life."

7. Stewart, "Concept of Quality of Life," 97.

8. Daniel Sulmasy, "The Last Word," 16 (November 2010): http://www.america magazine.org/content/article.cfm?article_id=12585&comments=1

9. L. Niebroj, K. Bargie-Matusiewicz, and A. Wilczynska, "Toward the Clarification of Ideas: Medical Futility, Persistent/Obstinate Therapy and Extra/Ordinary Means," *Advances in Experimental Medicine and Biology* 755 (2013): 349–56.

10. Nancy Berlinger, "Wishful Thinking: On the Grammar of 'Hope' in the Language of Serious Illness," Presentation at Columbia University Seminar on Death, November 10, 2010.

11. See Stewart, "Concept of Quality of Life," 93–108.

12. U.S. Department of Health and Human Services, Administration on Aging, "A Profile of Older Americans: 2011," 5.

13. Rosalie A. Kane, Kristen C. Kling, Boris Bershadsky, Robert L. Kane, Katherine Giles, Howard B. Degenholtz, Jiexin Liu, and Louis J. Cutler, "Quality of Life Measures for Nursing Home Residents" *Journal of Gerontology: Medical Sciences* 58A, 1 (2003):

240–8. http://www.hpm.umn.edu/LTCResourceCenter/research/QOL/RAKane_et_al_QOL_NH_measures_2003.pdf

14. Jennifer Temel, Joseph A. Greer, Alona Muzikansky, Emily R. Gallagher, Sonal Admane, Vicki A. Jackson, Constance M. Dahlin, Craig D. Blinderman, Juliet Jacobsen, William F. Pirl, J. Andrew Billings, and Thomas J. Lynch, "Early Palliative Care for Patients with Metastatic Non-Small-Cell Lung Cancer," *The New England Journal of Medicine*, 8 (August 2010): 733–42.

15. Federal Nursing Home Reform Act, Omnibus Budget Reconciliation Act of 1987, Pub. L. No. 100–203, 101 Stat. 1330 *thru* 101 Stat. 1339 (1987).

16. Centers for Medicare and Medicaid Services, "MDS 2.0 Public Quality Indicator and Resident Reports," http://www.cms.gov/Research-Statistics-Data-and-Systems/Computer-Data-and-Systems/MDSPubQIandResRep/index.html. Accessed September 29, 2012.

17. Eric G. Tangalos, "MDS 3.0: Can This Release Be All Things to All People?" *Journal of the American Medical Directors Association* 13 (2012): 576–77.

18. http://www.cdc.gov/nchs/nnhs.htm. Accessed February 25, 2013.

19. Medicare.gov, "Nursing Home Compare," http://www.medicare.gov/NursingHomeCompare/search.aspx?bhcp=1. Accessed September 29, 2012.

20. Nicholas G. Castle, "What Is Nursing Home Quality and How Is It Measured?, Table 2," *The Gerontologist* 4 (2010): 426–42.

21. For details, see EPEC's website http://www.epec.net/

22. Atul Gawande, "Letting Go," *The New Yorker,* http://www.newyorker.com/reporting/2010/08/02/100802fa_fact_gawande?currentPage=all. Accessed September 29, 2012.

23. Joanne Lynn, "A Controlled Trial to Improve Care for Seriously Ill Hospitalized Patients: The Study to Understand Prognoses and Preferences for Outcomes and Risks of Treatments (SUPPORT)," *Journal of the American Medical Association* 20 (1995): 1591–98.

24. Manjula Kurella Tamura, Kenneth E. Covinsky, Glenn M. Chertow, Kristine Yaffe, C. Seth Landefeld, and Charles E. McCulloch, "Functional Status of Elderly Adults before and after Initiation of Dialysis," *New England Journal of Medicine* (2009); 361:1539-47 and Susan L. Mitchell, Joan M. Teno, Dan K. Kiely, Michele L. Shaffer, Richard N. Jones, Holly G. Prigerson, Ladislav Volicer, Jane L. Givens, and Mary Beth Hamel, "The Clinical Course of Advanced Dementia," *The New England Journal of Medicine* 361 (2009): 1529–47.

25. Family Health Care Decisions Act, New York State, Article 29-CC (2010).

26. Mitchell, et al., "The Clinical Course of Advanced Dementia," 1529–38.

27. "Interventions to Reduce Acute Care Transfers (INTERACT)," http://interact2.net/about.html. Accessed September 29, 2012.

28. "Medical Orders for Life-Sustaining Treatment," New York State Department of Health, http://www.health.ny.gov/professionals/patients/patient_rights/molst/. Accessed September 29, 2012.

29. The Center for the Study of Science & Religion, Columbia University Earth Institute, http://cssr.ei.columbia.edu/. Accessed September 29, 2012.

Chapter 12

The Evolving Role of Hospital Chaplains at the End of Life

Martha R. Jacobs and Linda S. Golding

*T*o be a hospital chaplain is to be a member of a countercultural band of highly trained, degreed, and certified itinerants—to be a stranger with a stranger, holding open the door to making meaning of life, of suffering, of illness, of disability, of death, and dying. Walking, standing, and sitting with people whose hearts and souls have been revealed to us but whose other identifying details we barely know. To be a chaplain surrounded by the soft underbelly exposed by illness, by misfortune, or by tragedy is to serve in a space created by grace. Is this different work than a generation ago? Will it be different a generation hence? Yes. Developments in science and medicine and changes in cultural practices in America's increasingly multicultural society make the journey through life, up to and including the end of life, different today from what it was when the profession first entered the hospital. To do a chaplain's work today is to hear those differences reflected in the patient, the family member, and the staff person, and to sensitively step into their reality, to hear how their body is responding and to find language to reflect it. The chaplain still acts as a mediator and facilitator, running errands, writing letters, offering prayers, and hearing joys, regrets, and confessions. The chaplain still takes a dying man's hand, holds a grief-stricken child, or sits with staff. But people and life grow more complex everyday and the chaplain must step into the challenge of blending spirit with professionalism, art with accountability. The chaplain needs to know more than religious requirements and creed.

WHERE THE CHAPLAIN IS ASKED TO WEAVE

"Spirituality and religion are an integral part of human culture, and as such, have the potential to shape individual lives and personalities."[1] So, today's chaplain navigates the redefinition of religious practice; the layered and interwoven paths of faith, spiritual connection, ethnic and language diversity, and sexual and gender fluidity; and the economic uncertainties that keep people struggling to hold onto what they believe is the safety net. What keeps a man, told he is at the end of his life, waking up in the morning? How does a woman continue to carry a baby whose twin has died *in utero?* Where does a mother draw strength to know that her daughter can survive the infections following a transplant? Or a father to understand that his son will not receive a transplant and will die? How does the husband know to reshape his hope for his wife from recovery to comfort care?

In the 21st century, the chaplain's work is being raised to a new level of visibility. Mainstream newspaper and magazine articles give the public a view of how people can summon their spiritual beings and help others reconnect to their own spiritual beings and resources in times of need. In the workplace, chaplains are being asked to strategize, assess, document, evaluate, and justify. How does a chaplain quantify the exchange of value that takes place in a hospital room? We are learning to communicate in language meaningful to medical and social work colleagues. How does a chaplain demonstrate value to the care team? We are learning to take our share of leadership as care teams shift from interdisciplinary to transdisciplinary, crossing boundaries to reach corners of need. We are doing spiritual assessments and approach patient rooms with an open heart, but with an awareness that we are part of the team and, therefore, require more than "the Spirit" to guide us. We are trained professionals who meet 29 competencies and fulfill several thousand hours of training before we become Board Certified Chaplains. We are the professionals in the field of chaplaincy care.

THE HISTORY OF HOSPITAL CHAPLAINCY

In order to understand where we are today, we need to go back to where we came from. In order to grasp how our roles have shifted from providing solely "religious" rites to having a voice and being looked to on the transdisciplinary team, we have to understand just how far we have come.

Initially, hospitals in America were charity institutions for the poor, gravely ill, and desperate and were defined by the social needs of those groups.[2] Many hospitals were founded by religious groups, where "moral as well as physical healing was part of many early hospital's orientations. Bibles were available, patients at some hospitals were required to attend religious services on Sundays and card-playing and other vices were forbidden."[3] By 1885 there were more than 150 Catholic hospitals in the United States; Jewish hospitals started to open in the 1850s as well. While they both met the needs of their particular religious constituency, they were open to everyone.[4] Nowadays we accept that a hospital may have a religious name, for example, St. Luke's, or Presbyterian, or St. Mary's, or Beth Israel, but the religious ties have become more and more tenuous.

In the late 1800s, when medicine was becoming a profession with clinical training and credentials, the "healers" became doctors and members of the clergy were confined to their houses of worship. Because hospitals became science based, "the role of clergy as health care providers—except at the deathbed—became an artifact, outside of hospitals run by religious orders."[5]

In 1926, a German-born evangelical pastor named Julius Varwig proposed that his church start a "hospital mission" in St. Louis's public institutions for the sick and poor. The church agreed; he accepted no funding for the position. "The church mission board's letter introducing Varwig to hospital officials recommended him 'to minister unto such of their sick and infirm who are without church affiliation and who may desire spiritual or other advice . . . with the sole intent of rendering a much needed service to suffering humanity.'"[6] "It is widely believed, but not documented that positions for religious leaders in all hospitals were seen as low status, and outpost assignments suitable for retired clergy and those who could not tolerate the rigors of parish ministry."[7]

Also around this same time, the writing of William James began to emerge as essential for those who would become involved as hospital chaplains. James's writing incorporated ideas about psychology and self-development and how they interfaced with religion, personality development, and pastoral care.[8] These new insights, combined with the Social Gospel movement, led to seminary students doing field work not in churches but in social service agencies. Episcopal priest, William Keller, spearheaded this movement, which coincided with a group of clergy and medical educators in Massachusetts bringing future ministers into hospitals for supervised training in caring for the sick. Their inspiration may have been William Osler, one of the founding professors of Johns Hopkins Hospital, who initiated, the now standard, residency program for future medical doctors to ensure that they would have direct patient contact as well as academic courses.

Richard Cabot, a prominent Harvard physician, wrote an essay in 1925 entitled "A Clinical Year for Theological Students" arguing that it was important for seminarians to have a year of clinical training.[9] Cabot collaborated with Anton Boisen, thought to be the father of Clinical Pastoral Education (CPE): an action-reflection-action method of learning designed to integrate content and process producing an intentional student-oriented learning experience that creates vital ministry formation. For example, a student visits with a patient who wants to talk about his coming death. The student deflects and, unaware of the deflection, shifts the conversation to sports or the weather. The action-reflection-action method helps the student review the visit with colleagues and supervisor and learn that he or she deflected the patient's desire to talk about death. With support from colleagues and supervisor, the student would then consider his or her own concerns and fears around dying and death. Then, the next time a patient introduces the topic of death, the student will be more aware of his or her own concerns and be more able to set them to one side in order to be fully present with the patient. Cabot believed in this firsthand study of human experience as a way to challenge seminarians to think theologically.

Anton Boisen called this work reading "the living human documents" and believed it was a necessary supplement to classroom training in the seminary experience.[10] While taking a class from Dr. William Lowe Bryan at Indiana University, Boisen learned that "at the peak of a human crisis there is a turning toward healing, toward reorganization, toward reconnection."[11] Boisen, over his time working at the Worchester Psychiatric Hospital, "developed the case study method as the written human document for theological reflection. Boisen developed a detailed guide that needed to be used in the process of gathering information about a person. The strength of this tool was its ability to help students learn how to reflect systematically about the human condition, both psychological and theological." That detailed guide, or case study, continues to be one of the foundational ways that professional chaplains are trained.

CASES IN THE LIVES OF TWO 21ST-CENTURY HOSPITAL CHAPLAINS

It is at that "peak of human crisis" that chaplains continue to work with patients and family members to help turn them toward healing, reorganization, and reconnection. The authors of this chapter have worked as hospital chaplains at a large metropolitan teaching hospital with 1,000 beds, several medium-sized urban hospitals with 500-700 beds, and a small community hospital with 300 beds. Like most hospital chaplains, we work daily as part of a transdisciplinary team including medical staff, social workers, physical therapists, occupational therapists, care coordinators, bioethicists, and hospital administrators to bring chaplaincy care to the practice of medicine to enhance the healing environment. Our role on the team has led us to participate in a variety of situations, a few of which are included below.

The case study method has helped chaplains to understand the human condition and be able to remain present with those who are struggling to recover from illness, or letting go when they are dying. In order to best show how the role of the chaplain has evolved, we are using here an abbreviated case study method. We present several cases that demonstrate how our role has evolved from the days of Julius Varwig to today's highly trained and informed chaplain. The cases are a collection of experiences from our work and that of our colleagues. They are particular and, at the same time, entirely general. For the sake of clarity, the chaplain's voice is reflected in first person.

CASE 1

Anna, 73 years old, had been admitted for a surgical intervention designed to prolong her life. The surgery itself had turned out to be more difficult than expected and the doctors did not expect Anna, now in a state of unconsciousness and in the ICU, to recover. Mercedes, 45 years old and the youngest of three children, was her mother's health-care proxy. Mercedes spoke Spanish and English fluently.

The ICU Charge Nurse paged me, the on-call chaplain, "The doctor has just told the family that the patient is not going to recover. They are not taking it well, especially her daughter, Mercedes. We would all appreciate your coming over." Mercedes sat with a few family members and a young doctor in the conference room on the unit. She burst into tears at my arrival, saying this must mean her mother really would not recover, really would die.

Mercedes began to wail in Spanish and in English as family members came and went, each asking her to "be calm, be strong." I sat a few feet away from the flow of family. When Mercedes began to stamp the floor with her feet, I moved to sit next to her. She grabbed my arm, repeating over and over "I cannot accept that my mother is dying. I will not accept it. She must live. I should die instead." She whimpered and clung to me. My verbal contribution had been a series of "hmmm's." After a while, Mercedes, the young doctor, and I were alone in the room.

I asked Mercedes to tell me about her mother—her character, how she spends her time, who she loves, and who loves her. She told me about her mother.

I suggested she and I go see her mother—talk to her, sing to her, play music for her. Mercedes stopped crying and stood up. Calmly and with purpose, she led the way to her mother's room. Other family members gathered outside the room, having heard that Mercedes was going to see Anna. Without hesitation, Mercedes walked to the head of her mother's bed. Anna appeared sturdy under the blankets amidst the array of plastic tubing. For some time, Mercedes spoke and sang to her mother in Spanish. She then asked the nurse for a pair of scissors. The nurse and I watched Mercedes cut two long, black locks of hair from her mother's head. She placed them on some paper to "wrap up for my sisters because they always wanted her hair." The sisters came into the room and Mercedes gave them the locks that curled together into a complete circle.

Mercedes looked at me, told me she now understood that her mother was going to die soon and she sat down in the chair next to the bed to wait. Some hours later, the Catholic priest was called to anoint Anna who died the next day.

Commentary

The chaplain invited the daughter to talk about her mother and to enter the space of her mother's reality. This created an opportunity for Mercedes to step away from her own position. As Mercedes engaged with Anna, in Anna's actual reality of approaching death, rather than in Mercedes' reality of desired ignorance, not being able to consider Anna's coming death, Mercedes was able to set aside her position of "I will not accept it. She must live. I should die instead." Mercedes was able to recall Anna the person and to consider in what ways, through which characteristics Mercedes represents her. Instead of telling Mercedes to face her mother's coming death, as the medical staff was doing, the chaplain modeled accepting the death. Instead of engaging Mercedes through religious beliefs or Scriptural quotes, the chaplain engaged her by modeling presence. Although no religious dialogue took place, the two shared a meaningful spiritual and ritual experience as Mercedes cut her mother's hair. Is it important for the chaplain to share thoughts about Delilah cutting Samson's hair or Matthew 10:30 "But the very hairs of your head are all numbered"? Surely not. This moment was sacred to Mercedes and perhaps represented a kind of passing on of Anna's strength (Samson) and God's awareness of the hairs on her head. As Anna was moving from life to death, the chaplain and the nurse were able to support and witness this ritual without needing to define it or make sense of it. Rather, the reflection came afterward.

CASE II

The patient, George, was Chinese, elderly and frail, and had sustained a devastating brain hemorrhage. His wife spoke only Mandarin. His English-speaking adult children tried their best to navigate between the culture of an American hospital and the culture of their Mandarin-speaking Buddhist parents. George died just around the morning shift change several days after his admission to the hospital. His children approached the Charge Nurse and Patient Care Director about their desire for the Buddhist ritual of an extended period of chanting following the death of a Buddhist. Their priest was on his way and the "extended period" would ideally be eight hours from the time he began. This would mean the body would remain in the single room for eight hours raising concerns about hospital and morgue procedures and bed needs. The unit staff sought guidance from Patient Services and also asked me as the unit's multifaith chaplain to act as a mediator and translator of meaning between the family and the hospital.

The family expressed their concern about overstepping their rights and the hospital expressed concern about being culturally insensitive. Neither wanted to make a direct demand or decision. By walking back and forth along the hallway of the unit and practicing patient and impartial mediating, listening, and reflecting skills, I was able to bring the two parties together to make arrangements that both could embrace. The family embarked on the eight-hour ritual with the understanding that the hospital would do everything it could to avoid the need for the room. In the event the room was required, the family would adjust and conclude their prayers appropriately.

The eight hours passed without incident. The family and priest expressed their gratitude, the staff expressed their pleasure at being able to support the family, and the hospital was able to demonstrate its own institutional ability to respond to the diversity of needs of its patients and families.

Commentary

The chaplain was part of the team helping to negotiate and integrate the spiritual and religious needs of the family with the practical needs and Joint Commission responsibilities of the hospital. "An independent, not-for-profit organization, The Joint Commission accredits and certifies more than 19,000 health-care organizations and programs in the United States. Joint Commission accreditation and certification is recognized nationwide as a symbol of quality that reflects an organization's commitment to meeting certain performance standards."[12] The importance of such certification to the reputation of a health-care institution explains the hospital's concern about adhering to recommended procedures after the patient's death. The chaplain's ability to negotiate among all these interests, in addition to caring for the chaplaincy needs of patients and families, shows the chaplain's versatility and professionalism.

How does this kind of intervention fit into the continuum of spiritual and religious care offered by a chaplain? Contemporary America is replete with cultural and religious diversity. It is virtually impossible to know enough about any situation to be authoritative. It is often the case that each member of the team contributes to forwarding a resolution to a question. In this case, the chaplain helped to normalize the family's request to the hospital staff and helped the hospital staff investigate and understand its available choices. The chaplain supported the family in its desire to access its specific spiritual and religious resources during this time of transition and supported the hospital in its desire to demonstrate its cultural competence.

CASE III

Jimmy was a painter of some renown. Diagnosed with a degenerative autoimmune disease that appears to be rapidly progressing, he and his wife had been to several hospitals during the last year in search of "the" treatment plan. By "the" treatment plan, Jimmy and his wife meant they were seeking a cure or at least a way to manage Jimmy's symptoms so that he would be able to function in his accustomed ways. Jimmy had several upcoming commissions but had difficulty speaking and seeing as well as holding and controlling his paintbrush. Marion, his wife of 40 years, who was also his business partner, took detailed notes of every medical encounter, and questioned every piece of information and medication. As the care providers rotated, the nature of Marion's involvement in the patient's care was noted: She pointed out discrepancies revealing what was noted as her anger and disbelief. The medical staff felt that her attitude was becoming a hindrance to good and appropriate care for Jimmy and intruded into the time needed to care for other patients.

I was called because the staff wanted extra support for this patient and his wife, as well as extra support for themselves. When I entered the room, both Jimmy and Marion were very welcoming. In the room was a sheaf of color photocopies of some of Jimmy's work, his biography, and a small stack of notebooks reflecting notes from the recent hospital stays. Marion quickly showed me the color photocopies and the biography, telling me about the search for the right treatment and making comments about the care providers. Marion led most of the conversation, interpreting for Jimmy when he spoke. We engaged around music and art, about how they were managing with the illness and prolonged hospital stays. Marion said, "We are doing fine," while Jimmy gave me a sideways thumb and a twisted face meaning "mediocre." When Jimmy asked for a notebook and pen, Marion was disparaging about my ability to read his handwriting, which was actually quite clear. Jimmy wrote down his concerns—"work to do," "can't look after myself," "what will tomorrow bring?" Marion laughed nervously, "Sweetheart, I'm here to help you." "Jimmy," I said, "what about your spirit? Do you follow a spiritual or religious path?" "Catholic," he wrote. "Are there aspects of your faith that are helping you right now?" "Nope," he wrote. He looked at me and we both laughed. Marion's voice had receded. "Is there something we can do together that would be helpful?" I asked. "Pray," Jimmy said in a croaky voice. "What shall we pray for?" "Mrp," he said. And then he wrote, "Hope."

Commentary

The staff had made clear to the chaplain and to others that both the patient and his wife were taking a lot of their time, were demanding and challenging. The multifaith chaplain is trained to hear and meet patients and families where they find themselves, and to reflect on the situation using theology and psychology. While this case could have a religious component, it is certain that through illness and hospitalization Jimmy and Marion were experiencing the loss of autonomy and identity, both individually and as a couple. The chaplain engaged with the couple in ways that reflected and reminded them of their everyday life when they were not dealing with illness or hospitals. The chaplain was able to wait until enough trust had been established to see if prayer was of interest and asked the patient to define the content of the prayer. The assistance provided was a combination of spiritual, religious, and humanistic support.

CASE IV

David had late-stage metastatic lung cancer. Although he had known for a couple of years that something was wrong, he did not pursue diagnosis. The previous summer, he was feeling so poorly he went to a doctor for tests. At a family gathering, he looked gaunt and ill but professed to feeling fine and not worried about the coming test results. The family talked with each other about how David looked but nobody felt able to approach him. David and his wife Barbara have two adult children: Joan, who is very closely tied to her dad, and RJ, whose complex behavioral diagnosis caused a major rupture in his life and the life of his parents.

When David was hospitalized after some months, following a series of treatments, the extended family was notified that he was ill and close to death. People traveled to visit him, to shake their heads about not knowing sooner, to offer support to Barbara and Joan. RJ was not around. Since David was at least nominally Catholic, a priest had come to visit him at the hospital to offer him communion and a healing anointing. The hospital stay was a bridge from life to dying to death, as it was clear that David was dying.

I visited the family just as the referral for hospice care had been made. David would be transferred to a residential hospice within the next several hours. Barbara, the health-care proxy, and Joan were panicky. Although they had agreed to the transfer, they still struggled with the reality of what hospice meant. They were coming to grips with the fact that David was not going to receive any more attempted curative treatment and that he was really going to die. Neither Joan nor Barbara wanted to visit the proposed hospice and did not want to use the word with David. "We have told him he is going to a really nice rehab place to get stronger," reported Joan. "We don't want him to think he is dying." Both Barbara and Joan were firm about not talking with David about death. After visiting with David, who was mostly nonresponsive, I sat with Joan and we talked about her dad and about what hospice could mean for the family.

To Joan, hospice meant her dad would be left to die in discomfort while she and her mother looked on helplessly. We looked at the hospice website, considered definitions of "palliative care," discussed that David likely knew his condition. I raised the possibility that, without the aggressive and invasive interventions that had proven ineffective and with adequate pain medications David might have some energy for conversation and listening to music, and more space for quality of life during his last days. Joan asked, "You mean hospice might give us a little more time together?"

David died a week later. Joan felt the gift of the week was inestimable. "We talked about everything, he helped me so much," she wrote me. "I never imagined hospice might provide the kind of time and space we had. More people should understand that."

Commentary

The chaplain was able to press gently on the family's sore spot and to trust that Joan would be able to withstand the discomfort. The press was not for the sake of pain or for the sake of relief of pain. Does the chaplain need to quote Job 5:18 "For he wounds, but he also binds up; he injures, but his hands also heal" or is it more appropriate for the chaplain to simply keep it in mind? What about the short passage from a 19th-century liturgical poem by a Moroccan rabbi: "Heal my pain faithful God, for you excel at the art of healing"?

CASE V

Isaac was born with a heart defect that put him on the list for a transplant. At age two, he received his transplant and was beginning to thrive. During a routine procedure, something happened and Isaac had a stroke. He ended up in the ICU, surrounded by Mom, Dad, and grandparents. Mom wanted prayer every day. She dictated a specific routine to the chaplain or to the Catholic priest each day, a routine that included touching Isaac while offering prayer. The Department of Pastoral Care received calls for a chaplain or a priest two or three times a day. Mom seemed to connect more to the presence of a representative of God rather than to God or prayer. One night, a nurse paged the on-call chaplain at 2 A.M. to say Mom was requesting prayer. Taking into account that both a chaplain and a priest had been to see Mom and Isaac during the day, I decided to speak with Mom on the phone to try to hear what had prompted her current concerns. Nothing had changed, she just felt like some prayerful company. We talked on the phone for almost an hour, during which time Mom repeated the circumstances and the worries she had told each of my colleagues. She also talked about the financial condition of the family and of her need for medication.

The next day, the department made a plan for providing support to Mom, Isaac, and the family so that the time spent with the family was appropriate to their needs as well as to the staffing in the department. A representative spoke with the Social Work Department to try to address some of the social and behavioral concerns raised. We detailed which chaplains, which priest, how often we would come by. We communicated the plan to the family and to the unit and all proceeded well until the relationship between Isaac's parents and grandparents began to fall apart. Mom was accusing Dad and the grandparents, her in-laws, of interfering with Isaac's care. She wanted them banned from visiting. Then Dad spoke about Mom's psychiatric condition and asked that she be banned from visiting. The family members were sneaking around, attempting to avoid one another.

A chaplain colleague sat with Mom one day and became curious about the seeming loss of perspective and boundaries: Mom lashed out at the nurses, accused Dad of causing the need for the transplant and she insisted on more specific behaviors and rituals for prayer. The chaplain brought the case social worker and the Charge Nurse into the room and Mom was eventually brought to the Psychiatric Emergency Room for evaluation. Mom expressed relief rather than the anger the staff and family had expected. She spent several weeks on the Psychiatric Unit, with daily, supervised visits with Isaac and family members.

As Mom was being released from the Psychiatric Unit, Isaac was stable enough for transfer to a physical rehabilitation facility.

Commentary

Because the medical staff and the patient's mother called regularly, the chaplains and priests believed their presence provided important support to the family. It seemed that they were able to offer the presence of God in ways that helped the family through the days and nights. Eventually, it became apparent that the religious need was not as pressing as being able to call for people and have them arrive. Mom could not exercise any control over Isaac's condition or over when a doctor or nurse would provide information or solace. She focused this understandable desire for control on requesting pastoral care. In time, the chaplains were able to set boundaries that reduced the pressure on the staff, on the Department of Pastoral Care, and even on the family. The chaplains could stand in for, and deliver, "God's grace," and they evaluated the situation using a range of nontheological measures.

CASE VI

Bert, 59, and Janey, 37, met in South Korea when he was taking a year to teach English. She was his student. They fell in love, married, moved back to his hometown in the United States and had a child, Amanda. Bert's father was Catholic, his mother Jewish. As an adult, Bert made the decision to convert to his father's religion. He had survived many illnesses over the last 15 years but this time he had been in an unconscious state in his local hospital for three months due to encephalitis. Janey was Bert's health-care proxy. She was Presbyterian. She was self-possessed and still. Amanda, 18, had attended 12 years of Catholic school. A senior, she was waiting to hear the results of her college applications. She was opinionated and angry. Bert's mom, Lydia, was 85 and had lived with Bert, Janey, and Amanda since her husband's death 10 years ago. She held no religious affiliation at this time, "I gave up on religion a long time ago." Janey reported that she and Lydia had argued from the day they met, principally about what each considers "best" for Bert in any given situation. Bert's sister lived in another part of the country and was in contact by telephone. Both Bert and Janey were successful professionals in demanding careers.

Janey moved Bert from the local hospital to a large, urban hospital seeking a fuller diagnosis and curative care and healing. The new medical team had run tests for weeks but was not able to find a cause that assisted them in resolving Bert's current condition. One day, the medical team called a family meeting to discuss goals of care and I was asked to attend. The team believed there was no curative plan to offer the patient; that it was time to begin to discuss comfort care. Prior to the evening meeting, I met with the family in Bert's room to get to know the family a bit and to explain my role as part of the team. I told them that I was there to be present for the family and for the medical team, to listen in order to be a spiritual advocate, a neutral witness to the conversation, and to offer nonmedical ears and support. Janey and Amanda were open and discussed some of their concerns. Lydia, Bert's mom, yelled at the unconscious man, "It's enough already. Wake up, Bert. Listen to your mother. Wake up!" and hit her head with her fists.

At the meeting, the doctor and the nurse practitioner began the conversation with wanting to discuss the option of limiting Bert's treatments. Janey was still while her daughter and her mother-in-law exploded with emotions and suggestions for additional tests and interventions. The team responded patiently and gently went over the details of Bert's condition once again. Janey asked, "Are you saying there is no hope?" I entered into the conversation to understand how Janey was defining hope in that moment, what she could tell us about her husband's possible wishes given his current medical condition. Together with the medical team and the family, we considered the changing nature of hope and Janey asked for 48 hours to make a decision about limiting the medical interventions. Again, daughter and mother-in-law exploded. They went to separate corners of the room. When the storm calmed, the medical team left and I stayed on.

At first we sat without talking. After a while Janey said, "I have been worried about this for a long time." "About what?" I asked. "That I would have to decide to stop medical interventions and accept that Bert will die. I brought him here to put off making that decision." "What are you hoping for now, this evening?" "That I have the courage to make the decision, that my daughter and his mother won't hate me, that Bert forgives me." "Forgives you for?" "We have had so much discord in our marriage. We have had so many differences to overcome and I have not really tried my hardest."

One evening, after making the decision to stop curative and diagnostic interventions and to head toward comfort care, Janey told me about some of the discord and differences in the marriage. She wept. She spoke about her inability to talk about her marriage or about Bert's current condition with her family in Korea, her friends, or her pastor. "I don't want to impose on them." As the tears subsided, Janey turned to me and said, "I have just understood why people talk with a pastor. I feel so much better having told you all this, even though I know it is too late to make it up with Bert." "It is not too late" I said. "You can talk with Bert. Touch him, hold his hand, tell him what you want to tell him. You can connect with him, the spirit of love and forgiveness is in the room with you both." She nodded and began.

Several days later, Janey told the team she was ready for Bert to be extubated. She knew this meant he would die. She said she felt that his soul had already left his body and that the medical care was being given to a body, a shell. Bert made his own decision and died of a cardiac arrest the day before the extubation. His wife, his daughter, and his mother were with him holding his hands.

Commentary

The body is a document the chaplain is taught to read. Janey was still, caught between Amanda's anger at her father, Lydia's anger with herself, and her own disappointment. She was immobilized until she found the language to release herself. Bert was trapped in a liminal space until Janey was able to relinquish her anger with him. Psalm 118:24 comes to mind "This is the day the Lord has made; let us rejoice and be glad in it." That is, today is the day to make amends, to speak the truth, to take a stand. Amanda was a whirlwind of energy as she came up with new ideas and opinions. Lydia was trying to experience a physical sensation of pain to make an unreal situation more real. But Janey, in her stillness, held the energy to make the decisions. As she released the tears, she released her defended position and she released Bert. Is this summary theological? Psychological? Magical thinking? Janey never wanted to pray with the chaplain but she wanted to talk. Janey reported she never felt God's presence in Bert's room but that she felt it with a stranger on the street who prayed with her. It is difficult to define exactly what the chaplain did to support the family as well as the team but it is clear that the interventions took hold.

CONCLUSION ABOUT THE EVOLVING ROLE OF CHAPLAINS

The 2012 Pew Forum on Religion & Public Life study on religious affiliation in America offers 15 major religious categories with which participants can define their religious identity. These categories contain dozens of denominations for further refining. According to this study of 35,556 participants, the category with the fourth largest number of respondents is Unaffiliated (16.1%), after Evangelical Protestant (26.3%), Catholic (23.9%), and Mainline Protestant (18.1%). Of the Unaffiliated, self-defined Atheists account for 1.6 percent and self-defined Agnostics for 2.4 percent. The remaining respondents, amounting to 12.1 percent, define themselves as "nothing in particular."[13] Looking at these numbers in a broader context, the Unaffiliated represent the largest non-Christian group, followed at some distance by Jews (1.7%), Buddhists (0.7%), and Muslims (0.6%).[14]

Wendy Cadge, in her book *Paging God,* quotes one chaplain, who in response to Wendy's question about how chaplaincy has changed, said "We see a patient or family whether or not they have a religious affiliation and work with them to access the resources which help them cope with the crisis. For some, this means traditional resources of prayer and ritual. For others, it means supportive conversation. . . . [or] teaching guided relaxation, or exploring options about their medical treatment."[15]

Dr. Cadge points out that, ". . . the meaning of the term *spiritual* shifted from describing aspects of people's experiences within specific religious traditions to describing how people find meaning in any part of their lives. Chaplains today see themselves as providing spiritual support not only when they pray with patients, as they would have in the past, but as they speak with them about pets, family members, favorite places, and anything else that provides meaning and purpose."[16]

Russell Dicks, a CPE-trained chaplain, in 1935, became the second such trained chaplain at Massachusetts General Hospital. Dicks also worked with Richard Cabot. In 1939, Russell Dicks delivered a lecture at the American Protestant Hospital Association entitled "The Work of the Chaplain in a General Hospital." In that lecture, Dicks defined the CPE-trained chaplain not as someone who conducts religious rituals, but as a person interested in patients' physical recoveries and their "spiritual growth." A chaplain "knows that in suffering and stress, people are either thrown back or else they gain confidence in the fundamental nature of things and it is the chaplain's hope to steady them in any way he can during such stress."[17]

Today, chaplains are moving beyond being on a "mission" from their affiliated place of worship. Today's chaplains bring an open, nonjudgmental presence to assist patients, family members, and staff as they work through living and dying and the life and death decisions that have to be made. Today's chaplains bridge the religio-spiritual and the cultural and socioeconomic spectra. They are trained in mediation, bioethics, and psychology. They understand medical issues and pain management, have a basic understanding of a range of religious traditions and rituals, and possess a keen sense of the hospitals' parameters and ethos. Hence they are referred to as providers of "chaplaincy care," a service more encompassing than is usually meant by spiritual or religious care.

As the human condition becomes more complex it is more challenging to find the path of simplicity of thought, emotion, and action that can support a patient, family, and staff during end of life. As chaplains we continue to grow, expanding our knowledge as we integrate more fully into transdisciplinary teams that care for patients across age, race, social class, sexual orientation, and religion. We support those for whom an understanding of spirituality includes the fullest expression of their humanity and those for whom the word spirituality has little or no meaning.

The evolving role of chaplains at the end of life includes the view that the journeys that are life and that are the passage from life through dying and death offer a chance to mark a person's existence. The chaplain can witness and reflect the connection between the human and the transcendent, can help a patient or family or staff member create and see the markers that define a person's existence. Individual chaplains are responsible for finding religious or spiritual meaning or God's presence for themselves but it is the chaplain's gift to keep open that very space for those experiencing loss or life-changing health-related issues.

NOTES

1. Lynne Ann DeSpelder and Albert Lee Strickland, *The Last Dance: Encountering Death and Dying* (New York: McGraw Hill, 2005), 60.

2. Wendy Cadge, *Paging God: Religion in the Halls of Medicine* (Chicago: The University of Chicago Press, 2012), 21.

3. Ibid., 21.

4. Ibid., 22.

5. Bioethics Forum, http://www.thehastingscenter.org/bioethicsforum/post.aspx?id=704. Accessed February 2, 2013.

6. Ibid.

7. Cadge, *Paging God*, 23.

8. Ibid.

9. Cadge, *Paging God*, 24–25.

10. http://www.acpe.edu/NewBoisen_bio.html. Accessed February 2, 2013.

11. Ibid.

12. http://www.jointcommission.org/about_us/about_the_joint_commission_main.aspx

13. http://religions.pewforum.org/affiliations. Accessed March 2, 2013.

14. Ibid.

15. Cadge, *Paging God*, 19.

16. Ibid., 20–21.

17. Ibid., 28.

Chapter 13

Before Their Time: The Need for Communication When They Die Young

Nathan Ionascu

T his chapter offers an overview of child and adolescent mortality in the United States. It reviews statistical data and describes some of the conditions that cause these premature deaths, as well as points to some important advances and remaining barriers to health and survival of our young. Infancy and adolescence are the age groups with the highest death rates among preadults. In addition to illnesses, teens and young adults face deadly threats from violence and accidents. To reduce the mortality rates from these causes also requires improved communication. We need to view adolescent deaths as a serious public health problem; and we need to better educate this age group about risk factors and the importance of changing certain behaviors. When a life-limiting condition has been diagnosed, whether in a neonatal infant or a teen, or at any age for that matter, it is essential to have good, clear communication among medical staff, patients, and their families, so that difficult treatment choices can be appropriately addressed. The chapter concludes with recommendations for improving the dying process and relieving the suffering, both physical and existential, of the children who have been diagnosed with terminal conditions, as well as their parents and siblings. Improving how all of us—society as a whole and, notably, the medical professionals and patient families—communicate must be a priority if the journey through life is to be as good as possible, even when the road is unexpectedly shortened.

MY FIRST EXPERIENCE WITH CHILD MORTALITY

As a young physician in Romania, fresh out of training at the University of Bucharest medical school hospitals, I was assigned by the government to be the physician for a village in the Carpathian mountains, in the north of the country. My first encounter with a dying child happened there, on a cold November night, when I was asked to come to a villager's house to see his sick child.

After a 45-minute walk uphill on country roads and across some private properties as shortcuts, the child's father, who had come with the request and was my guide, opened the door to his home. In a small room, about six by four feet, surrounding the bed in which lay a pale, sweaty, comatose child were the grandparents, three siblings, and the mother who was wiping the child's forehead with a moist cloth. On a windowsill by the child's headboard was a lighted candle. The air in the room was extremely stuffy and even I found it difficult to breathe. When everyone except the parents had left the room, I was able to examine the child, who was four years old, and determined that he had meningitis. He had been sick with a high fever, vomiting, and complaining of severe headaches and nausea for over a week.

The parents refused any treatment and definitely rejected hospitalization, saying they wanted their child to die at home, surrounded by his family, and that it was G-D's wish to take his soul to heaven. I was angry. I felt betrayed by the midwife, who in this remote rural area handled medical care for children as well as obstetrics, besides filling the role of nurse both for my patients and those seen by the general practitioner. She must have known of this sick child for quite a few days, and I was dismayed at the parents' decision. Two days later I was told that the child had died, and I had trouble understanding why I had been asked to make the house call so late in the course of his disease, and when no treatment was accepted.

A couple of weeks later I was invited for Sunday lunch at a friend's house. The husband was the village postmaster and his wife worked at the Village Hall, keeping the vital statistics among other records. As this child's death was still gnawing and bothering me for lack of understanding, I asked them about it. Sure enough they knew of the case, and told me that the midwife had suspected a serious infection and offered to call me, in order to arrange for an ambulance to take the child to the county hospital. However, the parents had firmly refused, saying that if it was G-D's will to take his soul, then so be it—the will of the Lord shall be done. As I mentioned previously, the community was high up in the mountains, and the only hospital was in the valley in the town where the county seat was located; it would have taken an ambulance about four to five hours to drive the tortuous road to pick him up, and another two-and-half hours to bring him down to the hospital. So when the child became comatose, the midwife advised them to call me promptly to see the child, as otherwise I might not sign the death certificate, and the priest would not allow the child to be buried without it. I had my answer: I had been called upon to enable the parents to follow the rituals of their faith, not to practice medicine. I understood then, that as a physician, there would be healing roles for me to perform that were not taught in medical school.

THE PROBLEMS AT HAND

While much has changed in the world of medicine since my first experience with a dying child, emotional and psychological issues similar to those I encountered continue to beleaguer the medical profession in the delicate cases of a child facing death. Graduates of American medical schools generally start out with the same disadvantage as I did: a lack of training in how to connect with patients and their families, beyond suggesting curative treatments. We need to develop good systems and practices, so that clear communications can occur among the parties involved; and we need to teach sensitivity on the part of the medical team to the family's cultural and religious traditions, so that suffering can be minimized for patients as well as their loved ones.

It is encouraging to see that attention to this problem is slowly growing. Medical schools are gradually adding courses—albeit mostly electives—that teach future physicians how to conduct conversations on difficult topics, how to empathize with their patients and offer support beyond medical interventions. Most American medical schools have also introduced courses on medical ethics, with lessons about "Death and Dying." In spite of these encouraging beginnings, we have a long way to go to improve the journey to the end in the 21st century, especially for the young who by statistical measures should not even be on this road yet for many decades.

Communication at the bedside of a dying child, and all it entails—cultural sensitivity, translating medical terminology into everyday language, making choices, setting goals, and drawing up treatment plans—is one of the two main areas addressed in this chapter. The other subject given highlight, deals with greater societal problems that cause premature death, in the absence of a disease, among adolescents.

A general and a statistical overview offers background material that shows why I am focusing on infants and adolescents in my discussion of pediatric death, although much of my general discussion is applicable to all age groups of children and, incidentally, to adult care as well. In concluding, I propose systemic changes that could improve how events with deadly outcomes are managed and controlled in the 21st century, so we can spare our children and their parents unnecessary agony.

NOT ALL CHILDREN HAVE THE SAME SURVIVAL ODDS

Child mortality has variables across several spectra. Although there have been large absolute reductions in the level of infant and child mortality rates over time as well as a reduction in the absolute levels of differences across socioeconomic groups, relative inequality among racial and socioeconomic groups did not diminished over the 20th century. By comparing child and infant mortality in the United States using data from several surveys across the 20th century, Michael R. Haines has uncovered indicators of inequality in the death rates based on the occupations of the parents, their level of education, family income, race, ethnicity, and residence, among other factors.[1] When we formulate intervention to improve the current situation, we need to pay special attention to the most vulnerable groups to assure that progress is achieved across the socioeconomic field.

Minor variations in reporting exist, but most statistics of neonatal, child, and adolescent mortality divide the deaths into the groups I use here: *Perinatal mortality* includes only deaths between fetal viability (22 weeks gestation) and the end of the seventh day after delivery; *neonatal mortality* only deaths within the first month (or 28 days) of life; *postneonatal* mortality only deaths after 28 days of life but before one year; *infant mortality* all deaths before the first birthday; *child mortality* all deaths from age 1 through 12, with a separate group—*under-five mortality*—for deaths between birth and the fifth birthday; and *adolescent mortality* includes deaths from 13 to 18 years of age.

The United States Center for Disease Control (CDC) reports mortality data in increments of five years, which means that teenagers are divided into the age groups of 10–14 and 15–19. An analysis of the data from the CDC shows that the leading three causes of death within the principal age groups in childhood and adolescence in 2010 were as follows: *Neonatal:* preterm delivery, asphyxia, and severe infections, such as sepsis and pneumonia; *infants:* developmental and genetic conditions present at birth, sudden infant death syndrome (SIDS), and all conditions associated with prematurity and low birth weight; *1—4 years:* accidents, and developmental and genetic conditions that were present at birth, and cancer; *5–14 years:* accidents, cancer, and homicide; *15–24 years:* accidents, homicide, and suicide.[2]

If we look at the death rate of these age groups we find that in 2010, the highest death rate among these groups was for infants: 614 per live births of 100,000. The rate of the remaining groups were in order of magnitude: ages 15–19, 49.4 per 100,000; ages 1–4, 26.5 per 100,000; ages 10–14, 14.3 per 100,000; and ages 5–9, 11.5 per 100,000.[3] In brief, infants have by far the highest risk of dying prematurely followed by adolescents.

Looking closer, at the underlying facts, we see that African American children are at a far higher risk than white children. While the fertility rate was higher for African American women than for white women through the 1980s, their infants' mortality rate was 50–60 percent higher than that of white infants. Then, between 1980 and 2000, the infant mortality rate for African American infants was double and triple that for white infants. Variables that are thought to influence the numbers for African Americans as compared with whites include sexual activity at a much younger age, more single parent (maternal) families, lack of medical insurance, poverty, and lack of contraceptive knowledge and adherence.[4]

ADVANCES IN CHILD SURVIVAL

Worldwide almost 9 million children under the age of five die each year, which means that a child dies every four seconds. But, this alarming rate is actually improving: between 1990 and 2010, a 35 percent decline in child mortality has been recorded.[5] Many factors combine to cause child mortality, but the greatest concern is undernutrition, which is responsible for half of all child deaths worldwide.

The reduction in infant mortality in the United States can be attributed to technological advances in the care of the pregnant women and their unborn babies. Child and adolescent mortality are influenced by a range of societal changes and developments in our culture. Social factors, such as reduced poverty and public health programs, installations of clean, potable water systems, and generally cleaner environments, better nutrition, vaccines, and antibiotics all played major roles in the reduction of child mortality. Advances in medical technology and pharmacology were, of course, also substantial factors.

As a result, in the past 50 years many childhood diseases have been eradicated, many others have greatly improved outcomes, and some chronic conditions are much better managed, enabling the patients to have extended useful and productive lives. Yet despite these advances, children still do die and there are some diseases or conditions for which we still do not have effective curative interventions, either short term or long term.

While it is not surprising that the fetal death ratio, along with neonatal and infant mortality rates all decreased by over 50 percent during the period 1950–1980 (with smaller incremental decreases to 1998), from 1940 onward the fetal death ratio is not uniform around the country. It has been consistently lower in Massachusetts than in the rest of the country. Likely contributing factors, in the 19th century, were the presence of the Harvard Medical School, established in 1782 and the opening of Boston's Children's Hospital in 1869; both helped to shape medicine and the care of children in the United States and beyond.

Among significant advances that sprang from these and other institutions, Dr. James Gamble developed a method for intravenous feeding of infants and children in 1922. His method has since saved the lives of countless children at risk of dying of dehydration from diarrheal diseases and continues to do so to this day. In 1938, Dr. Robert Gross successfully surgically corrected a congenital cardiovascular defect, thus starting the field of pediatric cardiac surgery.

In 1954, Dr. John Enders and colleagues were the recipients of the Nobel Prize for successfully culturing the polio virus, enabling the development of polio vaccines. This work, begun in 1949, led to the announcement by Dr. Thomas Francis in 1955 of the results of the field trials of Dr. Jonas Salk's polio vaccine: "The vaccine works. It is safe, effective and potent."[6] Whereas close to 58,000 Americans were stricken by polio in 1952, there were only 1,312 cases by 1961.[7] That was a year before Albert Sabin's oral vaccine went into wide use, after which cases of polio in the United States effectively fell to zero. Yet, despite these advances, there are still sporadic, small outbreaks of polio in the United States, most typically among Amish and ultraorthodox Jewish communities where children are not vaccinated for religious reasons. Larger outbreaks have occurred around the world, due to misinformation, anti-vaccine propaganda, or lies spread to stir up political fervor. As *Time* magazine reported in 2013, referring to the Taliban in Pakistan and Afghanistan: "All viruses fight back against their eradication. Polio is the only one with a propaganda wing and an armed militia on its side."[8]

An important development in the fight against child mortality was the first surgical correction in 1983 of Hypoplastic Left Heart Syndrome (HLHS), a defect in which an infant is born without a left ventricle—a condition incompatible with life. My first encounter with this condition was in 1969. I was on duty in the emergency department of a regional hospital in Maryland, when a pediatric colleague brought his nine-weeks-old baby. The baby had stopped breathing while feeding on a bottle of formula at home. The child had been delivered at full term, was the family's fourth child, and perfectly normal at birth with standard growth and developmental milestones. He was chubby with an adorable face and blue eyes. He had simply stopped breathing during the feeding, became limp, and had no detectable heartbeat on arrival to the emergency room. All our efforts to resuscitate the baby were fruitless, and I signed the diagnosis as "Dead on arrival (DOA)." The autopsy revealed that the baby had the congenital cardiac anomaly known as a Hypoplastic Left Ventricle or Hypoplastic Left Heart Syndrome (HLHS).

As I had never before encountered the condition, and knew nothing about it, I called the National Library of Medicine in Bethesda, Maryland, and went there to do a computer search. The computers in those days, late 1960s, were in two large rooms, enormous metal cabinets, covering the long walls from floor to ceiling. A computer savvy librarian helped me and I found only about eight cases described in the world literature, none from the United States. The condition was congenital, no other family members had it, and it was always fatal, usually shortly after birth.

In 1987, a colleague was faced with another case of HLHS, which he related to me: Dr. Kevin McCreary said he was busy seeing patients in his office when the nurse handed him the phone with the words: "It's the nursery and they have an emergency." The nurse at the other end of the line told him that a newborn, who was going to be his patient, appeared quite sick and had a very rapid heartbeat and poor pulses in her extremities, and she asked him to come over promptly.

Once in the newborn nursery, after having examined the newborn, Dr. Mc-Creary realized that the baby had a major cardiac problem, as the chest and face appeared purple while the lower part of the body and the extremities were pale and limp. So he called the transport team from the Neonatal Intensive Care Unit (NICU) of a major tertiary care teaching medical center to come and transfer the baby to its unit. He also proceeded to place an umbilical catheter in order to be able to give the baby fluids, glucose, and eventually medication. Once the transport/transfer team arrived, they took over. The team had its own specially equipped ambulance with bassinets for premature and term newborns, oxygen, a neonatology fellow, an intensive care nurse, and a respiratory therapist. The newborn's father decided to follow the ambulance to the medical center.

After finishing his workday, Dr. McCreary called the medical center's NICU to find out how the transferred newborn was doing. He spoke to the neonatology fellow and requested to be called as soon as the cardiac ultrasound was done and they had a diagnosis for the newborn's condition. Around 4 A.M. he received the long-awaited phone call, and to his dismay was told that the baby had a HLHS.

Early the next morning Dr. McCreary went to see the baby's mother. She was extremely anxious, not knowing what was so wrong that her baby had to be transferred hours after birth. Dr. McCreary told her that her baby had a very serious congenital heart malformation and that her newborn's life was in G-D's hands, as she might not live a normal life, like her two-year-old sister.

Meanwhile, unbeknown to Dr. McCreary, at the medical center, a pediatric neonatology fellow had told the father that his baby would not survive the condition, but that they would transfer the baby to another major medical center's NICU in Philadelphia, where a nationally renowned pediatric cardiac surgeon does heart transplants and could give the baby a new heart. However, when they called Children's Hospital of Philadelphia, the famous surgeon was traveling on a speaking engagement and would not be back for 18 days. So the decision was made to transfer the baby to Boston Children's Hospital, where heart transplants were also done. The transport team then drove the baby and her father to a small airport and boarded a medevac plane to Boston. During the flight the baby developed bilateral pneumothoraces (a condition in which air gathers in the pleural sacs and effectively "blows out"—compresses the lungs), stopped breathing, and despite all resuscitative efforts, died. She was declared dead on arrival at Children's Hospital Emergency Department in Boston.

In the 1980s prenatal ultrasound became widespread, enabling physicians as well as the future parents to follow the fetal development inside the womb, and making possible early detection of congenital malformations. Subsequently, the first successful fetal repair of HLHS was performed in a 19-week-old fetus at Boston Children's Hospital in 2001.

DIFFICULT CONSEQUENCES OF ADVANCES IN TECHNOLOGY

A study of infant and child mortality with congenital heart defects (CHD) in England and Wales between 1959 and 2009 revealed that absolute numbers of CHD fell from 1,460 in 1959 to 154 in 2009. While in the five-year period between 1959 and 1963, 60 percent of all deaths due to CHD were among infants, that is children under one year of age, only 22 percent were in that category by 2004–2008. "Male babies continued to have higher death rates. Declining mortality across all age groups was observed for birth cohorts originating after 1989."[9] This substantial decrease in mortality for children with CHD resulted from technological advances in pediatric cardiac surgery, intensive care units, and medical support. While initially mortality in later childhood rose as infant deaths decreased, children born in the last 20 years experienced lower mortality throughout childhood.[10] It can be assumed that a similar decrease in mortality also occurred in the United States.

Advances in medical science and technology, the creation of NICUs in many medical centers, and the improved skills of neonatologists and pediatric surgeons have led to the survival and resuscitation of premature babies who might otherwise not have been viable. Interventions such as continuous positive airway pressure (CPAP), tracheostomies (ventilator support), gastrostomies (tube feeding), intravenous therapies (IVs), and surfactants are being used to save lives. All this sounds like good news but we need to look at the bigger picture.

Although giant steps have taken place in medical technology, pharmacology, and clinical developments since the 1970s, these advances have outpaced pediatricians' development of the skills needed to deal with life-limiting conditions and premature death, since all terminal conditions cannot be eradicated. Comforting a parent or a child faced with a life-limiting condition—families who are understandably upset, anxious, and trying to understand what has happened and why—should not lead to giving them false hopes. The odds against securing a newborn's heart, of it being compatible with this baby's immune system, and of being able to transplant it within 24–48 hours if the first two conditions were met, are astronomical.

INFANT MORTALITY

The World Health Organization (WHO) defines a live birth as any born human being who demonstrates independent signs of life, *including breathing, voluntary muscle movement, or heartbeat,* as long as they have reached 24 weeks gestation and at least 500 grams. Many countries, however, including certain European states and Japan, only count as live births cases where an infant breathes at birth, which makes their reported infant mortality rate (IMR) numbers somewhat lower, and raises their rates of perinatal mortality. In some countries, protocols that were established during the Soviet era define live births somewhat differently than WHO does. One difference is that a pregnancy ending at a gestational age of less than 28 weeks (or the newborn weighing less than 1,000 grams or measuring less than 35 centimeters in length) is considered premature and is classified as nonviable—even if signs of life are present at the time of delivery—unless the child survives for seven days. Only if the child survives the early neonatal period is he or she classified as a live birth.

A second difference concerns full-term births, that is, pregnancy ending at a gestation age of 28 weeks or more. The event is classified as a live birth if the child breathes at the time of delivery, but is considered a stillbirth if breathing is not evident at delivery, even though other signs of life are present. France, the Czech Republic, Ireland, the Netherlands, and Poland do not report all live births of babies under 500 grams and/or 22 weeks of gestation. Thus, some events classified as miscarriages or stillbirths in the registration system would be classified as live births and infant deaths according to the WHO definitions. Infants born at 22–23 weeks of gestation have 90 percent mortality rate. The first week of life is the riskiest week for newborns.

An estimated 2 million babies die within their first 24 hours each year worldwide. American babies are three times more likely to die in their first month of life than children born in Japan, and newborn mortality is 2.5 times higher in the United States than in Finland, Iceland, or Norway. This represents a difficult issue to address, as it will require the concerted efforts of health educators in schools, public health funded interventions in all communities, and access to early prenatal care—especially among those women with lower incomes and education levels.

A new dangerous trend in the United States is the skyrocketing abuse of prescription drugs, that is, painkillers, among young pregnant women, who are passing on the addiction to their newborn babies. University of Michigan research revealed that the number of infants born addicted to opiates, especially prescription Oxycontin and Vicodin, tripled from 2000 to 2009 to over 13,500 per year.[11] These babies, born to opiate-addicted mothers, are often premature and underweight, and suffer painful and dangerous withdrawal symptoms, such as seizures, breathing problems, and feeding difficulties. They also risk overdosing on the morphine and methadone needed to treat their addiction and wean them from the more dangerous opiates. This process is not only expensive, but also translates into weeks of treatment in NICUs. Recent data show that about 16 percent of pregnant teenagers and almost 8 percent of pregnant young women 18 to 25 years old use illicit narcotic drugs. This is really a public health emergency.[12]

SUGGESTED CHILD MORTALITY SOLUTIONS

Simple interventions can significantly reduce child mortality around the world. Foremost among them are improving the nutritional status of children, improving maternal health, reducing the impact of HIV, malaria, and other serious diseases, and providing safe water and sanitation. In the United States, preadult mortality rates can also be improved by addressing some of these areas, but most urgent would be to manage the death rate for the very youngest babies. Babies born before term have become the greatest concern in our country. They need more intensive care at birth and thereafter, tend to need more remedial medical, physical, psychological, and developmental therapies, and sometimes, after a stormy period—die way too soon. Not to mention the added stress and high expense outlays that their care requires.

PRETERM BABIES

Advancements in medicine and technology have made it possible for premature and seriously ill babies to live right through the risk period and eventually lead normal lives. Yet this same technology, in the hands of well-intentioned neonatologists working in state of the art NICUs, has prolonged the death of some premature infants and the suffering of their parents, as well as their extended families. As we move further into the 21st century and increase our arsenal of possible interventions, it will be just as important that pediatricians acquire the ability to recognize those therapies that may be harmful, that is, prolong the dying process, or therapies that lead families to have false hope of cure. Focusing on interventions that prolong suffering when the outcome is inevitable can take away energy that may be needed for palliative treatments and preparing for the last days of life.

The high percentage of preterm babies is the main cause of the high IMR in the United States. This country "does a good job of saving babies when they are born preterm," Marian F. MacDorman, PhD, said, "The problem we have is prevention, preventing that preterm birth, and that's where we are in trouble." The climate of medical management has changed over the past 15–20 years in the United States. Back in the day, if a woman had high blood pressure, they might put her in the hospital and wait until the baby is more mature. Physicians today seem more likely to want to deliver the baby early.[13] Sometimes preterm deliveries are done electively to prevent further complications, maternal or fetal, but they are not always successful.

In most high-risk pregnancies when the risk of premature delivery is imminent, the obstetrician, neonatologist, parents, and a social worker will weigh the risks of an early delivery and decide whether to pursue resuscitation at the time of birth for a baby under 1,000 grams or 24 weeks gestation. Once the decision is made the newborn will receive the whole resuscitative effort and be reevaluated within the week. Some of these babies survive with major disabilities, poor quality of life, and eventual shortened life spans, causing an enormous hardship not just on their families but also on society at large. During the agonizing days and weeks following their births, as all efforts and attention are concentrated on their survival, their siblings are often neglected, the parents are overstressed, and the family suffers financial strain.

A GOOD EXAMPLE OF A SOLUTION IN NEONATAL CARE

Since the beginning of the 21st century, some attempts are made to implement palliative care in the NICU for babies with a poor prognosis. In a study of parental perspectives on the withdrawal of artificial nutrition and hydration (WANH) in a tertiary-level NICU, one theme related by the parents of the babies involved in WANH "included the virtues of good communication, the importance of relationship building, admitting the uncertainty of prognoses, and the ways of sharing information. The reason for WANH was predicted poor outcome due to severe neurological injury or disease."[14] Positive factors were the ability of the parents to spend quality time with their infants, to create tangible memories, and the professional qualities and virtues of the caregivers. Negative factors were ascribed to breakdowns in the continuity and constancy of the palliative care team: "The team is constantly changing, so few people actually know the patient and can recognize how the baby is doing/changing over time. Consistency of care and continuity will provide parents with increased peace of mind and help reduce overall stress and anxiety."[15]

We must therefore focus on improving communication, both horizontally within families and vertically between families and physicians. There is an ongoing need to develop more extensive professional education for all those involved in end-of-life care, in both ethical and legal fields, as well as to improve communication skills among staff working with pediatric patients and their families. "Families and surrogates need to have a framework within which information has meaning and validates their relationship with the patient. This framework should also validate the surrogate's sense of themselves as loving, caring, responsible people faced with life-and-death decisions in the midst of shock, loss, possibly guilt, and grief. Surrogacy is both a cognitive and an affective task."[16]

All newborns with life-threatening conditions should be resuscitated and treated post delivery. Each baby's condition and progress should also be reassessed after a week *post partum* or sooner, and frequently thereafter, to determine if further interventions and continuing treatment will be needed for survival. At no time should the neonatologist and the parents find themselves in adversarial positions, rather they should be partners working toward achieving the best outcome and least suffering for that particular infant.

For instance, we treated a term newborn with anencephaly: lack of a brain—markedly reduced—and a thin layer of white cerebral tissue surrounding a cystic mass that occupied most of the cranial cavity. The baby looked otherwise perfectly normal, with a cherubic face. His young parents concentrated on feeding and nurturing him, despite the dismal prognosis. When the baby's sucking reflex diminished, the parents felt desperate as the baby started losing weight. A gastrostomy was performed and the baby was started on tube feedings, which the mother religiously administered. The main purpose of the gastrostomy, besides feeding the baby, was to alleviate the parents' guilt feelings and give them time to adjust to their baby's premature and untimely death. After a few bouts of aspiration pneumonia and subsequent hospitalizations, the baby stopped gaining any weight, the tube feedings became harder to accomplish, and eventually the baby died. The tube feedings through the gastrostomy enhanced the parents' feeling of self-worth, assured them that they did *everything* for their baby, and eased their deep grief and the subsequent bereavement.

"With dying children and their families, vulnerability is at a peak for emotional and cultural reasons."[17] In the field of pediatric palliative care and hospice, where the parents as surrogate decision makers have special authority—there is concern "about the capacity of these 'natural' and customarily recognized surrogates to fulfill the obligations of their role, given circumstances of emotional distress, family tensions and conflict, the concurrent needs and interests of other children in the family, and the like."[18]

ADOLESCENT MORTALITY

"Adolescence is, by definition, a period of profound transition from the near complete dependence of childhood to the self-determination of adulthood. As such, it is a period defined by emerging cognitive and problem-solving abilities, evolving emotional maturity, and growing psychosocial skills. . . . mastery of these skills is a gradual and step-wise process that begins long before the age of 18, and continues well into the third decade of life, or beyond. . . . Despite medical progress, many adolescents will face serious medical challenges; an estimated 3,000 will die annually as the result of chronic illnesses, including cancer, cardiovascular diseases (e.g., congenital heart disease), pulmonary diseases (e.g., cystic fibrosis), AIDS, renal disease, metabolic disorders, neurologic diseases (e.g., muscular dystrophy or spinal muscular atrophy), and congenital anomalies."[19]

Michael Resnick of the University of Minnesota said that a study of adolescent deaths in 50 countries found the majority of deaths in young people was through incidents such as car accidents or reckless behavior—and that violence and suicide have also become key causes of death in this group. "The profound health and social changes that have accompanied economic development and urbanization are particularly toxic for young people in both high-income and low-income settings."[20]

Accidents and Violent Death

A study in 2009 by WHO found that 40 percent of adolescent deaths were due to injuries and violence. Accidents are, by far, the leading cause of death among children and adolescents.[21]

In the 1950s, mortality in the 1–4 age group far exceeded that of all other age groups in all regions studied. But in the 50 years up to 2004, death rates in children aged 1–9 fell by 80 to 93 percent, mostly due to reductions in deaths from infectious disease. In contrast, declines in death rates in those aged 15–24 years were only about half that in the younger children, largely because of increases in injury-related deaths, particularly in young men.[22]

By the start of the 21st century, injuries—from incidents such as car crashes and street or gang violence—were responsible for 70–75 percent of all deaths in young men aged 10–24 in all the regions studied. By 2004, suicide and violence were responsible for between a quarter and a third of deaths in young men aged 10–24 years, and death rates in young men aged 15–24 are now two to three times higher than in boys aged 1–4.[23]

In 2007, 13,299 adolescents aged 15–19 years died of various causes, representing a rate of 61.9 per 100,000. Unintentional injury remains the leading cause of death among this age group, accounting for nearly half of all deaths among adolescents. The mortality rate for unintentional injury was 30.3 per 100,000. Homicide was the second leading cause of death, with a rate of 10.4 per 100,000, followed by suicide, with a rate of 6.9 per 100,000. The mortality rate of males in this age group was notably higher than that of females (86.9 versus 35.7 per 100,000, respectively). Racial and ethnic disparities also exist, with non-Hispanic black adolescents experiencing a mortality rate of 85.7 per 100,000, compared to rates of 58.0 and 57.9 per 100,000 among non-Hispanic whites and Hispanics, respectively. (This is all data from 2007.)[24]

Motor vehicle traffic was the leading cause of unintentional injury death among adolescents in 2007. Nearly half of deaths due to motor vehicle accidents occurred among vehicle occupants, while in 40 percent of the deaths the situation was not specified; a small percentage of motor vehicle deaths occurred among motorcyclists, pedestrians, and bicyclists.[25]

The second leading cause of unintentional injury death among adolescents was poisoning, followed by drowning, other land transport (such as all-terrain vehicle crashes), and fires or burns. However, when intentional injuries such as homicide and suicide are included, death by firearms becomes the second leading cause of injurious death. Nearly three-quarters (71%) of firearm deaths were homicides, while 23 percent were suicides; the remainder was unintentional, unknown, or due to legal intervention. Firearms accounted for 85 percent of homicide deaths and 43 percent of suicide deaths; suffocation, such as hanging, was the second leading cause of suicide death, accounting for another 42 percent.[26]

"Every year, more than 30,000 people, the equivalent of ten times the victims of 9/11, die of gunshot wounds; 55% of these are suicides. Another 60,000 are wounded, requiring long-term and expensive treatments, and rehabilitation. . . . is it 'too late' for any law to stop the slaughter in a nation with 300 million guns?"[27]

Guns kill one person every 20 minutes in the United States, and yet they are almost free of federal restrictions. To drive a car however, one must pass written and driving tests, wear seat belts, and follow safety laws.

Homicide

Homicide is one of the most disturbing causes of death among children and adolescents. Sociologists feel that the increase of gangs, teenage homicide, teenage suicide, teenage pregnancy, school dropout, and other problems are a reflection of a rapidly changing society and family structure. Homicide is a complex issue, which does not have a simple remedy.

Suicide

Overall teenage suicide rates for all races in the 1990s were higher than those in the 1980s. It is important to watch teens for signs of *stress, depression, and suicidal behavior.* Two-way communication between the troubled adolescent and parents or persons of trust is extremely important in preventing adolescent suicide. Four out of five people between the ages of 9 and 21 at least temporarily show some form of mental illness, including depression, anxiety, Obsessive-Compulsive Disorder, and addiction, according to a Duke University study of 1,420 children over 12 years of age.[28] We have to remove the stigma from mental disorders, said study coauthor E. Jane Costello. "We shouldn't be surprised that the brain has problems, just like the rest of the body."[29]

We also have to consider the homeless youth, those who sleep on the streets and resort to the street economy to stay alive: prostitution, drug dealing, robbery, and so on. Precise numbers about this population are unavailable, but according to a study done by the United States Department of Health and Human Services in 1986, as many as 2 million youth in the United States were homeless and as many as 200,000 lived as permanent residents of the streets at that time.[30]

Most of them have been exposed to neglect, abuse, malnutrition, venereal diseases, and addictive drugs, including alcohol and other substances. They all experience to varying degrees tremendous loss: parental divorce, death of family members and friends, and the devastation of physical and sexual abuse. All these events are known to often lead to chronic depression. Many of these young men and women have a poor body image that undermines their self-esteem; for most of them their education has been disrupted or is unavailable. The normal struggles and confusions of adolescence are exacerbated and "acting out" behavior is common. They live a stressful life of pain and hardships, and have a lower life expectancy, many succumbing to street gangs, stray bullets, or homicides.[31]

Illegal drugs and guns are readily available on the streets and in our neighborhoods. Young people get to drive cars at a young age, not yet having acquired the maturity to appreciate that a car handled improperly can lead to death. Street gangs have taken over some city areas, and more young people are homeless and trying to survive in the street economy and environment.[32]

ADOLESCENTS WITH LIFE-LIMITING DISEASE

Children with serious heart disease, incurable cancers, and other life-limiting conditions do not dominate the mortality statistics, but thousands of them die every year in the United States. Their agonizing long-term illnesses present problems of a very special kind. Because they are under 18 years of age, their parents—not they—are the decision makers when it comes to treatment choices. This can create excruciating situations in a family.

FINDING COMMON GROUND AND CONTROLLING THE BALANCE ACT

There has been a major shift in how our contemporary culture and society views and addresses death and dying in children and adolescents. The premature—for it is most often premature and mostly unexpected—death of a child or adolescent deeply affects the immediate and extended families, their friends, classmates, even the members of the caring medical team, and often their teachers. This is reinforced by the commonly held view that a parent is not supposed to survive a young child: we have in every language a name for a child who loses a parent, she or he is an orphan; someone who loses a spouse is a widow or widower; but there is no word in any language for someone who has lost a child.

The tragedy of a child's death was always true. However, two developments in late 20th and early 21st centuries have unsettled previous patterns: in the case of a child patient (1) the parents are brought into the decision-making process to a much greater degree than ever before and (2) medical advances have produced complex interventions that make possible extended survival. I will look briefly at these relatively new aspects of pediatric and adolescent care here and the consequences they have.

The almighty doctor authority no longer rules. Together at the bedside of a child with a life-limiting diagnosis, the parents—or the child's guardians—and the physicians who care for these young patients oftentimes perceive and express different realities. The language used by the physicians may be clear to someone who is medically trained but confusing to parents or misunderstood by them; obtuse language may also be used by the doctor, more or less deliberately, to hide a dire prognosis that he or she does not want to convey. Cultural and religious practices also participate in constructing different context for a discussion about dying. In general, religion plays a less prescriptive role in our society than it once did, and parents may start questioning why a compassionate and forgiving G-D will allow their child to die, adding complex metaphysical content to an already bewildering conversation.

Palliative care that provides physical, psychological, social, and spiritual care to these families is often the solution that provides the best care for both the child and his or her parents. However, the palliative care team is typically brought in too late in the course of the disease process, or not at all. Often the intervention is delayed because the physician is fearful of suggesting something that might sound to the parents like "giving up." The term palliative care has, in spite of the best efforts of those in the field, come to be viewed—and be presented by some sectors of the media—in the negative light of surrender. As a result, the lay public, as well as many medical professionals, have many misgivings about, and a poor understanding of, how palliative care works and how it can improve the quality of life for youngsters with life-limiting diagnosis, as well as for those around them.

Even those physicians and parents who do understand the concept of palliation and the role it can play—participate in a balancing act, akin to the necessary balancing act between the *Yang* and the *Ying* in traditional Chinese medicine. Most parents will insist on having everything medically possible done for their sick child, while bemoaning the suffering that is being inflicted and trying to reassure themselves that it will be temporary and well worthwhile in view of the child's survival and hoped for cure. There is the dedication and all too often the days and nights spend at the sick child's bedside, while being aware that the siblings are being neglected or left with relatives to fend for themselves. There is also the desire and utmost dedication of the treating physicians and medical staff to overcome the disease and defeat death, while fully aware of the suffering the therapy causes to their young patients. Finally, into this precarious balancing act, also enters the previously mentioned reluctance, on the part of the medical staff, to tell the parents the full truth about a dire prognosis, while being aware that they are not following either the Hippocratic Oath or ethical guidelines.

I will add one more note to my previous story about my friend Dr. McCreary who was so engaged in the life of the baby with HLHS. Over the next few days following the baby's death, Dr. McCreary' used his best efforts and skills to persuade the parents to bring the baby's body back from Boston for a Christian funeral in their church, as the Boston hospital had offered to take care of their baby daughter's burial and the parents were very distraught about what to do. This behavior on the part of Dr. McCreary demonstrates how the role of the physician who travels with us on the journey to the end has changed in many ways since the late 1980s. At that time, Dr. McCreary saw it as his duty to oversee, what he perceived as the best way for the entire family to heal after the infant's death. In the second decade of the 21st century, this task may have been assumed by a social worker or chaplain, and a physician who thus stepped into the family's personal life would possibly be accused of meddling.

While a lot of things have changed for the better, our society today is more fragmented. Doctors are more specialized and only rarely look to solve issues beyond their professional expertise; religious leaders play a lesser role in guiding their flock; and extended families are dispersed—meaning that new mothers do not have available the support and wisdom of their own mothers. This in turn has led to the need of developing social services, such as specific psychological support and bereavement groups for parents, siblings, and schoolmates of the dying or deceased children. This is largely for the good, but I also advocate here that attending physicians be given time and professional space to develop a trusting relationship with their patients, an atmosphere in which a careful plan and goals of care can be drawn up after in-depth conversations about values, choices, and personal circumstances.

Too seldom are the goals of care for any individual child or adolescent patient included in a comprehensive discussion about a life-limiting illness, or accident, that might lead to end of life. Goals of care include clarifying the benefits and burdens of any treatment recommendation, or therapeutic intervention. Individualized medical decisions should be made by the medical team members, who know the patient. The team should work out the plan together with the patient, if he or she is mature enough to understand the treatment's consequences, as well as with the family, who knows best the patient's values and goals. Such a shared decision-making process would analyze the benefits and burdens of each therapeutic option in light of the patient's prognosis, values, and religious and ethnic background, in order to establish the goals of care. A thorough conversation would evaluate if a specific intervention will provide the benefit of prolonging the child's quality of life without suffering, or be a burden by prolonging the child's dying process. Any discussion about the goals of care should include options for end-of-life care and the relief of pain, all other symptoms, and suffering, through the provision of palliative care provided under the hospice umbrella.

"End-of-Life care for children is not clinically straightforward, and the ethical challenges it poses for society and for health care professionals are complex and difficult. Relating to dying children with justice, respect, and compassion is not simply a case of ethical conduct toward human beings in general . . . but should consider the best interests of the patients, other children in the family, the extended family, as well as the members of the medical team."[33]

CONCLUSION

To summarize, "over the past 150 years life expectancy has doubled, increasing from 38.3 years in 1850 to 76.7 years in 1998. Childhood mortality greatly affects life expectancy, which was low in the mid-1800s, in large part because infants and children's mortality rates were so high. Today the infant mortality rate is under one percent in the United States. Factors behind the growing longevity include the acceptance of the germ theory of disease, programs of public health and personal hygiene, better medical technology, better diets, education, higher incomes, availability of more drugs and vaccines, and the emergence of health insurance."[34]

Giant steps have been made in fighting disease, especially infectious diseases, in repairing joints and bones, opening up clogged blood vessels, enabling amputees to walk again, and more. We are benefiting today from medical–surgical advances and innovations that were unheard or undreamed of 50 years ago. Yet human nature has not changed that much, people continue to cause harm to themselves: smoking, food and drug addictions, assaulting, murdering, and maiming others.

"In the past 40 years or so, life near the end of life has been invaded and colonized by hard medical technologies. Their benefit in prolonging life can be great, but their destructive potential is alarming. They can destroy the delicate social ecology of families and the tissue of meaning that dying children, their parents, and families need in order to get a grip on the terrible thing that has befallen them."[35]

"When it was technologically impotent, medicine (together with religion) presided over social rituals and cultural meaning during the dying process. Relationships and identities were repaired and renewed—with family and friends at hand, with an opportunity to reconcile with those estranged, to forgive and to ask forgiveness. Today, medicine and medical treatment decisions set up a dynamic that makes that ecology unstable at best, impossible at worst."[36]

While the public health push to curb cigarette smoking has been successful to a degree, automatic weapons of mass destruction with magazines holding 10 to 100 bullets are widely available, even though they too represent a major public health hazard. While there is better sanitation, clean water, many more pharmaceutical products, and laws to protect the environment, a lot still needs to be done. New technologies, such as smartphones and cellular tablets, are now used by teenagers and young people while driving, causing distraction and often leading to accidents and loss of life not just of the drivers but also their passengers and drivers in other cars.

The learning curve on how to communicate with patients, how to relieve pain and suffering—be it physical, existential, or psychological—has not kept up with the tremendous advances in medical technology and procedures. The development of palliative care and hospice, especially for children, lags behind that for adults, and they are being underutilized. There is a great need for physicians to become familiar with the benefits that a palliative care multidisciplinary team can offer, the advantages of having specially trained physicians and nurses in pain and symptoms management, and how they improve the quality of life for their patients with life-limiting conditions.

Medical care of newborns and infants is often complicated by prognostic uncertainty. Palliative care physicians have to balance the dual duties of telling the truth and not abandoning hope. To achieve this it is important to ascertain and clarify from the beginning the family values and ethnic, religious, and social backgrounds. In establishing goals of care, the team should focus on clarifying the goals in a culturally sensitive, family-centered manner, enabling the parents and baby's siblings of "living in hope." Patients, depending on their developmental stage, as well as their families experience the tension between hoping for a cure and living in hope. When members of the professional team are not sensitive and phrase the truth bluntly by saying "there is no chance for a cure" or "what you are asking is futile," it worsens communication and leads to suspicion and distrust. Such language may sound like giving up, dashing any hope, or even abandonment. It may lead to frustration, anger, confusion, and guilt for both the parents and the professional team. "Futility language can stand in the way of important family-centered end-of-life care and procedures. . . ." Because "of the uncertain time until a child's death, physicians should learn how to 'expect the unexpected' and adapt to 'a new normal.'"[37]

To continue on the road of medical technical advancements and improve the lives and health of children and adolescents who face a life-limiting condition, I propose a few measures that I think will be helpful:

- Education, at all levels of society, starting by the example of caring adults—at an early age—of what constitutes healthy diets, outdoor activities, and exercise and play. Our country at present has to deal with an epidemic of obesity as well as food and other addictions, as evidenced in the increased rate of children who develop Type II diabetes at earlier ages.
- Laws to preserve a clean and healthy environment need to be strengthened, and given teeth, so they can be enforced with serious penalties for infractors, rather than a light fine that is just considered the cost of doing business.
- Given the number of suicides by depressed teens, diagnosis and treatments for mental illness should be covered by all insurance plans, as mental disease can be just as serious and devastating as any other illness that affects any organ system.
- Public health, which to date is an orphaned medical field, needs to be strengthened, improved, funded, and empowered to increase the vaccination rate, with no religious or other exemptions. We know that the children

who are not vaccinated are at risk of spreading diseases in the community that some of today's younger pediatricians have never encountered.

- Public health, in its role to preserve health and life in the population at large, has an important role to play in educating school-age children about cigarettes, sexually transmitted diseases, use or abuse of guns, and the danger of addictive substances, be it alcohol, marijuana, or painkillers. Public health's mandate to educate and actively intervene in the general population's addictive problems also needs to be enhanced.

- Medical schools, medical training programs, and universities at large need to educate physicians and students about the art of sensitive communication, about not just curing but also caring in a compassionate way, and about the ethics of death and dying, as "nobody leaves this world alive."

- Ultimately, nothing can ever completely take away the burdens and the pain that accompany the challenges faced by a seriously ill child and his or her family, both before and after the child's death. In today's society, in this century, most decisions about children's health and disease processes should be a team effort by the parents or legal guardians, physicians, social workers, and clergy, focused on the best interest of the child or adolescent, and for that to happen and be done well, we—professional groups and families—all need to take the time to learn to communicate with one another.

NOTES

1. Michael R. Haines, "Inequality and Infant and Childhood Mortality in the United States in the Twentieth Century," *NBER Working Papers* 16133, National Bureau of Economic Research, Inc., June 2010, http://ideas.repec.org/p/nbr/nberwo/16133.html. Accessed March 24, 2013.

Michael R. Haines, "Fetal death ratio, neonatal mortality rate, and maternal mortality by race: 1850-1998," *Historical Statistics of the United States,* Vol. 1, Millennial Edition (Cambridge, UK: Cambridge University Press, 2006), 458, 473–82.

2. National Vital Statistics System, National Center for Health Statistics, CDC, "10 Leading Causes of Death by United States—2010," http://www.cdc.gov/injury/wisqars/pdf/10LCID_All_Deaths_By_Age_Group_2010-a.pdf. Accessed March 9, 2013.

3. "Vital Statistics Online," CDC National Center for Health Statistics, http://www.cdc.gov/nchs/data_access/Vitalstatsonline.htm.

"Compressed Mortality, 1999–2010," CDC National Center for Health Statistics, http://wonder.cdc.gov/cmf-icd10.html. Accessed March 25, 2013.

4. Susan B. Carter, Michael R. Haines, Richard Sutch and Gavin Wright, "Race and Ethnicity: Population, Vital processes and Education." *Historical Statistics of the United States,* Vol. 1, Millennial Edition (Cambridge, UK: Cambridge University Press, 2006), 10.

5. United Nations, *The Millennium Development Goals Report,* "Goal 4 Reduce Child Mortality" (Addendum: 2011), 2. See also Carter et al., eds., *Historical Statistics of the United States,* Vol. 2, 376–77; Roy Porter, ed., *The Cambridge Illustrated History of Medicine* (Cambridge, UK: Cambridge University Press, 1996).

6. "Salk Vaccine Announcement (1955)," University of Michigan History and Traditions, 1995, http://president.umich.edu/history/markers/salk.html. Accessed March 24, 2013.

7. Michael R. Haines, "Occupation and Social Class during Fertility Decline: Historical Perspectives," in *The European Experience of Declining Fertility: 1850–1970,* eds. John Gillis, David Levine, and Louis Tilly (Cambridge, MA: Blackwell, 1993), 193–226.

Daniel Scott Smith, "The Number and Quality of Children: Education and Marital fertility in Early Twentieth-Century Iowa," *Journal of Social History* 30, 2 (1996): 367–92.

8. Jeffrey Kluger, "Polio and Politics: A Great Scourge May Soon Be Gone, but War, Distrust, and Even the Death of Osama Bin Laden Could Get in the Way," *Time,* January 14, 2012, http://www.highroadsolution.com/file_uploader2/files/time+polio+full+story.pdf. Accessed March 25, 2013.

9. R. L. Knowles, C. Bull, C. Dezaleux, and C. Wren, "Mortality with Congenital Heart Defects in England and Wales 1959–2009: Exploring Technological Change through Period and Birth Cohort Analysis," *Archives of Disease in Childhood* 97, 10 (October 2012): 861–65. doi: 10.1136/archdischild-2012–301662.

10. Ibid.

11. Carter et al., eds., *Historical Statistics of the United States 2006,* Vol. 2, 639–52. United States Substance Abuse and Mental Health Administration Services (SAMHSA), "Preliminary Results from the 1997 National Household Survey on Drug Abuse," 1998, http://www.samhsa.gov/data/nhsda/nhsda97/toc1.htm

12. Ibid.

13. Marian F. MacDorman, Eugene Declercq, Fay Menacker, and Michael H. Malloy, "Infant and Neonatal Mortality for Primary Cesarean and Vaginal Births to Women with 'No Indicated Risk,' United States, 1998–2001 Birth Cohorts," *Birth* 33, 3 (September 2006), 175–82, doi: 10.1111/j.1523–536X.2006.00102.x.

14. D. S. Diekema and J. R. Botkin, "Forgoing Medically Provided Nutrition and Hydration in Children," *Pediatrics* 124, 2 (August 1, 2009): 813–22.

15. Jonathan Hellmann, Constance Williams, Lori Ives-Baine, and Prakesh S. Shah, "Withdrawal of Artificial Nutrition and Hydration in the Neonatal Intensive Care Unit: Parental Perspectives," *Archive of Diseases in Childhood: Fetal and Neonatal Edition* 98, 1 (January 2013): F21–5. doi: 10.1136/fetalneonatal-2012 301658.

16. Bruce Jennings, "Dying at an Early Age: Ethical Issues in Pediatric Palliative Care," in *Living with Grief: Children and Adolescents,* eds. Kenneth J. Doka and Amy S. Tucci (Washington, DC: Hospice Foundation of America, 2008), 115.

17. American Academy of Pediatrics Committee on Bioethics, "Informed consent, Parental Permission, and Assent in Pediatric Practice," *Pediatrics* 95, 2 (February 1, 1995), 314–17.

18. Jennings, "Dying at an Early Age: Ethical Issues in Pediatric Palliative Care," 110.

19. Kristin Meade and Sarah Friebert, "Informed Decision Making and the Adolescent Patient," in *End-of-Life Ethics: A Case Study Approach,* eds. Kenneth J. Doka, Amy S. Tucci, Charles A. Corr, and Bruce Jennings (Washington, DC: Hospice Foundation of America, 2012), 232.

20. E. A. Reder and J. R. Serwint, "Until the Last Breath: Exploring the Concept of Hope for Parents and Health Care Professionals during a Child's Serious Illness," *Archives of Pediatric and Adolescent Medicine* 163, 7 (July 2009): 653–57. doi: 10.1001/archpediatrics.2009.87.

21. J. Q. Xu, K. D. Kochanek, S. L. Murphy, B. Tejada-Vera, "Deaths: Final Data for 2007," *National Vital Statistics Reports* 58, 19 (May 20, 2010): 1–73.

22. "Compressed Mortality, 1999–2010," CDC National Center for Health Statistics, http://wonder.cdc.gov/cmf-icd10.html

23. C. Podell, "Adolescent Mourning: The Sudden Death of a Peer," *Clinical Social Work* 17, 1 (1989): 64–78.

24. Michael C. Clatts, Deborah J. Hillman, Aylin Atillasoy, and W. Rees Davis, "Lives in the Balance: A Profile of Homeless Youth in New York City," in *The Adolescent Alone: Decision Making in Health Care in the United States,* eds. Jeffrey Blustein, Carol Levine, and Nancy Neveloff Dubler (Cambridge, UK: Cambridge University Press 1999), 139–59.

25. L. A. Fingerhut and J. C. Kleinman, "Mortality among Children and Youth," *American Journal of Public Health* 79, 7 (July 1989): 899–901.

26. Xu et al., "Deaths: Final Data for 2007."

27. Editor's letter, "Our Dysfunctional Romance with Violence," *The Week* (December 28, 2012–January 4, 2013): 3.

28. Charles A. Corr and Donna Corr, eds., "Suicide and Life-Threatening Behavior," in *Death and Dying, Life and Living,* 7th ed. (Belmont, CA: Wadsworth, 2012), 543–75.

29. E. J. Costello, "Developments in Child Psychiatric Epidemiology," *Journal of American Academy of Child and Adolescent Psychiatry* 28 (1989): 836–41.

30. Ibid.

31. Jeffrey Blustein and Jonathan D. Moreno, "Valid Consent to Treatment and the Unsupervised Adolescent," in *The Adolescent Alone: Decision Making in Health Care in the United States,* eds. Jeffrey Blustein, Carol Levine, and Nancy Neveloff Dubler (Cambridge, UK: Cambridge University Press, 1999), 100–110.

32. B. S. Carter, "Ethical Dilemmas When the Patient Is an Infant: Uncertainty and Futility," in *End-of-Life Ethics: A Case Study Approach,* eds. K. J. Doka, A. S. Tucci, C. A. Corr, and B. Jennings (Washington, DC: Hospice Foundation of America, 2012), 209–18.

33. Jennings, "Dying at an Early Age: Ethical Issues in Pediatric Palliative Care," 99. See also Bonnie Tong and Hannah I. Lipman, "Whose Bed?" *Hastings Center Report* 43, 2 (March–April 2013): 14. doi: 10.1002/hast.153.

34. Richard H. Steckel, "Alternative Indicators of Health and the Quality of Life" in *Unconventional Wisdom: Alternative Perspectives in the New Economy,* ed. Jeff Madrick. (New York: Twentieth Century Fund, 2000).

35. Jennings, "Dying at an Early Age: Ethical Issues in Pediatric Palliative Care," 110–11.

36. S.R. Kaufman, "And a Time to die: How American Hospitals Shape the End of Life." Cited in Jennings, "Dying at an Early Age: Ethical Issues in Pediatric Palliative Care," 111.

37. M.B. Morrissey and B. Jennings, "A social ecology of health model in end of life decision making: Is the law therapeutic?" *New York State Bar Association Health Law Journal* 11, 1 (Winter 2006), 51–60. See also M. Green and J.S. Palfrey, eds., *Bright Futures: Guidelines for Health Supervision of Infants, Children, and Adolescents,* 2nd ed. rev. (Arlington, VA: National Center for Education in Maternal and Child Health, 2002).

174.9

Clinical Diagnosis: 174.9
It's a suspicious lump.
A mass.
When you see it on the radiologist's image it looks like a chalk mark
A quiet little moon in the summer sky.
Nothing to spoon in June over.
When you see it in the picture, it doesn't scare you.

174.9

A pretty little picture
And only when you remember that your rent is 1100 a month and you
have 700, when you count your money and you remember that all of it
comes from your leaving the house every morning at 7am in order to
beat the crowd on the subway and have time for a Starbuck's before the
attorneys come in, before the SEC starts calling your boss. Only when
you remember

Only then do you start to understand
what those guys might have felt
sailing past the Sirens and the one eyed monsters,
with nothing but the sky and the starshapes named after gods
for cover.

Catherine Rogers

Section III

Redrawing the Map

Chapter 14

Advance Directives and Hospice Care: Cost Savers at the End

Edward J. Lusk, Nellie Selander,
and Michael Halperin

*I*n the first years of the second decade of the 21st century, the United States
*finds itself in the midst of grave fiscal conditions. In addition to overall economic
instability, the cost of health care has exploded over the past half-century. There
is a particular concern, given the aging baby-boomer population, that escalating
end-of-life health-care costs will overwhelm the health-care delivery system. To
help remedy some of these problems we put forth a plan we call the "KLS Action
Plan." The plan's two fundamental principles are to expand the use of advance
directives and to encourage the use of hospice and palliative care at the end of life.
We proffer several interrelated actions that promote the cause of hospice and the
preparation of advance directives, and we discuss the connection between signing advance directives and electing hospice. Implementing the steps we propose,
we believe, would substantially reduce the cost of end-of-life care. Importantly, it
would also increase the potential of a dignified death.*

INTRODUCTION: THE RISING COST OF
HEALTH CARE AND THE BABY BOOMERS

National attention is focused on rising health-care costs, and for good reason. In the United States, health-care spending amounted to 5 percent of

gross domestic product (GDP) in 1960; by 2008, it had risen to 17 percent of GDP, or $2.4 trillion, and the United States led all G-20 countries in per capita spending.[1] In a 2009 report, the Social Security Advisory Board projected that health-care spending would grow to 20 percent of GDP by 2018. Nevertheless, various studies have found that this spending is not necessarily associated with improved health outcomes.[2] Up to 30 percent of health-care spending may be wasteful, meaning it could be reduced without affecting health outcomes.[3] Some economists attribute these skyrocketing costs to an increase in the use of intensive care, coupled with high prices for that care.[4]

An example of this American phenomenon—increasing costs without improving health outcomes—is the infant mortality rate: a crucial marker of a nation's health. Among 30 of the most advanced economies, the United States, with an infant mortality rate of 6.1 out of every 1,000 live births, ranked ahead of only Mexico, Turkey, and Chile in 2010.[5] Further, of select countries evaluated by the Health Resources and Services Administration, we are embarrassed to note that the United States' infant mortality rate slipped from 12th in 1960 to 31st in 2006.[6] During this time, health-care spending escalated from 5 percent of GDP to 17 percent of GDP.[7]

Central to the discussion about growing expenditures in the coming decades is the demographic bulge caused by those born between1946 and 1964. This population—the babyboomers—began aging into the Medicare benefit in 2011 and will be in need of potentially expensive late-in-life and end-of-life health care in coming decades. While only 5 percent of Medicare beneficiaries die each year, approximately 27 percent of Medicare outlays are spent on the last year of life, according to a survey published in 2001.[8] While a survey offering exact comparables is not available for later years, media reports, such as a CBS 60 Minutes program in 2010, have featured experts who vouch for the disproportionately high health-care cost for the elderly in the last days and months of their lives.[9] The government has forecast that 44 percent of the increase in Medicaid and Medicare costs through 2035 will be attributable to the aging population.[10] Whatever the exact numbers are, suffice it to say, we can assume that the portion spent on health care in the last months of a person's life is proportionally much larger than during earlier periods—not surprising, given that most of the people who die have serious illnesses.

The Patient Protection and Affordable Care Act (PPACA), signed into law by President Obama on March 23, 2010,[11] has as its principal intention to expand access to care. This will require a significant expansion of the health-care delivery system at all levels. The cost of such expansion is staggering.[12] Questions that emerge include: Is there the political will to effectively redistribute income by expanding health care? Is there waste? Is there a better way to manage the system?

Those who look at other developed countries and see the lower per person costs of health care and its smaller percentage of GDP may answer that the

United States needs to emulate these systems and institute universal health care with a single, government insurer and find a workable mechanism—and appropriate euphemism—for rationing care. Whatever the merits of the health care systems in Europe, Canada, and Japan, they are not feasible to implement in the United States in the time available to address the aging baby-boomer generation. The growth of this population has made it imperative for health-care delivery system planners to address, as efficiently as is currently politically feasible, the explosion in health-care spending over the past 50 years and the problems the baby boomers will present in the next 50 years. What we propose in this chapter can improve the current system without completely restructuring it.

COST REDUCTION INITIATIVES IN END-OF-LIFE HEALTH CARE

Recently, many different proposals have been presented—and implemented—by individual institutions and states to curtail health-care spending at all levels of government. A notable milestone on the road to better managed health care on a national level was the PPACA. Also known as ObamaCare, the goal of this act was to reduce the number of people in the United States without health insurance—a cohort estimated in 2010 to be 50 million people or 16.3 percent of the population[13]—and to reduce the cost of health care, including the cost of Medicare. One specific provision of the original House of Representatives' bill, House Resolution 3962, that did not make it through reconciliation with the Senate bill and into the final version of the PPACA, was intended to lower health-care costs by addressing care at the end of life. This statute would have required reimbursing health-care providers for end-of-life health-care counseling and provided funding for disseminating information on end-of-life planning.[14] Often, individuals at the end of life are subject to heroic and expensive medical interventions when—given the choice—they would prefer to avoid these often invasive and intense treatments.[15] These choices can be properly codified in legal documents through end-of-life counseling.

Attempts to pare down end-of-life health-care costs, such as the House bill's provisions for reimbursing end-of-life health-care counseling, are reasonable and timely, considering the aging baby-boomer population. Regrettably, no mention is made of end-of-life care in the final version of the PPACA, with the exception of a reference to children's choices at the end of life and a commitment to a future demonstration project to determine the relative cost of concurrent curative treatment and hospice, as compared with curative treatment alone or hospice care alone.[16] It is, however, a focus of this chapter: specifically we look at the potential gains of every adult having advance directives for health care and the potential for expanding the number of people enrolled in hospice or receiving palliative care at the end of life.

In the May/June 2012 Special Edition of *Nursing Economic$*, we offered an eight-point action plan, the KLS-Action Plan, to reduce end-of-life health-care costs in the United States.[17] We use this plan as the basis for this chapter. The KLS-Action Plan, derived from a synthesis of six articles contributed by experts in *Nursing Economic$*,[18] offers two principal recommendations: (1) increase the percentage of American adults with advance directives, and (2) develop a triage model that moves more patients, when appropriate and in accordance with patients' advance directives, into hospice and/or palliative care treatment plans at the end of life. Before we discuss these approaches in details, we need to briefly describe what is meant by hospice and palliative care, and by advance directives.

WHAT ARE HOSPICE AND PALLIATIVE CARE?

The understanding and definitions of hospice care and palliative care vary by country and to some extent by institution. The two distinct health-care models have partially overlapping definitions and in the United States are provided under different reimbursement provisions. From the patient's point of view, the treatments have many similarities. Both care models employ interdisciplinary teams and have holistic, family- and patient-centered philosophies of care. The World Health Organization's (WHO) definition of palliative care is "an approach that improves the quality of life of patients and their families facing the problems associated with life-threatening illness, through the prevention and relief of suffering by means of early identification and impeccable assessment and treatment of pain and other problems, physical, psychosocial and spiritual."[19]

The National Palliative Care Research Center (NPCRC) defines palliative care as "a health care specialty that is both a philosophy of care and an organized, highly structured system for delivering care" giving patients "relief from the symptoms, pain, and stress of a serious illness—whatever the diagnosis. . . . [Palliative care] is appropriate at any age and at any stage in a serious illness and can be provided along with curative treatment."

The Center for Advanced Palliative Care offers more details: "Palliative care treats people suffering from serious and chronic illnesses including cancer, cardiac disease such as Congestive Heart Failure (CHF), Chronic Obstructive Pulmonary Disease (COPD), kidney failure, Alzheimer's, HIV/AIDS and Amyotrophic Lateral Sclerosis (ALS). Palliative care relieves the symptoms of these diseases, such as pain, shortness of breath, fatigue, constipation, nausea, loss of appetite and difficulty sleeping. . . . The point of palliative care is to relieve suffering and provide the best possible quality of life for both the patient and family."[20]

Similar to palliative care, hospice care is a team approach to provide "expert medical care, pain management, and emotional and spiritual support expressly tailored to the patient's [and family's] needs and wishes."[21] Unlike palliative care, hospice care, according to the National Hospice and Palliative Care Organization (NHPCO), is designed for "people facing a lifelimiting illness," with a focus on "caring not curing."[22] Hospice care is a benefit under Medicare. "To be eligible to elect hospice care under Medicare, an individual must be entitled to Part A of Medicare and be certified as being terminally ill. An individual is considered to be terminally ill if the medical prognosis is that the individual's life expectancy is 6 months or less if the illness runs its normal course."[23] Hospice care can be offered in different settings. In 2011 the locations of hospice patients' deaths were: private residence (41.1%), a nursing home or other residential facility (24.9%), hospice inpatient facility (26.1%), or an acute care hospital (7.4%).[24] The proportion of hospice death in each of these locations varies from state to state, but hospice care in the patient's or a family member's home is the dominant model.

Palliative care can be used in concert with curative treatments on patients. Hospice care can, in theory, also be used in combination with curative treatments but in practice hospices rarely allow it. In signing up for the Medicare hospice benefit the beneficiaries must agree to forgo Medicare coverage for curative treatments of their condition. In 2012, for routine home care, which in 2012 accounted for more than 95 percent of patient days, hospice agencies were reimbursed $151 per patient per day, with a small regional difference accounting for cost differentials.[25] Since this amount has to cover all medical expenses for the patients, visits by team members, equipment, and medication, it is not possible for hospices to accept patients who want to continue to pursue expensive curative treatments.

The end goal of both hospice and palliative care is to improve the patient's quality of life, as well as the quality of life of his or her family. The KLS-Action Plan advocates the expansion of both hospice and palliative care. In order for that to happen, the general public, and especially those moving toward the end of life need to be informed that these are often optimal, medical care models.

WHAT ARE ADVANCE DIRECTIVES?

Spawned by the Patient Self-Determination Act of 1990, an advance directive is essentially a living will in which the future medical wishes of an individual are recorded and a surrogate is appointed for making the individual's medical decisions, should he or she be unable to make them.[26] There are no federally issued advance directives but all states have some form of officially sanctioned documentation, usually called Durable Power of Attorney for Health care or Health Care Proxy. These forms ask that the individual designate an agent or agents to speak for the principal in case he or she does not have capacity, as determined by—usually—two physicians. The agent—or surrogate—should have had in-depth conversations with the person they will speak for, so that decisions are certain to follow the patient's wishes. The basic document can be supplemented with a living will that enumerates care specifics, related to life-sustaining treatments. The PPACA lacks provisions to ensure that an advance directive is honored in states other than the one in which it was executed,[27] but in practice they are recognized across state lines.

When a patient is diagnosed with a serious illness and when his or her physician determines that the life expectancy of the person is probably less than one year, and especially if the patient has had repeated hospital admissions, additional advance directives specifically addressing wishes regarding life-sustaining treatments are often put place. These documents are labeled, depending on the state, Physician Orders for Life-Sustaining Treatment (POLST), Medical Orders for Life-Sustaining Treatment (MOLST), Physician's Orders for Scope of Treatment (POST), or Medical Orders for Scope of Treatment (MOST). They often include the patient's directives regarding life support, such as a ventilator, dialysis, blood transfusions, major surgery, and artificial nutrition and hydration. These orders are signed by the patient and the physician and carry the additional weight of a physician signature in the clinical setting. These documents are intended to travel with the patient from one care setting to the next. Among advance directives issued at a time when recovery to full health are not likely are Do Not Resuscitate (DNR) orders.

REDUCED EXPENSES WITH HOSPICE AND PALLIATIVE CARE

The NHPCO estimates that 44.6 percent of Americans—or 1,059,000 people—died in hospice care in 2011.[28]It is difficult to estimate how many of those who did not die on hospice could have benefited from that service, and how much money could have been saved if they had. In outlining the KLS-Action Plan we have calculated that if in a hypothetical environment we could make a straightforward swap between hospital beds and hospice beds, substantial savings could be made. Such a swap is not currently realizable in the scale needed and the trade-off measurements necessarily are crude, based on the average cost per day for a patient in a hospital bed and the average daily reimbursement paid under the hospice benefit. The hypothesis does not take into account the many variables. For example, if the swap consisted of patients who signed onto hospice only a few days before dying and remained in an acute care hospital or were checked into the hospital for pain and symptom management in the last few days of life, the saving may be minimal. In practice only a few of the many people who die in hospitals are likely to be candidates for hospice. Nevertheless on a macro scale there is no question that medical care in the hospital is more expensive than hospice care in the home or a nursing home.

Even in a hospital setting there is evidence that hospice and palliative care offers savings. Dr. Amy S. Kelley and colleagues of Mount Sinai School of Medicine in New York have published findings in March 2013, showing that expenditures for patients enrolled in hospice, as compared with matched patients not enrolled, demonstrated Medicare savings of between $2,561 and $6,430 per patient. The highest savings were for those enrolled in hospice for 15–30 days. The lowest, yet substantial, benefits were for enrollments of 53–105 days and for 1–7 days.[29] In analyzing dates from 2004 to 2007 another team of researchers determined that palliative care team consultations reduced hospital costs for Medicaid patients in four New York State hospitals as compared with a control group. The savings were on average $4,000 per patient who was discharged and over $7,500 for each patient who died in the hospital, with an average saving of $6,900.[30]

REDUCED EXPENSES WITH SIGNED ADVANCE DIRECTIVES

The KLS-Action Plan recommends requiring all adults to have advance directives long before entering the end of life. The authors consider it a moral imperative to ensure that individuals have a choice and a voice in how they die. Furthermore we believe that there could be substantial cost benefits if everyone had advance directives. One study, designed to determine what patient characteristics correlated with expenditures above and below the average during the last six months of life, found that, independent of regional differences, patient characteristics associated with higher than median expenditures at the end of life include decline in function, Hispanic ethnicity, and black race, as well as certain chronic disease such as diabetes, having family nearby, and a dementia diagnosis were associated with lower expenditures. Advance care planning had no association.[31] Nevertheless, we believe that if advance directives became more common nationwide, this would increase awareness about end-of-life options and would result in an increase in number of people choosing palliative and hospice care, which has proven to reduce health-care expenditures.

OVERCOMING BARRIERS TO COMPLETING ADVANCE DIRECTIVES

We believe the freedom to choose how you die is sacrosanct and that debates about cost control at the end of life must consider an individual's right to choose. But if Americans' wishes are to be honored, they must first be written down. And in turn, these documents must be retrievable and respected: the wishes stated must be honored and the selected surrogate heard.

Foundational to the KLS-Action Plan is that all individuals over 18 years old should have advance directives. The United States Department of Health and Human Services, the National Hospice Association, and the popular media have analyzed the many roadblocks that explain why only 20–30 percent of American adults have advance directives.[32] They range from misconceptions of the concept to apprehensions about being—and asking someone to be—a surrogate and are mostly rooted in lack of access to reliable information.

There may be a public assumption in the United States that all patients would choose aggressive curative measures—heroic measures—over palliative treatments at the end of life. Perhaps this predilection for aggressive measures stems from the fact, according to 2001 data, that "34 percent of Americans thought that modern medicine could cure almost any illness, whereas only 27 percent of Canadians and 11 percent of Germans thought this."[33] Such an overly optimistic belief in medical technology could be one of the reasons why so many American patients ask for every potentially curative treatment and device, no matter what the odds of success, or even without asking what the odds are or what the side effects or limitations in function may be in functional living. It may be part of the reason that so many individuals in permanent vegetative states are being kept alive in spite of the costly and scarce medical resources they consume. It may possibly be a contributing reason to why patients with terminal illnesses—in all but the three states, that is, Oregon, Washington, and Montana, where physician-assisted dying is legal—are restricted from using barbiturates prescribed by physicians to end their own lives.[34]

The assumption that aggressive medical care is always better than any alternative even permeated the polemic that ensued during the discussion about health-care reform in the United States House of Representative, when the discussion about provisions on palliative care information was misconstrued to suggest that the government would enact "death panels," that could effectively "pull the plug on granny."[35] Such ignorance, or deliberate misinformation, on the part of the nation's representatives in Congress demonstrates that efforts to control cost at the end of life in the United States will be incredibly difficult, politically.

The default mode in American hospitals in cases of serious illness is currently "full code," that is, doing everything medically and technologically possible to maintain life. Yet, surveys indicate that the majority of Americans would prefer to die at home, and that most do not.[36] This suggests that if people thought carefully about their wishes for care options at the end of life—which ideally one does when completing advance directives—then they would realize that they could not have "full code" at home and would instead ask for comfort care—palliative care or hospice—in their home. If, for example, they fully understood the risks of cardio pulmonary resuscitation (CPR) on a frail older body—fractured ribs, bruises—and the low survival rate for the elderly who receive CPR, they would be more likely to sign a DNR. Likewise if people understood the symptoms and side effects of certain treatments and devices, and compared the prognosis of the disease with and without these medical interventions, they would be more likely to specify that they wanted to forego them. Especially elderly individuals who have suffered a long period of illness and feel they have had a full life are likely in these situations to opt for comfort care. Thus the conversations with loved ones and physicians leading up to the completion of advance directives such as POLSTS and similar medical orders are likely to help reduce the number of times that ventilators are hooked up, dialysis treatments are extended, and energy draining chemotherapies are ordered.

Most people select a spouse, child, parent, or close friend as their surrogate, but the question of whom to assign as the surrogate can be thorny. Robert Gatter has noted that assigning the right to execute an individual's advance directive to a nonfamily member may result in the patient's wishes not being fully exercised due to the agent's fear of retribution or lawsuits.[37] In most states, the agent cannot be sued for wrongful action if he or she has acted in good faith; and lawsuits can, of course, be filed by a disgruntled relative even if the agent was a family member. At times an outsider—say, a friend of the patient—may be willing and able to make difficult decisions, in accordance with the patient's wishes, that a close family member would have had problems voicing.

Unresolved family conflicts can result in advance directives not being honored. A basic document assigning a trusted agent—surrogate—should be in place long before we find ourselves in the "seventh age." Mechanism have to be put in place to minimize situations in which family members who do not agree with the principal's wishes attempt to pressure the agent to go against those wishes. The surrogate and the principal should have had conversations that make it clear what wishes the principal has for his or her care at the end of life, but other family members, especially those who may disagree with the wishes, should also be included. Early, abundant, and open conversations among family members long before the crises occur have shown, at least anecdotally, to reduce these conflicts in the ICU.

To minimize conflicts and get a broad perspective, The KLS-Action Plan recommends that the decision-making team for a patient should be the patient and his or her family, case manager, nurses, and physicians. Currently, the law requires the patient to self-determine but, in fact, medical decisions are often made in groups with the patient relying on the input and judgment of his or her family as well as the medical team's expertise. In many cases, especially if the patient is an immigrant who has a poor grasp of English or the patient has much lower educational level than his or her children, the children act as language and cultural interpreters and become the de facto decision makers. A decision-making team helps the patient draft advance directive and collectively decides whether or not to start the patient on a hospice or palliative path. While we believe in each person's right to self-determination, we also encourage the development of more family-centered decision-making process.

Nurses, physicians, and other health-care providers should be required to adhere to the advance directives and be supportive of the surrogate who represents those wishes. Nevertheless, the hospital staff may be reluctant to execute the directives of the surrogate when it involves the withdrawal of life support if a relative opposes the action, because of the fear that they or the hospital will be sued. Since ultimately, it is the patient's right to have his or her wishes honored, it is important that the surrogate is someone who can stand up to pressure from relatives as well as the hospital or, even better, is someone who is able to reconcile all parties around the patient's directives.

In contentious situations a clearly written living will that accompanies the signed surrogate form can be useful; contrariwise a living will that does not precisely fit the actual circumstances—and it is impossible to write one that will fit all situations—can be fodder for further confusion and conflict. If a living will, which is not a legal binding document in many states, is written and included among the documents that is brought into the problematic situation, it can be helpful if it ends with a statement such as "If there are any questions about the interpretation of the above directives, I want my agent [NAME] to make any and all decisions for me"—a power, which is already granted in the surrogate form but may bear repeating.

Navigating information asymmetries—situations in which the patient, and his or her family and/or the surrogate do not fully understand all of the options a physician proposes—can be a very difficult and trying experience for all involved.[38] A myriad of other issues and situations require particular tact and communication skills on the part of medical professionals to carry out wishes in a sensitive manner: for example, questions related to euthanasia, the differential use of advance directives across different races/ethnicities, the cost of heroic neonatal care for low birth weight infants, and how to handle individuals without an advance directive.[39]

Finally, there is the issue of retrieving advance directives when they are needed. Once completed the forms are often lost, misplaced, or forgotten, and frequently not communicated to the relevant physician. Nancy Short indicated that 35 percent of advance directives that are executed cannot be located at the time that they are needed.[40] She advocates for a national registry of advance directives so that they can be accessed at the critical moments. The e-Directive Register of West Virginia offers a model.[41] Such a registry certainly makes sense; however, it would require a nontrivial cost to develop and maintain on a national scale.

For advance directives to function properly and make people consider hospice or palliative care over heroic and expensive treatments, they need to be clearly understood, completed correctly, and spread throughout the population. Beyond having in-depth conversations between the agent and the principal, we believe the following suggestions to be the essentialities in scripting effective advanced directives and increasing their prevalence:

1) Reimbursement policies should compensate health-care providers for helping their patients to complete advanced directives;

2) Advanced directives should be discussed and created in the context of an individual's community; and

3) Cost consequences should be transparently discussed as part of the intended effect of the advanced directives.

Informed discussion with a trusted medical provider in an unhurried setting provides a way to curtail the misconception that advance directives force individuals into a "Kevorkian-esque" decision-making state. Instead, health-care providers and end-of-life counselors should position advance directives as a way for individuals to codify their deepest wishes, which may, in turn, lead them to choose to receive hospice care at the end of life. Advance directives are simply one step in patients receiving care that is in line with their wishes.

There are numerous avenues to improving the reputation of advance directives. Wilkinson, Wenger, and Shugarman and Wholihan and Pace strongly advocate for counseling services supported by religious communities, as well as making health-care counseling services available widely in cities, states, and nationally.[42] Wholihan and Pace offer an excellent and detailed program for developing advance directives. Their plan has four pillars:

1) Defining community-based care: Where do these discussions take place?

2) Organizing the initiative

3) Integration of health information technology

4) Implementation

For example, in organizing the initiative Wholihan and Pace include important components: identify stakeholders and participants; include nonmedical personnel in wellness settings; identify resources, such as Five Wishes® and Respecting Choices® materials developed for the purpose of guiding conversations, as well as medical orders for life-sustaining treatment recognized in individual states, for example, POLST, MOLST, and MOST; and training of personnel in regard to values clarification and care planning needs to place the emphasis on the philosophy of exploring issues rather than merely obtaining a signed form during initial health-care encounters.

To this list of social in-person communication tools, the KLS-Action Plan suggests incorporating the use of social media and cyber networking, excellent vehicles for promoting awareness and completion of advance directives. Facebook™, Twitter™, and scores of other social networking sites are how many younger individuals transfer information. This younger audience is the target group that may be missed by traditional outreach and counseling services examined by the authors cited above.

Moving the advance directive discussion into the social networking sphere may help move this important conversation into a younger audience's communication channel. We consider this a critical aspect of the KLS-Action Plan. Perhaps Dr. Short, who turned 48 Doctor of Nursing Practice (DNP) students loose to "influence 1,000 people to sign an advance directive, living will, or POLST/MOST by the end of the semester,"[43] can offer the same sort of challenge to encourage other students to use social networking and social media to promote the same ideas.

We are enthusiastic about how social networking can be used in spreading awareness and promoting advance directives. It is a low-cost and potentially highly effective way to reach a younger generation and can also be used to explain hospice and palliative care options and make all generations familiar with these care models.

EXPANDING HOSPICE AND PALLIATIVE CARE AND OVERCOMING BARRIERS

The KLS-Action Plan recommends requiring that hospice and palliative care be available to all patients treated in hospitals or in facilities accepting Medicare, Medicaid, or other federal and state reimbursements or subsidies. The broad access to hospice and palliative care that the KLS-Action Plan advocates should be a fundamental right, taken for granted by all, including segments of the population that are currently underserved.

White (Caucasian) patients represented 82.8 percent of hospice patients in 2011;[44] white people represented 79.8 percent of all deaths in 2011.[45] Because minorities are underrepresented in hospice care, education about and, promotion of, this care model among minority groups could prove to be especially fruitful in increasing the number of people potentially opting for hospice. When such promotions are done it is important to recognize cultural differences and create care environments, including hiring multicultural providers that are comfortable for all groups.

To expand the use of hospice it may be helpful to create better support systems for surrogates to minimize hesitation for taking on that role, or asking someone to take it on. It is rarely easy for a surrogate to make the decision to abandon curative treatments and begin to travel with the patient down a hospice or palliative care route, even when it is clear that further curative attempts are futile. There is a rich literature that suggests that the psychological impact is profound on the individual designated as the patient surrogate.[46] After all, this person will be required to make a series of decisions that result, ultimately, in the patient's death. This is a weighty responsibility and the need for multidimensional—community, religious, family, and ethical—support has been documented.[47]

Counseling—a formal word for sensitive, unhurried, in-depth conversation during which the patient, surrogate, and family feel secure and "heard"—are an important part of good family-centered care. Wilkinson et al.'s findings are consistent with the excellent summary provided by Wholihan and Pace. The latter present information on the issue of counseling targeted at integrating all of the decision makers, not only in the development of the advance directive but also in enacting the treatment requested. The counseling services highlighted by Wholihan and Pace are extremely important in providing reasonable assurance that advance directives are enacted in such a way as to make the experience positive for all involved.[48]

A controlled trial of preference elicitation and advance directive completion with patients awaiting cardiac surgery did not find increased anxiety among patients or family members but did find increased congruence between patients and their families concerning preferences.[49] Such evidence shows that the feared psychological implications of acting as a patient's surrogate in end-of-life decision making are not supported by recent studies. In fact there seem to be positive effects of this relationship if it is handled with caution and care, and with proper counseling.

Better communication skills by medical providers continue to be a high priority, even though attention to this deficit has been increasing in the first decade and a half of the 21st century. Interventions to improve provider communication skills have demonstrated mixed results. Some show little effect, while other interventions have increased participants' knowledge, skills, and attitudes related to end-of-life care.[50] One study of (medical) fellows completing a geriatric medicine rotation focused on end-of-life care and found increased physician-reported preparation for care for dying patients.[51]

Song and Walsh et al. reviewed the literature on "breaking bad news" and advance directives discussion delivery methods with healthy and ill elderly, including the Study to Understand Prognoses and Preferences for Outcomes and Risks of Treatments (SUPPORT). They found that end-of-life discussions contributed to increased patient satisfaction with patient/provider communication, with no evidence of negative psychological adjustment or affective outcomes from these discussions.[52]

Beyond improving the cultural, social, and psychological conditions for making people receptive to hospice, it is also necessary to change the political will—as mentioned above—and to change the economics of hospice. The KLS-Action Plan advocates extending the traditional reimbursement mechanisms to include hospice and palliative care. This would mean that private insurance would be required to cover the services with little or no co-pay and that government sources of funding would help subsidize the expansion of these services. It would involve bringing palliative care and hospice care closer into line with one another. To erase the line between the two kinds of care may be

advantageous in that the transition to hospice care could be made more gradual and the often dreaded "H" word—for hospice—would be perceived less as
a death sentence. Attention needs to be paid, however, to several complicating
factors in merging the two in the mind of the public, the training of staff, and
in the reimbursement stream. Hospice currently is entirely focused on those
who are at the end of life and devotes all training of staff and services to the
holistic care of the patient and his or her family with this in mind. If it were
melded with other services hospice may risk watering down their mission and
only being able to offer reduced services. From the palliative care perspective,
merging with hospice may be seen as identifying too closely with death and
dying, and frightening off chronically ill patients who are not at the end of life
but could benefit from palliative care. That said, we believe that reforming the
hospice benefit so that it is less constricted than under current regulations
would serve both those who are dying and the nation's health-care budget.

In a discussion about the expansion of hospice and palliative care service,
the question of entitlement cannot be avoided. Who should get what and why?
This potentially contentious issue is best understood as it relates to derived
revenue and the requirement that it be redistributed. The derived revenue condition we propose is meant to open up or guarantee access to all potential patients who desire or qualify to be admitted to any program in the health-care
delivery system that is associated with any general or special derived redistribution revenues. Access also may be sought by anyone: the patient, the surrogate, or any agency espousing an interest in the specific individual. That is to
say that access must be guaranteed, as part of any regulations, to all American
citizens and permanent residents.

Further, we propose that a portion of the redistribution revenue be put into a
special revenue fund, the purpose of which is to provide the services needed to
increase the utilization of hospice and palliative care in the KLS-Action Plan by
currently underserved populations. This may seem like a revolutionary idea—
that is, granting access across such a wide range of possibilities—however,
this is the norm in most of the countries in the Euro-Zone.[53]

Traditional reimbursement sources, for example, Medicare in particular
now under the PPACA, will bear the cost of providing individuals with hospice and palliative care. The support of the health-care delivery system does
not solely fall on the federal government; state, counties, and municipalities
also have ability to collect taxes and distribute benefits, and so could qualify as
redistribution administrators, as they currently do in public school education.

Reimbursement through redistribution agreements should be as simple as
possible, following the usual concept of equitable redistributions. This may
sound daunting; however, simple rules such as "telescoping" where one first
exhausts any private insurance, then municipal, then state, and finally federal
can be employed. This may make the funding and reimbursement processes
simpler and more equitable. We also propose that the benefit is wealth and

income tested so that those who have substantial resources are obligated to pay a higher co-pay. Private insurers may be able to offer lower deductible contracts, especially insurance providers who traditionally supplement Medicare, such as AARP (formerly known as American Association of Retired Persons) plans. There is work to be done here, as the insurance industry has not yet accepted its role in adequately providing coverage to all individuals. Given the economic benefits possible from increasing the utilization of palliative and hospice care, we find extending traditional reimbursement schemes to cover palliative and hospice care to be a cost saving for the total health-care system.

If we are to expand hospice services across the board, the need to construct new hospice residences cannot be ignored. Approximately a quarter of hospice patients (26.1% in 2011[54]) die in a hospice residence facility and number is trending upward. We are proposing that legislation is passed to incentivize hospitals and other health-care institutions to create and expand such facilities. In some American cities the significant number of properties facing foreclosure proceedings (as of 2012) might become the sites of future hospice residences: To remove the blight municipalities have paid to demolish the buildings on a large number of the properties, and the banks that own the land are giving some of the lots away.[55] It is possible that deals can be struck so that inexpensive properties can be made available to agencies that want to expand their residential hospice services.

Acknowledging that nurses play a strong role in hospice and palliative care, the KLS-Action Plan recommends training more nurses in these specialties in order to meet the growing demand for hospice and palliative care service providers. In a health-care system with expanded palliative care and hospice services staffing more nurses with certifications in hospice and palliative care will be required. We expect the cost of the training to be part of the reimbursement mechanism.

ELNEC, the End-of-Life Nursing Education Consortium (ELNEC) project, is a national education initiative to improve palliative care. The project provides undergraduate and graduate nursing faculty, continuing education (CE) providers, staff development educators, specialty nurses in pediatrics, oncology, critical care and geriatrics, and other nurses with training in palliative care so they can teach this essential information to nursing students and practicing nurses.[56]

In 2011, the Institute of Medicine (IOM) rolled out an initiative to analyze the cost of alternative strategies related to educating nurses. In this report it was recommended that the proportion of nurses with a baccalaureate degree will increase from 50 percent in 2010 to 80 percent by 2020, the so-called 80/20 Initiative.[57] A Decision Support System (DSS) has been developed by Kovner et al. to estimate the feasibility and cost consequence of realizing the 80/20 Initiative.[58] One part of the DSS allows decision makers to identify the educational resources that would be used. Certainly this DSS could accommodate estimating the cost of education of hospice and palliative care-specialized nurses.

We support the clauses in the health-care reform acts that penalize hospitals for readmissions—and reward them for patient satisfaction.[59] As stated by Virginia Tilden and her colleagues, the concept is simple and fundamental to system change:

> . . . a heavier hammer for change is likely to come from those aspects of the 2010 Patient Protection and Affordable Care Act that pertain to CMS [Centers for Medicare and Medicaid Services] payments, such as penalties for hospital readmission, value-based and pay-for-performance plans, and other payment reforms that emphasize quality and penalize systems that deliver poor care.[60]

We propose that the government design a transparent and equitable audit for end-of-life health-care reimbursements. The development of advance directives with trained counselors helping to bring patients, families, nurses, physicians, and potentially clergy together to come up with a patient's treatment plan in accordance with their wishes and an understanding of expected outcomes should be fully reimbursed. This is intrinsic to the success of the KLS-Action Plan. These well-executed advance directives will result in treatment plans focused on expected outcomes. Treatment plans and outcome assessments are currently the standard in medical institutions that receive federal, state, and/or municipal funding; this is codified in the PPACA. We hope this rational and value-based system can be extended to include advance directive, as well as hospice and palliative care, as described in the KLS-Action Plan.

As the federal government is a major contributor to medical care reimbursements at the end of life through Medicare and Medicaid, we recommend that the Government Accountability Office (GAO) audit specific medical interventions often used at the end of life, both in the hospice and in the hospital context. These audits would set up a reimbursement standard, reimbursing at a higher rate for procedures that are both effective and cost efficient at the end of life and reimbursing at a lower rate for less effective, more costly interventions. There is certainly precedent for such a working practical model that requires an information generation, monitoring, evaluation, and decision making that leaves an audit trail to eliminate unnecessary medical procedures.[61] What we are proposing in the GAO audit linkage is no different and we therefore do not expect implementation difficulties of such an audit function for the KLS-Action Plan. We suggest health-care delivery system decision makers avidly pursue legislation that begins the process of engaging the GAO in auditing end-of-life health-care interventions.

Ultimately, consideration of cost control at the end of life must weigh an individual's right to choose to undergo heroic medical interventions, to receive those treatments alongside palliative care, or to simply choose hospice care. Difficult as it is to design the right formula for measuring effective care and efficiencies, if we are to control health-care costs, we cannot ignore these sensitive factors.

SUMMARY AND OUTLOOK

We have examined the KLS-Action Plan for reducing health-care expenditures and improving the end-of-life experience for the seriously ill, elderly, and dying. In brief, the key points we recommend are as follows:

1) All adults over the age of 18 with capacity should have an advance directive.

2) Hospice and palliative care should be made available to all who need and want these services.

3) The election of the hospice benefit should be a family decision in consultation with health-care providers.

4) Traditional reimbursement sources should bear the cost for universally available hospice and palliative care.

5) Government legislation should incentivize health-care institutions to create and expand hospice and palliative care facilities.

6) Social media should be used to promote the signing of advance directives and the use of hospice and palliative care.

7) More nurses should have a baccalaureate degree and should be encouraged to have hospice and palliative care training.

8) Value-based pay-for-performance should be instituted along with rewards for cost-efficient care.

Given that there are positive benefits that accrue to all parties involved in the creation of an advance directive—under the assumption of the wise use of counseling services in part supported by redistributed revenues—we are cautiously optimistic that increasing the number of advance directives is a practical expectation in the expanded health-care delivery system intrinsic to the PPACA. Further, we are hopeful that the benefits of hospice and palliative care can be properly communicated to the general public and attitudes about extending life at all cost will change.

The necessity of change in our health-service delivery system is now so evident that we will have to find the political will to address it. We need to continue the debate to move health-care policy in the right direction. What is not subject to debate is Nickitas' comment, "Unless we advocate personally, professionally, and politically, no American will be able to afford to die with dignity now and in the future. We will all die at some point, so why not create a culture that's comfortable with thinking and talking about death and dying?"[62]

NOTES

1. Sylvester J. Schieber, Dana K. Bilyeu, Dorcas R. Hardy, Marsha Rose Katz, Barbara B. Kennelly, and Mark J. Warshawsky, "The Unsustainable Cost of Health care" (Social Security Advisory Board Report, Washington, DC, 2009), 60. http://www.ssab.gov/documents/TheUnsustainableCostofHealthCare_graphics.pdf

2. Chris Peterson and Rachel Burton, "U.S. Health care Spending: Comparison with Other OECD Countries" (Congressional Research Service Report for Congress Domestic Social Policy Division report, Washington, DC, 2007), 65. http://assets.opencrs.com/rpts/RL34175_20070917.pdf. Victor Fuchs, "Perspective: More Variation in Use of Care, More Flat-of-the-Curve Medicine," *Health Affairs* web exclusive (2004). doi: 10.1377/hlthaff.var.104. Schieber et al., "The Unsustainable Cost of Health care."

3. "Waste in Health care: A $700 Billion Opportunity," *New England Health care Institute*, 2008, http://www.nehi.net/uploads/one_pager/waste_onepager__2011.pdf

4. Peterson and Burton, "U.S. Health care Spending."

5. "Health: Key Tables from OECD: 14. Infant mortality Deaths per 1,000 live births," OECD Library, October 30, 2012, http://www.oecd-ilibrary.org/social-issues-migration-health/infant-mortality-2012-2_inf-mort-table-2012-2-en

6. Gopal Singh and Peter van Dyck, "Infant Mortality in the United States, 1935–2007: Over Seven Decades of Progress and Disparities" (U.S. Department of Health and Human Services Health Resources and Services Administration report, Rockville, Maryland, 2010). http://ask.hrsa.gov/detail_materials.cfm?ProdID=4497

7. Schieber et al., "The Unsustainable Cost of Health care."

8. Christopher Hogan, June Lunney, Jon Gabel, and Joanne Lynn, "Medicare Beneficiaries' Costs of Care in the Last Year of Life," *Health Affairs* 20, 4 (2001): 188–95. doi: 10.1377/hlthaff.20.4.188.

9. "The Cost of Dying: End-of-life Care: Patients' Last Two Months of Life Cost Medicare $50 Billion Last Year: Is There a Better Way?" *60 Minutes,* August 8, 2010, http://www.cbsnews.com/stories/2010/08/05/60minutes/main6747002.Shtml

10. Schieber et al., "The Unsustainable Cost of Health care."

11. "The Patient Protection and Affordable Care Act," 111th Congress Public Law 111–48, 2010, March 23, 2010. http://www.gpo.gov/fdsys/pkg/PLAW-111publ148/pdf/PLAW-111publ148.pdf

12. Sue Ducat, "US Health Spending Projected to Grow an Average of 5.7 Percent Annually through 2021," *Health Affairs* (press release), June 12, 2012. http://www.healthaffairs.org/press/2012_06_12.php

13. Carmen DeNavas-Walt, Bernadette D. Proctor, and Jessica C. Smith, "U.S. Census Bureau, Current Population Reports, P60–243," *Income, Poverty, and Health Insurance Coverage in the United States: 2011* (Washington, DC: U.S. Government Printing Office, 2012), 21.

14. "2012 Legislative Blueprint for Action," *Hospice Association of America,* 2012, http://www.nahc.org/facts/HAALeg2012.pdf

15. Alexander Smith et al. "Half of Older Americans Seen In Emergency Department in Last Month of Life; Most Admitted to Hospital, and Many Die There," *Health Affairs* 31, 6 (2012): 1277–85. doi:10.1377/hlthaff.2011.0922.

16. Kathy L. Cerminara, "Health Care Reform at the End of Life: Giving With One Hand but Taking with the Other." Retrieved from http://www.aslme.org/print_ article. php?aid=460404&bt=ss

17. Christine Kovner, Edward Lusk, and Nellie Selander, "Affordable Death in the United States: An Action Plan Based on Lessons Learned from the *Nursing Economic$* Special Issue," *Nursing Economic$* 30, 3 (2012): 179–84.

18. Lisa A. Giovanni, "End of Life Care in the United States: Current Reality and Future Promise—A Policy Review [127–34]"; Marlene McHugh, Joan Arnold, and Penelope R. Buschman, "Nurses Leading the Response to the Crisis of Palliative Care for Vulnerable Populations [140–47]"; Brenda M. Nevidjon, "Death Is Not an Option—How You Die Is: Reflections from a Career in Oncology Nursing [148–52]"; Deborah Witt Sherman and Jooyoung Cheon, "Palliative Care: The Paradigm of Care Responsive to the Demands for Health Care Reform in America [153–62]"; Virginia P. Tilden, Sarah A. Thompson, Byron Gajewski, and Marjorie Bott, "End-of-Life Care in Nursing Homes: The High Cost of Staff Turnover [163–66]"; Dorothy J. Wholihan and Christine Pace, "Community Discussions: A Proposal for Cutting the Costs of End-of-Life Care," in *Nursing Economic$* 30, 3 (2012): 170–75.

19. "WHO Definition of Palliative Care," World Health Organization. http://www. who.int/cancer/palliative/definition/en/. Accessed March 19, 2013, quoted in McHugh, Arnold, and Buschman, "Nurses Leading the Response to the Crisis of Palliative Care for Vulnerable Populations," 141.

20. "Center to Advance Palliative Care," Community-Based Palliative Care. http:// www.capc.org/palliative-care-across-the-continuum/community-based/.   Accessed March 19, 2013.

21. "About Hospice and Palliative Care," National Hospice and Palliative Care Organization. http://www.nhpco.org/about/about-hospice-and-palliative-care. Accessed March 19, 2013.

22. Ibid.

23. "Centers for Medicaid & Medicare Services," Madicare/Hospice. http://www.cms. gov/site-search/search-results.html?q=hospice%20for%20medicare. Accessed March 20, 2013.

24. National Hospice and Palliative Care Organization, *NHPCO Facts and Figures: Hospice Care in America* (2012), 6. //www.nhpco.org/sites/default/files/public/ Statistics_Research/2012_Facts_Figures.pdf

25. Medicare Payment Advisory Commission, Chapter 11, "Hospice Services," *Report to the Congress Medicare Payment Policy,* March 2012 (Washington DC), 283. http://www.medpac.gov/chapters/Mar12_Ch11.pd.

26. "What Are Advance Directives?" Caring Connections. http://www.caringinfo. org/i4a/pages/index.cfm?pageid=3285. Accessed November 17, 2012.

27. "The Patient Protection and Affordable Care Act" and "2012 Legislative Blueprint for Action."

28. *NHPCO Facts and Figures: Hospice Care in America* (2012), 3.

29. Amy S. Kelley, Partha Deb, Qingling Du, Melissa D. Aldridge Carlosn, and R. Sean Morrison, "Hospice Enrollment Saves Money for Medicare and Improves Care Quality Across a Number of Different Lengths-of-Stay," *Health Affairs* 32, 3 (March 2013): 553–61.

30. R. S. Morrison, J. Dietrich, S. Ladwig, T. Quill, J. Sacco, J. Tangeman, and D. E. Meier, "Palliative Care Consultation Teams Cut Hospital Costs for Medicaid Beneficiaries," *Health Affairs* 30, 3 (2011): 454–63.

31. Amy S. Kelley, Susan L. Ettner, R. Sean Morrison, Qingling Du, Neil S. Wenger, and Catherine A. Sarkisian, "Determinants of Medical Expenditures in the Last 6 Months of Life," *Annals of Internal Medicine* 154, 4 (February 15, 2011): 235–42. http://annals.org/article.aspx?articleID=746807

32. "Advance Directives and Advance Care Planning" (U.S. Department of Health and Human Services Assistant Secretary for Planning and Evaluation Office of Disability, Aging and Long-Term Care Policy report to Congress, Washington, DC, 2008). http://aspe.hhs.gov/daltcp/reports/2008/ADCongRpt.pdf; "2012 Legislative Blueprint for Action"; Paula Span, "Why Do We Avoid Advance Directives?" *The New Old Age* (blog), April 20, 2009 (9:00 a.m.), http://newoldage.blogs.nytimes.com/2009/04/20/why-do-we-avoid-advance-directives/; "Facing Death: Facts & Figures," *Frontline*. http://www.pbs.org/wgbh/pages/frontline/facing-death/facts-and-figures/. Accessed November 17, 2012. Barbara Kass-Bartelmes and Ronda Hughes, "Advance Care Planning: Preferences for Care at the End of Life" (U.S. Department of Health and Human Services Agency for Health care Research and Quality, Rockville, Maryland, 2003). http://www.ahrq.gov/research/endliferia/endria.htm

33. Peterson and Burton, "U.S. Health care Spending," 37.

34. Thomas Hafemeister, "End-of-Life Decision Making, Therapeutic Jurisprudence, and Preventive Law: Hierarchical v. Consensus-Based Decision-Making Model Copyright," *Arizona Law Review* 41, 2 (1999): 329–73.

35. Jason Hancock, "Grassley: Government Shouldn't 'Decide When to Pull the Plug on Grandma,'" *The Iowa Independent* (Iowa), August 12, 2009, http://iowaindependent.com/18456/grassley-government-shouldnt-decide-when-to-pull-the-plug-on-grandma

36. W. F. Benson and N. Aldrich, "Advance Care Planning: Ensuring Your Wishes Are Known and Honored If You Are Unable to Speak for Yourself," *Critical Issue Brief* (Centers for Disease Control and Prevention, 2012). http://www.cdc.gov/aging/pdf/advanced-care-planning-critical-issue-brief.pdf

37. Robert Gatter, "Unnecessary Adversaries at the End of Life: Mediating End-of-Life Treatment Disputes to Prevent Erosion of Physician-Patient Relationships," *Boston University Law Review* 79, 5 (1999): 1091–137.

38. Wholihan and Pace, "Community Discussions," 172.

39. Eric Miller, "Listening to the Disabled: End-of-Life Medical Decision Making and the Never Competent," *Fordham Law Review* 74, 5 (2006): 2889–925.

40. Nancy Short, "The Final Frontier," *Nursing Economic$* 30, 3 (2012): 185–86.

41. http://www.wvendoflife.org/e-Directive-Registry

42. Anne Wilkinson, Neil Wenger, and Lisa R. Shugarman, "Literature Review on Advanced Directives", US Department of Health and Human Services, Office for Disability,

Aging and Long-Term Care policy, June, 2007. http://aspe.hhs.gov/daltcp/reports/2007/advdirlr.htm. Wholihan and Pace, "Community Discussions."

43. Short, "The Final Frontier," 186.

44. *NHPCO Facts and Figures: Hospice Care in America* (2012), 7.

45. U.S. Department of Health and Human Services, "Deaths: Preliminary Data for 2011," *National Vital Statistics Report,* October 10, 2012. http://www.cdc.gov/nchs/data/nvsr/nvsr61/nvsr61_06.pdf. Accessed March 19, 2013.

46. Wilkinson et al., "Literature Review on Advanced Directives."

47. Ibid., 23.

48. Wilkinson et al., "Literature Review on Advanced Directives"; Wholihan and Pace, "Community Discussions."

49. Mi-Kyung Song et al., "A Randomized, Controlled Trial to Improve Advance Care Planning Among Patients Undergoing Cardiac Surgery," *Medical Care* 43, 10 (2005): 1049–53.

50. Stewart Alexander et al., "A Controlled Trial of a Short Course to Improve Residents' Communication with Patients at the End of Life," *Academic Medicine* 81, 11 (2006): 1008–12; Solomon Liao, Alpesh Amin, and Lloyd Rucker, "An Innovative, Longitudinal Program to Teach Residents About End-of-Life Care," *Academic Medicine* 79, 8 (2004): 752–57; Marcos Montagnini, Basil Varkey, and Edmund Duthie, "Palliative Care Education Integrated into a Geriatrics Rotation for Resident Physicians," *Journal of Palliative Medicine* 7, 5 (2004): 652–59; Katya Robinson et al., "Assessment of the Education for Physicians on End-of-Life Care (EPEC) Project," *Journal of Palliative Medicine* 7, 5 (2004): 637–45; Georgette Stratos et al., "Faculty Development in End-of-Life Care: Evaluation of a National Train-the-Trainer Program," *Academic Medicine* 81, 11 (2006): 1000–1007; Amy Sullivan et al., "Teaching and Learning End-of-Life Care: Evaluation of a Faculty Development Program in Palliative Care," *Academic Medicine* 80, 7 (2005): 657–68.

51. Cynthia Pan et al., "There is Hope for the Future: National Survey Results Reveal that Geriatric Medicine Fellows are Well-Educated in End-of-Life Care," *Journal of the American Geriatric Society* 53, 4 (2005): 705–10.

52. Mi-Kyung Song, "Effects of End-of-Life Discussions on Patients' Affective Outcomes," *Nursing Outlook* 52, 3 (2004): 118–25; Raoul Walsh, Afaf Girgis, and Rob Sanson-Fisher, "Breaking Bad News 2: What Evidence is Available to Guide Clinicians?" *Behavioral Medicine* 24, 2 (1998): 61–72.

53. Peterson and Burton, "U.S. Health care Spending," 1.

54. *NHPCO Facts and Figures: Hospice Care in America* (2012), 6.

55. Bradley Dennis, "Banks Turn to Demolition of Foreclosed Properties to Ease Housing-Market Pressures," *The Washington Post* (Washington, DC), October 12, 2011, http://www.washingtonpost.com/business/economy/banks-turn-to-demolition-of-foreclosed-properties-to-ease-housing-market-pressures/2011/10/06/gIQAWigIgL_story.html

56. http://www.aacn.nche.edu/elnec. Accessed March 15, 2013.

57. IOM (Institute of Medicine), *The Future of Nursing: Leading Change, Advancing Health* (Washington, DC: The National Academies Press, 2011) http://www.thefutureofnursing.org/sites/default/files/Future%20of%20Nursing%20Report_0.pdf

58. Christine Kovner, Chou-Hsuan Lee, Edward J. Lusk, Carina Katigbak, and Nellie Selander, "Sustainability of the IOM 80/20 Nursing Initiative as Viewed through a Decision Support System Supporting "What-If" Capabilities," *Journal of Management and Sustainability* 3, 3(2013): 3–18. '

59. "Medicare to Penalize 2,217 Hospitals for Excess Readmissions," *Kaiser Health News,* August, 13, 2012, Updated on October 12 [2012] with revised data from Medicare. http://www.kaiserhealthnews.org/Stories/2012/August/13/medicare-hospitals-readmissions-penalties.aspx. Accessed March 14, 2013.

60. Tilden et al., "End-of-Life Care in Nursing Homes: The High Staff of Nursing Turnover," 163–66.

61. Carolyn Yocom and Kathleen King, "Program Integrity: Further Action Needed to Address Vulnerabilities in Medicaid and Medicare Programs" (testimony before the Subcommittee on Government Organization, Efficiency, and Financial Management, Committee on Oversight and Government Reform, U.S. House of Representatives, Washington, DC, June 7, 2012).

62. Donna Nickitas, "The Dialogue about Death and Dying: It's Time," *Nursing Economic$* 30, 3 (2012).

Chapter 15

Conspicuous Metabolism: Life Support and Life Extension as Luxury Goods

Kevin T. Keith

*T*he *seemingly science-fictional achievement of extreme life extension through medical technology is now held to be plausible, if not probable. However, the enabling technologies will likely remain unaffordable for the vast majority of the world's population. This renders life-support and life-extension technology a luxury good. Thereby, life itself becomes a luxury good. This leads to a first conclusion: continued development of life-support and life-extension technology will replicate, if not exacerbate, existing social divisions arising from inequalities of economic privilege and access to medical technology, by creating conditions* in which not just health-care *technology, but extended multiples of the human life span function as luxury goods on a free market. A luxury market in such technologies will have radically transformative social impact. How much so is expressed in a second conclusion: the availability of life-extension technology raises the possibility that medical technologies acting under market forces may bifurcate society into functionally distinct biomedical classes with ineffably different expectations, opportunities, and experiences. This framing leads to a third conclusion: the ethics of the development and implementation of life-support and life-extension technology are only incidentally issues for applied bioethics, but should instead be viewed as a question of social priorities and class dynamics with implications for the stability of the human species as a cohesive biological*

and social entity. Therefore, finally: issues related to extreme life-extension tech-
nology must be understood from a perspective of species-level interests—similar
to global warming or nuclear war—not from a social, professional-ethical, or
individualized perspective.

INTRODUCTION

Life is not what it used to be, or, rather, life span is not what it used to be for
those who can claim the benefits of the pills and potions that, increasingly,
stave off the postmortems medical care once universally promised. An old
surgeons' taunt of medical practitioners was that they had nothing to offer
but "pills, prayers, promises, and post-mortems". Surgeons in turn, of course,
were said to "bury their mistakes". Pathologists rounded out the internecine
slagging: they "know everything and do everything, but too late". If the wilder
prophecies of medical futurists hold good, all three of these descriptions may
become false by obsolescence.

The seemingly science-fictional goal of extreme life extension through
medical technology has now become common currency. There is, in some
quarters, a confident expectation that the extension of the average healthy
human life span on the order of decades, if not more, is a plausible, or even
probable, development in the very near future.

Technology is becoming available that hints at the potential for such great
increases in life expectancy. Existing life-support technology and treatments
for what would otherwise have been terminal diseases have had a dramatic
impact on the duration and quality of the end-years of life. More ambitious
is current research on what is often referred to as "life-extension" technology,
intended to revise our expectations of life span not on the order of a few years
or a few decades, but possibly on the order of multiples of the current average
human life span or even more.

Those technologies are already having a significant impact on what we understand to be the course of our lives, and on what we can expect in terms of
our average life span now and in generations to come, at least for those privileged to enjoy the health-care benefits available in affluent societies. Today,
sophisticated life-support technology, bringing extension of what would previously have been a short expectation of remaining life in the case of terminal
diseases, is commonplace, and the average human life span from beginning to
end has more than doubled since the 18th century.[1]

It has often been correctly noted that most of this gain in average life span is
the result of better nutrition and advances against easily controllable morbidity such as infectious disease. This may not have literally extended the natural
human life span so much as merely made available the years of natural life that
had commonly been lost to childhood diseases and epidemics. Even from this
perspective, however, it is clear that what had, at any given point in history,

been accepted as the "natural" limit of human life was merely contingent upon conditions of prevalent disease and available treatment that changed over time; there is no reason to assume our current average life span is any more immutable now than it was at any point in the shorter-lived past.

How much further this delay of the inevitable can be pushed is still an unanswered question, but the fact that life span can be extended by the application of health-care resources, to some degree at least, has already been established, and there is no reason to think continued progress in that direction is impossible.

How long one lives, or may live in the future, is thus determined not entirely by the merely physiological arc of one's bodily existence, but by one's degree of access to the medical technologies that take over and determine the path of life. As those technologies become more potent, and their effects more extensive, the difference in outcomes for those who do or do not have access to them will become more dramatic.

In this chapter I argue that the development of technologies of extreme life extension will be of such import for humanity as a whole that they must be regarded, and treated for policy purposes, in a manner entirely unlike that of almost any other medical technology. Because of the economic and social patterns surrounding the introduction of certain types of technologies, including those considered here, these developments, to the extent they become real, will present moral and practical challenges of global significance, to which moral reasoning must respond with concepts and values of global scope.

INCREASED LIFE SPAN: HOW REALISTIC?

Though the entire concept of life extension, or radically extended life support, may seem fantastical, there is enough serious and active interest in such projects to justify giving some attention to their potential consequences.

Life Support and Life Extension

As noted above, existing life-support technology offers the opportunity to extend life expectancy from a given point forward, that is, to extend the process of dying, pushing off an ending that would have come sooner without the application of modern treatments and technologies, and thereby grafting added years of life onto the very end of life. Significantly, this is an opportunity granted only to the dying: there is no technology currently available that extends the middle years of health, rather than the years of dying. Still, such terminal benefits are not despised by those who need and can access them.

These familiar technologies of life support, however, are only the meagerest wonders on offer. Extensions of the normal span of healthy human life—not extended dying but extended robust health and a longer life expectancy from birth onward—are seriously predicted, by scientists actively engaged in the pursuit of remaking human life from cradle to far-distant grave. This visionary, but nonetheless quite seriously pursued, technology progressing along a variety of avenues, the technical details of which are too complicated to be recounted here, promises increases in life span on the average of decades or even centuries. Such grandiose god-playing is taken seriously in the scientific community; however staggering to contemplate, it is not impossible it could succeed.[2]

For the purposes of this chapter, the term "life support" will be used to refer to treatments intended to stave off death for patients near the end of life, suffering from a serious or terminal illness. "Life extension" will be used to refer to treatments or technologies that increase the maximum human life span, working on all or most of the entire arc of life and not necessarily aimed at curing or slowing a particular immediate illness. The issues contemplated by this chapter are most acute in the case of life extension, but the discussion will address both forms of technology.

An Established and Active Field of Research

Life extension has grown into an active research project across academic, governmental, and private institutions. The American Aging Association was founded in 1970; its main purpose is to "promote biomedical aging studies directed toward slowing down the aging process(es);" it publishes its own journal and holds annual conferences on such topics as "Aging: Prevention, Reversal, and Slowing."[3] The International Association of Biomedical Gerontology has held biannual conferences since 1985. The Maximum Life Foundation declares it "will help reverse the human aging process by 2029."[4]

The term "negligible senescence," meaning a state in which advances in medical treatments and biotechnology reduce the rate of death faster than it increases from age alone, was introduced in the 1990s by Caleb E. Finch of the University of Southern California; there is today a SENS ("Strategies for Engineered Negligible Senescence") Foundation which seeks to develop "rejuvenation biotechnologies which comprehensively address the disabilities and diseases of aging" and holds its own biannual conferences.[5] There are professional journals with titles such as *Rejuvenation Research* and the *Journal of Anti-Aging Medicine,* though articles on the subject are also often found in prestigious mainstream journals such as the *Proceedings of the National Academy of Sciences,* the *Annals of the New York Academy of Sciences,* and *Nature.* Peripheral players include such mainstream institutions as the Defense Advanced Research Projects Agency (DARPA), commercial firms such as Advanced Cell Technology (ACT), Geron Corporation, and Human Genome Sciences, and research campuses including UC Irvine, UC Berkeley, Stanford, Cambridge University, and elsewhere.[6]

This work goes far beyond the fringes of geriatrics—a well-established clinical field offering mainstream treatments for conditions affecting the elderly—into realms that often garner suspicion or accusations of crackpotism.[7] But it is represented by numerous journals, increasing amounts of funding, and hundreds of active researchers who are increasingly willing to speak their dreams aloud.[8]

In fact, this futuristic technology, while not currently available, attracts such concern that during the George W. Bush administration the President's Council on Bioethics devoted part of its meeting session and subsequent report on developing biotechnologies to considering the social and medical impact of extensions of life span on the order of 100 years or more—a topic that the body took seriously enough that they considered it was something demanding moral contemplation at this time.[9]

As for the anticipated outcome of such research, estimates vary with the optimism (or recklessness) of the individual scientist. A common strategy is "compressed morbidity"—reducing age-related disease and debility to provide increased years of healthy life up to the apparent natural limit of about 120 years, without actually increasing that limit. Some researchers, however, claim they see no scientifically necessary limit to human life, while admitting they have not overcome the processes currently leading to senescence. Aubrey de Grey, easily the most prominent figure in the field and the scientific director of the SENS Foundation, breezily declares that the first person who will live to 150 years of age has already been born, and the first to live to 1,000 years will be born within the next 20 years.[10]

Objections and Counterexamples

Before proceeding, it should be acknowledged that these gleefully optimistic projections and estimates are anything but guarantees. The argument of this chapter rests on the possible consequences, projected far into the future, of the adoption of a technology that is, as of this writing, only in the early developmental stages. It is not certain that the technology will reach a practical stage at any point, or that its consequences will be as dramatic as discussed below. If life extension became practical but was limited to only 10 or 20 extra years of survival, the consequences would be significant but different from those considered here.[11]

Since there is, as has been argued above, at least some reason to believe that technological advances as significant as those speculated upon can in fact be reached, there is then corresponding reason to consider their impact, and that is the focus of the discussion below. But it is also true that the outcomes considered in this chapter could be evaded or moderated by a different, and less dramatic, technological development pathway.

For example, many medical technologies have different degrees of efficacy in different patients, resulting in a spectrum of health outcomes across the entire patient population. It is possible that life-extension technology would be of this type, such that it did not concentrate the benefits of distinctly and uniquely extended life spans among a select few, but rather produced a heterogeneous population with individual life expectancies varying across a broad distribution curve, much like today, though approaching a longer overall maximum life span. This would significantly ameliorate the "biological class" division described below.[12]

Moreover, an important counterexample is the case of the United States committing, in 1972, to universal, subsidized access to renal dialysis—one of the first modern life-support technologies to reach the market. That decision was largely driven by the then new specter of access to added years of life being determined by economic status or social evaluations conducted by self-appointed hospital committees. It is possible that the inequalities prophesied in this chapter, resulting from the introduction of even more disruptive life-extending technologies, would be forestalled by similar subsidies or guarantees of access. Instructively, as the costs of the dialysis program have soared, the U.S. Congress has declined to make a similarly open-ended guarantee of access to any other treatment. Still, the possibility exists.

Another counterexample, particularly relevant to this chapter, is found in the cases of speculative future technologies such as "transhumanism," neuroelectronic cognitive enhancement, and the like. These transformative but still fictional technologies seem to attract high-level pontificating about what the future of the human species should be, or what limits should be enacted for everyone for all times on modifications to natural human biology, but no actual steps have been taken to establish practical guidelines. As in the case of this chapter, perhaps, it may be easy to propose global solutions to problems that don't yet exist, but that is a far cry from enacting them. Even if the futuristic problems under consideration do come about, it is not clear that well-intended efforts to solve them in advance are likely to be of benefit.

So, there are reasons to imagine that the issues addressed in this chapter either will not arise in practical application of the technology in question, or are simply too speculative to be of concern. Honesty requires that acknowledgment, but the contrary possibility requires attention as well. It is to that possibility that the discussion below is directed.

MEDICAL TECHNOLOGY: AVAILABILITY, ACCESS, AND DISTRIBUTION

The impact of the kinds of technologies considered here on aging, senescence, life span, and the other biological desiderata of mortality, inevitably fascinates, possibly appalls. But, in a way perhaps not at first obvious, the nonmedical details of their implementation will turn out to be the most significant. Although the changes potentially to be wrought in the very scope and substance of a human life are dizzying to imagine, it is not the absolute impact of those changes, however significant they may be, that is at issue here.[13] The greatest impact on society at large will come from inequalities of access to such technologies, not from their mere function.

A society with an average age at death of 300 years will have a different pace and flavor, but not necessarily greater social conflicts, than one with an average life span of 75 years, assuming similar standard deviations, among other things. But one in which only some people live for 300 years and others cannot expect much more than 75 will be faced with conflicts of an unprecedented kind.

That is to say, it is the expectation of inequality, in regard to this particular, revolutionary technology that elevates issues associated with life extension to the level of significance argued for them here. That expectation is not a welcome one, but it cannot be dismissed, for reasons addressed below.

Dr. Jerry Nessel has criticized the "chauvinistic proposition" that "technology is only for the rich and chosen"—something he denies, citing the history of technological development.[14] This chapter implicitly endorses the chauvinistic proposition that technology is in fact for the rich and chosen, not as a preferred policy but as a descriptive observation that must be grappled with, especially in the case of technologies of such awesome and pervasive force.

Class Privilege and Medical Technology

It is already well documented that economic class and access to economic resources, especially health-care resources, are considerable determinants of life expectancy and the health-related outcomes of life. That will remain true as technology progresses.

However good our medical technology becomes, even if it extends beyond current capabilities of near-death life support to the point of actual life extension, taking advantage of those benefits will require access to the resources that make them possible. Inevitably, access to those resources will be, just as it is now, determined by economic class or by status within a society affluent enough to make those resources available to some of its citizens.

Life-support technology is today available largely in First World countries, but not to all their citizens, and largely unavailable in Third World countries. *Life-extension* technology is currently not available at all, but there is no question that if it becomes available it will be, in the beginning at least, concentrated in the more affluent countries, and the question of who within those countries has access to those technologies is a significant one as well. That is guaranteed by the economic process of advanced technology development, which requires resources only the most affluent societies possess and the products of which are then deployed for the benefit of those citizens or corporate stakeholders controlling the inventions.

Distribution of Life Support/Extension Is Inevitably Market Based

Access to medical technology, including life support, is essentially market based. Even in those countries with universal health-care coverage, limits are inevitably placed on what kinds of technological resources are available. As Erica Borgstrom notes, citizens cannot demand unlimited life-support technology under ordinary health-care coverage plans, even in countries guaranteeing access to health care for their citizens.[15] In the United States, which offers no such guarantee, access is a function of one's ability to afford sufficient health insurance, or to pay out of pocket. Thus, whether in a universal-access or free-market system, the global or individualized cost of health-care services determines the level of access individual patients enjoy. Health care is thus inevitably a market-based good, even in single-payer systems.

Beyond this, though, there is an essentially unregulated market in health care above the levels of the typical or universal basic coverage plans. Whatever basic minimum of health-care resources is guaranteed, if any, in most cases patients can buy care above that level, the limit to which is determined primarily by their private resources. The implication of this is that, since life-support and life-extension technologies are market-based goods, the benefits they offer are market-based goods.

Since Life Support/Extension Is a Market Commodity, Life Is a Market Commodity

The benefits that life-support and life-extension technologies offer are added years of life. It is currently possible to buy access to the life-support technology that extends life in the dying years, and when it becomes available it will be possible to buy access to the life-extension technology that gives a greater expectation of total life span. Buying access to such technology buys the added years of life the technology provides. You can buy life.

This is even more literally true when it is remembered that the technology in question, life extension, purports to extend human life span by multiples of its current average length, possibly into the hundreds of years. That is the equivalent of living multiple periods of time equal to one current life span—in essence living multiple extra lives after one's expected life span, in today's terms, has run out.

Life, or bonus years of life, or in fact extra lives, in addition to, or in comparison to, those afforded by an unmodified and only modestly technologized life span such as most people live today, is thus a market commodity. But it is a market commodity heavily dependent on advanced technologies still in development, which, as argued above, will almost undoubtedly be more expensive and less widely available than those medical technologies taken as commonplace today.

This purchased life will be available, or at least increased years of life will be available, only to those who can afford them. In other words, added years of life are essentially luxury goods.

LUXURY GOODS

"Luxury goods" is a term of art in economics. It refers to certain types of things available for sale in the marketplace that are distinct from other types of things.

Defining Luxury

The concept of luxury is familiar in an everyday sense: luxuries are the things we want but can't have. It is somewhat more difficult to define luxury in technical terms, but there have been attempts made:

Economic definition of luxury: goods for which demand increases with the income of the buyer. In technical terms: goods with an income elasticity.[16] In simple terms, by this definition luxury goods are those things rich people choose to buy and poor people can't afford.

Inherent quality definition of luxury: goods that are very high in quality, inherently desirable, or better than whatever else is on the market in that category of product. By this definition, luxuries are those things far exceeding in quality or performance a basic functional item of similar type—a Cadillac as compared to a Ford, for instance.[17]

Social definition of luxury: goods which convey, or indicate, social status with ownership.[18] By this definition, status as luxury is contingent on the broader social dynamic: the function of an item as a luxury, and its desirability, partly depend not only on having access to the goods in question but also the fact that few others have access to them.

Economists contrast luxury goods with "necessity goods"—goods for which demand is inelastic to price or income, that is, goods for which buyers will pay no matter what, because they must. Necessity goods are the things everyone has to buy: basic food, clothing, shelter, and so forth.

It is true these concepts are slightly ambiguous. But luxury nonetheless is a real and valid concept, and it defines categories of goods usually available to, or affordable by, only a limited and privileged subset of the population. This is true largely for economic reasons in the case of economic luxuries, by definition, and inherent-quality luxuries, which generally sell at a premium price.

There is also an important phenomenon by which access to social-status luxuries is deliberately restricted to maintain the prestige associated with them, for instance, in the case of country-club memberships, which are denied to some people who could otherwise afford to pay club dues in order to maintain the exclusivity of the membership privilege.

Life as a Luxury Good

The central conceit of this chapter is that the added years of life that can be purchased through health-care technology, either by means of life support or life extension, are a luxury good. That fact has moral and social implications greater, and more worrisome, than it may at first appear, and elucidating and responding to those concerns will be the burden of the rest of the discussion.

Health Care as a Luxury Good

By the kinds of definitions discussed above, health-care goods function on the open market as economic luxury goods. We see how much money affluent people willingly spend for spas and plastic surgery and exotic treatments. And it is well documented that the most affluent societies spend, annually, over $2,000 per person on health care at this time, while many of the least-developed countries spend amounts measured in one or two digits.[19] At both the individual and societal levels these demand curves rise with income (or GDP) and thus define a luxury in the technical sense, however necessary health care would seem to be. This becomes somewhat complicated: the curve of demand versus income doesn't rise indefinitely for health care; it levels off somewhat at a point beyond which there is limited benefit from continued expenditure. But it remains true that the affluent spend much more on health care than the nonaffluent do, and when comparing societies rather than individuals this difference becomes stark.

Added years of life are also obviously luxury goods of the inherent-quality type—almost everyone wants added years of life, regardless of cost. Empirical evidence is found in the common observation that vast amounts of health-care expenditures are concentrated in the final years of life or the final months of treatment for terminal illnesses, with greater expenditures by those of greater wealth for the acquisition of health-care services beyond the basic level more widely available to all.[20]

In addition, as will be touched on below, the consequences of life extension likely include a social-status-setting function that will be central to the moral issues associated with that technology. It is the self-perpetuating dynamic of social-status luxury goods, in particular, that is of special significance in this regard.

Luxury and Privilege of Access

What the affluent are buying with their luxury-level health care is better health and longer lives. The comparison between life spans in different countries bears this out (though the relationship between per-capita health-care spending and average life span is not entirely consistent).[21] But in respect of expenditures on life-support technologies specifically—technologies aimed at not just increasing health in general but specifically adding years of life to the expected end of life—the affluent in the private health-care market are buying added years to which the nonaffluent have no economic access at all.

Exactly how this plays out depends on the nature of the technologies to be developed. If life extension requires embryonic or germ-line genetic engineering—that is, if it is a benefit that must be acquired at or before birth, or by genetic inheritance—then it will be unavailable to any of the children of parents who cannot afford that technology at the crucial juncture. If it proves to be a treatment that could be taken later in life, then the hope arises of a kind of biological upward mobility—the lucky or industrious might be able to afford to acquire the treatment before time runs out. The types of class divisions that would arise from these different types of technologies would be different in effect, but real enough nonetheless.

FUTURISM: UTOPIAN AND SCIENTIFIC

Invariably, issues regarding life-extension technology, and even life-support technology to some extent, are addressed at a global level: "What will happen when we all live to 300 years?" In many discussions, there is an implicit assumption that when these kinds of technologies become available, or in the case of life support as they become more available, they will be available to everybody—the future will be one in which everyone will live to be 300 years old regardless of income, economic status, or the mechanisms of production and distribution of the relevant technology. This Utopian expectation of untrammeled access to such new technologies is wildly unrealistic. To their credit, the SENS Foundation includes "ensure widespread access" among their goals for the development of life-extension technology. But even here, they seem to assume implicitly that it can or will be done.[22]

Technology Development and Equality of Access

No technology is introduced without regard to the market-based forces driving technology through society. Taking as an example the personal computer, becoming widely available in the early 1980s, it remains true over 30 years later, even in affluent societies, that some people have access to computer technology and some people don't, even though it has become quite cheap in current dollar terms.

The idea that extremely technology-intensive health-care goods with dramatic societal impact will be made universally available without regard to cost, is, for the foreseeable future at least, simply false. Even if life-support technology were to become as cheap as computers today, it would not be universally available, as the example of computers themselves tells us.

Only a program of universal access by way of massive subsidy would reduce such technologies to the level of ordinary goods rather than luxuries. And here, the self-perpetuating nature of social-status luxuries takes on particularly malevolent significance. For economic reasons alone, a policy of universal subsidy will be opposed by powerful social forces. The technology, in its early phases at least, is likely to be limited in availability and highly expensive. The powerful classes that derive social privilege from access to such technology—in ways discussed below—will have no incentive to see that privilege diluted. Life-extension technology as a luxury good will thus remain a luxury good, available to the affluent classes, providing benefits only certain people can access, and making a distinction between classes on the basis of that access, for the foreseeable future.

From the description of technology, biology, and economic privilege given above, we are led to a preliminary conclusion pointing toward the general concern motivating this chapter:

First conclusion: *Continued development of life-support and life-extension technology will replicate, if not exacerbate, existing social divisions arising from inequalities of economic privilege and access to medical technology, by creating conditions in which not just health-care technology, but extended multiples of the human life span, function as luxury goods on a free market.*

SOCIAL IMPLICATIONS OF LIFE SUPPORT AND LIFE EXTENSION

Before proceeding to a consideration of the moral implications of putting life in the same economic category as Italian leather handbags, the human impact of the development of these still-imaginary technologies, and of their irregular and limited distribution through luxury channels, ought to be introduced. A brief consideration of the types of consequence that may be foreseen will be enough.

Economic Impact of Life Support

Among the most obvious consequences of introducing technologies that push death further off are the ways in which doing so would alter the balance of economic forces defining and organizing life today. With a potential working life of hundreds of years, the privileged few who are in a position to choose such a future for themselves will have economic opportunities that are not just hard to reach, but unreachable, for others.

Though, on the one hand, hundreds of years of labor seem an unattractive prospect, retirement planning over such a horizon becomes greatly simplified: it is only necessary to work long enough to save enough resources to be able to live on the interest thereafter, a task that is unmanageable for many in today's economy, but would be almost guaranteed of success for those with access to centuries' worth of compound interest. The reward would then be centuries of investment-income lotus-eating, while those still doomed to the much shorter current-average life span would, as today, be lucky to retire at all. That is, life extension as a luxury good brings not just extra lives, but extra lifetimes of comfort and ease, compared to the single one of nearly endless toil that is left behind.

A related benefit would be the opportunity to pursue as many careers as one likes: why not go to medical school at the age of 200, and law school at 300? There would be time enough for full careers in multiple professions with a lengthy retirement to come at the end, while others struggle to find fulfillment in a single working life. The same would be true for private pursuits or hobbies: there would be essentially no reason to deny oneself any pursuit or indulgence, or any skill or body of knowledge, in a life with room for many of today's life spans' worth of learning and activity.

Social Impact of Life Extension

Concomitant with the economic disruptions these changes in life span would bring are the changes in social patterns and practices depending, vitally but often invisibly, on what we currently understand our lives to be like. In a society in which human reproductive age is (presumably) unchanged, but average age at death has been pushed back hundreds of years, relations within life-extended families will be altered in ways that have never been seen or experienced. Successive generations, each born 25 years after their parents, will know not, at most, 4 grandparents, but 8 great-grandparents, 16 great-great-grandparents, and exponentially more even unto the 8th, 12th, or further generations.

For dynastic families of this type, family relations will take on a different aspect. Intrafamilial resources and assistance will flow down as water. Children may come to feel they are more peers than juniors to their own parents—separated from them in age by only a few decades, in a life extending through centuries. Lifelong marriage may come to seem unrealistic, and new forms of blended families be developed. "Family," and what it means to be a member of a family, will take on a new meaning that cannot now be guessed, but can neither be denied.

Life Extension and Class

In these ways, the existence of luxury goods conveying actual years of life would create a class division of a uniquely stark and unbridgeable nature. Those with access to the technology of seeming immortality would live lives so different from, and so extensive beyond, the life spans and life patterns of those lacking access that they would form in essence a *biological class*—a social subset defined by biological barriers others could not cross for reasons that were at bottom economic but which cashed out in terms of the embodied experience of life itself.

With truly revolutionary technologies—life extension on an order of multiples of the current average life span—the lives of those privileged to access it would be simply indescribable in terms of what we now understand as a human life and its component ages and experiences. What is "middle age" if you live 300 years? What does it imply to plan for your third decades-long career, or the birth of your great-great-great-great-great-great-grandchild, and what do you have in common with those who have just one chance to see their plans and goals through, and may not be sure they will ever see even their first grandchild? How can you be friends with another supposedly mature and experienced adult who is 200 years younger than you, and will die 100 years sooner?

It seems impossible that members of the long-lived population would be likely to marry, form friendships, or even collaborate on projects with those whose life spans are incongruent with theirs by a matter of hundreds of years. They would cleave to their own and—especially as they consolidated their economic power and privilege—drift into a way of life defined by biological and social patterns simply impenetrable by the short-lived, regardless of will or inclination on either side of the barrier. Such lives would be, in practical effect if not—at first—strict biological fact, those of a completely separate species.

This is a new form of class distinction—the creation of social classes defined in biological terms—that arises from the function of these technologies as luxury goods available only to the affluent in a market-based health-care distribution system, and from the likely consequences of such goods in the lives of those who do and do not have access to them.

Those consequences parallel, but would have vastly more pervasive and insidiously influential effects as, existing class distinctions arising in the health-care arena, such as unequal access to expensive treatments or intensive-care technology. While those inequalities may have significant impact in the lives of the privileged and nonprivileged, today's technology does not offer added decades, let alone multiple life spans, of healthy life.

The advent of biological class distinctions of that magnitude would be not just another example of economic inequality as it is currently known, but the beginning of the division of the species itself into incompatible populations living unrecognizably different lives. Those lives would be, in the one case, defined by their enjoyment of biological luxury goods acquired through an open—but not equally accessible—market that are the equivalent of actually renewed or multiplied human life spans, and in the other by the denial of such access and opportunity.

THE INTRODUCTION OF LIFE-EXTENSION TECHNOLOGY INTO THE PUBLIC SPHERE

The central burden of this chapter rests upon two assumptions arising from the arguments above: first, life-extension technology, when it is introduced, will be distributed through a free market without guarantee of universal access, in the nature of a luxury good available only to the economically privileged; second, the effects of that technology will be of dramatic magnitude, adding decades or entire extra life spans to the ordinary human life span of today.

If either of these aspects of the technology's implementation prove to be less divisive—that is, if the technology proves more easily available to a wider range of people, or its effects produce a less dramatic difference in life expectancy between those who do and do not have access to them—the most extreme consequences predicted by the argument above would be ameliorated, lessening the moral significance argued for them below. However, the divisive outcome previously described follows from the economic patterns attributed to luxury goods and the history of health-related and technological luxuries in the late 20th century, as well as the predictions made by scientists in the field regarding the most dramatic of the consequences to be expected from life-extension technologies. Its probability is more than merely speculative.

The scope and significance of such consequences in the lives of those who embrace this technology—as well as those who cannot—pushes us another step toward a conclusive appreciation of the impact of the technology in question:

*Second conclusion: The availability of life-extension technology raises the possibility that medical technologies acting under market forces may bifurcate society into functionally distinct **biomedical classes** with ineffably different expectations, opportunities, and experiences in living.*

IS THE ADVENT OF BIOLOGICAL CLASS A SIGNIFICANT MORAL ISSUE?

Although this second conclusion is unmistakably dramatic, it may be overstated. Before concluding—as will be considered below—that the rise of "biological classes" will have some unique moral import, it must be considered whether this is different from, or worse than, the consequences of class divisions as they are felt today, including in regard to access to biomedical technologies.

Class Inequality as Such Is Not the Central Moral Issue

Luxuries as such are not objectionable. In a society that does not demand absolute equality of wealth or circumstance—as few or none today do—there will be those who have more of what is desirable than do others. If inequality does not arise from circumstances or economic forces that are themselves objectionable (in every case a complicated question), and does not entail the denial of actual necessities to some in the provision of luxuries to others, the existence of such class distinctions, and the distribution of luxuries they make possible, does not by itself demand intervention.

That the ability to purchase health-care resources is such a determinant of access to, literally, vital necessities such as health and longevity, in societies with free-market-based health-care programs, is an especially blunt illustration of the power of class to impose detrimental inequalities, aside from mere inequalities of access to luxury goods. But the impact of that inequality is mediated, in today's health-care context, in two ways.

First, most affluent societies have chosen to guarantee universal access to reasonable necessity-level health-care resources, thus class-based privileges provide access only to luxury-level health-care goods such as cosmetic surgery, better hospital-room amenities, and so forth. Second, currently-available health-care technology, particularly life-support technology, though impressive, is still limited in the absolute benefits it can bring. Life support, today, often merely extends the dying process for debilitated or moribund patients. Interventions which can truly bring years of good health are often simple and not technology intensive, such as better diet, antibiotics, and vaccinations. So the actual advantage in absolute terms that access to health-care luxury goods can bring, today, is relatively modest, and certainly nothing at a level that overtly divides societies in terms of expectations and outcomes related to life expectancy. Again, this remains true largely within individual, affluent societies. The life span advantage of the most affluent societies, compared to members of nonaffluent societies, can be as much as 100 percent. The U.S. Census Bureau reports life expectancies at birth, in 2010, of less than 39 years in Angola and over 81 years in Spain. But even that is a comparison of extremes that are likely to converge in the future, assuming continued improvements in the global political and economic situation. It pales in comparison to the many multiples of life span touted for the revolutionary technologies discussed in this chapter.[23]

The claim that the inequalities of health and life contemplated in this chapter do in fact rise to a level far more severe, and objectionable, than the already-existing health-related class distinctions of today, must be demonstrated before any further conclusions about them can be reached.

Revolutionary Health-Care Luxuries Not Only Reflect, But Impose, Inequalities

For the reasons given above, today's health-care inequalities do not and cannot create new classes or functional taxonomies of the human species. And if the current fitful but real global leveling trend toward greater economic prosperity and access to technological benefits continues, those existing inequalities should diminish, not increase. But extreme life extension would give its beneficiaries lives so removed from the pace and content of those we live today that that privileged class would constitute its own biological community, ineluctably divergent from the community of the mortality-poor it had sprung from.

This analysis depends on the expectation that such technologies would in fact be luxury goods—that is, available on the free market, but not guaranteed to all. It seems obvious that would be true at least at first, when such new technologies can be expected to be expensive and dependent upon treatments or equipment that will not immediately be widely available. Beyond that, however, luxury status can have a self-perpetuating quality.

Those who control access to luxury goods may choose to keep them exclusive (as in the case of restrictive housing covenants before the Civil Rights Movement). And the mere indulgence of certain luxuries by those who can afford them may, by itself, have the effect of exaggerating already-existing inequalities of access. This is, for example, the case in germ-line genetic engineering, the benefits of which may remain unobtainably expensive for the lower classes, but which, once acquired, would then be inherited naturally by successive generations of the upper class at no further cost.

As a proof-of-concept example, the pattern of health-care technologies assuming an initial, and then permanent, luxury status has already been seen in the case of in vitro fertilization (IVF), which is by now a mature technology but remains very expensive and largely restricted to the affluent classes.

When billions of the world's people, and even significant fractions of the populations of affluent societies, still cannot benefit from such commonplace technologies as computers and IVF, decades after their introduction, there is no reason to imagine an exotic and revolutionary technology such as life extension will remain anything but a very exclusive luxury good long after the affluent classes have begun to employ it.

The Persistence of Biological Class Division Is a Moral Issue

Although class inequality may be justifiable in some cases, particularly in the distribution of luxury or non-necessary goods, that conclusion incorporates the assumption that most luxury goods do not mediate vital or otherwise necessary aspects of people's lives. When social luxuries perpetuate inequalities of moral significance, as in the case of racially restrictive housing covenants, those inequalities are less justifiable. When such inequalities produce class divisions of such magnitude as to affect the social functioning of the species itself—and to the systematic detriment of the less affluent or privileged— that moral significance is magnified to an unprecedented degree. The potential for such divisions to become biologically or socially self-reinforcing extends the scope of that problem through ages and generations.

MEDICAL ETHICS AND THE EXTENDED-LIFE CLASSES

As was noted, inequalities and class divisions, in regard of health care and much else, already exist. There is much that can be said about the advisability of such inequalities and the means of managing them, but that discussion sits within, and is addressed by the tools and concepts of, ordinary economic, political, and philosophical analysis. It may be, however, that those tools and concepts are inadequate to the treatment of the issue at hand, comprehending not merely distinctions within but the actual bifurcation of human society and even the human species itself.

Medical Ethics Is Not Capable of Addressing Species-Level Moral Issues

In particular, medical ethics does not seem to have the tools to address society-level impacts of medical technologies, let alone impacts of such magnitude as to actually remake the society in which they arise.

Perhaps in part because most market-oriented societies lack mechanisms for authoritatively setting global social values, and particularly because luxury-goods markets, by their nature, stand outside the distributive mechanisms of the welfare state, global policy-setting regarding equality of access to limited-availability medical luxuries is uncommon. Regulations driven by supposed moral concerns, such as in the cases of abortion or physician-assisted suicide, are relatively common, but questions of scope of access, even in countries guaranteeing a minimal level of health care, are typically motivated more by budgetary concerns than by a top-level policy regarding the average life span, or types of class relations, or intergenerational dynamics, that have been chosen as explicit broad goals for their societies.

Medical ethics has tended to focus on clinical applications of familiar moral precepts, for the purposes of decision making in individual cases, or policy setting regarding particular practices. Society-level concerns such as the differential impact of health care on women, minorities, and other groups, the potential for health-care practices to challenge or reinforce social patterns and stereotypes, or the abusive nature of certain practices such as drug testing in the Third World, among many others, have often been raised, but even these are issues of the direct impact of particular policies, not in most cases a push for lofty goals for the entire species. Even the issue of equality of access—central to the argument of this chapter, and a recurrent hot topic in medical ethics—is typically addressed as a financial management issue.

Thus, when practices arise portending changed conditions of life for humanity in the most general sense, the recognized tools and perspectives of medical ethics are not expansive enough, nor do they command universal-enough consensus, to encompass the scope and sweep of the issue.

The Moral Issue in Life Extension Arises Fundamentally from Class, Not Medicine

Furthermore, given the class dynamics of the issue of extreme life extension, as described above, even though the technology itself addresses the most fundamental aspects of human biology and human life, it is not, in its employment, distribution, and final consequences, essentially a medical issue. It is rather an issue of indirect social engineering through class-based differences in access to a transformative experience. That experience—the extension of life expectancy for oneself or one's offspring—is biological in nature, since it is its impact on species-level biology that leads to differences in experiences of life having such dramatic consequences. But those consequences—the issue of real moral significance—are ones of social stability, equality, and the future of the human species as such.

Third conclusion: The ethics of the development and implementation of life-support and life-extension technology are only incidentally issues for applied bioethics, but should instead be viewed as a question of social priorities and class dynamics with implications for the stability of the human species as a cohesive biological and social entity.

THE CONTROLLING MORAL PERSPECTIVE

If we create a society in which there are essentially two distinct human species, defined not by their ability to interbreed, but by differences in access to economic resources resulting in dramatically different life spans, we will have changed human society in a way that has never been countenanced, and which has to be addressed as a question of species-level significance.

Such questions are few, but they have a defining quality: they cannot be avoided or evaded. Life will change for those who do not or cannot buy extra lives, because those who can have done so. When the most economically powerful class removes itself to its purchased immortality, how those left behind are regarded and treated will inevitably be different even if they themselves have no truck with the technology in question. Unlike with simpler luxuries, or even luxuries of health care such as are currently available, the advent of transformational luxury goods will change not just the lives of those few who can afford them, within the limited scope of its immediate biomedical impact, but the nature and future of humanity itself, for both its new privileged biological class and the remnant untransformed majority.

In a society divided into two distinct and different biological classes, the lives of both classes must be very different from those lived in a world where such distinctions do not arise. The employment of technologies with such effects is, therefore, a moral issue that comprehends the future and interests of the entire human species, not merely of those who directly access or make use of that technology.

What Moral Perspective Is Available for Issues of Such Magnitude?

There are in fact issues of such scope, other than the fictional one addressed here. Their existence and our understanding of them do not provide solutions to the problem posed by the potential of human life extension, but they at least provide an example of how issues, with such expansive moral import, have been considered in the past.

Issues of this type are those that threaten species-level harms, imposed on all or almost all individuals regardless of their personal choice to participate in or endorse the technological changes giving rise to them. Most important moral or social issues are not of this type: there are many issues having great significance for a given society or even internationally, and which threaten or oppress individuals without their choice or endorsement, but which do not give rise to transformational impact at the species level. An example might be economic exploitation: many workers lack basic necessities, and some societies are systematically exploited for gain by more powerful others, but, as unjust as that may be, it directly affects only those directly involved, and not by necessity. Exploitation occurs because some with power choose to abuse vulnerable others; it is not an inevitable feature of work itself. But there are other issues that embroil all of humanity in dangers which cannot be avoided, as an inevitable consequence of the practice in question. Those are issues of the type this chapter contemplates.

Examples of this type may be nuclear war, global warming, or the worst excesses of environmental degradation. In these cases, the introduction or use of certain transformative, that is, destructive, technologies threatens devastating consequences for everyone who lives on the planet. The powerful elites who make the decisions to use these technologies thereby choose life, death, and a transformed future for everyone else, without their input or agreement.

Because of the potential magnitude of consequences of these decisions, their moral significance can only be addressed from a global perspective. This explains the particular horror with which antinuclear activists regard discussions of the "tactical" or "limited" use of nuclear weapons, perceiving that such use would immediately or eventually escalate to the level of global harm threatened by full-scale nuclear war. Planning for such individual-scale uses without comprehending global consequences is thus a way of ensuring the worst outcome. In addition, because of their transformative nature, policy decisions about technologies of this type must be made before they are deployed.

We have not solved the problems posed by the threat of nuclear war, and in the cases of global warming or environmental disaster it may already be too late to avoid even the worst possible consequences. But one legacy of having at least contemplated them is that we now recognize there are such things as global-level moral issues. And we have at least some history of analysis, planning, and even cooperation in addressing them at the global policy level.

Life-Extension Technology Must Be Addressed Using the Moral Tools Developed for Other Issues of Global, Species-Level Consequence

Given the transformative potential of extreme life-extension technology as a luxury good both defining and creating species-level class distinctions, it must be addressed as equal in significance to other moral issues of global impact such as nuclear war or global warming:

Fourth conclusion: Issues related to extreme life-extension technology must be understood from a perspective of species-level interests, similar to global warming or nuclear war, not from a social, professional–ethical, or individualized perspective.

CONCLUDING REMARKS

The final conclusion above, namely that "life extension is very important," may seem rather weak tea. At the end of a labored argument about health care, economics, class, and social dynamics, it offers only a moral categorization, not a proposed solution to the identified problem. But defining the moral scope of a problem and determining the level of analysis and policy making at which it must be addressed are important preliminary steps, and, as was noted, problems of this scope are notoriously difficult to bring to practical resolution.

One thing this conclusion does is help to avoid the error of miscategorizing and minimizing the issues portended by technologies of this type. Life extension and similarly fanciful technological proposals enjoy great popularity with the futurist-minded or transhumanist communities, and others who are fascinated by technology in and of itself. It is tempting to think they are just more-exotic forms of medical technology, to be addressed with the familiar tools of medical ethics and policy setting. For some cutting-edge medical projects—individual human body enhancement with relatively minor impact on bodily functioning, for instance—that is probably true. In other cases—as I have argued throughout—it is not, but those cases, because they are rare and because their dynamics are both indirect and hard to predict, may be hard to recognize.

Assuming luxury technologies promising transformation at the level of the species can be treated as just another issue of health-care financing or equality of access could be an oversight analogous to that of humanity's long indifference to global climate change. The problems they threaten may be irreversible before we realize they have occurred. Forewarning ourselves may provide the opportunity to identify and respond to the problem before we make our mistakes.

And, finally, though the discussion herein is focused on the exotic and as-yet-undeveloped technology of life extension, it may make clear the type of analysis that should be employed with other transformative technologies, especially, but not exclusively, in the realm of biology and medicine. That technologies employed at the level of the individual, as biomedical treatments quintessentially are, may have indirect effects that change conditions of life for everyone, even in societies where such technologies are unavailable, is a new possibility and a new way of perceiving the moral issues that technology raises. It necessitates developing the conceptual flexibility to recognize such transformative technologies and employ the breadth of perception and moral analysis they demand. Acknowledging that need may broaden the scope of this chapter's conclusion, even if it brings it no nearer a solution to the problems addressed.

NOTES

1. Caleb E. Finch and Eileen M. Crimmins, "Inflammatory Exposure and Historical Changes in Human Life Spans," *Science* 305 (2004): 1736–39.

2. For a general overview of one major project aimed at life extension, by one of the central figures in the field, see Aubrey D. N. J. de Grey, *Ending Aging: The Rejuvenation*

Breakthroughs that Could Reverse Human Aging in Our Lifetime (New York: St. Martin's Griffin Press, 2008).

3. http://www.americanaging.org/history.html. Accessed October 1, 2012.

4. http://www.maxlife.org/mission.asp. Accessed October 2, 2012.

5. www.sens.org.

6. Brian Alexander, "Don't Die, Stay Pretty: Introducing the Ultrahuman Makeover," *Wired* 8.01 (January 2000): 184.

7. In 2006, in response to a highly critical article by medical writer Sherwin Nuland, *Technology Review* magazine announced a $20,000 prize for any essay by a scientist demonstrating the SENS project was "unworthy of learned debate." There were numerous entries but the judges declared none had met the challenge. A half-prize was awarded to the best submission received. http://www.mprize.com/index.php?pagenam e=newsdetaildisplay&ID=0104. Accessed October 1, 2012.

8. Aubrey D. N. J. de Grey, "Biogerontologists' Duty to Discuss Timescales Publicly," *Annals of the New York Academy of Science* 1019 (2004): 542–45.

9. The President's Council on Bioethics, *Beyond Therapy: Biotechnology and the Pursuit of Happiness,* Washington, DC, October 2003. http://bioethics.georgetown .edu/pcbe/reports/beyondtherapy/index.html

10. "Who Wants to Live Forever? Scientist Sees Aging Cured," *Reuters* (July 4, 2011). http://www.reuters.com/article/2011/07/04/us-ageing-cure-idUSTRE7632ID20110704. Accessed October 1, 2012.

11. The author is grateful to Christina Staudt, PhD, for this point.

12. The author is grateful to Kristin Nelson, MA, for this point.

13. For a detailed consideration of the social impact of life extension, and the ethics of the issues that raises, see Kevin T. Keith, "Life Extension: Proponents, Opponents, and the Social Impact of the Defeat of Death," in *Speaking of Death: America's New Sense of Mortality,* ed. Michael K. Bartalos (New York: Praeger Publishing, 2008), 102–51.

14. Jerry Thomas Nessel, "Opportunities and Obstacles Towards Postponing Death and Postponing Dying," presented at the Third Austin H. Kutscher Memorial Conference, Columbia University, March 24, 2012.

15. Erica Borgstrom, "Ensuring a Good Death—English Policy for and Experiences of End-of-Life Care," presented at the Third Austin H. Kutscher Memorial Conference, Columbia University, March 24, 2012

16. Howard J. Sherman, E. K. Hunt, Reynold F. Nesiba, and Phillip A. Ohara, *Economics: An Introduction to Traditional and Progressive Views* (New York: M. E. Sharpe, 2008), 326.

17. Interestingly, price itself is often taken as a mark of quality by consumers—thus a certain product may induce consumers to pay a high price for its perceived prestige simply because its price is high. Charles W. Lamb, Joe F. Hair, Jr., and Carl McDaniel, *Essentials of Marketing* (Mason, OH: Thomson South Western College Publishing, 2008), 487.

18. Such goods are sometimes termed "Veblen goods," in reference to Thorstein Veblen's theory of "conspicuous consumption," A. Mitchell Polinsky and Steven Shavell, *Handbook of Law and Economics,* Vol. 2 (Amsterdam: North Holland Press, 2007), 1542.

19. http://ucatlas.ucsc.edu/spend.php. Accessed October1, 2012.

20. Samuel Marshall, Kathleen M. McGarry, and Jonathan S. Skinner, "The Risk of Out-of-Pocket Health Care Expenditure at End of Life," National Bureau of Economic Research Working Paper Number 16170, July 2010.

21. Ibid.

22. www.sens.org

23. http://www.census.gov/compendia/statab/2012/tables/12s1339.pdf.   Accessed September 30, 2012.

Chapter 16

Solidarity, Mortality: The Tolling Bell of Civic Palliative Care

Bruce Jennings

No man is an Iland, intire of it selfe; every man is a peece of the Continent, a part of the maine; . . . any mans death diminishes me, because I am involved in Mankinde; And therefore never send to know for whom the bell tolls; It tolls for thee.

—John Donne[1]

*T*his chapter argues that dying cannot be understood properly, or responded to well, without recourse to the connections between the dying experience and the larger social structures that make up a social and civic community. End-of-life care should respect persons and promote their well-being and flourishing, and it is fundamentally a public health issue. Inadequate end-of-life care is a function of a failing system of health-care and communal provision. To develop this perspective the chapter discusses the basic conception of what end-of-life care is—what kinds of relationships among care givers and care recipients are involved, what kinds of motivations drive those interactions, and what kinds of underlying assumptions about the self and its social ecology are at play. It also presents an analysis of the concept of solidarity in social policies and practices connecting those who are dying and those who are not. Finally, the chapter argues that we must develop a new kind of end-of-life care system that extends *beyond professional expertise and consumerism to encompass the capacities, resources, and social capital of entire communities. I call this new system civic palliative care. The moral awareness of solidarity can enable us to accomplish this.*

In *The Sociological Imagination,* C. Wright Mills formulated an important distinction between "personal troubles of milieu" and "public issues of social structure."[2] These are different ways of seeing and different ways of understanding the experience of self and world. To exercise the sociological, or, as I would prefer to say, the "civic," imagination is to move from viewing events or experiences as personal troubles to viewing them as public issues. This imagination has to do with reality as it is, not fantasy. It connects forces at work in history and society with the shape of one's own life, thoughts, and feelings.

The purpose of this chapter is to reflect on how we might come to see death, dying, and end-of-life care as "public issues" rather than as "personal troubles." This, I believe, is one fundamental change in perception that will be essential in the coming population explosion of aging in the 21st century. Mills defines troubles as those things that "occur within the character of the individual and within the range of his immediate relations with others; they have to do with his self and with those limited areas of social life of which he is directly and personally aware." In contrast, issues "have to do with the organization of many such milieu into the institutions of an historical society as a whole."[3]

In these terms, death and dying would appear to be the quintessential examples of troubles in human life. Do not the process of dying and the experience of end-stage illness constrict our lives and attention, contract the circumference of the circle of our activities and engagements, and progressively narrow the scope of our self-identity? We become preoccupied with our disease, our symptoms, and our medical treatments. We become deeply embodied—and more consciously aware of our embodiment—than at previous times of health. In that sense, at least, dying is the phenomenological extension of aging, during which we also become more conscious of bodies that we had heretofore ignored as if they were more or less on automatic pilot. Moreover, when dying we tend to move away from the public world and into the intimate household of our families and close friends.

Yet, even though dying throws us into the troubles of personal milieu, this is not the whole truth about it. Dying cannot be understood properly, or responded to well, without recourse to the connections between the dying experience and the larger social structures and connections that make up a social and civic community. End-of-life care is often viewed as exclusively a problem for clinical medicine, but it is also a public health issue.[4] Indeed, it is my contention that *our ethical ideals of a good dying experience and just care for the dying person depend upon our appreciation of these matters as public issues. Dying and care giving are human activities that are fundamentally conditioned and informed by larger civic and social structures.* What I intend by "good" dying here involves the conditions of presence, compassion, effective relief of suffering, and support in the sustaining of a sense of agency and meaning; and "just" care involves fairness, autonomy, dignity, and respect. Inadequate end-of-life care is neither a personal trouble nor a family failing primarily; it is a function of a failing civic system of health care and communal provision.

These failures are complex and have multiple causes, not the least important of which involve financial motivation and incentives, on the one hand, and matters of power, status, and control, on the other. In this chapter, though, I leave such matters aside in order to concentrate on the shaping power of ideas and cultural conceptions and values. If we do not critically reexamine several of the basic notions that we all bring to the topic of the care of the dying, then financial, political, and professional reforms may not be successful, if they can even be initiated in the first place.

Accordingly, I shall explore in some detail two cultural conceptions that I regard as fundamental, but relatively neglected, topics in end-of-life care ethics. The first is the basic conception of what end-of-life care is: what kinds of relationships among care givers and care recipients are involved, what kinds of motivations drive those interactions, and what kinds of underlying assumptions about the dying self and its social ecology are at play. The second conception to be explored is the meaning and analysis of solidarity: what kind of connection and identification can exist between those who are dying and those who are not, and what are the motivational and moral implications of such a connection, or the lack thereof.

WHAT DO WE DO WHEN WE CARE FOR THE DYING?

It is often said that America is a culture that denies death. Yet, there is a growing recognition of the dilemmas that high technology medicine has created for critically and terminally ill persons, and a dawning recognition of the staggering social problems that loom in the graying of the baby-boom generation. Looming ahead is the specter of dying bad deaths—deaths with inadequate palliative support, inadequate compassion, and inadequate human presence and witness; deaths preceded by a dying marked by fear, anxiety, loneliness, and isolation; and deaths that efface dignity and deny individual self-control and choice.

The fact is that too many Americans approach death without adequate medical, nursing, social, and spiritual support.[5] In the last stage of a long struggle with incurable, progressive diseases such as cancer, heart or lung disease, AIDS, Alzheimer's, Parkinson's, or amyotrophic lateral sclerosis, the pain of too many is untreated or inadequately controlled. Their depression or other mental health problems are not addressed. Debilitating physical symptoms rob them of energy, dignity, and sometimes the will to carry on. Family members who provide care are stressed, inadequately supported by professionals, and often rendered ill themselves by the ordeal. Patients who wish to remain in familiar surroundings at home are often forced to spend their final days or weeks in a hospital or nursing home. Neither dying patients nor their families are provided with the kind of emotional and spiritual support they desire and need.

Death is an inevitable aspect of the human condition. Dying badly is not. Yet it usually cannot be avoided by single individuals and families acting alone. Dying badly is a social problem that requires a civic solution. It is an artifact of the way our health-care system is organized and financed. And it is a product of a failure of civic imagination and solidarity—our inability to perceive dying and the care near the end of life as a civic issue and our lack of what I shall call the solidarity of a shared mortality.

The population of seniors in the United States is projected to more than double over the next 40 years, rising from 35 million in 2000 to over 88 million by 2050. At that time, one in five Americans will be age 65 or older. Those 80 and above will be the most populous age group in the country—32.5 million or 7.4 percent of the population.[6] America's chronic care, long-term care, and end-of-life care systems (if they can even be called that, so fragmented and patchwork, are they) are nowhere near ready to face the human demands that these demographic trends will create.[7] The challenge now is to design a more adequate health-care system and infrastructure.[8] This is necessary across the entire life span, of course, but especially important during the last year or two of life, during which incurable, progressive chronic disease that erodes quality of life reaches a time when technological intervention to prolong life may become both futile and harmful.[9]

The problems and shortcomings of end-of-life care in the United States have not gone unnoticed, of course. For the past 40 years, from the establishment of the first hospice program in 1973, and the landmark New Jersey Supreme Court decision in the Karen Ann Quinlan case in 1976, to the 1990 United States Supreme Court decision in the case of Nancy Beth Cruzan, a movement to empower and protect dying persons has been underway. This can be characterized as a consumerist reform, as I will explain more fully below, and this shift was monumental. There is no question of going backward to reembrace paternalistic medical control in end-of-life decision making, but consumerist reform has now reached the limits of its viability. What is needed today, and indeed what has been quietly forming and building up pressure since the 1990s, is another complex shift in orientation for end-of-life care represented by the philosophy of what might be called "civic (or social) palliative care." This represents a movement of tectonic plates in our moral imagination and caring practices, so to speak, to produce a new conceptual foundation for end-of-life care ethics and new institutional structures for end-of-life care practice. It is the shift from an individualistic perspective to one that is relational, civic, and communal.

THREE ORIENTATIONS OF CARE NEAR THE END OF LIFE

There are three different ways of answering the question: "What are we doing when we give or receive end-of-life care?" The first answer is that we are trying to save or rescue the person from that which is undermining function and might eventually (but not yet) cause death. Alternatively, we can view medical treatment and care as a commodity or service that is consumed to further the individual person's interests, as defined by the patient in accordance with his or her underlying biological condition, values, beliefs, and preferences. Finally, we can see end-of-life care, as is the case with all forms of care generally, as the creation of a system or "ecology" of assisting, affirming relationships that support and sustain the person's capabilities for meaning, self-esteem, and agency, even as the person is living with, and in spite of, a life-limiting illness.

The first of these is an activity that involves *benevolent medical control and compliance*. It fights death in the hope of staving off or defeating it. It focuses on the biological system of the dying person and the technological manipulation of it. The second is an activity that involves providing *consumer-oriented medical services*. It facilitates the person's chosen manner of facing the approach of death. It focuses on planning and decision making in terms of a benefits versus burdens calculus. The third is an activity that can be called *civic palliative care* (as distinct from only pain control or symptom management, which might be thought of as personal palliative care). It creates a social and cultural lifeworld for a person who has been adapted to her changing physical and psychological needs brought on by the terminal stage of illness. It focuses on the meaning and quality of living during the last chapter of one's life.

The benevolent medical control conception perceives the person confronted with a life-limiting illness as the victim of an attack; this model enlists medicine as the defender and rescuer of the endangered victim. The medical services conception sees dying persons as socially unencumbered selves, with separate, individualistic interests, still planning and directing their plan of life right up to the end—for instance, dying consumers enlisting medicine in the quest to control the dying process in accordance with preferences and values. The civic palliative care concept sees dying persons, not as self-sufficient or self-sovereign individuals, but as relational and interdependent selves. It defines the situation of dying persons in social, emotional, and transactional terms; that is, dying is a process that takes place within a system of interrelationships and a network of shared meanings, both private and public. Benevolent medical control is centered on need; medical service on individual interests and rights; and civic palliative care on human flourishing in community.

I shall elaborate on these three orientations in a moment. First, let me say that I do not offer these distinctions in order to conclude that one is appropriate and the others misguided. This is not a question of correct or incorrect ways of perceiving, thinking, and feeling. Human life and experience are multifaceted and complex; each of these orientations survives because it helps in some way to make sense of the experience of dying. Most people and society as a whole cling to the medical treatment model, but often at great cost to the dying person, who experiences the ordeal of aggressive but futile life-sustaining treatment, and to the families and other loved ones who watch.

However, I do believe the civic or social or relational orientation holds the greatest promise to guide the ethical treatment of persons with incurable, irreversible terminal illness and their families. The remaining and as yet unfulfilled promise of good dying and just caring requires a countervailing vision to offset the medical orientation and the will to power in the face of death. It also requires a fundamentally different way of conceiving the personhood of the patient, the context of communication and care giving, and the goals of care.

BENEVOLENT MEDICAL CONTROL

Medical treatment is fundamentally about power. A patient's power derives from the physician's power and from the power of medical science and technology to rescue the patient from illness and to preserve and prolong life. Indeed, power is so basic to the way we have come to think about medical care that we don't often state it explicitly. Power colors the way we think and feel about illness, disability, and hope. In the context of death and dying, it is a profound obstacle to the acceptance of biological limits to what we can control.

Our predominant cultural image of disease or illness is that of a foreign invader, something that attacks us and against which we must be defended. This enemy will deprive us of what is supremely valuable to us, either life itself or life as we ideally wish to live it. There is never a time when this attack is natural or should be accepted.

Medical control is a perspective that reinforces—and is reinforced by—the military metaphors commonplace in our cultural ideology of medicine. The patient and physician enter an "alliance" in which the technical armamentarium of medicine is used to defend the patient and attack the invader. Such metaphors tend to rationalize any pain, suffering, or disruption of personal life that the patient and those around him or her are asked to endure: The more deadly the enemy, the greater the sacrifice that may be required to win the war. The body becomes a battleground, and patients go to war on themselves.

Seeing the illness as a threatening intruder allows us to externalize and objectify it, and makes the illness extrinsic and foreign to the person, even though it is inside the body. Illness represents a temporary identity imposed on the person by an alien source, an estrangement that thwarts self-determination and the pursuit of life's normal goals. Similarly, illness undermines well-being because well-being is taken to mean a state of being well without—not in spite of—illness; a state of being for which illness is an Other.

The desire to have power and control over death often takes precedence over dignity and quality of life. This is shown by people's willingness to submit to temporary pain, suffering, and dependency on others in return for access to the possible beneficial forces of scientific knowledge and technological interventions that may overpower death. How else to explain the willingness to undergo the significant risks of major surgery and difficult rehabilitation? How else to explain the willingness to put up with the side effects of powerful cancer treatments, and even to clamor for acceptance into experimental treatment programs?

At bottom, the medical control orientation renders patients passive, submissive, and reactive. From the patient's perspective the paradox of medical treatment is that one must relinquish power in order to gain power. The tacit contract of the medical perspective is roughly as follows. The physician says to the patient: "You suspend your normal activities and expectations for a while, give me your body, which I may use roughly, but out of care and concern, not out of malice, and I will give you back your life, your healthy function restored as much as humanly possible, and extra time."

Acute medical treatment aimed at cure or life-prolongation often entails a crisis in one's sense of place and the relationship between self-identity and place. Institutionalization, even in the most benign of hospitals or nursing facilities, inherently involves the abandonment of one's personal identity and everyday roles and the assumption of a very different persona and role. The so-called patient role or sick role is a condition of passivity and temporary exemption from ordinary social norms and expectations. While you undergo the suffering, exposure, and helplessness of submitting to treatment, you are socially and morally indulged by those to whom you have entrusted your life. This experience can precipitate a feeling of loss of self-identity. It can cause an alienation from one's past—and perhaps even from what one fears will be the future—at the very time when it is precisely that past that one is desperate to regain. Moreover, it can involve a detachment from one's family and closest loved ones who, still healthy and whole, reside on the other side of the looking glass.

CONSUMING MEDICAL SERVICES

The medical control orientation is paternalistic. In medical ethics and the law there has been a strong shift away from physician paternalism and patient passivity, and the style of discourse has changed from military metaphors to commercial ones. With the idea of defeating death still hovering in the background, end-of-life care in the medical services conception is about providing services that are in keeping with the interests, preferences, and values of the patient as a separate and unique individual. Accordingly, power and authority in the decision-making process have shifted from the expert physician to the sovereign consumer of that expertise, and in hospitals, as in hardware stores, "the customer is always right." Depending on the patient's personal goals, this arrangement may lead to an attempt to deny death through aggressive life-sustaining treatment, or to accept it through decisions to forgo life-sustaining treatment and transfer into a hospice program. In this orientation, the main concern about the power of medical technology is not that it may be unsuccessful and ineffective, but that it may be wrongly used or forgone: that it will fall into the wrong hands—a greedy physician, a malevolent or uncaring family member, or the state.

In addition to these concerns about power, the emergence of the medical services orientation in end-of-life decision making focuses on respect for the dignity and self-sovereignty of the patient. Lethal illness is still the enemy, but the patient's body is no longer a battlefield commanded by physician-generals; it is now the private property of the patient. The physician who imposes unwanted or burdensome treatments is a trespasser; the one who fails to provide wanted and beneficial treatment is a poor steward; and both are accountable to the landlord.

However familiar this commercial rhetoric and neoliberal individualistic orientation may be, the medical services conception is out of step with the experiences and values of many dying patients and their families. In rejecting medical paternalism in favor of individual consumerism in end-of-life care, the law has created a decision-making process that very few people, and not always even lawyers themselves, can understand; a process that is difficult to navigate successfully during times of extreme illness and emotional turmoil.

CIVIC PALLIATIVE CARE AND SOCIAL ECOLOGY

Understanding the ethical dimension of end-of-life care (including hospice and palliative care) requires more than a traditionally individualistic conception of rights and interests; it requires that we shift our focus from the individual interests' orientation to a social ecology orientation. In biology and environmental science, ecology is the study of the systemic interaction and interdependency of various organisms among themselves and with their inorganic environment. Social ecology applies the same systems approach to the complex nexus of social and cultural relations among human beings, with their extraordinarily diverse and powerful cognitive, affective, and communicative capacities.

The notion of social ecology is an essential element of the emergence of a civic palliative care. This orientation is particularly apt with regard to the human experience of dying and death.[10] Intense, highly charged and delicate, and invested with meanings that are at once intimately personal or private and necessarily social and public, dying is a particularly complex social performance that takes place in an exceedingly dense or thick cultural environment. This enactment of the dying process can destroy the delicate social ecology of families and the tissue of meaning that dying patients and families need in order to get a grip on the terrible thing that has befallen them. When it was technologically impotent, medicine (together with religion) presided over social rituals and cultural meaning during the dying process. Relationships and identities were repaired and renewed—with family and friends at hand, with an opportunity to reconcile with those estranged, to forgive and to ask forgiveness. Today, medicine and medical treatment decisions set up a dynamic that makes that ecology unstable at best, impossible at worst.[11]

To improve end-of-life care, liberation of the patient from the paternalism of the medical control orientation is necessary, but far from sufficient. Law, ethics, and policy must also come to grips with fundamentally communal and public—not private—issues of mortality and meaning. We sometimes seem to act as though dying were solely the concern of the dying person. This vision is too narrow. What happens in dying—like what happens in life—is shaped by and shapes social relationships. This is one of the key insights of civic palliative care.

Central to the task of developing the concept of civic palliative care are the concepts of personhood and relationships—or, more precisely, *personhood in and through relationships*. These concepts have been profoundly shaped and defined by the individualistic notions of patient rights and interests now governing treatment decision making at the end of life. The quotidian moral experience of our familial and relational lives as selves—our social embeddedness as persons—serves as an essential corrective to the aspiration for control and individualistic independence, moderating and civilizing, so to speak, the will to power and the will to die strictly on one's own terms.

Civic palliative care combines respect for developmental personhood with respect for the inherent dignity of all human beings and respect for their need for fidelity, presence, mutuality, and solidarity. It acknowledges, as it were, that we are all citizens of a republic of suffering and mortality.[12] To be spared death is to navigate those relationships and meanings intact through the shoals of a crisis and to attain survival; to die well is to preserve, and perhaps repair, those relationships right up until the end, and even beyond in the memory of those who do survive.

SOLIDARITY, MORTALITY

The challenge facing us is to rebuild, reinforce, and reinterpret our laws, institutions, and practices around the acknowledgment that dying is interpersonal, not strictly individualistic. With this in mind I turn now to the concept of solidarity. Although not entirely absent from discussions of end-of-life care, particularly in the language of the hospice movement, solidarity has not been sufficiently drawn upon and deployed to make the case for broader moral, political, and financial support for universal access to high-quality palliative care.[13] Moreover, at least in the interpretation of the concept of solidarity that I articulate below, solidarity has a social and motivational trajectory that will reinforce political support for the care of the dying. It will enable us to see palliative care as a fundamental civic responsibility and function. Solidarity grows out of what Mills meant by the sociological imagination—its contextualizing gestalt shift of political and historical understanding and its discernment of connections among human beings that are obscured by structures of wealth, power, and privilege.

We can begin to get a better sense of what solidarity means by examining the nature of a society and a self that has lost or rejected the concept. Imagine a society in which the interests of each individual (including one's health status and the circumstances of one's own dying) are seen as *sui generis* and fundamentally distinct from the interests of others. Call it a society of instrumental, incidental cooperation. If my interests are fulfilled and yours are not, then I gain and you lose; I am fortunate, you unfortunate; I am skillful and successful, and you are not. Sometimes, to be sure, my success may depend in some way on your success and cooperation, but then your success is only an instrument of mine, not a constituent feature of it, and your success is valuable to me only incidentally, only *en passant,* as it were. If I can do without your cooperation, I shall: all the more to be secure, self-reliant, and independent.

In the lifeworld of such a society the same perspective would be extended to the distribution of health and disease and to the collective meaning given to the experience of a particular state of health by each individual. If I am healthy and you are sick, your low level of health does not affect in any way my high level of health because we are essentially separate beings. Of course, your illness may affect my future health, through infection or in some other way, but that involves merely an external connection between your health status and mine. There is no internal connection such that your condition is actually a constitutive element of my condition. The factors leading to health (or illness) are assessed for each individual separately and serially. The same holds for someone's dying. *PaceDonne*, it does not diminish me fundamentally. We all die our own deaths, separately. We are all alone together.

Consider now a self devoid of solidarity. A vision of the individual agent unencumbered, as it were, by solidarity is a vision that stresses the uniqueness of each person and emphasizes difference and separation rather than sameness and commonality. Instrumental ties are the limit of relationality. Any more robust, intrinsically valuable, or identity-constituting connection with others is precluded as something that stunts or effaces the self. In an alternative solidaristic perspective, connection could be seen instead as an enabling or empowering medium of self-realization.[14] The interests of the individual are pursued through instrumental forms of cooperation, strategic action, and normative commitments, but those interests are constituted prior to and independently of such transactions, not in and through them. Personhood here is not seen in terms of those dimensions of the human condition that incline one toward solidarity and related concepts—our common human vulnerability and insufficiency as physically embodied and socially embedded creatures of need, desire, and want.[15]

The society of instrumental cooperation also has a delimited normative vocabulary with which to evaluate and justify its governance and common rules of conduct. This is primarily the language of negative rights, liberties, and obligations, such as the "right to be let alone,"[16] on the normative side, and the language of interests, utilities, and preferences on the motivational side. Health policies that regulate health-care financing, health-care delivery, and public health programs in such a society are subject to a calculus of risk–benefit ratios, means-end rationality, and the balancing of individual rights of self-determination with obligations of self-restraint. In the final analysis, such obligations can really only be grounded on enlightened considerations of self-interest. There is no moral encumbrance here, no normative push of commitment or obligation, no motivational pull of mutual recognition and resemblance; there is simply the logic of collective action, in the sense of individuals happening to act self-interestedly together.

This delimited moral vocabulary, and this delimited scope of available commitments and motivations for individual and civic agency, leaves out something that is fundamental to the successful enterprise of end-of-life care in modern societies. Those who are dying are among the least valuable assets in a society limited to instrumental cooperation and self-interest. *On what basis do we articulate the ethical reasons why we should expend resources and care for the dying?* When the conversation centers, as it so often does these days, on how hospice and palliative care are justified by the fact that they are cost-effective ways to provide care to persons in the last year or few months of their lives, this fundamental question gets swept under the rug. The justification of civic palliative care is based on its goodness (the facilitation of human flourishing) and rightness (equitable respect for the dignity and worth of all persons); its efficiency, real and valid though it is, is but a means to those ends. The moral pull or calling of those ends cannot be understood coherently without recourse to the concept of solidarity.

SOLIDARITY IN FOUR DIMENSIONS

I want to now offer an interpretive account of solidarity that will provide a grounding for civic palliative care (among other health policies and social welfare practices).[17] This account is based on the idea that expressing what is called solidarity involves a social action or practice of proximity, public identification, and support— in a word, it involves a standing up. With this in mind, I take solidarity to be a practice with four phases or dimensions. The basic dimension of solidarity is as a form of *standing up beside.* In addition, there are three developmental dimensions of solidarity: *standing up for, standing up with,* and *standing up as.*

Standing Up Beside

This is solidarity's characteristic gesture and stance as a moral action. Solidaristic moral action can be undertaken by both individuals and groups. Solidarity is a form of active engagement, not simply passive support. It is an intentional, engaged form of agency. It is purposive and motivated by a public commitment that exposes the agent to social visibility and potentially to risk and harmful consequences.

When you stand up beside a person (including one who is dying), a group, an organization, or even an idea or ideal, you make yourself visible; it is an inherently and necessarily public gesture. One can perhaps "take a stand," in the sense of making a moral or normative commitment in the privacy of one's life, behind the closed doors of one's conscience, or in the safety of one's circle of friends, but that is not solidarity. Solidarity requires both taking a stand and standing up. This public posture also carries with it a sense of urgency and moral importance to both the agent being seen and to those who are looking. One stands up beside someone or something because one has something of importance to say, so that one can be seen and heard. Civic palliative care is a public standing up beside the dying.

In solidarity as standing up one is elevating one's moral and social awareness and commitment: one is moving upward toward justice, such as the redress of the oppression or denigration of others, or the reduction of racial disparity in health, and an increase in equality of personal dignity and respect. And one is moving laterally from where one is (apart) to a place closer (beside) to where one ought to be and is needed by others. This standing, this public agency, is one gesture in the realization of a moral imagination. Of course, there are many other motivations, including narcissistic ones, for calling attention to oneself, but this communal and moral seriousness is the semantic resonance that the notion of solidarity as standing up beside carries with it.

Exercising the moral imagination through the agency of solidarity may put one in harm's way. But it is a mistake to make solidarity a joyless and dour virtue. In a way characteristic of the ambivalence of the concept of solidarity, it is both sacrificial of the self in a certain sense, and liberating and enhancing of the self in another. However that may be, solidarity runs counter to the prime directive of self-interest maximization that is so predominant in our society and health-care system today.

Standing Up For

This suggests an intention to assist or advocate for the Other. Oftentimes the Other is a stranger, and not necessarily a human individual: one can stand up for other species, an ecosystem, or a cultural way of life. The Other for whom one stands up in solidarity is someone whose situation presumably is problematic either because of how they are seen by others (stigma) or because of what is being done or happening to them, such as suffering from an incurable, terminal illness.

Standing up for is only the first stage of the development of solidarity, and it is a relatively weak form. The reason is that this mode of solidarity can imply a continued differentiation, even condescension, in the relationship between those individuals or groups standing up and those others who are being stood up for. This kind of solidarity can advocate for improved treatment or benefits for an oppressed or vulnerable group, but does not necessarily challenge the underlying basis for their subordinate social status. Advocacy-for can become a self-perpetuating rather than a self-transcending mode of action. Inasmuch as it does not undermine the structural inequalities, it serves to perpetuate the need for its own continuing existence.

Standing Up With

The third dimension of solidarity goes some way toward avoiding the trap of relating to the Other as victim or as persons whose situation can (and should) be ameliorated but cannot structurally be transformed. Moving from *relationality for* to *relationality with* is meant to signal that solidarity involves the entry into the lifeworld of the Other. Doing so entails changes in one's initial prejudgments and perspectives, and solidarity as standing with requires an openness to this possibility.

To put this point slightly differently, there is something in the imaginative dynamic of moving from *for* to *with* that is transformative of the solidarity relationship so that a (supportive) stranger-to-stranger relationship begins to develop, perhaps not all the way to a relationship that should be called friendship (*philia*, as Aristotle understood it) but at least to a stronger kind of fellowship and mutual recognition of one's self in the face of the Other, "*mon semblable, mon frère*," as Baudelaire put it. Relating to other people or groups in the specificity of their values and vocabularies of self-interpretation simultaneously develops respect for the specific standpoints of others.[18] Being with in this sense also reveals a level of commonality between the parties to this kind of solidarity that resides in the capacity for intercultural and transpersonal interpretive understanding.[19] The difference created by the specificity of lifeworlds resides within the commonality of the ability to understand lifeworlds other than one's own. Solidarity contains the possibility of being common readers of the diverse and distinct lives we each author.

Standing Up As

Obviously this suggests a yet stronger degree of identification between the agents of solidaristic support and the recipients of such support. However, what I have in mind here has nothing to do with "going native" as a form of solidarity in a diverse, multiracial, multiethnic society. For agents engaged in the practice of solidarity who reach this mode of relationship, it is not a question of denying diversity or doing away with the continuing obligation to recognize and respect difference. The solidarity of standing up as involves finding an overarching connection that does not negate diversity at all, but rather establishes the grounds of its respect, protection, and continuation. This is the notion at work in the phrase *E pluribus unum,* for example; although the point I am making here is that one can also find plurality reaffirmed, even strengthened, in acknowledging an overarching sameness.

It is very important not to overlook this interplay between the perspectives of sameness and difference. In end-of-life care, for example, there has been an extensive discussion of the impact of cultural and ethnic diversity on the use of advance directives, treatment decision making, and the role of family members. Much of that discussion has emphasized difference so strongly, making the cultural divide separating dying patients and health-care professionals so broad, that practically the only framework within which to understand the caring and the decision-making relationship is the notion of consumerism of medical services. This notion of solidarity in the sense of standing up as provides an alternative to that unfortunate conceptual dead end.

FORMING THE MORAL IMAGINATION OF SOLIDARITY

To move from the first of these dimensions of solidarity through the second and third to the fourth is to move in the direction of greater imaginative creativity and range in the moral life. Standing up for depends upon a kind of abstract moral commitment to support the application of general norms to the life situation of the Other as a creature with a certain moral status. It thereby embraces common moral rules or principles, such as equal protection of the law and universal human rights, without more fully embracing the lived reality and distinct perspectives of the Other. Standing up with involves adopting a perspective that is more internal to the lifeworld and the contextually meaningful agency of the Other. Standing up as returns to generality, but this time synthesizing the general system of justice and human rights with the context of meaningful agency, motivation, and self-identity, thereby synthesizing cosmopolitan humanity with a particular manifestation of humanness in a specific place and time. Standing up as is the solidarity of humanity, or more fully expressed, the solidarity of being embodied, vulnerable, metabolic, and social organisms. It is also the solidarity of mortality.

BUILDING CIVIC PALLIATIVE CARE

There are some fundamental aspects of the human condition and human experience that naturally lead us up a path of increasing moral awareness. In the world of human relationships, solidarity traces one such path; we grow in moral awareness as we go from understanding ourselves as in relationship for others, through being in relationship with others, to an understanding of being in a relationship as others: "oneself as another," as philosopher Paul Ricoeur expressed it.[20] A serious reflection on death and dying is one occasion, some would say the foundational occasion, for this sort of moral growth and learning.

My thought in this chapter has been that taking the next step in achieving this moral growth requires that we develop a new kind of end-of-life care system, one that extends beyond professional expertise and consumerism to encompass the capacities, resources, and social capital of entire communities. I call this new system civic palliative care. The moral awareness is that solidarity not only requires us to develop this community based end-of-life care system but also enables us to do so by laying the foundation for a social consensus on behalf of comprehensive palliative care that will gain political support. Then we will create communities that understand, in the spirit of John Donne, that the dying of every person affects all persons. And it does so precisely because we are connected by more than instrumental utility and self-interest, fear and desire for security. We are connected by a shared ontology of interdependency, meaning, and a life embedded in time and change, ending in death.

Civic palliative care is based on three characteristics of the original hospice philosophy of care. First, civic palliative care has a calling, a mission. By providing expert, experienced care and symptom management, it responds to the call—the imperative—that issues forth from the sheer suffering of a human being and from the common humanity one shares with that person, and those close to her. Second, civic palliative care is flexible and dynamic in developing new partnerships and connections with the assets and capabilities found in local communities. In these communities the palliative care organization is not so much an expert authority, or a mere vendor of services (albeit precious services), but is an active citizen and member. Third, civic palliative care provides continuity of care giving and care planning, across a broad continuum of settings and services, as the patient moves along a trajectory of chronic, debilitating, and life-limiting illness. These characteristics reflect goals that hospice has sought to adhere to; but their implications extend well beyond what we currently designate as "hospice" alone. They also provide elements for a restructuring of the entire system of care in the final chapter of life.

At the heart of this new vision—and a system that could embody its practice—is the notion of care for the "condition" of the dying person, that is to say, the social being of the person. The object of civic palliative care is the patient's embodied and relationally embedded personhood, not just her disease, symptoms, or isolated body and self. Palliative care and hospice are often referred to as "holistic" forms of care, focusing on the psychological and social aspects of the patient's lived experience of the disease or the implications of the disease state for family members or others. The notion of caring for a total human situation or condition implies a respect for the integrity and participation of both patient and family members. It also betokens an active process of controlling symptoms and handling aspects of everyday life so that they do not undermine the kinds of relationships, reminiscences, communication, feelings, and activities that the patient finds meaningful and that give remaining life its positive quality.

Civic palliative care must thoroughly understand how to negotiate the fissures and crevices of the American health-care system. It will be in a good position to know when the fabric of a local community and its social capital are in need of repair. In the future aging society, universal access to insurance coverage will only come on the condition of greater accountability and cost containment. Civic palliative care builds upon hospice, which has always had a capitated payment arrangement and has found ways to coordinate care among many providers. Therefore, civic palliative care should be well positioned in the emerging health-care system. It offers perhaps the most promising way to provide enhanced continuity across institutional settings and to assist patients and families who are wrestling with complex clinical and personal decisions.

Having someone serving as a broker, health-care advocate, or "case manager" in a bewildering system can often be just as important to patients and families as the provision of medical and nursing care and symptom management. Civic palliative care will be a system of *condition-focused management achieving continuity of care across a continuum of services.* In addition to focusing on the care of those facing a terminal illness, civic palliative care will be active in the delivery or development of programs for individuals who want symptom management and adaptive counseling even as they find their way through the labyrinth, too often a dark one, of an ongoing chronic illness. It will also serve those facing the debilitating effects of aging or those in need of bereavement in the wake of sudden and catastrophic death of loved ones, or even of one's fellow citizens or their children.

Palliative care and hospice must develop new organizational forms if they are to function in this way. The development of such new forms of financing and delivery for civic palliative care will tax the political courage of health policy makers and the creativity of palliative care and hospice leaders. It will also require that policymakers begin to combine health care with social care, and the combination of civic palliative care and other initiatives of civic renewal can provide the model for doing so.[21] While the first expression of civic palliative care may be care of the dying, in the final reckoning, the scope of its mission and contribution will grow. Civic palliative care will take its place within a wide array of other civic and service organizations as an active participant, a plain member and citizen, of a just, healthy, caring, and resilient civic community.

NOTES

1. John Donne, "Devotions upon Emergent Occasions," Meditation XVII, in *The Complete Poetry and Selected Prose of John Donne,* ed. Charles M. Coffin (New York: Random House, 1952), 441.

2. C. W. Mills, *The Sociological Imagination* (New York: Oxford University Press, 1959), 8.

3. Ibid., 8.

4. J. Cohen and L. Deliens, eds.,*A Public Health Perspective on End-of-life Care.* (Oxford: Oxford University Press, 2012). J. K. Rao, L. A. Anderson, and S. M. Smith, "End-of-life Is a Public Health Issue," *American Journal of Preventive Medicine* 23, 3 (2002): 215–20. J. Stjernswärd, K. M. Foley, and F. D. Ferris, "The Public Health Strategy for Palliative Care," *Journal of Pain and Symptom Management* 33, 5 (2007): 486–93.

5. M. J. Field and C. K. Cassell, eds., *Approaching Death: Improving Care at the End of Life* (Washington, DC: National Academy Press, 1997). This sobering conclusion is reflected in the findings of The Last Acts Coalition, Means to a Better End: A Report on Dying in America Today (Washington, DC: Partnership for Caring, November 2002).

6. L. B. Shrestha and E. J. Heisler, *The Changing Demographic Profile of the United States* (Washington, DC: Congressional Research Service, 7–5700, 2011), http://www.fas.org/sgp/crs/misc/RL32701.pdf

7. J. Lynn, "Living Long in Fragile Health: New Demographics Shape End-of-life Care," in *Improving End-of-Life Care: Why Has it Been so Difficult?* ed. B. Jennings, G. Kaebnick, and T. H. Murray, Hastings Center Special Report 35, 6 (November/December 2005): S14–18.

8. C. Schoen, R. Osborn, S. K. H. How, M. M. Doty, and J. Peugh, "In Chronic Condition: Experiences of Patients with Complex Health Care Needs, in Eight Countries, 2008," *Health Affairs* 28, 1 (2009): w1–w16. L. O. Gostin, J. I. Boufford, and R. M. Martinez, "Future of Public's Health: Vision, Values and Strategies," *Health Affairs* 23, 4 (2004): 96–107.

9. J. Lynn, *Sick To Death and Not Going to Take It Anymore!: Reforming Health Care for the Last Years of Life* (Berkeley, CA: University of California Press, 2004).

10. M. B. Morrissey and B. Jennings, "A Social Ecology of Health Model in End-of-Life Decision Making: Is the Law Therapeutic?" *New York State Bar Association Health Law Journal* 11, 1 (Winter, 2006), 51–60.

11. S. R. Kaufman, *And a Time to Die: How American Hospitals Shape the End of Life* (New York: Scribner, 2005).

12. D. G. Faust, *This Republic of Suffering: Death and the American Civil War* (New York: Vintage, 2009).

13. The normative and empirical literature on solidarity is very large in both philosophy and the social sciences. Important works that bring solidarity to bear explicitly on bioethics include B. Prainsack and A. Buyx, *Solidarity: Reflections on an Emerging Concept in Bioethics* (London: The Nuffield Council, 2011). R. ter Meulen, W. Arts, and R. Muffels, eds.,*Solidarity in Health and Social Care in Europe* (Dordrecht: Kluwer Academic Publishers, 2001). S. L. Bartky, *Sympathy and Solidarity* (London: Roman and Littlefield, 2002). K. Bayertz, "Four Uses of Solidarity," in *Solidarity,*ed. K. Bayertz (Dordrecht: Kluwer Academic Publishers, 1999). H. Brunkhorst, *Solidarity: From* Civic Friendship to a Global Legal Community (Cambridge, MA: MIT Press, 2005).

14. A. E. Komter, *Social Solidarity and the Gift* (Cambridge: Cambridge University Press, 2005).

15. R. Forst, "How (Not) to Speak about Identity," *Philosophy and Social Criticism* 18, 3/4 (1992): 293–312.

16. This is Justice Lewis Brandeis's famous phrase in Olmsted v. United States, U.S. 438, 478 (1928).

17. The development of my thinking about the concept of solidarity has benefited greatly from collaboration with Angus Dawson, Professor of Public Health Ethics and Head of Medicine, Ethics, Society & History at the University of Birmingham in the UK.

18. J. Dean, "Reflective Solidarity," *Constellations* 2, 1 (1995): 114–40. J. Dean, *Solidarity of Strangers* (Berkeley, CA: University of California Press, 1996).

19. Forst, "How (Not) to Speak about Identity," 293–312.

20. P. Ricoeur, *Oneself as Another* (Chicago: University of Chicago Press, 1992).

21. See C. Sirianni and L. Friedland, *Civic Innovation in America: Community Empowerment, Public Policy, and the Movement for Civic Renewal* (Berkeley, CA: University of California Press, 2001).

(*JANOS retreats a little from SANDOR, from the pain of memory. SANDOR gently reaches out to him again.*)

SANDOR

I wouldn't call it blue. Fifty years I'm looking in this river, but I wouldn't call it blue.

(*Still JANOS cannot respond. SANDOR starts to leave. Perhaps he should give JANOS his privacy. But JANOS doesn't want to be left alone with the pain and the questions.*)

(*JANOS considers a moment. Perhaps there is a connection possible between them after all. On the other hand, JANOS thinks SANDOR is a hopeless romantic.*)

JANOS

Of course it's blue. What is it, pink? Water is blue!
(*They will agree to disagree.*)

From Burnt *by Robi Polgar and Catherine Rogers*

Conclusion: A Letter
from a Fellow Traveler

Christina Staudt

In the United States we have 100 percent mortality. When announced aloud, this statement rarely fails to send a ripple of astonished discomfort through an audience, or garner a self-conscious laugh from an individual person who hears it for the first time in conversation, as if a deep, slightly dirty secret has just been revealed. The introductory chapter of volume I of *Our Changing Journey to the End* references Geoffrey Gorer's *The Pornography of Death,* published in 1955[1] as the starting point of a slowly emerging interest in mortal matters in a time when such subjects were rarely mentioned. In the subsequent decades the nation began to look at death and the needs of the dying with increasing engagement. In 2013, the discourse on dying and grief is plentiful. Nevertheless, a trace of inappropriateness lingers at the mention of death's universal effect.

Dr. Richard Selzer, an eminent surgeon and best-selling author was asked to describe in an essay for this volume how his views on death, dying, and medical care have evolved from his personal perspective since the mid-20th century, and especially since his publication of *Mortal Lessons: Notes on the Art of Surgery* (1976) and *Letters to a Young Doctor* (1982). He responded:

August 30, 2012

Dear Christina Staudt,

Many thanks for your invitation to contribute to the volume on Dying in America. Several things make me hesitate to accept it. One is my age which is 84+ and entering the prime of my senility would make of accepting an uncertain promise. It is true over the course of decades I have changed my feelings about dying quite radically. I no longer look upon longevity as a blessing. It can be a misfortune in which one is forced to observe the inevitable deterioration of mind and body that comes with advanced age or incurable illness. I have come to doubt that the medical profession is doing its patients a service in prolonging life at any cost. As a practicing surgeon and a professor of surgery for many years, I presided over the death of many people, and each time, I felt a sense of having failed. Back then, dying was an abstraction that applied to other people—the human race, of which I was a member.

But with age, I think of dying as my own termination, a personal event. Of course, I am intellectually accepting of death as Man's fate, but that too is a generalization. Quite frankly, I have come to think of death as a welcome release from whatever sorrow and suffering will come.

As a doctor, I am in full support of Assisted Death for those who have intractable pain or insupportable mental or physical limitations. I would want that for myself. It is a reversal of the old battle cry of the revolution: Give me liberty or give me death". For me, it would be "Give me liberty AND give me death."[2]

I could pursue this further, but not in the form of an essay of some thousands of words aimed at publication. Again, thanks for the invitation. I sincerely regret having to turn it down.

Cordially,
Richard Selzer.

This thoughtful letter—published here by permission—elicits a few reflections on my part that serve as the conclusion of this volume.

. . . my age which is 84+ . . .

Dr. Selzer has exceeded his life expectancy at birth by 17 years. As a newborn, white, American male in 1929, he was expected to live until age 57. At 84, in 2013, actuarial tables predict he will live another six and a half years.[3] The average life expectancy for a baby born in 2015 is projected to be 78.9 (boys, 76.4 and girls 81.4 years).[4] Impressive strides have been made, yet, the life expectancy for the average person in Japan, Macau, and Singapore is about eight years longer than in the United States. In about 40 countries around the world, people have a higher life expectancy than Americans.[5]

The averages hide tremendous inequalities by race and ethnicity, sex and gender, geography and access to health care, education, occupation, and economic status, as well as psychosocial factors.[6] Overall in the United States, Hispanic females have the longest life span and black males the shortest. Cross-correlating race and state, among the extremes are Asian Americans in New Jersey and Native Americans in South Dakota, the former living, on average, 26 years longer than the latter. As an example of the range in one metropolitan area in California, those living in a section of Orange County from Newport Beach to Laguna Hills have a life expectancy of about 88 years; whereas the life expectancy in the Watts neighborhood of Los Angeles is about 73 years, or 15 years less.[7] For a newborn boy in Watts the picture is even grimmer, reflecting the deadly danger of being a disadvantaged, young black man in an area of urban poverty.

Life expectancy is not race-determined but correlates extensively with life style and socioeconomic status. Once people reach retirement age, the differences between blacks, whites, and Hispanics are evened out to within a year, and by age 80, black persons have longer life expectancy than whites. The gap between the life expectancy for blacks and whites narrowed between 2000 and 2009 from 5.5 years to 4.3 years. The nation's poorest state, Mississippi, has the lowest life expectancy with 74.8, and Hawaii, the highest with 80.[8]

The gap between the "haves" and the "have-nots" widened in the first decade of the 21st century; even as the average (mean) standard of living has increased, the poorer groups have lost ground.[9] Is this something that we, as a society care to reframe in order to make the journey to the end more equal? Or, will we in the future talk about two different journeys, one longer luxury ride for the affluent and a more modest, shorter one for the poor? The idea that some people may be spending the last days of their lives in a hospital's five-star accommodation is not just utopia—or dystopia, depending on one's point of view. Some hospitals already offer luxury hotel accommodations with concierge and butler services for those who are willing to pay the price.[10] The vast inequities in custodial personal care that this arrangement permits can be seen as somewhat mitigated by the excessive price of this extravagance. The rooms generate profits for the hospital's bottom line and may help everyone be served better.

. . . entering the prime of my senility . . .

I know nothing about Dr. Selzer's personal health condition so cannot judge if he is expressing a reality for himself or just the odds that face him. Alzheimer's and other dementia are on an upward trajectory as a cause of death, with Alzheimer's alone the fifth leading cause of death in the United States, claiming

85,000 lives in 2011. Other illness and injuries present an even greater threat, depending on one's genetic history and lifestyle.

A decade into the 21st century, approximately 2.5 million people die every year in the United States. By decree from the CDC, none of them succumb to "natural causes" or "old age."[11] The two leading causes of death are heart disease and cancer, accounting for about 600,000 and 575,000 deaths, respectively. They are followed by chronic lower respiratory diseases (145,000), and stroke (130,000), unintentional injuries (125,000), Alzheimer's (85,000), diabetes (75,000), influenza and pneumonia (55,000), kidney disease (45,000), and suicide (40,000).[12]

Because of the rapid upward trend of the Alzheimer's curve with the baby boomers entering the age groups when Alzheimer's presents itself in large numbers, this disease receives a lot of attention. Unless a way is found to cure or contain Alzheimer's, one of the great challenges for coming decades is to rethink the care settings that we create for those afflicted by the disease so that their treatment is humane, for them as well as for their loved ones.

The map of the top 10 causes of death may be substantially redrawn in the decades ahead. A cure for cancer has been predicted for decades. Notable success has been recorded in detecting, diagnosing and treating breast cancers through new screening methods and genetic advances, providing increasingly individualized treatments. With the research trends, for all malignant tumors moving further toward gene therapy and immunology, new optimism surfaces about the potential that living with cancer is more likely than dying from one of the many types it presents. Promising drugs may lower our risk for heart disease, stroke, kidney disease, and diabetes. Many deaths are preventable, or vastly reducible, but require changes in personal lifestyle and life choices, as well as systemic societal restructuring with realignment of priorities and allocation of resources. The direction of these last variables is perhaps the most challenging parts of the matrix to predict. To further complicate any prophesy, history has shown that it is also advisable to factor in the degree to which a disease is championed by popular celebrities, as well as which will resonate with members of Congress.

> *. . . I have changed my feelings about dying quite radically.*
> *I no longer look upon longevity as a blessing. . . .*

If Dr. Selzer has changed his outlook, in all likelihood, so have others his age. The prospect of growing old may be seen as a misfortune in which one is forced to observe the inevitable deterioration of mind and body that comes with advanced age or incurable illness. It is reasonable to expect that many elderly may look with nostalgia and longing to the time a few decades ago when serious deterioration resulted in a relatively brief period of survival, rather than, as now, several years of survival in an often physically and mentally severely compromised condition. Since palliative care is designed to mitigate this frail condition and offer comfort, it is be the model of care that can offer Dr. Selzer and others hope rather than despair at the prospect of a long life, regardless of all health-care settings. In addition to more palliative care services in home care, nursing homes, and hospitals, where they are currently growing, we can expect to see new specialized residential palliative care facilities.

> *. . . I have come to doubt that the medical profession is doing its*
> *patients a service in prolonging life at any cost . . .*

In different ways, this issue is being addressed by almost all of the contributors in this volume. As their chapters suggest, a resolution of Dr. Selzer's doubt will not be achieved until the issue is broadened to include the whole health-care system, and as Bruce Jennings has suggested, making the end-of-life condition not just a medical problem but a broader civic issue, a public health concern that requires coordinating social and medical services. We need to think about the things that serve patients long before the issue comes down to hooking a patient up to life support. We need to ask ourselves how we have ended up in a situation where we do not question the right of an elderly and frail person to have almost any medical treatment regardless of cost, but we will not pay for him or her to get help with the tasks of daily living: bathing, cooking, or shopping. Why does most of our insurance system not reimburse the small cost for occupational therapists to advise on hazards in the home, rather than paying for the setting of broken bones and subsequent rehabilitation?

> *Back then, dying was an abstraction that applied to other people,*
> *the human race, of which I was a member.*

Our approach to death will in the future be shaped by the population's increasingly broad-based exposure to death. We can envision including death and end-of-life education courses at all stages, starting at the high school and college levels and reaching into medical schools, seminaries, law schools, and schools of social work, as well as other professional and academic programs. The college courses will likely be taught in philosophy departments and will look at death from an abstract perspective, as exemplified by *Death*, a collection of lectures compiled by Shelly Kagan from a 2007 eponymous course at Yale University.[13] Advanced graduate courses will offer practitioners the tools they need to better empathize in their work with those at the end of life and to realize that, indeed, we are all members of the same human race. Cases in point are *A Clergy Guide to End-of-Life Issues* (2011) by Martha R. Jacobs, often assigned in seminaries, and the program at Columbia

University described in Volume I, Chapter 6: A Narrative Medicine Curriculum to Reframe Death and Dying.

> *. . . I think of dying as my own termination, a personal event. . . .*
> *I have come to think of death as a welcome release from*
> *whatever sorrow and suffering will come.*

Since the passing of the Self-Determination Act in 1991, the personalization of death increasingly has become an assumed characteristic of the American way of dying. However, in order to succeed in fulfilling this ideal and die in the place and manner of one's choosing, it is necessary to take an active preparatory role in one's own death. This is an area where a positive trend can be discerned in the period since the passing of the Self-Determination Act. Not everyone, but many are looking for ways that will give them control over their final days and a growing number of websites offer assistance on the national and local levels.[14]

The unexpected happens unexpectedly and everyone needs to do some basic planning in case of a sudden accident or illness. It is important to think about what one's goals are in life and how they would pertain to the end. Sharing one's thoughts with loved ones is probably the single most important way to assure that one's directives are followed. Circumstances change, so a written living will trying to cover all possible scenarios is not likely to be effective in a clinical setting but in-depth discussions with a trusted person who is assigned as an agent is a flexible vehicle to maneuver among the many sensitive decisions in the maze-like health-care system. The health-care proxy or power of attorney for health care—the name varies from state to state—allows for appointing a person—a surrogate who speaks for the principal in case the principal does not have capacity. Surveys that poll how many people in the United States have appointed a health care agent vary in estimate from 10 percent to almost 40 percent. Regardless of what number is accurate, we can expect a large increase in this number in the second and third decade of the 21st century as education spreads and baby boomers realize the importance of the documents—advance directives—that allow a personalized journey even when the capacity to express one's choices is gone.

Other types of more detailed advance care planning such as physicians' orders (MOLST and POLST), Do Not Resuscitate orders (DNRs), and other directives help communicate wishes in case of severely life-limiting conditions. They are likely to grow in prevalence in situations when the physician determines that he or she would not be surprised if death occurs within a year. This "not-surprised-if-deceased-in-a-year" standard gained currency when Joanne Lynn presented it in *Sick to Death and Not Going to Take It Anymore!* (2004).[15] has been adopted by many physicians with elderly and seriously ill patients as an indication of when to initiate discussions with them about DNRs and other medical directives.

*As a doctor, I am in full support of Assisted Death for those who
have intractable pain or insupportable mental or physical
limitations. I would want that for myself.*

Physician-assisted suicide (PAD) is controversial in America and is only legal in three states (Oregon, Washington, and Montana). In those states, it only accounts for one percent or less of all deaths.[16] The law has been introduced in other states and where it may pass is uncertain. In the Netherlands, which has the world's most liberal policy for PAD, about three percent of those dying take advantage of the law.[17] It is safe to assume that even if PAD is approved by many states, it will account for only a small number of deaths if it retains the same form as the current laws, which require request by a person with capacity. Dr. Selzer—and others—may gain a sense of control over their fates, but PAD laws would have no impact on those who die without capacity, nor on the large numbers, the over 90 percent who have stated that they would not consider taking advantage of the law under any circumstances.[18] Compared to palliative care, the PAD movement is likely to reshape very little about the way people die in America.

*. . . I presided over the death of many people, and each time,
I felt a sense of having failed.*

Physicians commonly report a sense of failure when a patient dies. The medical specialty of palliative care is beginning to reframe the concept of "failure." It has no place in a situation when someone is dying who is frail and elderly or has a serious, incurable illness but is given comfort, symptom management, and compassion until the end, to the best ability of those who are present. All of us will eventually "expire," to use a common hospital term, so when death occurs it cannot *per se* be a failure. That term may be appropriate if the team of medical providers fails to palliate or the family creates an atmosphere around the dying person that is contrary to what he or she would have wished, if there is negligence, or if the dying person feels abandoned.

That the progression of an incurable illness is a "battle" that is lost when the person dies is an unfortunate—and common—notion that has seeped into the vocabulary by way of our campaigns to find cures for difficult diseases, such as cancer. The "war against cancer" can be won if we find a cure or a way to subdue it, the way the Salk vaccine can be seen to have won the war against polio, but no human being can win a battle against the ultimate deterioration of the body. It is meant as a compliment when we say that someone fought a valiant battle before death—but the expression needs rephrasing. The all-out fight is not optimal for everyone. In the spirit of palliative care philosophy we may say simply that he or she died on his or her own terms.

Those terms might mean employing every last medical intervention and experimental treatment. It may mean peacefully falling into a permanent sleep after saying to loved ones what, according to Ira Byock, are the four things that matter most: "please forgive me, I forgive you, thank you, I love you."[19] It may mean a combination of both. Or neither. But no fight was lost and no one was a failure. Hospice volunteers are trained to be attentive and present at the bedside of a dying person and to follow his or her lead. In future decades, we may hear that a deceased "was a good leader on the journey to the end."

> *It is a reversal of the old battle cry of the revolution:*
> *"Give me liberty or give me death." For me,*
> *it would be "Give me liberty AND give me death."*

The full sentence of Patrick Henry's call to action, delivered in Virginia, on March 23, 1775 was "I know not what course others may take; but as for me, give me liberty or give me death!" Like Henry's, Dr. Selzer's statement, is personal. Henry made his speech in a public space with the purpose of arousing his fellow Virginians to rise up against the British, while Selzer's words are not a battle cry. They are one individual's plea and epitomize the personal engagement with death in America in the 21st century. Other men and women of the "greatest generation" will call for physician aid in dying, but many more will be looking for long-term care services in their homes to live out their days in as dignified a manner as possible.

As the population ages and becomes more frail, the demand will escalate for custodial home care to help with baths, dressing, meal preparation, shopping, and errands, as well as for adult day care and transportation to doctors' appointments and social events. The need for help with handyman chores, bill paying, managing insurance forms and other practical aspects of life will increase. Houses will need to be refitted with handlebars in the bathroom, nonskid rugs, and personal alarm and monitoring systems. Medicare covers none of these services and in America no comprehensive network of resources is in place to meet these basic nonmedical needs.

A few innovative community programs have penetrated the firewall between medical services and social services on a local level, but bolder action and substantial resource allocation will be needed to meet the call for a personalized and dignified last stage of life for all. For that to occur we need to marshal political will and personal commitment. Is America ready to take on the challenge, at the national as well as grassroots level, of developing and executing plans that reshape our social systems and communal attitudes? Will we pledge to accommodate and serve our fellow travelers on their journey to the end?

NOTES

1. Geoffrey Gorer, "The Pornography of Death," in *Death, Grief, and Mourning in Contemporary Britain* (London: The Cresset Press, 1965). U.S. Edition: *Death, Grief, and Mourning* (Garden City, NY: Doubleday, 1965). Paperback Edition (Garden City, NY: Doubleday-Anchor, 1967), 192–99.

2. Richard Selzer, a personal letter to Christina Staudt, dated August 30, 2012.

3. Elizabeth Arias, "United States Life Tables, 2008," *National Vital Statistics Reports* 61, 3 (September 24, 2012). http://www.cdc.gov/nchs/data/nvsr/nvsr61/nvsr61_03 .pdf

4. United States Department of Census, "Table 104. Expectation of Life at Birth, 1979 to 2008, and Projections, 2010–2020," *Compendium of Statistical Abstracts,* 2010. http://www.census.gov/compendia/statab/2012/tables/12s0104.pdf

5. Central Intelligence Agency, "Country Comparison: Life Expectancy at Birth," *The World Fact Book*, https://www.cia.gov/library/publications/the-world-factbook/ rankorder/2102rank.html. Accessed April 1, 2013. The Fact book lists the United States as no. 50 but many of the countries listed are small areas that administratively are part of other nations. European Union 79.76 and US 78.49.

6. See Christina Staudt and Marcelline Block, eds., *Unequal before Death* (Newcastle upon Tyne: Cambridge Scholars Press, 2012).

7. Kristen Lewis and Sarah Burd-Sharps, *A Century Apart: New Measures of Well-Being for U.S. Racial and Ethnic Groups*, Measure of America, A Project of Social Science Research Council, 2010. http://www.measureofamerica.org/wp-content/uploads/2010/04/A_ Century_Apart.pdf. Human Development Report, 2011, *A Portrait of California— California Human Development Report 2011,* http://www.measureofamerica.org/ california/media-release/

8. http://www.census.gov/compendia/statab/2012/tables/12s0104.pdf

9. http://inequality.org/income-inequality/ and http://inequality.org/wealth-inequality/. Accessed April 1, 2013.

10. Nina Bernstein, "Chefs, Butlers, Marble Baths: Hospitals Vie for the Affluent," *New York Times,* January 21, 2012. http://www.nytimes.com/2012/01/22/nyregion/chefs-butlers-and-marble-baths-not-your-average-hospital-room.html?pagewanted= all_r=0

11. Since 1983, US statistical reports do not list "natural" death or "old age" as causes; every death is assigned a medical diagnosis or a mortal injury (an accident, homicide or suicide, or an act of nature or war), which is deemed the "cause" of death.

12. Numbers rounded to the nearest 5,000. Donna L. Hoyert and Jiaquan Xu, "Deaths: Preliminary Data for 2011," *National Vital Statistics Reports* Volume 61, Number 6 (Hyattsville, MD, 2012), http://www.cdc.gov/nchs/data/nvsr/nvsr61/nvsr61_06 .pdf

13. Shelly Kagan, *Death* (New Haven, CT: Yale University Press, 2012).

14. http://www.caringinfo.org/i4a/pages/index.cfm?pageid=1, http://getyourshittogether .org/, LiveWithCare.org

15. Joanne Lynn, *Sick to Death and Not Going to Take It Anymore!* (Berkeley, CA: University of California Press, 2004)

16. Judy Schwarz, "Assisted Dying in Legal and Illegal Environments: Experiences of Patients, Families and Clinicians," oral Presentation at the Columbia University Seminar on Death meeting on February 13, 2013.

17. STATLINE Centraal Bureau voor der Statestiek, Deaths by medical end-of-life decision; age, cause of death, changed on July 11, 2012. http://statline.cbs.nl/StatWeb/publication/?VW=T&DM=SLen&PA=81655ENG&LA=en. Accessed April 1, 2013.

18. Refers to Oregon, Judith Schwarz, Columbia University, 2013.

19. Ira Byock, *The Four Things That Matter Most—A Book About Living* (New York: Simon and Schuster, 2004).

Afterword

J. Harold Ellens

Richard P. Feynman (1918—1988) was one of the most remarkable scholars, teachers, and physicists that ever lived. In the last years of 1987 he lay stricken with two types of incurable cancer: Liposarcoma and Waldenström's Macroglobulinemia. For months he was moderately comatose from the medications necessary to control his pain. One day he awakened quite coherent and in his cryptic style observed to his wife, "This business of dying surely takes a hell of a long time." His final recorded words, after an unsuccessful surgical intervention, were, "I'd hate to die twice. It's so boring." Then he was gone. His was the traditional way of dying. The process was an ordeal for him, despite his insuppressible comic commentary. We who read of his final journey to the end can palpably feel the insupportable anguish and the prolonged assault his suffering inflicted upon this remarkably lovely and heroic human being.

Somewhat in contrast to this was the death of Stanley Ellens (1934–2011),* a real 21st-century demise that reflected many of the constructive principles enunciated and urged in this volume and its companion. Stanley suffered in his late 70s from a congenital pulmonary disorder. During the last five years of his life the difficulty grew progressively more problematic for the physicians to treat. During the last year he needed to receive intravenous antibiotics nearly every week, often daily for a week or 10 days. Progressively his normal active life became impossible. Finally he was hospitalized in a coma

---

*· Stanley Ellens (December 6, 1933–July 8, 2012) is the brother of J. Harold Ellens, the coeditor of this work.

for nearly a week. When he was released from the hospital he moved rapidly to auction his personal possessions, successfully sold his property, bought a condo for his wife near his son's home, moved his wife there, and instructed his family regarding his financial affairs and his final wishes.

The day after he dotted the last I and crossed the last T, as it were, his suffering returned and he was returned to hospital where he was placed on a ventilator and an oxygen mask. Again he fell into a coma that lasted for three days. Then he awakened, saw that his family was gathered around him, greeted each of them in a hearty personal way and took his leave of them, and then called the nurse to remove the ventilator and oxygen mask, and in a matter of minutes he died. This was typical of Stanley's style. It was his decision. He had been in charge during his life. He was decisive about his death. The focus of this two-volume set of publications about death is on a trajectory of that kind of well-supported self-determination in our newly developing style for our journey to the end.

Bibliography

60 Minutes. "The cost of dying: End-of-life care: Patients' last two months of life cost Medicare $50 billion last year: Is there a better way?" *60 Minutes* video. August 8, 2010. http://www.cbsnews.com/stories/2010/08/05/60minutes/main6747002.Shtml.

Abadir, Peter M., Thomas E. Finucane, and Matthew K. McNabney. "When Doctors and Daughters Disagree: Twenty-Two Days and Two Blinks of an Eye." *Journal of the American Geriatrics Society* 59 (2011): 2337–40.

Adamy, Janet. "US Ties Hospital Payments to Making Patients Happy." *The Wall Street Journal,* October 14, 2012.

Adler, Linda. "Understanding Patient Advocates and Patient Navigators." Accessed February 6, 2013. http://www.thedoctorweighsin.com/understanding-patient-advocate-and-patient-navigators.

The Administration on Aging (AoA). "Aging Statistics." Accessed March 18, 2013. http://www.aoa.gov/AoARoot/Aging_Statistics/index.aspx.

Akesson, Lynn. "The Message of Dead Bodies." In *Bodytime: On the Interaction of Body, Identity and Society,* edited by Susanne Lund and Lynn Akesson, 157–82. Sweden: Lind University Press, 1996.

Albert, Marilyn, Steven T. DeKosky, Dennis Dickson, et al. "The Diagnosis of Mild Cognitive Impairment due to Alzheimer's Disease: Recommendations from National Institute from Aging and Alzheimer's Association work group." *Alzheimer's & Dementia* 7 (2011): 1–10.

Albert, S. M. "Quality of Life in Patients with Alzheimer's Disease as Reported by Patient Proxies: Construction of the Sf-36." *Journal of the American Geriatrics Society* 44 (1996): 1342–47.

Albom, Mitch. *Tuesdays with Morrie.* New York, NY: Broadway Books, 1997.

Alexander, Brian. "Don't Die, Stay Pretty: Introducing the Ultrahuman Makeover." *Wired* 8.01 (January 2000). http://www.wired.com/wired/archive/8.01/forever.html.

Alexander, Stewart, Sheri A. Kleitz, Richard Sloane, and James Tulsky. "A Controlled Trial of a Short Course to Improve Residents' Communication with Patients at the End of Life." *Academic Medicine* 81 (2006): 1008–12.

Almack, Katheryn, Jane Seymour, and Gary Bellamy. "Exploring the Impact of Sexual Orientation on Experiences and Concerns about End of Life Care and on Bereavement for Lesbian, Gay, and Bisexual Older People." *British Sociological Association* 44, 5 (2010): 908–24.

Alzheimer's Association. "2011 Alzheimer's Disease Facts and Figures." *Alzheimer's & Dementia* 7 (2011): 208–44.

American Academy of Family Physicians. "Positions and Policies: Cultural Proficiency Guidelines." Last modified 2011. Accessed July 30, 2013. http://www.aafp.org/afp/2005/0201/p515.html

American Academy of Hospice and Palliative Medicine. Fellowship Program Directory. Accessed March 22, 2013. http://www.aahpm.org/fellowship/default/fellowshipdirectory.html.

American Academy of Hospice and Palliative Medicine. "Hospice Medical Director Certification." Accessed March 23, 2013. http://www.aahpm.org/certification/default/hmdcert.html.

American Academy of Hospice and Palliative Medicine. Palliative Care & Hospice Education and Training Act. Accessed March 22, 2013. http://www.aahpm.org/uploads/pcheta_summary2012.pdf.

American Academy of Pediatrics Committee on Bioethics. "Informed consent, Parental Permission, and Assent in Pediatric Practice." *Pediatrics* 95, 2 (February 1, 1995): 314–17.

American Aging Association. "History." Accessed October 1, 2012. http://www.americanaging.org/history.html.

American Association of Colleges of Nursing. "End-of-Life Nursing Education Consortium (ELNEC)." Accessed March 24, 2013. http://www.aacn.nche.edu/elnec.

American Medical Directors Association. "The Nursing Home Medical Director: Leader and Manager (White Paper A11, Becomes Policy March 2011)." 2011.

American Veterinary Medical Association. "Veterinarian's Oath." http://www.avma.org/KB/Policies/Pages/veterinarians-oath.aspx.

Ariès, Philippe. *The Hour of Our Death.* New York: Vintage Books, 1982.

Astow, Alan B., and Beth Popp. "The Palliative Care Information Act in Real Life." *New England Journal of Medicine* 364 (May 19, 2011): 1885–87.

Atkinson, David William. *The English Ars Moriendi.* New York: Lang, 1992.

Bank, Justin. "Palin vs. Obama: Death Panels". The Factcheck Wire. August 14, 2009. Accessed March 22, 2013. http://www.factcheck.org. /2009/08/palin-vs-obama-death-panels/.

Barnato, Amber, Denise Anthony, Jonathan Skinner, Patricia Gallagher, and Elliott Fisher. "Racial and Ethnic Differences in Preferences for End-of-Life Treatment." *Journal of General Internal Medicine* 24, 6 (2009): 695–701.

Barrett, Ronald K. "Death and Dying in the Black Experience." *Journal of Palliative Medicine* 5, 5 (2000): 793–99.

Bartky, S. L. *Sympathy and Solidarity.* London: Roman and Littlefield, 2002.

Bayertz, K. "Four Uses of Solidarity." In *Solidarity,* edited by K. Bayertz, 3–28. Dordrecht: Kluwer Academic Publishers, 1999.

Becker, Ernest. *The Denial of Death.* New York: Free Press, 1973.

Berlinger, Nancy. "From Julius Varwig to Julie Dupree: Professionalizing Hospital Chaplains." *Bioethics Forum,* January 25, 2008. Accessed February 2, 2013. http://www.thehastingscenter.org/bioethicsforum/post.aspx?id=704.

Berlinger, Nancy. "Wishful Thinking: On the Grammar of 'Hope' in the Language of Serious Illness." Presentation at the Columbia University Seminar on Death, New York, NY, November 10, 2010.

Blustein, Jeffrey, and Jonathan D. Moreno. "Valid Consent to Treatment and the Unsupervised Adolescent." In *The Adolescent Alone: Decision Making in Health Care in the United States,* edited by Jeffrey Blustein, Carol Levine, and Nancy Neveloff Dubler, 100–10. Cambridge University Press, 1999.

Bomba, Patricia, and Charles P. Sabitino. "POLST: An Emerging Model for End-of—Life Care Planning." *The Elderlaw Report,* XX, 7 (Feb. 2009): 1–5.

Borgstrom, Erica. "Ensuring a Good Death—English Policy for and Experiences of End-of-Life Care." Presentation at the Third Austin H. Kutscher Memorial Conference, Columbia University, New York, NY, March 24, 2012.

Boston, Patricia, Anne Bruce, and Rita Schreiber. "Existential Suffering in the Palliative Care Setting: An Integrated Literature Review." *Journal of Pain and Symptom Management* 41, 3 (2011): 604–18.

Brain Series 2. "Generalized Defects in Cognition: Alzheimer's Disease." Broadcast 23 February 2012 by PBS.

Bregman, Lucy. "Spirituality: A Glowing and Useful Term in Search of Meaning." *Omega* 53, 1 (2006): 5–26.

Breitbart. Vicki. "My Mother Was Not Alone." *Health Advocacy Bulletin: The Journal of the Health Advocacy Program at Sarah Lawrence College* 19, 2 (Fall 2012): 1–12.

Brody, Jane. *Jane Brody's Guide to the Great Beyond—A Practical Primer to Help You and Your Loved Ones Prepare Medically, Legally, and Emotionally for the End of Life.* New York: Random House, 2009.

Brunkhorst, H. *Solidarity: From Civic Friendship to a Global Legal Community.* Cambridge, MA: MIT Press, 2005.

Buiting, H. M., J. K. M. Gevers, J. A. C. Rietjens, B. D. Onwuteaqka-Philipsen, P. J. van der Mass, A. van der Heide, and J. J. M. van Delden. "Dutch Criteria for Due Care for Physician Assisted Dying in Medical Practice: A Physician Perspective." *Journal of Medical Ethics* 34, 9, e12 (2008): 234–37.

Bullock, Karen. "The Influence of Culture on End-of-Life Decision Making." *Journal of Social Work in End-of-Life & Palliative Care* 7, 1 (2011): 83–98. doi 10.1080/15524256.2011.548048.

Bullock, Karen, Sarah McGraw, Karen Blank, and Elizabeth Bradley. "What Matters to Older African Americans Facing End-of-Life Decisions? A Focus Group Study." *Journal of Social Work in End-of-Life & Palliative Care* 1, 3 (2005): 3–19.

Buyon, Julie, and Marsha Hurst. "The Patient Advocate in Palliative Care: Bridging the Structural Divide at the End of Life." In *Unequal Before Death,* edited by Christina Staudt and Marcelline Block, 124–37. Newcastle: Cambridge Scholars Publishing, 2012.

Byock, Ira. *Dying Well: Peace and Possibilities at the End of Life.* New York: Riverhead Books, 1987.

Byock, Ira. *The Four Things That Matter Most—A Book About Living.* New York: Simon and Schuster, 2004.

Cadge, Wendy. *Paging God: Religion in the Halls of Medicine.* Chicago: The University of Chicago Press, 2012.

Cairnes, A. W. *Carnap and 20th Century Thought: Explications and Enlightenment.* Cambridge: Cambridge University Press, 2007.

California Health Care Foundation. "Attitudes Towards End-of-Life Care in California." http://www.chcf.org/publications/2006/11/attitudes-toward-endoflife-care-in-california.

California Health Care Foundation. *S n a p s h o t: Final Chapter: Californians' Attitudes and Experiences with Death and Dying.* Oakland, CA, 2012. February 2012. http://coalitionccc.org/documents/FinalChapterDeath Dying.pdf.

Callanan, Maggie, and Patricia Kelly. *Final Gifts: Understanding the Special Awareness, Needs, and Communications of the Dying.* New York: Bantam Books, 1993.

Caring Connections. "What are advance directives?" Accessed November 17, 2012. http://www.caringinfo.org/i4a/pages/index.cfm?pageid=3285.

Carr, Deborah. "Racial Differences in End-of-Life Planning: Why Don't Blacks and Latinos Prepare for the Inevitable?" *Omega* 63, 1 (2011): 1–20.

Carrión, Iraida. "When do Latinos use Hospice Services? Studying the Utilization of Hospice Services by Hispanic/Latinos." *Social Work in Health Care* 49, 3 (2010): 197–210.

Carrión, Iraida, and Karen Bullock. "A Case of Hispanics and Hospice Care." *International Journal of Humanities and Social Sciences* 2, 4 (2012): 9–16.

Carter, B. S. "Ethical Dilemmas When the Patient is an Infant: Uncertainty and Futility." In *End-of-life Ethics: A Case Study Approach,* edited by K. J. Doka, A. S. Tucci, C. A. Corr, and B. Jennings, 209–18. Washington, DC: Hospice Foundation of America, 2012.

Carter, Rosalynn. "Foreword." In *Handbook for Mortals: Guidance for People Facing Serious Illness,* edited by Joanne Lynn, Joan Harrold, and The Center to Improve the Care of the Dying, xiii–xiv. New York: Oxford University Press, 1999.

Carter, Susan B., et al., eds. *Historical Statistics of the United States,* Volumes 1 and 2. Millennial Edition. Cambridge, UK: Cambridge University Press, 2006.

Casarett, D. J., J. Karlawish, and I. Byock. "Advocacy and Activism: Missing Pieces in the Quest to Improve End-of-Life Care." *Journal of Palliative Medicine* 5, 1 (2002): 3–12.

Cassel, E. J. "The Nature of Suffering and the Goals of Medicine." *New England Journal of Medicine* 306, 11 (1982): 639–645.

Cassell, Joan. *Life and Death in Intensive Care.* Philadelphia: Temple University Press, 2005.

Castle, Nicholas G. "What Is Nursing Home Quality and How Is It Measured?" *The Gerontologist* 50, 4 (2010): 426–42.

Center for Medicare & Medicaid Services. *MLN Matters,*R Number MM7857. July 20, 2012. Accessed March 24, 2013. http://www.cms.gov/Outreach-and-Education/Medicare-Learning-Network-MLN/MLNMattersArticles/downloads/MM7857.pdf.

Center to Advance Palliative Care. *A State by State Report Card on Access to Palliative Care in Our Nation's Hospitals.* Accessed July 30, 2013. http://www.capc.org/reportcard/.

Center to Advance Palliative Care. *2011 Public Opinion Research on Palliative Care.* Accessed March 19, 2013. http://www.capc.org/tools-for-palliative-care-programs/marketing/public-opinion-research/2011-public-opinion-research-on-palliative-care.pdf.

Center to Advance Palliative Care (CAPC), GetPalliativeCare. Retrieved January 1, 2013 from www.getpalliativecare.org.

Center to Advance Palliative Care. Palliative Care Leadership Centers.TM Accessed March 24, 2013. http://www.capc.org/palliative-care-leadership-initiative/overview.

Centers for Disease Control. "Deaths: Preliminary Data for 2011." National Vital Statistics Reports. Volume 61, No. 6, October 10, 2012. Accessed March 17, 2013. http://www.cdc.gov/nchs/data/nvsr/nvsr61/nvsr61_06.pdf.

Centers for Disease Control and Prevention. "National Nursing Home Survey." Accessed March 12, 2013. http://www.cdc.gov/nchs/nnhs.htm.

Centers for Medicare & Medicaid Services. "Medicare.Gov Nursing Home Compare." Accessed March 12, 2013. http://www.medicare.gov/NursingHomeCompare/search.aspx?bhcp=1&AspxAutoDetectCookieSupport=1.

Centers for Medicare & Medicaid Services. "MDS 2.0 Public Quality Indicator and Resident Reports." Accessed March 12, 2013. https://www.cms.gov/Research-Statistics-Data-and-Systems/Computer-Data-and-Systems/MDSPubQIandResRep/index.html.

The Center for the Study of Science and Religion, Columbia University Earth Institute. "Welcome." Accessed March 12, 2013. http://cssr.ei.columbia.edu/.

Center to Advance Palliative Care. "Community-Based Palliative Care." Accessed March 19, 2013. http://www.capc.org/palliative-care-across-the-continuum/community-based/.

Cerminara, Kathy. "Health Care Reform at the End of Life: Giving with One Hand but Taking with the Other." *American Society of Law, Medicine and Ethics Blogs and Forums.* June 7, 2010. http://www.aslme.org/print_article.php?aid=460404&bt=ss.

Chambliss, Daniel. *Beyond Caring: Hospitals, Nurses, and the Social Organization of Ethics.* Chicago: University of Chicago Press, 1996.

Chan, Lisa S., Mary Ellen Macdonald, and S. Robin Cohen. "Moving Beyond Ethnicity: Examining Dying in Hospital Through a Cultural Lens." *Journal of Palliative Care* 25, 2 (2009): 117–24.

Chapter 8, 2010 Laws of New York, A.7729-D (Gottfried et al.) and S. 3164-B. (Duane et al.). Section 2 of Chapter 8 amends New York Public Health Law to create "Article 29-CC Family Health Care Decisions Act."

Clatts, Michael C., Deborah J. Hillman, Aylin Atillasoy, and W. Rees Davis. "Lives in the Balance: A Profile of Homeless Youth in New York City." In *The Adolescent Alone: Decision Making in Health Care in the United States,* edited by Jeffrey Blustein, Carol Levine, and Nancy Neveloff Dubler, 139–59. Cambridge University Press, 1999.

Clifford, Jack, Jr. et al. "Hypothetical Model of Dynamic Biomarkers of the Alzheimer's Pathological cascade." *Lancet Neurology* 9 (2010): 119–28.

Cohen, J., and L. Deliens, eds. *A Public Health Perspective on End-of-life Care.* Oxford: Oxford University Press, 2012.

Cohen, Lilian. "Racial/Ethnic Disparities in Hospice Care: A Systematic Review." *Journal of Palliative Medicine* 11, 5 (2008): 763–68.

"Compressed Mortality, 1999–2010." CDC National Center for Health Statistics. http://wonder.cdc.gov/cmf-icd10.html.

The Commonwealth Fund. Accessed March 25, 2013. http://www.common wealthfund.org/Charts/Testimony/Caring-for-an-Aging-America/T/Two-thirds-of-Medicare-Spending-is-for-People-with-Five-or-More-Chronic-Conditions.aspx.

Congressional Research Service. Domestic Social Policy Division. *U.S. Healthcare Spending: Comparison with Other OECD Countries.* By Chris Peterson and Rachel Burton. RL34175. Washington, DC: United States Government Printing Office, 2007. Accessed March 24, 2013. http://assets.opencrs.com/rpts/RL34175_20070917.pdf.

Corr, Charles A., and Donna Corr, eds. "Suicide and Life-Threatening Behavior." In *Death and Dying, Life and Living*, 543–75. Belmont, CA: Wadsworth, 2012, 7th edition.

Costello, E. J. "Developments in Child Psychiatric Epidemiology." *Journal of American Academy of Child and Adolescent Psychiatry* 28 (1989): 836–41.

Cox, Cathy R., Jamie L. Goldenberg, Tom Pyszczynski, and David Weise. "Disgust, Creatureliness and the Accessibility of Death-Related Thoughts." *European Journal of Social Psychology* 37 (2007): 494–507.

Craig-Shapiro, Rebecca, et al. "Biomarkers of Alzheimer's Disease." *Neurobiology of Disease* 35 (2009): 128–40.

Crawley, Lavera. "Racial, Cultural, and Ethnic Factors Influencing End-of-Life Care." *Journal of Palliative Medicine* 8, Supplement 1 (2005): S58–69.

Cristakis, Nicolas A., and Elizabeth E. Lamont. "Extent and Determinants of Error in Doctor's Prognoses in Terminally Ill Patients: Prospective Cohort Study." *British Medical Journal* 320, 7233 (2000): 469–73.

Csikai, Ellen, and Elizabeth Chaitin. *Ethics in End-of-Life Decisions of Social Work Practice*, Chicago: Lyceum Books Inc, 2006.

The Dartmouth Institute for Health Care Policy and Clinical Practice. "The Dartmouth Atlas of Health Care." Accessed March 24, 2013. http://www.dartmouthatlas.org/keyissues/issue.aspx?con=2944.

de Grey, Aubrey D. N. J. "Biogerontologists' Duty to Discuss Timescales Publicly." *Annals of the New York Academy of Science* 1019 (2004): 542—5.

de Grey, Aubrey D. N. J. *Ending Aging: The Rejuvenation Breakthroughs That Could Reverse Human Aging in Our Lifetime*. New York: St. Martin's Griffin Press, 2008.

Dean, J. *Solidarity of Strangers*. Berkeley, CA: University of California Press, 1996.

Dean, J. "Reflective Solidarity." *Constellations* 2, 1 (1995): 114–40.

Dennis, Bradley. "Banks Turn to Demolition of Foreclosed Properties to Ease Housing-Market Pressures." *The Washington Post*, October 12, 2011. Accessed March 24, 2013. http://www.washingtonpost.com/business/economy/banks-turn-to-demolition-of-foreclosed-properties-to-ease-housing-market-pressures/2011/10/06/gIQAWigIgL_story.html.

Department of Health and Human Services. HealthCare.Gov. Last modified February 6, 2013. http://www.healthcare.gov/law/features/rights/bill-of-rights/index.html.

DeSpelder, Lynne Ann, and Albert Lee Strickland. *The Last Dance: Encountering Death and Dying*. New York: McGraw Hill, 2005.

Diekema, D. S., and J. R. Botkin. "Forgoing Medically Provided Nutrition and Hydration in Children." *Pediatrics* 124, 2 (August 1, 2009): 813–22.

Dobsha, Steven K., Ronald K. Heintz, Nancy Press, and Linda Ganzini. "Oregon Physician's Responses to Requests for Assisted Suicide: a Qualitative Study." *Journal of Palliative Medicine* 7, 3 (2004): 451–61.

Donald, Merlin. *A Mind So Rare.* New York: Norton & Norton & Co., 2002.

Donne, J. "Devotions upon Emergent Occasions." Meditation XVII. *The Complete Poetry and Selected Prose of John Donne,* edited by Charles M. Coffin,. New York: Random House, 1952.

Duffy, Sonia, Frances Jackson, Stephanie Schim, David Ronis, and Karen Fowler. "Racial/Ethnic Preferences, Sex Preferences, and Perceived Discrimination Related to End-of-Life Care." *Journal of American Geriatric Society* 51, 7 (2006): 150–57.

Durkheim, Emile. *The Elementary Forms of Religious Life.* New York: Free Press, 1965.

Earp, Jo Anne L., Elizabeth A. French, and Melissa B. Gilkey. *Patient Advocacy for Health Care Quality: Strategies for Achieving Patient-Centered Care.* Sudbury, MA: Jones and Bartlett Publishers, 2007.

Edmonds, Brownsyne Tucker. "Moving Beyond the Impasse: Discussing Death and Dying with African American Patients." *Obstetrics and Gynecology* 117, 2 (2011): 383–87.

Ehrenreich, Barbara. *Bright Sided: How Positive Thinking Is Undermining America.* New York: Henry Holt and Company, 2009.

Emery, Nathan J., and Nicola S. Clayton. "The Mentality of Crows: Convergent Evolution of Intelligence in Corvids and Apes." *Science: New Series* 306 (December 2007): 1903–7.

Englehardt, Tristram, H. *The Foundations of Bioethics.* New York: Oxford University Press, 1996, 2nd edition.

EPEC. "About Us." Education in Palliative and End-of-life Care (EPEC). Accessed March 12, 2013. http://www.epec.net/.

Faber-Langendoen, Kathy, and Paul Lanken. "Dying Patients in the Intensive Care Unit: Forgoing Treatment, Maintaining Care." *Annals of Internal Medicine* 133, 11 (December 2000): 886–93.

Fagerlin, Angela, and Carl E. Schneider. "Enough: The Failure of the Living Will." *The Hastings Center Report* March–April (2004): 30–42.

Faust, D. G. *This Republic of Suffering: Death and the American Civil War.* New York: Vintage, 2009.

Fausto, James. Palliative Care PowerPoint Presentation to St. Barnabas Hospital and Montefiore Medical Center. December 8, 2011.

Feifel, Herman. *The Meaning of Death.* New York: McGraw-Hill, 1959.

Field M. J., and C. K. Cassell, eds. *Approaching Death: Improving Care at the End of Life.* Washington DC: National Academy Press, 1997.

Finch, Caleb E., and Eileen M. Crimmins. "Inflammatory Exposure and Historical Changes in Human Life Spans." *Science* 305 (2004): 1736–39.

Fingerhut, L. A., and J. C. Kleinman. "Mortality among Children and Youth." *American Journal of Public Health* 79, 7 (July 1989): 899–901.

Finucane, Thomas E. "Care of Patients Nearing Death: Another View." *Journal of American Geriatrics Society* 50 (2002): 551–53.

Firestone, Robert, and Joyce Catlett. *Beyond Death and Anxiety.* New York: Springer, 2009.

Fischer, Stacy M., Angela Sauaia, and Jean Kutner. "Patient Navigation: A Culturally Competent Strategy to Address Disparities in Palliative Care." *Journal of Palliative Medicine* 10, 5 (2007): 1023–28.

Fleming, Chris. "U.S. Health Spending Projected to Grow an Average of 5.7 Percent Annually through 2021." *Health Affairs Blog,* June 12, 2012. http://healthaffairs.org/blog/2012/06/12/health-spending-growth-projected-to-average-5-7-percent-annually-through-2021/.

Forst, R. "How (Not) to Speak about Identity." *Philosophy and Social Criticism* 18, 3/4 (1992): 293–312.

Fried, Terri R., John O'Leary, Peter Van Ness, and Liana Fraenkel. "Inconsistency Over Time in the Preferences of Older Persons with Advanced Illness for Life-Sustaining Treatment." *Journal of the American Geriatrics Society* 55 (2007): 1007.

Frolik, Lawrence A. "Is a Guardian the Alter Ego of the Ward?" *Stetson Law Review* 37 (2007): 53–86.

Frolik, Lawrence A., and Linda S. Whitton. "The UPC Substituted Judgment/Best Interest Standard for Guardian Decisions—A Proposal for Reform." *University of Michigan Journal of Law Reform* 45 (2012): 729–60.

Frontline. "Facing Death: Facts & Figures." Accessed November 17, 2012. http://www.pbs.org/wgbh/pages/frontline/facing-death/facts-and-figures/.

Fuchs, Victor. "Perspective: More Variation in Use of Care, More Flat-of-the-Curve Medicine." [0]*Health Affairs* web exclusive (2004). Accessed March 24, 2013. http://content.healthaffairs.org/content/early/2004/10/07/hlthaff.var.104.citation.

Ganzini, Linda, et al. "Attitudes of Patients with Amyotrophic Lateral Sclerosis and Their Caregivers Toward Assisted Suicide." *New England Journal of Medicine* 339 (1998): 967–73.

Ganzini, Linda, Elizabeth R. Goy, and Steven K. Dobsha. "Prevalence of Depression and Anxiety in Patients Requesting Physician's Aid in Dying: Cross Sectional Survey." *British Medical Journal* 337, 7676 (2008): 966–71.

Gatter, Robert. "Unnecessary Adversaries at the End of Life: Mediating End-of-Life Treatment Disputes to Prevent Erosion of Physician-Patient Relationships." *Boston University Law Review* 79 (1999): 1091–1137.

Gawande, Atul. "Letting Go." *The New Yorker* August 2 (2010): 36–49.

George Washington University School of Medicine and Health Sciences. *Graduate Medical Education Resident Manual.* 2004.

Giovanni, Lisa A. "End of Life Care in the United States: Current Reality and Future Promise—A Policy Review." *Nursing Economic$* 30 (2012): 127–34.

Goldenberg, Jamie L., Tom Pyszczynski, Jeff Greenberg, Sheldon Solomon, Benjamin Kluck, and Robin Cornwell. "I am Not an Animal: Mortality Salience, Disgust, And the Denial of Human Creatureliness." *Journal of Experimental Psychology* 130 (2001): 427–35.

Gostin, L. O., J. I. Boufford, and R. M. Martinez. "Future of Public's Health: Vision, Values and Strategies." *Health Affairs* 23, 4 (2004): 96–107.

Gray, William H., III. "Omnibus Budget Reconciliation Act of 1987." In *IV,* edited by 100th United States Congress, H.R. 3545. Washington DC, 1987.

Green, James W. "Physician Assisted Suicide: *Death on Request.*" In *The Picture of Health: Medical Ethics and the Movies,* edited by Henri Colt, Silvia Quadrelli, and Lester Friedman, 405–9. New York: Oxford University Press, 2011.

Green, M., and J. S. Palfrey, eds. *Bright Futures: Guidelines for Health Supervision of Infants, Children, and Adolescents.* Arlington, VA: National Center for Education in Maternal and Child Health, 2002, 2nd edition rev.

Greenberg, Jeff, Sheldon Solomon, and Tom Pyszczynski. "Terror Management Theory of Self-Esteem and Cultural Worldviews." *Advances in Experimental Social Psychology* 29 (1997): 65.

Greenberg, Jeff, Tom Pyszczynski, and Sheldon Solomon. "The Causes and Consequences of a Need for Self-Esteem: A Terror Management Theory." In *Public Self and Private Self,* edited by R. F. Baumeister, 189–212. New York: Springer-Verlag, 1986.

Greenberg, Saadia. *A Profile of Older Americans: 2011.* United States Department of Human and Health Services Administration on Aging, 2011. http://www.aoa.gov/Aging_Statistics/Profile/2011/docs/2011profile .pdf.

Grenier, K. Allen, Subashan Perera, and Jasjit Ahluwalia. "Hospice Usage by Minorities in the Last Year of Life: Results from the National Mortality Followback Survey." *Journal of American Geriatric Society* 51, 7 (2003): 970–78.

Groopman, Jerome. *How Doctors Think.* Boston: Houghton Mifflin, 2007.

Hafemeister, Thomas. "End-of-Life Decision Making, Therapeutic Jurisprudence, and Preventive Law: Hierarchical v. Consensus-Based Decision-Making Model Copyright." *Arizona Law Review* 41 (1999): 329–73.

Haines, Michael R. "Inequality and Infant and Childhood Mortality in the United States in the Twentieth Century." *NBER Working Papers* 16133, National Bureau of Economic Research, Inc., June 2010. Accessed March 24, 2013. http://ideas.repec.org/p/nbr/nberwo/16133.html.

Haines, Michael R. "Occupation and Social Class during Fertility Decline: Historical Perspectives." In *The European Experience of Declining Fertility: 1850–1970,* edited by John Gillis, David Levine, and Louis Tilly, 192–226. Cambridge, MA: Blackwell, 1993.

Hampel, Harald, et al. "Biomarkers for Alzheimer's disease: Academic, Industry, and Regulatory Perspectives." *Nature Reviews Drug Discovery* 9 (2010): 560–74.

Hancock, Jason. "Grassley: Government shouldn't 'decide when to pull the plug on grandma.'" *The Iowa Independent,* August 12, 2009. Accessed March 24, 2013. http://iowaindependent.com/18456/grassley-government-shouldnt-decide-when-to-pull-the-plug-on-grandma.

Hardin, Steve B., and Yamin A. Yusufaly. "Difficult End-of-Life Treatment Decisions: Do Other Factors Trump Advance Directives?" *Archives of Internal Medicine* 164 (2004): 1531–32.

Hauser, Joshua. "Navigation and Palliative Care." *Cancer* 117, S15 (2011): 3583–89.

Healy, Melissa. "Quiet Deaths Don't Come Easy." *Los Angeles Times.* February 05, 2013.

Hellmann, J., et al. "Withdrawal of Artificial Nutrition and Hydration in the Neonatal Intensive Care Unit: Parental Perspectives." *Archive of Diseases in Childhood: Fetal and Neonatal Edition* 98, 1 (Jan. 2013): F21–5. doi: 10.1136/fetalneonatal-2012301658.

Herman, Louis M. "Cognition and Language Competencies of Bottlenosed Dolphins." In *Dolphin Cognition and Behavior: A Comparative Approach,* edited by R. J. Schusterman, J. Thomas, and F. G. Woods, 221–51. Hilldale, NJ: Laurence Erlbaum Associates, 1986.

"Hippocratic Oath." *Microsoft® Encarta® Online Encyclopedia.* 2000.

Hirschman, Karen B., Jennifer M. Kapo, and Jason H. T. Karlawish. "Why Doesn't a Family Member of a Person with Advanced Dementia Use Substituted Judgment When Making a Decision for That Person?" *American Journal of Geriatric Psychiatry* 14 (2006): 659–67.

Hogan, Christopher, June Lunney, Jon Gabel, and Joanne Lynn. "Medicare Beneficiaries' Costs of Care in the Last Year of Life." *Health Affairs* 20 (2001): 188–95. doi: 10.1377/hlthaff.20.4.188.

Hospice Association of America. "2012 Legislative Blueprint for Action." Accessed March 24, 2013. http://www.congressweb.com/nahc/docfiles/12-HAA-LegBP-Inside.pdf.

Humphrey, Hubert H. Remarks at the dedication of the Hubert H. Humphrey Building, November 1, 1977, Congressional Record, November 4, 1977, vol. 123, 37287.

Hurst, Marsha, Martha E. Gaines, Rachel N. Grob, Laura Weil, and Sarah Davis. "Educating for Health Advocacy in Settings of Higher Learning." In *Patient Advocacy for Health Care Quality,* edited by Jo Anne L. Earp, Elizabeth A. French, and Melissa B. Gilkey, 481–506. Sudbury, MA: Jones and Bartlett Publishers, 2008.

Huxley, Aldous. *Island.* New York, NY: Harper Perennial Modern Classics, 1962.

Interventions to Reduce Acute Care Transfers (INTERACT). "About INTERACT." Accessed March 12, 2013. http://interact2.net/about.html.

Institute of Medicine. "The Future of Nursing: Leading Change, Advancing Health." Washington, DC: The National Academies Press, 2011. Accessed March 24, 2013. http://www.thefutureofnursing.org/sites/default/files/Future%20of%20Nursing%20Report_0.pdf.

Anonymous. "A Piece of My Mind: It's over, Debbie." *Journal of the American Medical Association* 259, 2 (1988): 272.

James, Vaughn E. "No Help for the Helpless: How the Law Has Failed to Serve and Protect Persons Suffering from Alzheimer's Disease." *Journal of Health & Biomedical Law* 7 (2012): 407–49.

Jenkins, Todd, Kathryn Chapman, Christine Ritchie, Donna Arnett, Gerald McGwin, Stacey Cofield, and H. Michael Maetz. "Hospice Use in Alabama, 2002–2005." *Journal of Pain and Symptom Management* 41, 2 (2011): 374–82.

Jennings, Bruce. "Dying at an Early Age: Ethical Issues in Pediatric Palliative Care." In *Living with Grief: Children and Adolescents,* edited by Kenneth J. Doka and Amy S. Tucci, Washington, DC: Hospice Foundation of America, 2008.

Johnson, Kimberly, Maragatha Kuchibhatla, and James Tulsky. "What Explains Racial Differences in the Use of Advance Directives and Attitudes Toward Hospice Care?" *Journal of the American Geriatrics Society* 56, 10 (2008): 1953–58.

The Joint Commission. *Advanced Certification for Palliative Care Programs.* Accessed March 22, 2013. http://www.jointcommission.org/certification/palliative_care.aspx.

Joyce, James. *Ulysses,* New York: Random House, 1990.

Kagan, Shelly. *Death.* New Haven, CT: Yale University Press, 2012.

Kagawa-Singer, Marjorie, and Leslie Blackhall. "Negotiating Cross-Cultural Issues at the End of Life: 'You Got to Go Where He Lives.'" *Journal of the American Medical Association* 286, 6 (2001): 2993–3001.

Kamal, Arif H., et al. "Community-Based Palliative Care: The Natural Evolution for Palliative Care Delivery in the U.S." *J Pain Symptom Manage,* November 15, 2012. doi: 10.1016/j.jpainsymman.2012.07.018.

Kane, Rosalie A., Kristen C. Kling, Boris Bershadsky, Robert L. Kane, Katherine Giles, Howard B. Degenholtz, Jiexin Liu, and Louis J. Cutler. "Quality of Life Measures for Nursing Home Residents." *Journal of Gerontology: Medical Sciences* 58A, 1 (2003): 240–48. http://www.hpm.umn.edu/LTCResourceCenter/research/QOL/RAKane_et_al_QOL_NH_measures_2003.pdf.

Kastenbaum, Robert J. *Death, Society, and Human Experience.* Boston: Allyn and Bacon, 2001.

Kaufman, Sharon. *And a Time to Die: How American Hospitals Shape the End of Life.* New York: Scribner, 2005.

Keith, Kevin T. "Life Extension: Proponents, Opponents, and the Social Impact of the Defeat of Death." In *Speaking of Death: America's New Sense of Mortality,* edited by Michael K. Bartalos, 102–51. New York: Praeger Publishing, 2008.

Kelland, Kate. "Who wants to live forever? Scientist sees aging cured." *Reuters,* July 4, 2011. Accessed October 1, 2012. http://www.reuters.com/article/2011/07/04/us-ageing-cure-idUSTRE7632ID20110704.

Kelley, Amy S., Susan L. Ettner, R. Sean Morrison, Qingling Du, Neil S. Wenger, and Catherine A. Sarkisian, "Determinants of Medical Expenditures in the Last 6 Months of Life." *Annals of Internal Medicine* 154 (2011): 235–42. http://annals.org/article.aspx?articleID=746807.

Kelley, Amy S., et al. "Hospice Enrollment Saves Money For Medicare And Improves Care Quality Across A Number Of Different Lengths-Of-Stay." *Health Affairs* 32, 3 (2013): 552–61.

Kessler, David. *The Needs of the Dying: A Guide for Bringing Hope, Comfort, and Love to Life's Final Chapter.* New York: Harper Collins, 2000.

Kleinman, Arthur. *The Illness Narratives, Suffering, Healing and the Human Condition.* New York: Basic Books, 1988.

Kleinman, Arthur, and Peter Benson. "Anthropology in the Clinic: the Problem of Cultural Competence and How to Fix It." *PLoS Medicine* 3, 10 (2006): 1673–76.

Kluger, Jeffrey. "Polio and Politics. A Great Scourge May Soon Be Gone, but War, Distrust, and Even the Death of Osama Bin Laden Could Get in the Way." *Time,* January 14, 2012. Accessed March 25, 2013. http://www.highroadsolution.com/file_uploader2/files/time+polio+full+story.pdf.

Knowles, R. L., C. Bull, C. Dezaleux, and C. Wren. "Mortality with Congenital Heart Defects in England and Wales 1959–2009: Exploring Technological Change Through Period and Birth Cohort Analysis." *Archives of Disease in Childhood* 97, 10 (October 2012): 861–65. doi: 10.1136/archdischild-2012-301662.

Ko, Eunjeong, Sunhee Cho, and Monica Bonilla. "Attitudes Toward Life-Sustaining Treatment: The Role of Race/Ethnicity." *Geriatric Nursing* 33, 5 (2012): 341–49.

Kolata, Gina. "Doubt on Tactic in Alzheimer's Battle." *New York Times,* August 18, 2010.

Komter, A. E. *Social Solidarity and the Gift.* Cambridge: Cambridge University Press, 2005.

Kovner, Christine, Chuo-Hsuan Lee, Edward J. Lusk, Carina Katigbak, and Nellie Selander. "A Demonstration of the Use of "What-If " Analysis in Challenging Decision Making Situations: The Case of the IOM 80/20 Nursing Initiative." *Journal of Management and Sustainability* 3, 3 (2013): 3–18.

Kovner, Christine, Edward Lusk, and Nellie Selander. "Affordable Death in the United States: An Action Plan Based on Lessons Learned from the *Nursing Economic$* Special Issue." *Nursing Economic$* 30 (2012): 179–84.

Kübler-Ross, Elisabeth. *On Death and Dying.* New York: Macmillan, 1969.

Lamb, Charles W., Joe F. Hair, Jr., and Carl McDaniel. *Essentials of Marketing.* Mason, OH: Thomson South Western College Publishing, 2008.

The Last Acts Coalition. *Means to a Better End: A Report on Dying in America Today.* Washington, DC: Partnership for Caring, November 2002.

Lawton, Julia. *The Dying Process: Patients' Experiences of Palliative Care.* London: Routledge, 1997.

Leas, Robert. "The Biography of Anton Theophilus Boisen." *Association for Clinical Pastoral Education, Inc.* Accessed February 3, 2013. http://www.acpe.edu/NewBoisen_bio.html.

Leibniz, Gottfried. *The Monadology.* Translated by Robert Latta. Last modified January 30, 1999. http://www.rbjones.com/rbjpub/philos/classics/leibniz/monad.htm.

Lewis, Terrie. "Pain Management for the Elderly." *William Mitchell Law Review* 29 (2002): 223–44.

Liao, Solomon, Alpesh Amin, and Lloyd Rucker. "An Innovative, Longitudinal Program to Teach Residents about End-of-Life Care." *Academic Medicine* 79 (2004): 752–57.

Lifton, Robert J. *The Broken Connection.* Washington DC: American Psychiatric Press, 1979.

LiveSTRONGTM. Advancing Joint Commission Palliative Care Certification in Cancer Centers. Accessed March 24, 2013. http://www.livestrong.org/What-We-Do/Our-Actions/Programs-Partnerships/Community-Engagement/Programs/Advancing-Palliative-Care.

Luce, John M. "End-of-Life Decision Making in the Intensive Care Unit." *American Journal of Respiratory Critical Care Medicine* 182 (2010): 6.

Lupu, Dale. "Estimate of Current Hospice and Palliative Mmedicine Physician Workforce Shortage." *Journal of Pain and Symptom Management* 40, 6 (Dec. 2010): 899–911.

Lynn, Joanne. "A Controlled Trial to Improve Care for Seriously Ill Hospitalized Patients: The Study to Understand Prognoses and Preferences for Outcomes and Risks of Treatments (Support)." *Journal of the American Medical Association* 274, 20 (1995): 1591–98.

Lynn, Joanne, Janice Lynch Schuster, and Joan Harrold. *Handbook for Mortals: Guidance for People Facing Serious Illness.* New York: Oxford University Press, 1999.

Lynn, Joanne. "Living Long in Fragile Health: New Demographics Shape End-of-life Care." In B. Jennings, G. Kaebnick, and T. H. Murray eds., "Improving end-of-life care: Why has it been so difficult?" *Hastings Center Report* (special report) 356, 2005: S14–18.

Lynn, Joanne. *Sick To Death and Not Going to Take It Anymore!: Reforming Health Care for the Last Years of Life.* Berkeley, CA: University of California Press, 2004.

MacDorman, Marian F., Eugene Declercq, Fay Menacker, and Michael H. Malloy. "Infant and Neonatal Mortality for Primary Cesarean and Vaginal Births to Women with 'No Indicated Risk,' United States, 1998–2001 Birth Cohorts." *Birth* 33, 3 (September 2006): 175–82. doi: 10.1111/j.1523-536X.2006.00102.x.

Marshall, Jeffrey A. "Power of Attorney—Key Issues for Elder Care Planning." *Pennsylvania Bar Association Quarterly* 74 (2003): 160–67.

Marshall, Samuel, Kathleen M. McGarry, and Jonathan S. Skinner. "The Risk of Out-of-Pocket Health Care Expenditure at End of Life." National Bureau of Economic Research Working Paper Number 16170, July 2010.

Marzuk, Paul, et al. "Increased Risk of Suicide in Persons with AIDS." *Journal of the American Medical Association* 259 (1988): 1333–37.

Maximum Life Foundation. "Mission Statement." Accessed October 2, 2012. http://www.maxlife.org/mission.asp.

Mayeux, Richard. "Early Alzheimer's Disease." *New England Journal of Medicine* 362 (2010): 2194–201.

Mazanec, Polly, Barbara Daly, and Aloen Townsend. "Hospice Utilization and End-of-Life Care Decision Making of African Americans." *American Journal of Hospice & Palliative Medicine* 27, 8 (2010): 560–66.

McHugh, Marlene, Joan Arnold, and Penelope R. Buschman. "Nurses Leading the Response to the Crisis of Palliative Care for Vulnerable Populations." *Nursing Economic$* 30 (2012): 140–47.

McKinley, Elizabeth, Joanne Garrett, Arthur Evans, and Marion Danis. "Differences in End-of-Life Decision Making Among Black and White Ambulatory Cancer Patients." *Journal of General Internal Medicine* 11 (1996): 651–56.

McPhee, S. J., et al. "Finding our way-perspectives on the close of life." *Journal of the American Medical Association* 284, 19 (2000): 2512–13.

Meade, Kristin, and Sarah Friebert. "Informed Decision Making and the Adolescent Patient." In *End-of-Life Ethics: A Case Study Approach,* edited by Kenneth J. Doka, Amy S. Tucci, Charles A. Corr, and Bruce Jennings. Washington, DC: Hospice Foundation of America, 2012.

Medicare Benefit Policy Manual. Chapter 9—Coverage of Hospice Services Under Hospital Insurance. Accessed March 25, 2013. http://www.cms.gov/Regulations-and-Guidance/Guidance/Manuals/Downloads/bp102c09.pdf.

Medicare Payment Advisory Commission. *Report to the Congress Medicare Payment Policy.* Chapter 11, "Hospice Services." Washington, DC: United States Government Printing Office, 2012. Accessed March 24, 2013. http://www.medpac.gov/chapters/Mar12_Ch11.pdf.

Medicare Payment Advisory Commission. *Report to the Congress: Medicare Payment Policy.* Chapter 12: Hospice services; 265–67. March 2013. Accessed March 25, 2013. http://www.medpac.gov/chapters/Mar13_Ch12 .pdf.

Meisel, Alan, and Kathy L. Cerminara. *The Right to Die, The Law of End-of-Life Decisionmaking.* New York: Wolters Kluwer, 2011, 3rd edition.

Miller, Eric. "Listening to the Disabled: End-of-Life Medical Decision Making and the Never Competent." *Fordham Law Review* 74 (2006): 2889–925.

Mills, C. W. *The Sociological Imagination.* New York: Oxford University Press, 1959.

Mitchell S, J. Teno, D. Kiely, M. Shaffer, R. Jones, H. Prigerson, L. Volicer, J. Givens, and M. B. Hamel. "The Clinical Course of Advanced Dementia." *The New England Journal of Medicine* 361, 16 (2009): 1529–38.

Montagnini, Marcos, Basil Varkey, and Edmund Duthie. "Palliative Care Education Integrated into a Geriatrics Rotation for Resident Physicians." *Journal of Palliative Medicine* 7 (2004): 652–59.

Morris, J. N., R. Jones, S. Morris, and B. E. Fries. *Attachment 13: Proximity to Death: A Modeling Tool for Use in Nursing Homes.* Hebrew Rehabilitation Center for Aged Research and Training Institute, Contract No. 500-95-0062; and interRAI.

Morrison, R. Sean, Jessica Dietrich, Susan Ladwig, Timothy Quill, Joseph Sacco, John Tangeman, and Diane E. Meier. "Palliative Care Consultation Teams cut Hospital costs for Medicaid Beneficiaries." *Health Affairs* 30 (2011): 454–63.

Morrissey, M. B., and B. Jennings. "A Social Ecology of Health Model in End of Life Decision Making: Is the Law Therapeutic?" *New York State Bar Association Health Law Journal* 11, 1 (Winter 2006): 51–60.

Nachman, Dorothy D. "Living Wills: Is It Time to Pull the Plug?" *The Elder Law Journal* 18 (2011): 289–333.

National Association of Social Workers. "Code of Ethics." Last modified 2008. http://www.socialworkers.org/pubs/code/code.asp?print=1.

National Consensus Project for Quality Palliative Care. *Clinical Practice Guidelines for Quality Palliative Care* 3rd edition 2013. Accessed March 24, 2013. http://www.nationalconsensusproject.org/Guidelines_Download2 .aspx.

National Hospice and Palliative Care Organization. *2012 Edition NHPCO Facts and Figures: Hospice Care in America.* Accessed March 1, 2013. http:// www.nhpco.org/sites/default/files/public/Statistics_Research/2012_ Facts_Figures.pdf.

National Hospice and Palliative Care Organization. "About Hospice and Palliative Care." Accessed March 19, 2013. http://www.nhpco.org/about/ about-hospice-and-palliative-care.

National Hospice and Palliative Care Organization. "Hospice and Palliative Care." Last modified 2012. http://www.nhpco.org/i4a/pages/index.cfm?pageid=4648&openpage=4648.

National Hospice and Palliative Care Organization. *NHPCO Standards of Care for Hospice Programs*. Accessed March 24, 2013. http://www.nhpco.org/standards.

National Hospice and Palliative Care Organization. *NHPCO Facts and Figures: Hospice Care in America*. 2012. Accessed March 24, 2013. http://www.nhpco.org/sites/default/files/public/Statistics_Research/2012_Facts_Figures.pdf.

National Institute for Health Care Management Foundation. "The Concentration of Health Care Spending." *NIHCM Foundation Data Brief* July 2012. Accessed March 18, 2013. http://www.nihcm.org/images/stories/DataBrief3_Final.pdf.

National Institutes of Health RePORT. NIH Grants Funded by the American Recovery and Reinvestment Act of 2009. Accessed March 22, 2013. http://www.report.nih.gov/recovery/arragrants.cfm.

National Journal and The Regence Foundation. *Living Well at the End of Life: A National Conversation* (Public Data). Accessed July 31, 2013. http://syndication.nationaljournal.com/communications/NationalJournalRegenceToplines.pdf.

National Journal and The Regence Foundation. *Living Well at the End of Life: A National Conversation* (Physicians' Data). http://www.cambiahealthfoundation.org/media/release/11152011njeol.html, Accessed July 31, 2013.

National Vital Statistics System, National Center for Health Statistics, CDC. "10 Leading Causes of Death by United States—2010." Accessed March 9, 2013. http://www.cdc.gov/injury/wisqars/pdf/10LCID_All_Deaths_By_Age_Group_2010-a.pdf.

Naylor, Mary, et al. "Advancing Alzheimer's Disease Diagnosis, Treatment and Care: Recommendations from the Ware Invitational Summit." *Alzheimer's & Dementia* 8 (2012): 445–52.

Niebroj L., K. Bargiel-Matusiewicz, and A. Wilczynska. "Toward the Clarification of Ideas: Medical Futility, Persistent/Obstinate Therapy and Extra/Ordinary Means." *Advances in Experimental Medicine and Biology* 755 (2013): 349–56.

Nessel, Jerry Thomas. "Opportunities and Obstacles Towards Postponing Death and Postponing Dying," Presentation at the Third Austin H. Kutscher Memorial Conference, Columbia University, New York, NY, March 24, 2012.

Nevidjon, Brenda M. "Death Is Not an Option—How You Die Is: Reflections from a Career in Oncology Nursing." *Nursing Economic$* 30 (2012): 148–52.

New England Health care Institute. *Waste in Health care: A $700 Billion Opportunity.* 2008. Accessed March 24, 2013. http://www.nehi.net/uploads/one_pager/waste_onepager__2011.pdf.

New York State Department of Health. "Medical Orders for Life-Sustaining Treatment (Molst)." Accessed March 12, 2013. http://www.health.ny.gov/professionals/patients/patient_rights/molst/.

New York State Department of Health. "Palliative Care Access Act (PHL Section 2997-d): Palliative Care Requirements for Hospitals, Nursing Homes, Home Care and Assisted Living Residences (Enhanced and Special Needs)." Accessed March 24, 2013. http://www.health.ny.gov/professionals/patients/patient_rights/palliative_care/phl_2997_d_memo.htm.

Nickitas, Donna. "The Dialogue about Death and Dying: It's Time." *Nursing Economic$* 30 (2012): 147.

Nolan, Marie T., Derek P. Narendra, Johanna R. Sood, Peter B. Terry, AlanB. Astrow, Joan Kub, Richard E. Thompson, and Daniel P. Sulmasy. "When Patients Lack Capacity: The Roles that Patients with Terminal Diagnoses Would Choose for Their Physician and Love Ones in Medical Decisions." *Journal of Pain Symptom Management* 30 (2005): 342–53.

Olmsted v. United States, U.S. 438, 478 (1928).

Oregon Public Health Division. *Characteristics and end-of-life care of 596 DWDA patients who have died from ingesting a lethal dose of medication as of February 29, 2012, by year, Oregon 1998–2011.* http://public.health.oregon.gov/ProviderPartnerResources/EvaluationResearch/DeathwithDignityAct/Documents/year14-tbl-1.pdf.

Oregon Public Health Division. *Death with Dignity Act Requirements.* http://public.health.oregon.gov/ProviderPartnerResources/EvaluationResearch/DeathwithDignityAct/Documents/requirements.pdf

Oregon Public Health Division. *Oregon's Death with Dignity Act—2011.* http://public.health.oregon.gov/providerpartnerresources/evaluationresearch/deathwithdignityact/documents/year14.pdf

Organisation for Economic Co-operation and Development. "Health: Key Tables from OECD: 14. Infant mortality Deaths per 1,000 live births." Accessed October 30, 2012. http://www.oecd-ilibrary.org/social-issues-migration-health/infant-mortality-2012-2_inf-mort-table-2012-2-en.

"Our Dysfunctional Romance with Violence." Editor's Letter. *The Week,* December 28, 2012–January 4, 2013.

Oxford English Dictionary. Oxford University Press.

Pan, Cynthia X., Sharon Carmody, Rosanne M. Leipzig, Evelyn Granieri, Amy Sullivan, Susan D. Block, and Robert M. Arnold. "There is Hope for the Future: National Survey Results Reveal that Geriatric Medicine Fellows are Well-Educated in End-of-Life Care." *Journal of the American Geriatric Society* 53, 4 (2005): 705–10.

Patel, Kant, and Mark Rushefsky. *Health Law Politics and Policy in the United States.* Armonk, NY: M.E. Sharpe, 2006, 3rd edition.

The Patient Protection and Affordable Care Act. U.S. Public Law 111–148, 111th Congress (2010). Accessed March 24, 2013. http://www.gpo.gov/fdsys/pkg/PLAW-111publ148/pdf/PLAW-111publ148.pdf.

Perlman, Robert A. "Ethics Committees, Programs and Consultations." Last modified February 19, 2013. http://depts.washington.edu/bioethx/topics/ethics.html.

Piven, J. S. *Death and Delusion.* Westport, CT: Information Age Publishing, 2004.

Podell, C. "Adolescent Mourning: the Sudden Death of a Peer." *Clinical Social Work* 17, 1 (1989): 64–78.

Polinsky, A. Mitchell, and Steven Shavell. *Handbook of Law and Economics, Volume 2.* Amsterdam: North Holland Press, 2007.

Pontin, Jason. "The SENS Challenge." *Technology Review,* July/August 2005.

Pontin, Jason. "Is Defeating Aging Only a Dream?" *Technology Review,* July/August 2006. Accessed October 1, 2012. http://www.mprize.com/index.php?pagename=newsdetaildisplay&ID=.

Porter, Roy, ed. *The Cambridge Illustrated History of Medicine.* Cambridge, UK: Cambridge University Press, 1996.

Prainsack, B., and A. Buyx. *Solidarity: Reflections on an Emerging Concept in Bioethics.* London: The Nuffield Council, 2011.

The President's Council on Bioethics. *Beyond Therapy: Biotechnology and the Pursuit of Happiness.* Washington, DC, October 2003. http://bioethics.georgetown.edu/pcbe/reports/beyondtherapy/index.html.

Querfurth, Henry, and Frank LaFerla. "Alzheimer's Disease." *New England Journal of Medicine* 362 (2010): 329–44.

Quill, Timothy E. "Personal Reflections n the Meaning of Our Brand." *AAHPM Quarterly* 13, 2 (Summer 2012): 4–5.

Quill, Timothy. "Physician-Assisted Death in the United States: Are the Existing 'Last Resorts' Enough?" *Hastings Center Report* 38, 5 (2008): 17–22.

Quill, Timothy E., and Amy P. Abernethy. "Generalist plus Specialist Palliative Care—Creating a More Sustainable Model." *New England Journal of Medicine* 368 (2013): 1173–75. doi: 10.1056/NEJMp1215620.

Radner, Dasie, and Michael Radner. *Animal Consciousness.* New York: Prometheus Books, 1996.

Rao, J. K., L. A. Anderson, and S. M. Smith. "End-of-life Is a Public Health Issue." *American Journal of Preventive Medicine* 23, 3 (2002): 215–20.

Rau, Jordan. "Medicare To Penalize 2,217 Hospitals For Excess Readmissions." *Kaiser Health News,* August 13, 2012. Accessed March 14, 2013. http://www.kaiserhealthnews.org/Stories/2012/August/13/medicare-hospitals-readmissions-penalties.aspx.

Reder, E. A., and J. R. Serwint. "Until the Last Breath: Exploring the Concept of Hope for Parents and Health Care Professionals during a Child's Serious

Illness." *Archives of Pediatric and Adolescent Medicine* 163, 7 (July 2009): 653–57. doi: 10.1001/archpediatrics.2009.87.

Reith, Margaret, and Malcolm Payne. *Social Work in End-of-Life and Palliative Care.* Chicago: Lyceum Books Inc, 2009.

Ricoeur, P. *Oneself as Another.* Chicago: University of Chicago Press, 1992.

Robinson, Katya, Sharyn Sutton, Charles F. von Gunten, Frank D. Ferris, Nicholos Molodyko, Jeanne Martinez, and Linda L. Emanuel. "Assessment of the Education for Physicians on End-of-Life Care (EPEC) Project." *Journal of Palliative Medicine* 7 (2004): 637–45.

Rosenberg, Charles E. *The Care of Strangers: The rise of the American Hospital System.* New York: Basic Books, 1987.

Ruhnke, Gregory, Sandra Wilson, Takashi Akamatsu, Takaaki Kinoue, Yutaka Takashima, Mary Goldstein, Barbara Koenig, John Hornberger, and Thomas Raffin. "Ethical Decision Making and Patient Autonomy: A Comparison of Physicians and Patients in Japan and the United States." *Chest* 118, 4 (2000): 1172–82.

Sabatino, Charles P. "The Evolution of Health Care Advance Planning Law and Policy." *The Milbank Quarterly* 88 (2010): 211–39.

Sachs, Greg. "Dying from Dementia." *New England Journal of Medicine* 361 (2009): 1595–96.

"Salk Vaccine Announcement (1955)." University of Michigan History and Traditions, 1995. Accessed March 24, 2013. http://president.umich.edu/history/markers/salk.html.

Savva, George M., et al. "Age, Neuropathology and Dementia." *New England Journal of Medicine* 360 (2009): 2302–09.

Schoen, C., R. Osborn, S. K. H. How, M. M. Doty, and J. Peugh. "In Chronic Condition: Experiences of Patients with Complex Health Care Needs, in Eight Countries, 2008." *Health Affairs* 28, 1 (2009): w1–16.

Scott, Gale. "Preparing for the Last Waltz. Hospitals have Mixed Feelings about Providing Palliative Care as Mandated by Law." *Crain's New York Business,* March 18, 2012. www.crainsnewyork.com/article/20120318/sub303189992.

Seale, Clive. "Heroic Death." *Sociology* 29, 4 (1995) 597–613.

Searight, H. Russell, and Jennifer Gafford. "Cultural Diversity at the End of Life: Issues and Guidelines for Family Physicians." *American Family Physician* 71, 3 (2005): 515–22.

Segen, J. C. *McGraw-Hill Concise Dictionary of Modern Medicine.* New York: McGraw-Hill Medical, 2005.

Shaw, Gina. "New Opportunities for Palliative Care in Medical Education." *AAMC Reporter* July 2012. Accessed March 22, 2013. http://www.aamc.org/newsroom/reporter/july2012/297224/palliative-care.html.

Sherman, Deborah Witt, and Jooyoung Cheon. "Palliative Care: The Paradigm of Care Responsive to the Demands for Health Care Reform in America." *Nursing Economic$* 30 (2012): 153–66.

Sherman, Howard J., E. K. Hunt, Reynold F. Nesiba, and Phillip A. Ohara. *Economics: An Introduction to Traditional and Progressive Views*. New York: M. E. Sharpe, 2008.

Short, Nancy. "The Final Frontier." *Nursing Economic$* 30 (2012): 185–86.

Shrank, William H., Jean S. Kutner, Terri Richardson, Richard A. Mularski, Stacy Fischer, and Marjorie Kagawa-Singer. "Focus Group Findings about the Influences of Culture on Communication Preferences in End-of-Life Care." *Journal of General Internal Medicine* 20, 8 (2005): 703–9.

Shrestha, L. B., and E. J. Heisler. *The Changing Demographic Profile of the United States*. Washington, DC: Congressional Research Service, 7–5700, 2011. http://www.fas.org/sgp/crs/misc/RL32701.pdf.

Sirianni, C., and L. Friedland, *Civic Innovation in America: Community Empowerment, Public Policy, and the Movement for Civic Renewal*. Berkeley: University of California Press, 2001.

Sisneros, Jose, Catherine Stakeman, Mildred Joyner and Catheryne Schmitz. *Critical Multicultural Social Work*. Chicago: Lyceum Books Inc, 2008.

Smith, Alexander K., Ellen P. McCarthy, Ellen Weber, I. S. Cenzer, W. John Boscardin, Jonathan Fisher, and Kenneth Covinsky. "Half Of Older Americans Seen in Emergency Department in Last Month of Life; Most Admitted to Hospital, and Many Die There." *Health Affairs* 31 (2012): 1277–85. doi:10.1377/hlthaff.2011.0922.

Smith, Alexander, Rebecca Sudore, and Eliseo Pérez-Stable. "Palliative Care for Latino Patients and their Families: Whenever We Prayed, She Wept." *Journal of the American Medical Association* 301, 10 (2009): 1047–57.

Smith, Daniel Scott. "The Number and Quality of Children: Education and Marital Fertility in Early Twentieth-Century Iowa." *Journal of Social History* 30, 2 (1996): 367–92.

Social Security Advisory Board. *The Unsustainable Cost of Health care*. By Sylvester J. Schieber, Dana K. Bilyeu, Dorcas R. Hardy, Marsha Rose Katz, Barbara B. Kennelly, and Mark J. Warshawsky. Washington, DC: United States Government Printing Office, 2009. Accessed March 24, 2013. http://www.ssab.gov/documents/TheUnsustainableCostofHealthCare_graphics.pdf.

Somerville, Jacqueline. "The Paradox of Palliative Care Nursing Across Cultural Boundaries." *International Journal of Palliative Nursing* 13, 12 (2007): 580–87.

Song, Mi-Kyung. "Effects of End-of-Life Discussions on Patients' Affective Outcomes." *Nursing Outlook* 52 (2004): 118–25.

Song, Mi-Kyung, Karin T. Kirchhoff, Jeffrey Douglas, Sandra Ward, and Bernard Hammes. "A Randomized, Controlled Trial to Improve Advance Care Planning Among Patients Undergoing Cardiac Surgery." *Medical Care* 43 (2005): 1049–53.

Span, Paula. "Why Do We Avoid Advance Directives?" *The New Old Age Blog*. April 20, 2009. http://newoldage.blogs.nytimes.com/2009/04/20/why-do-we-avoid-advance-directives/.

Stanton Chapple, Helen. *No Place for Dying: Hospitals and the Ideology of Rescue.* California: Left Coast Press, 2010.

Starr, Paul. *The Social Transformation of American Medicine.* Basic Books, 1982.

Staudt, Christina, and Marcelline Block, eds. *Unequal Before Death.* Newcastle: Cambridge Scholars Press, 2012.

Steckel, Richard H. "Alternative indicators of Health and the Quality of Life." In *Unconventional Wisdom: Alternative Perspectives on the New Economy,* edited by Jeff Madrick, 189–206. New York: Century Foundation Press, 2000.

Stein, Gary, and Karen Bonuk. "Physician–Patient Relationships Among the Lesbian and Gay Community." *Journal of the Gay and Lesbian Medical Association* 5, 3 (2001): 87–93.

Stein, Gary, Patricia Sherman, and Karen Bullock. "Educating Gerontologists for Cultural Proficiency in End-of-Life Care Practice." *Journal of Educational Gerontology* 35, 11 (2009): 1008–25.

Steinhauser, Karen E., et al. "Factors Considered Important at the End of Life by Patients, Family, Physician, and other Care Providers." *Journal of the American Medical Association* 204, 19 (November 15, 2000): 2476–82.

Stewart, Anita L. "The Concept of Quality of Life of Dying Persons in the Context of Health Care." *Journal of Pain and Symptom Management* 2 (February 1999): 93–108.

Stjernswärd, J., K. M. Foley, and F. D. Ferris. "The Public Health Strategy for Palliative Care." *Journal of Pain and Symptom Management* 33, 5 (2007): 486–93.

Stratos, Georgette, Sara Katz, Merlynn Bergen, and James Hallenbeck. "Faculty Development in End-of-Life Care: Evaluation of a National Train-the-Trainer Program." *Academic Medicine* 81 (2006): 1000–1007.

Sullivan, Amy M., Matthew D. Lakoma, J. Andrew Billings, Antoinette S. Peters, Susan D. Block, and the PCEP Core Faculty. "Teaching and Learning End-of-Life Care: Evaluation of a Faculty Development Program in Palliative Care." *Academic Medicine* 80 (2005): 657–68.

Sulmasy, Daniel. "The Last Word: The Catholic Case for Advance Directives." *America* November 29, 2010, 13–16.

Sulmasy, Daniel P., Mark T. Hughes, Richard E. Thompson, Alan B. Astrow, Peer B. Terry, Joan Kub, and Marie T. Nolan, "How Would Terminally Ill Patients Have Others Make Decisions for Them in the Event of Decisional Incapacity?" *Journal of the American Geriatric Society* 55 (2007): 198.

The SUPPORT Principal Investigators. "A controlled trial to improve care for seriously ill hospitalized patients: the Study to Understand Prognoses and Preferences for Outcomes and Risks of Treatments (SUPPORT)." *Journal of the American Medical Association* 274, 20 (1995): 1591–88.

Svenson, Arthur G. "Montana's Courting of Physician Aid in Dying. Could Des Moines Follow Suit?" *Politics and the Life Sciences* 29, 2 (2010): 2–16.

Tangalos, Eric G. "MDS 3.0: Can This Release Be All Things to All People?" *Journal of the American Medical Directors Association* 13, 7 (2012): 576–77.

Tamura M. K., K. E. Covinsky, G. M. Chertow, K. Yaffe, S. Landefeld, C. E. Mc-Culloch. "Functional Status of Elderly Adults before and after Initiation of Dialysis." *The New England Journal of Medicine* 361, 16 (2009): 1539–47.

Taylor, Janelle S. "The Story Catches You and You Fall Down: Tragedy, Ethnography, and 'Cultural Competence.'" *Medical Anthropology Quarterly* 17, 2 (2003):159–81.

Temel, Jennifer S., Joseph A. Greer, Alona Muzikansky, Emily R. Gallagher, Sonal Admane, Vicki A. Jackson, Constance M. Dahlin, Craig D. Blinderman, Juliet Jacobsen, William F. Pirl, J. Andrew Billings, and Thomas J. Lynch. "Early Palliative Care for Patients with Metastatic Non-Small-Cell Lung Cancer." *The New England Journal of Medicine* 363 (2010): 733–42.

Teno, Joan, et al. "Change in End-Of-Life Care for Medicare Beneficiaries." *Journal of the American Medical Association* 309, 5 (2013): 470–77.

Tilden, Virginia P., Sarah A.Thompson, Byron Gajewski and Marjorie Bott. "End-of-Life Care in Nursing Homes: The High Cost of Staff Turnover." *Nursing Economic$* 30 (2012): 163–66.

ter Meulen, R., W. Arts, and R. Muffels, eds. *Solidarity in Health and Social Care in Europe.* Dordrecht: Kluwer Academic Publishers, 2001.

Tervalon, Melanie, and Jann Murray-Garcia. "Cultural Humility versus Cultural Competence: a Critical Distinction in Defining Physician Training Outcomes in Multicultural Education." *Journal of Health care for the Poor and Underserved* 9, 2 (1998):117–25.

Thomas, Katie. "Trials for Alzheimer's Drug Halted After Poor Result." *New York Times,* August 6, 2012.

Thomas, Roger, Donna M. Wilson, Christopher Justice, Stephen Birch, and Sam Sheps. "A Literature Review of Preferences for End-of-Life Care in Developed Countries by Individuals with Different Cultural Affiliations and Ethnicity." *Journal of Hospice and Palliative Nursing* 10, 3 (2008): 142–61.

Tong, Bonnie, and Hannah I. Lipman. "Whose Bed?" *Hastings Center Report* 43, 2 (March–April 2013): 14. doi: 10.1002/hast.153.

Trivers, Robert. *The Folly of Fools: The Logic of Deceit and Self-Deception in Human Life.* New York: Basic Books 2011.

True, Gala, Etienne Phipps, Leonard Braitman, Tina Harralson, Diana Harris, and William Tester. "Treatment Preferences and Advance Care Planning at End of Life: The Role of Ethnicity and Spiritual Coping in Cancer Patients." *Annals of Behavioral Medicine* 30, 2 (2005): 174–79.

The University of California at Santa Cruz Atlas of Global Inequality. "Health care Spending." Accessed October 1, 2012. http://ucatlas.ucsc.edu/spend.php.

U.S. Census Bureau. "An Older and More Diverse Nation by Midcentury." Last modified 2008. http://www.census.gov/newsroom/releases/archives/population/cb08-123.html.

U.S. Census Bureau. Current Population Reports. *Income, Poverty, and Health Insurance Coverage in the United States: 2011.* By Carmen DeNavas-Walt,

Bernadette D. Proctor, and Jessica C. Smith. P60-243. Washington, DC: U.S. Government Printing Office, 2012.

U.S. Census Bureau. "Overview of Race and Hispanic Origin: 2010." Last modified 2011. http://www.census.gov/prod/cen2010/briefs/c2010br-02.pdf.

U.S. Census Bureau, Statistical Abstract of the United States. "Table 1339. Births, Deaths, and Life Expectancy by Country or Area: 2010 and 2020." 2012. Accessed September 30, 2012. http://www.census.gov/compendia/statab/2012/tables/12s1339.pdf.

U.S. Department of Health and Human Services. Agency for Health care Research and Quality. "Advance Care Planning, Preferences for Care at the End of Life: Research in Action." By Barbara Kass-Bartelmes and Ronda Hughes. 03-0018. Rockville, Maryland, 2003. http://www.ahrq.gov/research/endliferia/endria.htm.

U.S. Department of Health and Human Services. Centers for Disease Control and Prevention. "Advance Care Planning: Ensuring Your Wishes Are Known and Honored If You Are Unable to Speak for Yourself." By William F. Benson and N. Aldrich. 2012. Accessed March 24, 2013. http://www.cdc.gov/aging/pdf/advanced-care-planning-critical-issue-brief.pdf.

U.S. Department of Health and Human Services. Centers for Disease Control and Prevention. National Center for Health Statistics. "National Vital Statistics Report, Deaths: Preliminary Data for 2011." By Donna L. Hoyert and Jiaquan Xu. Hyattsville, MD, 2012. Accessed March 19, 2013. http://www.cdc.gov/nchs/data/nvsr/nvsr61/nvsr61_06.pdf.

U.S. Department of Health and Human Services. Centers for Medicaid and Medicare Services. "Hospice." Accessed March 24, 2013. http://www.cms.gov/Medicare/Medicare-Fee-for-Service-Payment/Hospice/index.html.

U.S. Department of Health and Human Services. Health Resources and Services Administration. *Infant Mortality in the United States, 1935–2007: Over Seven Decades of Progress and Disparities.* By Gopal K. Singh and Peter C. van Dyck. Rockville, MD, 2010. Accessed March 24, 2013. http://ask.hrsa.gov/detail_materials.cfm?ProdID=4497.

U.S. Department of Health and Human Services. Planning and Evaluation Office of Disability, Aging and Long-Term Care Policy. "Advance Directives and Advance Care Planning." HHS-100-03-0023. Washington, DC, 2008. Accessed March 24, 2013. http://aspe.hhs.gov/daltcp/reports/2008/ADCongRpt.pdf.

U.S. Government Printing Office. *Electronic Code of Federal Regulations.* Part 418-Hospice Care. Accessed March 25, 2013. http://www.ecfr.gov/cgi-bin/text-idx?c=ecfr&sid=818258235647b14d2961ad30fa3e68e6&rgn=div5&view=text&node=42:3.0.1.1.5&idno=42.

United Nations. *The Millennium Development Goals Report,* "Goal 4 Reduce Child Mortality." Addendum, 2011.

US Library of Congress. Congressional Research Service. *The Changing Demographic Profile of the United States.* By Laura Shrestha, et al. CRS Report RL32701. Washington, DC: Office of Congressional Information and Publishing, March 31, 2011.

"US Religious Landscape Survey." *The Pew Forum on Religion and Public Life.* http://religions.pewforum.org/affiliations.

United States Substance Abuse and Mental Health Administration Services (SAMHSA). "Preliminary Results from the 1997 National Household Survey on Drug Abuse." http://www.samhsa.gov/data/nhsda/nhsda97/toc1.htm.

Van der Lee, Marije L. "Depression and Physician Assisted Dying." *British Medical Journal* 337, 7676 (2008): 941–42.

"Vital Statistics Online." CDC National Center for Health Statistics. Accessed March 25, 2013. http://www.cdc.gov/nchs/data_access/Vitalstatsonline.htm.

Walter, Tony. *The Revival of Death.* London: Routledge, 1993.

Walter, Tony. "Spirituality in Palliative Care: Opportunity or Burden?" *Palliative Medicine* 16, 2 (2002): 133–39.

Walsh, Raoul, Afaf Girgis, and Rob Sanson-Fisher. "Breaking Bad News 2: What Evidence is Available to Guide Clinicians?" *Behavioral Medicine* 24 (1998): 61–72.

Webley, Erin. "Law, Insouciance, and Death in the Emergency Room." *The Elder Law Journal* 19 (2011): 256–87.

West Virginia Center for End-of-Life Care. "e-Directive Registry." Accessed March 24, 2013. http://www.wvendoflife.org/e-Directive-Registry.

Westbrook, David A. *Navigators of the Contemporary: Why Ethnography Matters.* Chicago: University of Chicago Press, 2008.

Wholihan, Dorothy J., and Christine Pace. "Community Discussions: A Vision for Cutting the Costs of End-of-Life Care." *Nursing Economic$* 30 (2012): 170–75.

Wise, Stephen M. *Drawing the Line: Science and the Case for Animal Rights.* New York City: Basic Books, 2003.

World Health Organization. "WHO Definition of Palliative Care". Accessed March 18, 2013. http://www.who.int/cancer/palliative/definition/en/.

Xu, J. Q., K. D. Kochanek, S. L. Murphy, and B. Tejada-Vera. "Deaths: Final Data for 2007." *National Vital Statistics Reports* 58, 19 (May 20, 2010): 1–73.

Yalom, Irvin. *Existential Psychotherapy.* New York: Basic Books, 1980.

Yang, Lucie, et al. "Brain Amyloid Imaging—FDA Approval of Florbetapir F18 Injection." *New England Journal of Medicine* 367 (2012): 885–87.

Yeo, Gwen, and Nancy Hikuyeda. "Cultural Issues in End-of-Life Decision Making Among Asians and Pacific Islanders in the United States." In *Cultural Issues in End-of-Life Decision Making,* edited by K. Braun,

J. H. Pietsch, and P. L. Blanchette, 101–26. Thousand Oaks, CA: Sage, 2000.

Yocom, Carolyn, and Kathleen King. "Program Integrity: Further Action Needed to Address Vulnerabilities in Medicaid and Medicare Programs." Testimony before the Subcommittee on Government Organization, Efficiency, and Financial Management, Committee on Oversight and Government Reform, U.S. House of Representatives, Washington, DC. June 7, 2012.

CASES

Cruzan v. Director, Missouri Department of Health, 497 U.S. 261 (1986).

Compassion in Dying v. Washington, 79 F.3d 790 (9th Cir. 1996).

In re Grant, 747 P.2d 445 (Wash. 1987), *modified,* 757 P.2d 534 (Wash. 1988).

In re Guardianship of Browning, 568 So. 2d 4 (Fla. 1990).

In re Quinlan, 355 A.2d 647 (N.E. 1976).

Schoendorff v. Society of New York Hospital, 105, N.E. 92 (N.Y. 1914).

ORGANIZATIONS

Sarah Lawrence Health Advocacy Program (www.slc.edu/graduate/programs/health-advocacy/index.html)

Alliance of Professional Health Advocates (APHA) (http://aphadvocates.org/)

National Association of Health Advocacy Consultants (NAHAC) (http://nahac.memberlodge.com/)

Professional Patient Advocate Institute (PPAC) (http://www.patientadvocatetraining.com/)

The Center for Patient Partnerships, University of Wisconsin. (http://www.patientpartnerships.org)

Stanford School of Medicine. (http://ptadvocacy.stanford.edu/)

The University of North Carolina (http://www.northcarolina.edu/)

STATUTES

Patient Self-Determination Act of 1990, Pub. L. No. 101–508.

Agreements with Providers of Services, 42 U.S.C. 1395 cc (a).

About the Editors

CHRISTINA STAUDT (PhD in Art History, Columbia University) is the Chair of the Columbia University Seminar on Death, a monthly colloquium focused on timely inquiries of dying, death, and grief. She is the lead organizer of three interdisciplinary conferences sponsored by the Seminar. The cofounder and President of the Westchester End-of-Life Coalition, a Board Member of a local hospice, and Cancer Support Team, she initiates and directs programs and speaks in the public and professional arena to foster education around mortality and mourning. She is the coeditor of and wrote the Introduction to the anthologies *The Many Ways We Talk About Death in Contemporary Society* (Mellen 2009) and *Unequal Before Death* (Cambridge Scholars Publishing 2012); and contributed chapters on the literature of death and dying and on the imagery of death after 9/11 for *Speaking of Death—America's New Sense of Mortality* (Michael K. Bartalos, ed., Praeger 2009). An active hospice volunteer for 15 years, with a focus on assisting the actively dying and their families, she sits by the bedside of those at the end of life and is an advocate for improving the end-of-life experience for patients and their families.

J. HAROLD ELLENS (PhD in Psychology of Human Communications, Wayne State University; PhD in Second Temple Judaism and Christian Origins from the University of Michigan) is a retired university professor of Philosophy and Psychology, retired Presbyterian Theologian and Pastor, retired U.S. Army Chaplain (Colonel), Executive Director Emeritus of the Christian Association for Psychological Studies, and Founding Editor and Editor in Chief of the *Journal of Psychology and Christianity*. He has published extensively on the interface of psychology and religion/spirituality. His recent publications include *The Destructive Power of Religion* (4 vols, 2004), *Psychology and the Bible*

(4 vols, with Wayne Rollins, 2004), *God's Word for our World, A Festschrift for Professor Simon John De Vries* (2 vols., 2004), *Sex in the Bible* (2006), *Text and Community, A Festschrift Commemorating Professor Bruce M. Metzger* (2 vols, 2007), *Radical Grace: How Belief in a Benevolent God Benefits Our Health* (2007), *Understanding Religious Experience: What the Bible Says About Spirituality* (2007), *Miracles: God, Science, and Psychology in the Paranormal* (3 vols, 2008), *The Spirituality of Sex* (2009), *Probing the Frontiers of Biblical Studies, A Festschrift in Honor of Professor David J. A. Clines* (2009), *The Son of Man in The Gospel of John* (2010), *The Healing Power of Spirituality: How Faith Helps Humans Thrive* (3 vols, 2010), *Honest Faith for Our Time: Truth Telling about the Bible, the Creed, and the Church* (2010), *Light from the Other Side: The Paranormal as Friend and Familiar* (2010), *Explaining Evil* (3 vols, 2011), *Psychological Hermeneutics of Biblical Themes and Texts, A Festschrift in Honor of Wayne G. Rollins* (2012), *A Dangerous Report: Challenging Sermons for Advent and Easter* (2012), *God's Radical Grace: Challenging Sermons for Ordinary Time(s)* (2012), *Heaven, Hell, and Afterlife: Eternity in Judaism, Christianity, and Islam* (3 vols, 2013), and *Winning Revolutions: The Psychology of Successful Revolts for Freedom, Fairness, and Rights* (3 vols, 2013). He has authored or coauthored 226 published volumes, 176 professional journal articles, and 282 review articles. He is a psychotherapist in private practice. He may be contacted at www.jharoldellens.com and at jharoldellens@juno.com.

About the Contributors

KAREN BULLOCK, PhD, LCSW, is Professor and Head of the Department of Social Work, College of Humanities and Social Sciences, North Carolina State University. Dr. Bullock earned an MS in social work from Columbia University and a PhD from Boston University. She has more than 20 years of experience as a mental health practitioner. She trained in Epidemiology and Child Psychiatry at Albert Einstein and Columbia-Presbyterian medical centers in New York City prior to receiving her PhD. Since that time, her research and clinical practice have been in the areas of health disparities, cultural competence, aging, and end-of-life care. Dr. Bullock has published and presented nationally and internationally on health-care disparities and end-of-life care issues. She has served on several community and national boards including the Social Work Hospice & Palliative Care Network (SWHPN), the National Association of Social Work (NASW), National Council on Race and Ethnic Diversity (NCORED), Hartford Hospital's Ethic Committee in Hartford, Connecticut, and as Chair of the NASW Mental Health Committee.

MIRIAM PIVEN COTLER, PhD, received an MSPH and PhD from the UCLA School of Public Health. She is currently a visiting professor in the graduate Bioethics Institute at Loyola Marymount University and Professor Emeritus at CSUN where she served as Department Chair and directed the Center for Health care Ethics and Policy. She is consultant to ethics programs at several hospitals and the California Medical Association Council on Ethical Affairs, and a member of several editorial boards. She has served as visiting professor, the UCLA School of Public Health, the UNESCO steering committee for teaching medical ethics and for research ethics, as well as cochair of the Los Angeles County Bar Association Bioethics Committee. Dr. Cotler has over 65 publications and has presented invited papers throughout the world.

MAURA L. DEL BENE, APRN, ACHPN, PMHNP-BC, ANP, is a nurse practitioner specializing in Palliative Medicine within WESTMED Medical Group where she provides advanced pain and symptom management, long-term planning, and advance decision making for patients diagnosed with serious illness. She is a medical staff member of Lawrence Hospital Center and White Plains Hospital. She received an MS in nursing from Columbia University. She is licensed in New York State as a nurse practitioner and holds certifications in Hospice & Palliative Care and Psychiatry. She has specialty experience in neurologic illness (ALS, MS, and muscular dystrophy). She was previously Clinical Director of the Palliative Medicine Service at Lawrence Hospital Center and Director of Clinical Programming at the Multiple Sclerosis Comprehensive Care Center at New York University School of Medicine. She was assistant professor of Clinical Nursing at Columbia University, and Clinical Administrator at the Eleanor and Lou Gehrig MDA/ALS Research Center at Columbia University. She has directed research investigations and coauthored publications about palliative care and ALS. Her professional associations and committees include the Nurse Practitioner Association of NY and the American Academy of Hospital and Palliative Medicine.

LAWRENCE A. FROLIK, JD, received his BA from the University of Nebraska where he was elected to Phi Beta Kappa and his JD *cum laude* and his LLM. from Harvard Law School. Frolik, a nationally recognized scholar and lecturer on legal issues of aging, including end-of-life planning, is Distinguished Faculty Scholar and Professor of Law at the University of Pittsburgh School of Law. His books include *Everyday Law for Seniors* (Paradigm Press with Whitton), *Residence Options for Older or Disabled Client* (ABA Press), *The Law of Later-Life Health Care and Decision Making* (ABA Press), *Advising the Elderly or Disabled Client* (2nd ed. with Brown) (Warren, Gorham, & Lamont), *Elder Law in a Nutshell* (5th ed. with Kaplan, West), and the casebooks *Elder Law: Cases and Materials* (5th ed. with Barnes, LexisNexis) and *The Law of Employee Pension and Welfare Benefits* (3rd ed. with Moore, LexisNexis).

LINDA S. GOLDING, MA, has been Staff Chaplain at New York-Presbyterian Hospital (CUMC and MS-CHONY) since 2010, working with patients, families, and staff at the bedside, in groups and individually. She serves as the Chaplain on the hospital's Ethics Committee and is a member of the Palliative Care Team. Golding cofacilitates an outpatient group on Chronic Illness and Spirituality, leads in-house workshops and didactics on Ambiguous Loss, Bioethics, Resilience, and Patient Charting, and is a visiting instructor for the hospital's Hospice and Palliative Medicine Fellows. Golding has completed Ackerman Institute for the Family workshops in Family Secrets, Forgiveness, Ambiguous Loss, Palliative Care; and the Ethics Consultation Skills Intensive at Montefiore Hospital (NY). Her undergraduate degree was in Music and she graduated from the Jewish Theological Seminary in 2013 with a master's in Jewish Studies and the Certificate of Pastoral Care & Counseling. Golding received a two-year Fellowship from Jewish Foundation for the Education of Women and a Career Development Grant from the Association of American University Women. She recently completed a study on the impact of spirituality on compassion fatigue. Her chapter in this book represents her first published work on chaplaincy.

JAMES W. GREEN, PhD, is Senior Lecturer Emeritus in the Department of Anthropology at the University of Washington, Seattle. His research interests include death in American popular culture, "spirituality" in the professional literature and in end-of-life care, and diversity issues related to dying. He has trained as a hospital chaplain as part of these interests. Earlier research included folk healing at religious shrines in Pakistan and cross-cultural social services. The latter led to three editions of *Cultural Awareness in the Human Services* (Allyn and Bacon, 1989). More recently, in papers for professional groups, he has critiqued "cultural competence" as a service goal, suggesting an ethnographic approach instead. His book, *Beyond the Good Death: The Anthropology of Modern Dying* (University of Pennsylvania Press), was published in 2008. In retirement, he continues to write and present papers, volunteers in local chaplaincy services, and is an avid wine collector.

MICHAEL HALPERIN, PhD, MBA, is Director of the Lippincott Library, the Library of the Wharton School. He has published extensively in both library and business literatures and is the coauthor of two books: *International Business Information* and *Research Guide to Corporate Acquisitions.* He is the creator, with Penn Libraries' Delphine Khanna, of the "Business FAQ," a business knowledge database, now shared by 25 major academic libraries in the United States and abroad. From 1976 until 1997, he was an adjunct professor at Drexel University's College of Information Science and Technology. In 2009, he received an award from the American Library Association for his contributions to the field of business reference. He holds a BA in History from Washington College, an MA in History from Temple University, and an MLS, an MBA, and a PhD (Information Studies) all from Drexel University.

NATHAN IONASCU, MD, born in Rumania, graduated from the "Carol Davila" Institute of Medicine and Pharmacyin, Bucharest. He practiced Pediatrics and Adolescent Medicine for five years in villages and small towns in Rumania, reducing infant mortality rate to zero in two rural agricultural communities. After arriving in the United States, he served a rotating Internship, followed by a Pediatric Residency, at Babies Hospital, New York Presbyterian Medical Center. He served in the U.S. Army Medical Corps as Post Surgeon during the Vietnam War. After discharge, he opened a pediatric office. Among other cases, he diagnosed and treated a child with Rickettsial Typhus fever, publishing his findings in the coauthored article "Typhus Group Infections in New York State: Presentation of Four Suspected Cases" in the *Annals of the New York Academy of Science*. He holds a Certificate in Bioethics from New York University. As a Board Member of the Westchester End of Life Coalition, and a Member of ChiPPs Palliative Care electronic newsletter editorial group (a division of NHPCO), the VA-Hospice Partnership, and Westchester Collaborative for Palliative Care, he has a special interest in educating professional and the general public and presents on issues related to bioethics, life-limiting conditions, hospice, and palliative care.

MARTHA R. JACOBS, MDiv, DMin, BCC, is a per diem chaplain at NY Presbyterian Hospital and Interim Pastor at First Congregational Church of Chappaqua, NY. She is an ordained minister of the United Church of Christ and has been a chaplain since 1991. A board-certified chaplain (Association of Professional Chaplains), Dr. Jacobs received her doctorate and master's in Divinity from New York Theological Seminary, where she is an adjunct professor in the doctoral program. She is on the faculty of the Blanton-Peale Pastoral Care and Counseling Institute. Her book, *A Clergy Guide to End-of-Life Issues,* is a mustread for clergy and seminarians. She has been the keynote speaker for medical staff, chaplains, clergy, lay leaders, and students, addressing end-of-life issues throughout the United States and was the keynote speaker at an International Symposium at Palais Universitaire in Strasbourg, France, in 2013. Dr. Jacobs has had many articles published in professional journals and recently her chapter "Creating a Personal Theology to Do Spiritual/Pastoral Care" was published in *Professional Spiritual & Pastoral Care: A Practical Clergy and Chaplain's Handbook.* She has received awards for advancing the field of professional pastoral care, including an award for her work at Ground Zero in 2001.

BRUCE JENNINGS, MA, is Director of Bioethics at the Center for Humans and Nature. He teaches ethics at the Yale University School of Public Health and the New York Medical College and also holds a faculty appointment at the Weill Medical College-Cornell University. He is Senior Advisor and Fellow at The Hastings Center, where he served from 1991 through 1999 as Executive Director. In 2011, Mr. Jennings was named editor in chief of the new fourth edition of the *Encyclopedia of Bioethics* (5 vols, Macmillan Reference, 2013). Mr. Jennings has been active in the end-of-life care arena and has published widely on ethical issues in hospital treatment, decision making, palliative care, and hospice. He was cofounder of the "Decisions Near the End of Life" program that was conducted in over 200 hospitals in 20 states from 1990 to 1996. He has served on the Board of Directors of the National Hospice and Palliative Care Organization, and the Board of Trustees of the Hospice and Palliative Care Association of New York State. He is coauthor of *The Hastings Center*

Guidelines for Decisions on Life-Sustaining Treatment and Care Near the End of Life: Revised and Expanded Second Edition (Oxford University Press, 2013).

KEVIN T. KEITH, MA, is an ethicist with interests in biomedical and technology issues. He has taught philosophy and bioethics at the undergraduate level, and served as an instructor in bioethics at two U.S. medical schools. He has served on an institutional review board for human research safety, and as consultant to a clinical ethics committee at a major urban teaching hospital. He has published and lectured in the areas of the ethics of life extension and "transhumanism," the role of rational analysis in informed consent and autonomous decision making, the sociopolitical aspects of biotechnology and bioethics, and the professional obligations and activities of medical ethicists, among others.

LINDA KOEBNER, MA, is a health advocate, who writes medical narrative with and for patients. Koebner provides comfort to patients through her work in animal-assisted therapy. Koebner visits hospice, children's rehabilitation centers, and palliative care units with her certified therapy dogs. A graduate of the Health Advocacy Masters program, Sarah Lawrence College, Koebner continues her advocacy work through action and education. An advocate for nonhuman animals throughout her career, Linda Koebner was captivated by chimpanzees in her childhood. In 1974, she became codirector of the Great Ape Protection Project. Funded through the National Science Foundation, Rutgers University and private support she created a new home in Florida for chimpanzees released from biomedical research. As executive director of Chimp Haven, she created a consortium of organizations and the National Institutes of Health to pass the CHIMP Act (Chimpanzee Health Improvement Maintenance and Protection). Chimp Haven was named the National Chimpanzee Sanctuary System and is currently home to 200 chimpanzees. Koebner was Director of Development for the Children's Museum of Manhattan and has developed programs and materials to interpret science for major national cultural institutions. She is the author of numerous books and articles.

ANTHONY J. LECHICH, MD, is an internist/geriatrician with long experience in the care of the frail elderly. Early in his career he served as the senior attending physician in the Chelsea Village Program for the homebound elderly and as director of the General Internal Medicine Residency program at St. Vincent's Hospital in Greenwich Village. Since 1993, he has been medical director and chief medical officer of the Terence Cardinal Cooke Health Care Center, a 729-bed long-term care facility in Manhattan serving a diverse population including individuals with late-stage Huntington's Disease, AIDS, End Stage Renal Disease, frail elderly, severely dependent children, and sub acute care. He has been a frequent workshop presenter for the American Medical

Director's Association on nursing home palliative care and has served as a mentor to students and attending physicians in his charge. He has passionately modeled the moral responsibility that practitioners must accept toward the achievement of a "good" death for those in their care.

EDWARD J. LUSK, PhD, is Professor of Accounting, College of Economics and Business, State University of New York [SUNY], Plattsburgh, and Professor Emeritus at the Department of Statistics, The Wharton School, The University of Pennsylvania. From 2001 to 2006 he held the Chair in Business Administration at the Otto-von-Guericke University in Magdeburg, Germany. He has also taught in China at the Shanxi University of Finance and Economics, Taiyuan, and The Shanghai Finance University, as well as at the Chulalongkorn University in Bangkok, Thailand. He has published more than 185 articles in peer-reviewed journals and texts including three articles in the *New England Journal of Medicine; Cancer; Hospice; Nursing Economic$; The Public Opinion Quarterly; Omega; The Accounting Review; Journal of Political Economy; Statistics and Probability; American Statistician; Management Science; Environmental Quality Management; Journal of the Operational Research Society; Gender, Work and Organizations;* and *International Journal of Forecasting.*

KERRIANNE P. PAGE, MD is an Assistant Clinical Professor of Medicine at Columbia University Medical Center and Medical Director and Senior Vice President of Clinical Effectiveness for Hospice and Palliative Care at Good Shepherd Hospice, a member of Catholic Health Services of Long Island. A graduate of Rutgers University and the New York University School of Medicine, Dr. Page has 20 years of experience and expertise caring for people with serious illness in her work as a primary care physician and hospice and palliative medicine specialist. She has received the Health Care Chaplaincy Wholeness of Life Award, and is a member of the American Academy of Hospice and Palliative Medicine and the American Medical Association. She is board certified in hospice and palliative care and internal medicine, and resides in Westchester County, New York.

CATHERINE ROGERS is a performer and playwright whose most recent solo show, *The Sudden Death of Everyone,* has been seen in New York, Philadelphia, and Greece. Currently a graduate student in Narrative Medicine at Columbia University, Catherine taught writing at New York University and was a Fulbright playwright-in-residence at Aristotle University, Thessaloniki, and the University of Athens. She holds the MFA in playwriting from the University of Texas where she was a James A. Michener fellow.

NELLIE SELANDER, MA, earned her Master of Urban Planning degree from New York University's Robert F. Wagner Graduate School of Public Service in

2012 and Bachelor of Arts with honors in American Studies from Stanford University in 2007. She currently serves as Project Coordinator for the Columbus Downtown Development Corporation and Capitol South Community Urban-Redevelopment Authority. Nellie previously held positions as a research assistant to Professor Christine Kovner at New York University's College of Nursing and as project coordinator at Stanford in Washington. Nellie's policy interests include housing, community development, and related healthcare issues.

MARGARET SOUZA, PhD, is an Associate Professor at SUNY/Empire State College, Staten Island. She is a medical anthropologist who received her doctorate and MA in anthropology from the Graduate Faculty at the New School. She also holds an MA in Social Work from Wayne State University. Her research has focused on end-of-life issues in both acute care and long-term care facilities in New York City where she has served as a researcher, educator, and practitioner in nursing homes and in the acute care setting. Dr. Souza's continues to research end-of-life issues and presently is interviewing persons with life-threatening diagnosis. She also has been working on issues of bereavement in the context of a socially life-changing process. She has presented the findings from her research at national and international conferences.

MICHAEL TEITELMAN, MD, PhD, is a psychiatrist in private practice in New York City. Previously he was a psychiatrist in the AIDS Center of Mount Sinai Medical Center. He has also been an assistant professor in the Department of Philosophy, Columbia University. His publications include an essay on assisted suicide, "Not in the House: Arguments for the Exclusion of Physician Assisted Suicide from Hospital Practice"; on the ethics of access to medical care, "The Mental and the Dental: On the Vicissitudes of Compassion"; and on the foundations of philosophical theories of justice, "On the Theory of the Practice of the Practice of the Theory of Justice."

JASMIN VOLKEL, BA, holds a BA in Psychology from Duke University and a MSW from North Carolina State University. She has worked for several years at a community mental health, behavioral health, and substance abuse agency in Durham, North Carolina, called Triumph, LLC. During her time at Triumph, she became interested in social work and the importance of assisting those who lack access to appropriate resources. She is an intern and graduate research assistant with the Center for Family and Community Engagement, located at North Carolina State University. Her duties include facilitating focus groups, conducting interviews, assisting with the establishment of a youth-based advisory council, creating a qualitative survey, designing and implementing training curricula, evaluating data, and generating reports to the federal funders and the project's advisory councils.

SARA WALLER, PhD, is an Associate Professor of Philosophy at Montana State University, where she teaches *Other Animals* and *Mind and Consciousness*. Her research interests include human and animal minds and measures of intelligence and consciousness across species. She records vocalizations of dolphins, wolves, coyotes, and feral cats, and tries to understand principles for the inferences we make between vocalizations and cognition. This inquiry into the life of animal minds led to the article about how we understand the death of animals, and human death, as portrayed by the Hippocratic and Veterinary oaths. She has published articles on philosophy of mind and cognitive neuroscience in journals such as *Synthese, Journal of Cognitive Neuroscience,* and *Journal of Value Inquiry.*

Index